Enterprise Mac Security

OS X El Capitan

Third Edition

■ ■ ■

Charles Edge
Daniel O'Donnell

Apress®

Enterprise Mac Security

ISBN-13 (pbk): 978-1-4842-1711-5

ISBN-13 (electronic): 978-1-4842-1712-2

Managing Director: Welmoed Spahr
Lead Editor: Louise Corrigan
Development Editor: James Markham
Technical Reviewer: Jim Graham
Editorial Board: Steve Anglin, Pramila Balen, Louise Corrigan, Jim DeWolf, Jonathan Gennick,
    Robert Hutchinson, Michelle Lowman, James Markham, Susan McDermott, Matthew Moodie,
    Jeffrey Pepper, Douglas Pundick, Ben Renow-Clarke, Gwenan Spearing
Coordinating Editor: Jill Balzano
Copy Editor: Jim Compton
Compositor: SPi Global
Indexer: SPi Global
Artist: SPi Global

Distributed to the book trade worldwide by Springer Science+Business Media New York, 233 Spring Street, 6th Floor, New York, NY 10013. Phone 1-800-SPRINGER, fax (201) 348-4505, e-mail orders-ny@springer-sbm.com, or visit www.springeronline.com. Apress Media, LLC is a California LLC and the sole member (owner) is Springer Science + Business Media Finance Inc (SSBM Finance Inc). SSBM Finance Inc is a Delaware corporation.

For information on translations, please e-mail rights@apress.com, or visit www.apress.com.

Apress and friends of ED books may be purchased in bulk for academic, corporate, or promotional use. eBook versions and licenses are also available for most titles. For more information, reference our Special Bulk Sales–eBook Licensing web page at www.apress.com/bulk-sales.

Any source code or other supplementary material referenced by the author in this text is available to readers at www.apress.com. For detailed information about how to locate your book's source code, go to www.apress.com/source-code/.

To my sweet little Emerald, with all of my love!

– Charles Edge

Contents at a Glance

Contents

About the Authors

Charles S. Edge Jr. is a Product Manager at JAMF Software and the former CTO of 318, which at the time was the largest consultancy for Mac in the Entperprise. Charles maintains the Bushel blog at blog.bushel.com as well as a personal site at krypted.com.

Charles is the author of a number of titles on Mac OS X Server and systems administration topics going back to OS X 10.3, including a number of titles from Apress for Mac OS X. He has spoken at a variety of conferences including DefCon, Black Hat, LinuxWorld, Macworld, MacSysAdmin, X World, ACES, the Penn State Mac Admins Conferene, and the Apple WorldWide Developers Conference. Charles is the developer of the SANS course on Mac OS X Security and coauthor of its best practices guide to securing Mac OS X as well. Charles now lives in Minneapolis, Minnesota, with his sweet little daughter, Emerald.

Daniel (Dan) O'Donnell has been working with computers since the pre-GUI days when he was an undergraduate physics student. He touched his first Macintosh keyboard in 1984 and bought his first computer, a Mac SE, in 1987. He began working as a Mac administrator for the American Film Institute and UCLA Film School, then as a Mac admin and server manager in broadcast television production for NBC, then as chief enterprise Mac administrator and eventually Corporate Information Systems Security Officer for the RAND Corporation, a world renowned think tank in Southern California.

He has integrated OS X into Microsoft networks, and has configured Macs for US Government certifications in high security computing networks. He was the first person to introduce log aggregation with OS X into a high security government network environment.

Dan has presented on various aspects of the OS X operating system at Macworld, Mac IT Conference, Splunk User Conference and other technical conferences since 2007.

He is currently working on a project to incorporate another layer of security into OS X and other unix-like platforms.

About the Technical Reviewer

Jim Graham received a bachelor of science in electronics with a specialty in telecommunications from Texas A&M University in 1989. He was published in the International Communications Association's 1988 issue of ICA Communique ("Fast Packet Switching: An Overview of Theory and Performance"). He has worked as an associate network engineer in the Network Design Group at Amoco Corporation in Chicago, Illinois; as a senior network engineer at Tybrin Corporation in Fort Walton Beach, Florida; and as an intelligence systems analyst at both 16th Special Operations Wing Intelligence and HQ US Air Force Special Operations Command Intelligence at Hurlburt Field, Florida. He received a formal letter of commendation from the 16th Special Operations Wing Intelligence in 2001.

Acknowledgments

I'd like to first and foremost thank the Mac InfoSec community. This includes everyone from the people that design the black box to the people that dissect it and the people that help others learn how to dissect it. We truly stand on the shoulders of giants. Of those at Apple that need to be thanked specifically: Schoun Regan, Joel Rennich, Greg Smith, JD Mankovsky, Drew Tucker, Stale Bjorndal, Cawan Starks, Eric Senf, Jennifer Jones, and everyone on the development team. And of course the one and only Josh "old school game console ninja who has massive dogs" Wisenbaker! Outside of Apple, thanks to Arek Dreyer and the other Peachpit authors for paving the way to build another series of Mac systems administration books by producing such quality. And a special thanks to the late Michael Bartosh for being such an inspiration to us all to strive to understand what is going on under the hood.

The crew at 31JAMF Software also deserves a lot of credit. It's their hard work that gave me the time to complete yet another book!

And finally, a special thanks to Apress for letting us continue to write books for them. They fine-tune the dribble I provide into a well-oiled machine of mature prose. And I'll just include my co-author in the Apress family: Dan, thanks for the countless hours to make the deadlines and looking forward to the next round!

—Charles Edge

Introduction

A common misconception in the Mac community is that the Mac is more secure than any other operating system on the market. Although this might be true in most side-by-side analyses of security features right out of the box, what this isn't taking into account is that security tends to get overlooked once the machine starts to be configured for its true purposes. For example, when sharing is enabled or remote control applications are installed, a variety of security threats are often established—no matter what the platform is.

In the security sector, the principle of least privilege is a philosophy that security professionals abide by when determining security policies. This principle states that if you want to be secure, you need to give every component of your network the absolute minimum permissions required to do its job. But what are those permissions? What are the factors that need to be determined when making that decision? No two networks are the same; therefore, it's certainly not a decision that can be made for you. It's something you will need to decide for yourself based on what kinds of policies are implemented to deal with information technology security.

Security Beginnings: Policies

Security in a larger organization starts with a security policy. When looking to develop security policies, it is important that the higher-level decision makers in the organization work hand in hand with the IT team to develop their policies and security policy frameworks. A security policy, at a minimum, should define the tools used on a network for security, the appropriate behavior of employees and network users, the procedures for dealing with incidents, and the trust levels within the network.

The reason policies become such an integral part of establishing security in a larger environment is that you must be secure but also be practical about how you approach security in an organization. Security can be an impediment to productivity, both for support and for nonsupport personnel. People may have different views about levels of security and how to enforce them. A comprehensive security policy makes sure everyone is on the same page and that the cost vs. protection paradigm that IT departments follow are in line with the business logic of the organization.

On small networks, such as your network at home, you may have a loose security policy that states you will occasionally run security updates and follow a few of the safeguards outlined in this book. The smaller a network environment, the less likely security is going to be taken seriously. However, for larger environments with much more valuable data to protect, the concern for security should not be so flippant. For example, the Health Insurance Portability and Accountability Act (HIPAA) authorizes criminal penalties of up to $250,000 and/or 10 years imprisonment per violation of security standards for patient health information. The Gramm-Leach-Bliley Act establishes financial institution standards for safeguarding customer information and imposes penalties of up to $100,000 per violation.

Everyone in an organization should be concerned about security policies, because everyone is affected to some extent. Users are often affected the most, because policies often consist of a set of rules that regulate their behavior, sometimes making it more difficult for them to accomplish their tasks throughout their day. The IT staff should also be consulted and brought into the decision-making process since they will be required to implement and comply with these policies, while making sure that the policies are realistic given the budget available. In addition, you must notify people in advance of the development of the policy. You should contact members of the IT, management, and legal departments as well as a random sampling of users in your environment. The size of your policy development will be determined by the scope of the policy and the size of your organization. Larger, more comprehensive policies may require many people to be involved in the policy development. Smaller policies may require participation by only one or two people within the organization.

As an example, a restrictive policy that requires all wireless users to use a RADIUS server would incur IT costs not only from the initial install but also with the installs and configurations necessary to set up the RADIUS clients on each of the workstations. A more secure RADIUS server would also cause additional labor over other less secure protocols such as WEP. You also need to consider IT budgeting and staffing downtime.

When developing your actual policy, keep the scope limited to what is technically enforceable and easy to understand, while protecting the productivity of your users. Policies should also contain the reasons a policy is needed and cover the contacts and responsibilities of each user. When writing your policy, discuss how policy violations will be handled and why each item in the policy is required. Allow for changes in the policies as things evolve in the organization.

Keep the culture of your organization in mind when writing your security policy. Overly restrictive policies may cause users to be more likely to ignore them. Staff and management alike must commit to the policies. You can often find examples of acceptable use policies in prepackaged policies on the Internet and then customize them to fulfill your organization's needs.

A Word About Network Images

Whether you are a home user or a corporate network administrator, the overall security policy of your network will definitely be broken down into how your computers will be set up on the network. For smaller environments, this means setting up your pilot system exactly the way you want it and then making an image of the setup. If anything were to happen to a machine on your network (intrusion or virus activity, for example), you wouldn't need to redo everything from scratch. If you're in a larger, more corporate environment, then you'll create an image and deploy it to hundreds or thousands of systems using DeployStudio, NetInstall, Casper Suite, FileWave, or a variety of other tools with which you may or may not have experience.

Risk Management

By the end of this book, we hope you will realize that if a computer is plugged into a network, it cannot be absolutely guaranteed secure. In a networked world, it is not likely that you will be able to remove all of the possible threats from any networked computing environment. To compile an appropriate risk strategy, you must first understand the risks applicable in your specific environment. Risk management involves making decisions about whether assessed risks are sufficient enough to present a concern and the appropriate means for controlling a significant risk to your environment. From there, it is important to evaluate and select alternative responses to these risks. The selection process requires you to consider the severity of the threat.

For example, a home user would likely not be concerned with security threats and bugs available for the Open Directory services of OS X Server and Profile Manager. However, in larger environments running Open Directory, it would be important to consider these risks.

Risk management not only involves external security threats but also includes fault tolerance and backup. Accidentally deleting files from systems is a common and real threat to a networked environment. For larger environments with a multitude of systems requiring risk management, a risk management framework may be needed. The risk management framework is a description of streams of accountability and reporting that will support the risk management process for the overall environment, extending beyond information technology assets and into other areas of the organization. If you are managing various systems for a large organization, it is likely there is a risk management framework and that the architecture and computer policies you implement are in accordance with the framework.

All too often, when looking at examples of risk management policies that have been implemented in enterprise environments, many Mac administrators will cite specific items in the policies as "not pertaining" to their environment. This is typically not the case, because best practices are best practices. There is a reason that organizations practice good security, and as the popularity of Mac based network environments grows, it is important that administrators learn from others who have managed these enterprise-class environments.

As mentioned earlier, managing IT risk is a key component of governmental regulations. Organizations that fall under the requirements of Sarbanes-Oxley, HIPPA, or the Gramm-Leach-Bliley Act need to remain in compliance or risk large fines and/or imprisonment. Auditing for compliance should be performed on a regular basis, with compliance documentation ready and available to auditors.

Defining what is an acceptable risk is not something that we, the authors of this book, can decide. Many factors determine what is an acceptable risk. It is really up to you, the network administrator, to be informed about what those risks are so that you can make an informed decision. We will discuss options and settings for building out secure systems and a secure networked environment for your system. However, many of the settings we encourage you to use might impact your network or system in ways that are not acceptable to your workflow. When this happens, a choice must be made between usability and performance. Stay as close to the principle of least privilege as much as possible, keeping in mind that you still need to be able to do your job.

How This Book Is Organized

The first goal of this book is to help you build a secure image, be it at home or in the office, and then secure the environment in which the image will be used. This will involve the various options with various security ramifications, but it will also involve the network, the sharing aspects of the system, servers, and finally, if something drastic were to happen, the forensic analysis that would need to occur.

Another goal of this book is to provide you with the things to tell users not to do. Adding items to enforce your policy and security measures will help you make your network, Mac, or server like a castle, with various levels of security, developed in a thoughtful manner. To help with this tiered approach, we've broken the book down into five parts.

Part 1: The Big Picture

First, an introduction to the world of security on the Mac comprises Part 1:

Chapter 1, "Security Quick-Start": If you have time to read only one chapter, this is the chapter for you. In this chapter, we cover using the GUI tools provided by Apple to provide a more secure environment and the best practices for deploying them. We give recommendations and explain how to use these various features and when they should be used. We also outline the risks and strategies in many of their deployments.

Chapter 2, "Services, Daemons and Processes": In this chapter, we look at the processes that run on your computer. We look at the ownership, what starts processes and what stops them. This is one of the most integral aspects of securing a system and so we decided to look at it early in the book.

Chapter 3, "Securing User Accounts": Mac OS X is a multiuser operating system. One of the most important security measures is to understand the accounts on your system and when you are escalating privileges for accounts. This chapter explains how to properly secure these users and groups.

Chapter 4, "Permissions: POSIX and ACLs": Once you have secured your user accounts, you'll want to secure what resources each has access to. This starts with the files and folders that they can access, which we cover in Chapter 4.

Chapter 5, "Reviewing Logs and Monitoring": What good are logs if they aren't reviewed? In this chapter, we discuss what logs should be reviewed and what is stored in each file. We then move on to various monitoring techniques and applications and the most secure ways to deploy them in typical environments.

Part 2: Securing the Ecosystem

Part 2 gets down to some of the essential elements of security on a Mac:

Chapter 6, "Application Security: Signing and Sandbox": Apple has built a number of sophisticated security controls into Mac OS X. These give you the ability to control exactly which resources applications have access to. By controlling resource accessibility you can limit the damage that can be done by a rogue application or process.

Chapter 7, "The Internet: Web Browsers and E-mail": Safari, Firefox, Internet Explorer, Mail. app, and Entourage—with all these programs to manage, how do you lock them all down appropriately? In this chapter, we discuss cookies, Internet history, and browser preferences and when you should customize these settings. We also give some tips for third-party solutions for protecting your privacy. In addition, this chapter provides readers with best security practices for the mail clients that they likely spend much of their time using.

Chapter 8, "Malware Protection": Viruses, spyware, and root kits are at the top of the list of security concerns for Windows users. However, Mac users are not immune. In this chapter, we go into the various methods that can be used to protect Mac systems against these and other forms of malware.

Chapter 9, "Encrypting Files and Volumes": Permissions can do a good job in protecting access to files unless you have a system that has dubious physical security. An additional layer of security that you can take on top of permissions is to encrypt data. In Chapter 9 we look at encrypting the files, folders and even the boot volume of OS X.

Part 3: Securing the Network

Part 3 describes how you secure a Mac network:

Chapter 10, "Securing Network Traffic": As useful as securing the operating system is, securing the network backbone is a large component of the overall security picture. In this chapter, we explore some of the techniques and concepts behind securing the network infrastructure. This includes the common switches, hubs, and firewalls used in Mac environments and the features you may have noticed but never thought to tinker with. We also cover how to stop some of the annoying issues that pop up on networks because of unauthorized (and often accidental) user behavior.

Chapter 11, "Firewalls: IPFW and ALF": The firewall option in OS X is just a collection of check boxes. Or is it? We discuss using and securing the OS X software firewall, and we go into further detail on configuring this option from the command line. We also discuss some of the other commands that, rather than block traffic, allow an administrator to actually shape the traffic, implementing rules for how traffic is handled, and mitigate the effects that DoS attacks can have on the operating system.

Chapter 12, "Wireless Network Security": Wireless networking is perhaps one of the most insecure things that users tend to implement themselves. In this chapter, we cover securing wireless networks, and then, to emphasize how critical wireless security is (and how easy it is to subvert it if done improperly), we move on to some of the methods used to exploit wireless networks.

Part 4: Securely Sharing Resources

One of the biggest threats to your system is sharing resources. But it doesn't have to be. Part 4 covers the most common resources shared out from a Mac OS X computer, including the following:

Chapter 13, "File Services: AFP, SMB, and FTP": What is a permission model, and why do you need to know what it is, when all you want to do is allow people access to some of the files on my computer? Knowing the strategies involved in assigning file permissions is one of the most intrinsic security aspects of a shared storage environment. It is also important to understand the specific security risks and how to mitigate them for each protocol used, including AFP, FTP, and SMB, which are all covered in this chapter.

Chapter 14, "Web Security: Apache": Apache is quite possibly the most common web server running on the *nix platform. Entire books are dedicated to explaining how to lock down this critical service. In this chapter, we focus on the most important ways to lock down the service and some Apple-centric items of Apache not usually found in discussions about Apache on the *nix platform. We also provide you with other resources to look to if you require further security for your web server.

Chapter 15, "Securely Controlling a Mac": One of the most dangerous aspects of administration is the exposure of the very tools you use to access systems remotely. Many of these programs do not always need to be running and can be further secured from their default settings. In this chapter, we cover many of the methods for protecting these services and some of the ways that vendors should change their default settings to make them more secure. We also cover some of the ways you can secure these tools, and we help administrators make choices about how to best implement remote administration utilities to counteract these shortcomings.

Chapter 16, "Basic OS X Server Security": Mac OS X Server is very much like Mac OS X Client, without many of the bells and whistles and with a more optimized system for sharing resources. This is true with many server-based operating systems. Because a OS X server fills a different role in a networked environment, it should be treated differently from OS X. For this reason, we cover many of the security options that are available as well as those that are crucial to securing OS X Server. We also cover many of the security options from OS X that should specifically not be used in OS X Server.

Included with server security is directory services, which are critical to expanding technology infrastructures. By interconnecting all the hosts of a network, you are able to better control the settings and accounts on systems. In this chapter, we also focus on the ways to securely deploy OS X clients to various directory services and point out the items to ask for (if you are in a larger network infrastructure) or to set up in order to help make the directory service environment as secure as possible.

Part 5: Securing the Workplace

How secure is your work environment's network? This part explores security as it pertains to environments with multiple Mac computers connected on a network:

Chapter 17, "Network Scanning, Intrusion Detection, and Intrusion Prevention Tools": Host-based intrusion detection systems (IDS) are quickly becoming a standard for offering signature-based and anomaly-based detection of attacks. Some of these tools allow for augmenting the operating system settings to further secure the hosts on which they run. In this chapter, we provide a best practices discussion for deploying and using IDSs. We also cover the various attacks that have been developed over the past few years against IDS systems and explore add-ons for IDSs that provide rich aggregated data about the systems.

Chapter 18, "Backup and Fault Tolerance": If you don't have a backup plan now, then you will after you read this chapter. Backups are the last line of defense in a security environment. Backups are critical and should be provided in tiers. In this chapter, we describe some of the strategies for going about implementing a backup plan, from choosing the right software package to properly implementing it. We also cover some of the more common techniques for providing fault-tolerant services and the security risks that can be introduced by doing so.

The Big Picture

## Chapter 1

Security Quick-Start

Ready to start securing your Mac? Let's get right into it. Keep in mind that this chapter is meant to be a quick-and-dirty start to securing your Mac, for the "I don't have time to dive into the nitty-gritty, I need to get my Mac secured right away" readers. This chapter will give you just the basics to get your Mac secure quickly, and although it will leave you with a fairly secure system, it's not as comprehensive as the subsequent chapters, where we'll fine-tune your Mac's settings. For a more thorough understanding of OS X security and the tools you can use to secure your Mac, we urge you to continue reading beyond the basics. Beginning in Chapter 2, you'll be introduced to all the other intricacies surrounding securing the Mac OS, diving deeper into the larger concepts of what is covered here in this quick-start.

Securing the Mac OS X Defaults

Because it is built on a Unix architecture, OS X is a fairly secure and stable operating system right out of the box. Unix, at its core, is designed for high-end server architecture, web servers, and the like. Therefore, it was designed with security needs in mind. However, it is a commonly held misconception that the Mac cannot be made any more secure in the graphical user interface (GUI) of the operating system and can only be further secured through the Unix command line. On the contrary, there are a number of security settings to configure right in the System Preferences Security section. And there are many ways we can and should make Mac OS X more secure without dabbling with the command line.

In fact, right out of the box, there are many security holes within the Mac OS, and they were left intentionally. Why? In the world of operating systems, there is a balancing act between an operating system's ease of use and how secure it is. If you've tinkered with various operating systems, you've seen that the most cumbersome of the lot tend to be those that require more verification windows to make sure you really want to do what you're trying to do. This can prove rather frustrating when performing even the most basic of tasks. When the engineers at Apple redesigned their OS from the ground up, they considered security very heavily, but they also considered usability. In many cases, they decided to err more on the side of user-friendly interaction than obtrusive "allow" and "deny" windows, establishing a reputation as one of the most user-friendly computer systems available. Many security features are disabled by default. This provides an easy-to-use machine while still allowing the user to implement more advanced security measures at their discretion, but it can also leave the machine open to exploits through these security holes.

Many of the features of OS X are already fairly secure without changing anything, with little or no trade-off to functionality. In fact, certain features should not be changed unless changing them is absolutely required; for example, you should not enable the root account unless you need to run a process that requires it, as is the case with programs such as Carbon Copy Cloner. Root is a very powerful feature, and enabling it is a huge security risk if other security measures are not implemented to offset the activation, such as disabling root after using it. Many security breaches occur because users forget to put security settings back the way they were.

Now that we've got that out of the way, let's start discussing some of the places where we can improve the Mac's security right away.

Customizing System Preferences

Probably the best (and most obvious) place to start is in your computer's System Preferences pane, located in the dock or under the Apple menu. Believe it or not, seemingly innocuous settings can be used to exploit some of the Mac's core features. By optimizing System Preferences, we can provide a higher level of protection than is provided right out of the box. And we can cover the most important security options all in the first chapter!

Let's start with the Accounts pane.

Users & Groups

One of the most important concepts to understand in OS X security is that a Mac running OS X is running a multiuser operating system. Every machine has at least one user account and one local administrative account (sometimes referred to as the *root* account), which, if enabled, has the ability to take ownership of all the files on the system as well as to kill any processes on the computer without giving anyone a chance to save their work (via the kill command). As with any multiuser operating system, multiple accounts on the machine create multiple points of entry for potential breaches in security. Therefore, it is important to make sure each point of entry is properly secured.

The first way to do that is actually quite simple: by using strong passwords. Let's say that again one more time for emphasis: *use strong passwords*. Your system is only as secure as your passwords are strong. All too often, a computer is compromised because its password is simply *password,* or the user's first name, or the name of the company. In OS X, Apple created the Password Assistant to counteract this alarming trend by assisting the user with some fairly advanced password techniques (more on that shortly).

If you haven't set your password yet, let's do that right now. To set a password, open the Users & Groups preference pane and click your account name. (Make sure the padlock at the bottom of the pane is unlocked. If it isn't, you'll need an administrator account and password to unlock it.) To the right, you'll see a Change Password button (see Figure 1-1).

The name is typically your full name or the full name you may have entered when the account was created. The short name is a shortened version of the name (the first letter of the first word and the full second word by default).

> **Note** We'll discuss users and groups in detail in Chapter 3, but we will touch on a few of the important points in this section: disabling login items, setting account types, and basic user security.

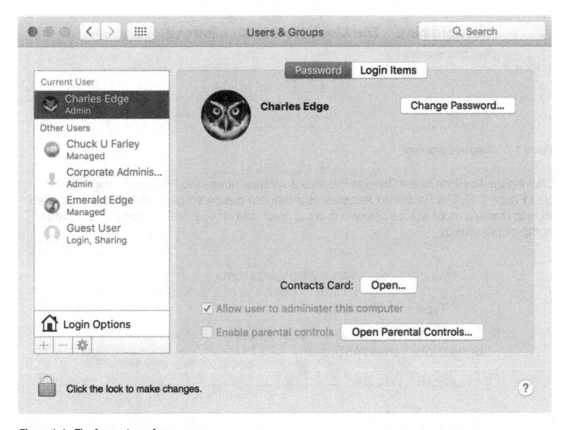

Figure 1-1. The Accounts preference pane

To change the password, click the Change Password button on the Accounts preference pane. A smaller window will appear, requesting that you enter the old password once and the new password twice (see Figure 1-2).

Figure 1-2. Changing a password

Clicking the key icon in the Change Password window opens the Password Assistant (see Figure 1-3). The Password Assistant is a random password generator that can be used to help create a more secure password. It's a great utility if you need suggestions for more complex passwords.

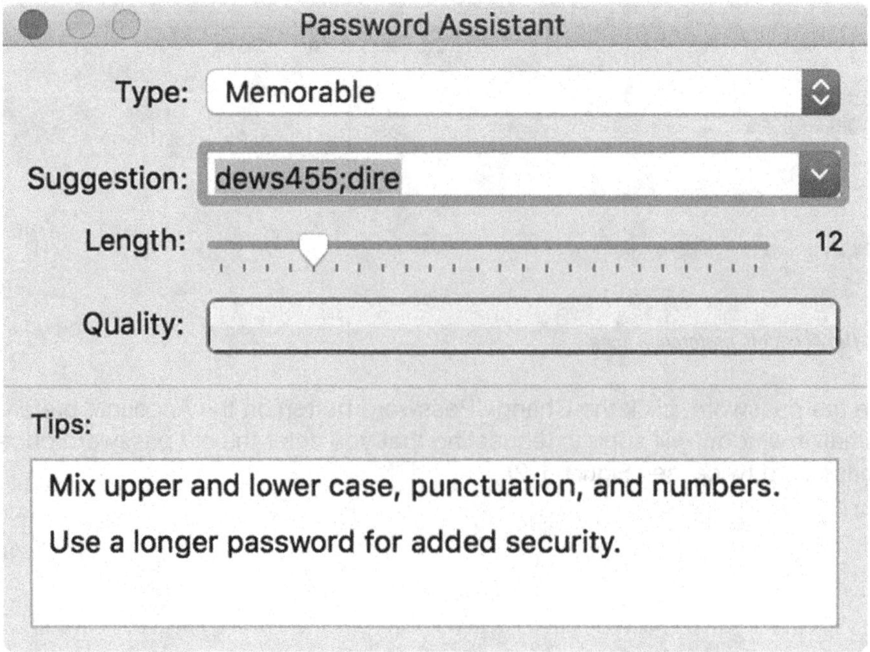

Figure 1-3. Password Assistant

If your password is still *password* or your name or the name of your company, it's time to change it. Right now. We'll wait.

> **Tip** When setting passwords, it's a good practice to make them as complex as possible by including numbers, letters, or special characters, such as !, @, #, or $ (and not just using those characters to substitute similar letters). The more complex the character selection, the more secure the password can be. This is where the Password Assistant really comes in handy.

The final note about passwords is that Apple has been slowly merging the experience of using an iCloud password and that of using an OS X password. In OS X 10.11, when you click Reset Password and create new accounts, you'll have the choice to use an iCloud password as your user password, allowing you to, for example, reset these online. As you can see in Figure 1-4, the process of configuring an iCloud password is pretty straightforward; just click the Use iCloud Password button. However, for an enterprise organization, the jury is still out on whether using iCloud passwords is a good idea.

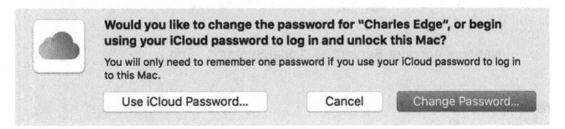

Figure 1-4. iCloud user passwords

Login Options

You can further refine the security options in the Users & Groups preference pane by customizing the default settings of its Login Options button. To change the settings, click the Login Options button, which is located below the various accounts. (Again, you may need to click the padlock icon and access this screen as an administrator.) The first option to change on the resulting screen (Figure 1-5) is "Automatic login." If it's currently set to On, we'd recommend setting it to Off. This gives you some control over who can access the computer when it's first turned on.

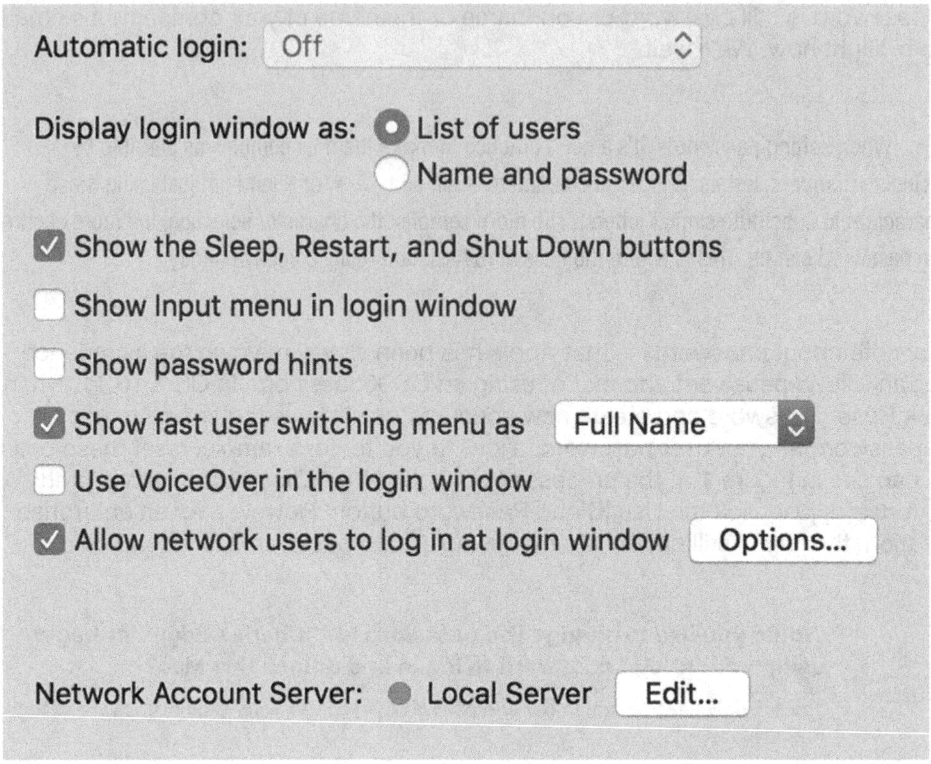

Figure 1-5. Login options

The Login Options screen is where you'd enable the root user (which we recommend you only do when you're performing tasks that absolutely require the root account to be enabled). To enable the root user, click the Join or Edit button (according to the state the system is in) next to Network Account Server. Click the Open Directory Utility button (make sure to click the lock in the Directory Utility window) and then click Edit in the top menu and choose Enable Root User or, if the root account is enabled, click Disable Root User to turn it back off.

Next, the "Display login window as" option (Figure 1-5) enables you to display either a list of users or a blank field for the username and password at login. Quite often, users use their photo and real name when configuring their user account, which can be a security concern if an attacker were able to grab control of the machine (they'd know what they look like and what their real name is). We highly recommend that you enable root and configure the option to require a full name and password be typed in to log in.

If the computer is in a workgroup setting and more than one user needs to access it, we also recommend turning off the "Show the Restart, Sleep, and Shut Down Buttons" option, which is enabled by default. When you disable this option, these buttons will be hidden at the login window if the computer were to be logged off due to inactivity or by another user. Some systems provide services for other users, and disabling that option helps to ensure that users have access to those services.

If you are using a stand-alone computer or if you do not use a directory service (we'll cover Open Directory further in Chapter 16), uncheck the "Allow network users to log in at login window" box.

Passwords

The Show Password Hints option can be helpful if you need a hint to remind yourself of your password. But use caution here: this is a prime example of a security hole that can be easily exploited. While the hint box can help you to remember your password, it can also give someone trying to guess your password valuable insight into what the password may be. Put some thought into it and use an obscure connection to the password, something only you would know.

For example, "My dog's name," may seem harmless enough, but an acquaintance familiar with you and your pets would find it extremely easy to guess your password. Something like "bone sleuth with numbers" might jog your memory and be obvious to you, but not so obvious to others. Or use something that looks like a password and jogs your memory. Again, there is no substitute for the use of strong passwords. And whatever you do, do not enter the actual password into the password hint field (trust us, it happens all the time). One-word answers are guaranteed to be the first words that will be attempted when guessing your password.

> **Note**   You should also change your password routinely. But given the choice between a somewhat secure password and never rotating your password, we recommend a somewhat secure password. Not everyone can do both, but when you can, you should.

Administrators

The administrative user should be logged in only when administrative tasks (changing passwords, configuring network settings, and so on) are necessary; not for everyday work. This is a key component of Unix system administration and a good way to keep users from accidentally harming the system. Limit the administrative access to the machine only to the users who absolutely need it (this includes your own account if you use the machine regularly). To remove administrative access for a user, click the account in the Accounts pane and click the user for whom you'd like to change access. Uncheck the box "Allow user to administer this computer." (See Figure 1-6.)

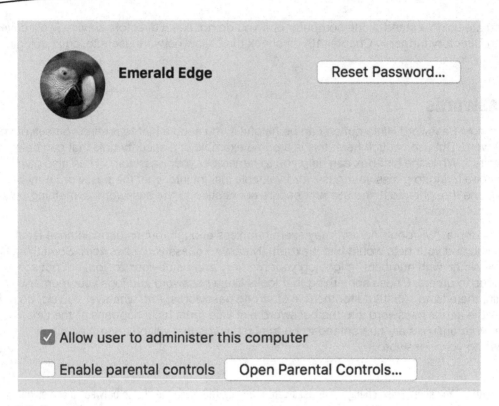

Figure 1-6. User settings

Fast User Switching is a convenient way to allow a user to log in to multiple accounts concurrently. It poses a security risk, however, because it is possible to access or alter processes (and files not in the user's home directory) run by other users. Fast User Switching should be used only for specific reasons, such as testing different versions of software. As a security precaution, it should not be left running unattended.

Another way to safeguard against abuse is to limit administrative access to those who absolutely need it. Better yet, if Fast User Switching is a feature you are not likely to use, disable it by unchecking the "Show fast user switching" menu option (shown in Figure 1-5 earlier).

Security & Privacy Preferences

Another place to change the default settings to make the machine more secure is in the Security preference panel (see Figure 1-7). Here, you will find options for enabling many of the miscellaneous security features that Apple has developed, as well as disabling some less secure features. This panel has become the default place to look for security features that don't fit into any specific section of System Preferences.

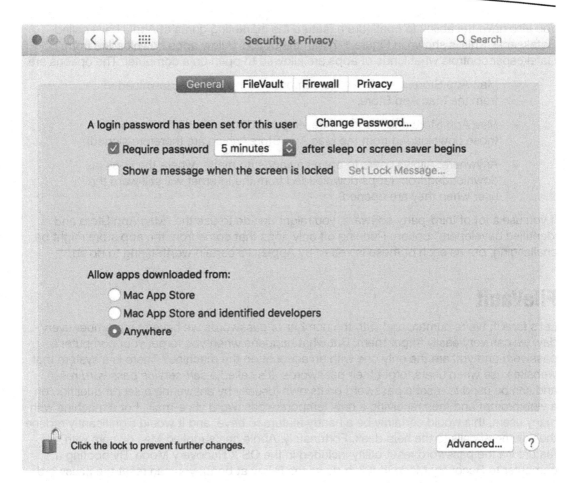

Figure 1-7. Security preference pane, General tab

General

Under the General tab is the option "Require a password [time interval] after sleep or screen saver begins." This will require that a password be used to wake the computer after it has gone to sleep or after the screen saver has been activated. This feature is absolutely critical and is not enabled by default. You can also specify a time when the password can be required after the machine has woken up. We cannot overstress the importance of enabling this option and specifying that the machine require a password immediately. Assigning a key or hot corner (moving the cursor to a corner of the screen to activate the display) to put a system to sleep allows you to put your machine to sleep when you are finished using it. Later in this chapter we will review setting up automatic sleep, the hot corner, and screen saver options.

The option "Show a message when the screen is locked" will show users a message when the screen is locked. This message can be set to inform users of your organization's security policy or instruct people who find a lost computer how to return it to your organization.

You also have the ability to configure a feature the marketing gurus at Apple have called Gatekeeper. This is shown in Figure 1-7 with the option "Allow apps downloaded from." Gatekeeper controls what kinds of apps are allowed to open on a computer. The options are

- Mac App Store: Only allow the computer to install Apps downloaded from the Mac App Store.

- Mac App Store and identified developers: Only allow signed apps and those downloaded from the Mac App Store (which are therefore signed).

- Anywhere: Allows users to open any apps no matter where the app was downloaded from (apps downloaded from the Internet will still warn the user when they are opened).

If you use a lot of third-party software, you might decide to use the "Mac App Store and identified developers" option. Running off only apps that come from the app store might be challenging, but as each of these is vetted by Apple, it's certain worth trying to do so.

FileVault

Let's face it: we're human, and with the number of passwords we have to remember every day, we can very easily forget them. But what happens when you forget your computer's password and you are the only one with an account on the machine? There is a system that websites use when users forget their passwords. It's called a *self-service password reset* and can be used to reset a password on its own (usually by answering a secret question on a web prompt and then receiving a new temporary password via e-mail). For a machine with many users, this would certainly be a handy feature to have, and it would significantly reduce the volume of calls to the help desk. Fortunately, Apple has supplied Mac owners with this feature via the password reset utility included in the OS X Recovery Mode. By booting a computer to Recovery Mode (holding down the R key at boot), you can reset the password. A very handy feature indeed.

But what if your computer fell into the wrong hands, and you wanted to limit someone's ability to access your data if they were able to reset the password? Many of us travel with laptops that, if stolen and their passwords reset, would give users access to data they shouldn't be able to access. If a teacher's computer were rebooted by a student, they'd have access to tests, children would have access to their parent's website viewing habits, employees would have access to confidential data about other employees, and so on—all if they were able to get physical access to our computers while we were away. The ability to reset a password easily introduces you to a feature of the OS X security preferences that protects data, even if the password is reset using Recovery Mode: FileVault. This option removes the ability to access data on a computer, even if the password is reset, by encrypting the contents of the boot volume.

Note   The FileVault feature is only as strong as the password protecting the account.

To use FileVault, you need to set it up in the Security preference pane. Open System Preferences, and click Security. Then click the FileVault tab to see a screen similar to Figure 1-8 and choose Turn On FileVault.

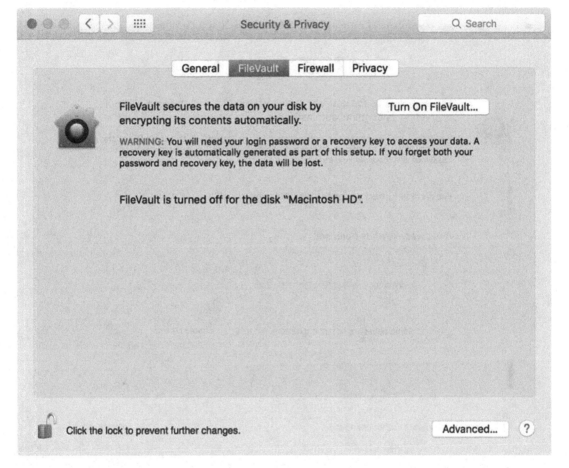

Figure 1-8. Setting up FileVault

You will then be prompted to restart your computer before enabling FileVault. Click Restart to reboot the computer and complete starting the FileVault encryption process. Once restarted, you will be prompted to restart the computer again and the encryption process will start.

Note If you suspect that others will enable FileVault to encrypt their computers, such as students, children, or employees, then setting up an institutional recovery key before they can enable FileVault will help ensure that you will always be able to log into any FileVault disk images that are created by other users on the system.

At the login screen, you will be able to log in as the user who enabled FileVault. Once logged in, allow other users to authenticate to the computer using the Enable Users button in the FileVault pane of the Security System Preference, as you can see in Figure 1-9.

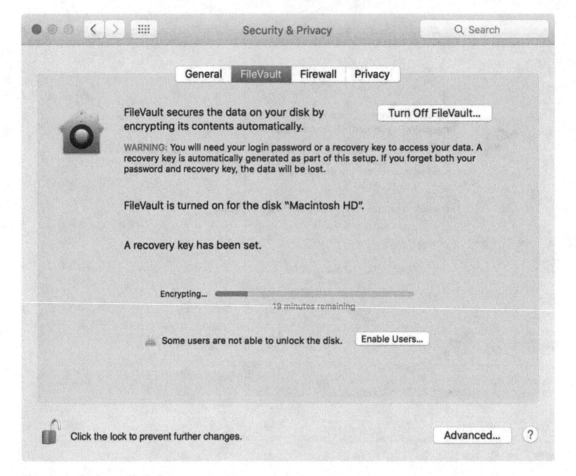

Figure 1-9. Setting up FileVault

If you want to change FileVault settings later, you can do so by returning to the Security preference pane and clicking the FileVault tab again. Your options include disabling FileVault completely (which can be helpful in troubleshooting).

> **Note**   There will be a little impact to the user experience on the computer when FileVault is first setup. The computer will run a little slow while the hard drive is being encrypted. Additionally, because of the restarts, you may find the computer will not be usable for a good 10 to 20 minutes after FileVault is enabled.

Firewall

The OS X firewall is a software-based application firewall built into the operating system designed to block unwanted network traffic. It is disabled by default, and unless you know that enabling it causes incompatibility issues with other operating systems or file systems, you should enable it. Doing so is a simple process: simply open System Preferences and click Security & Privacy and then the Firewall tab. From here, click the Turn On Firewall button, shown in Figure 1-10.

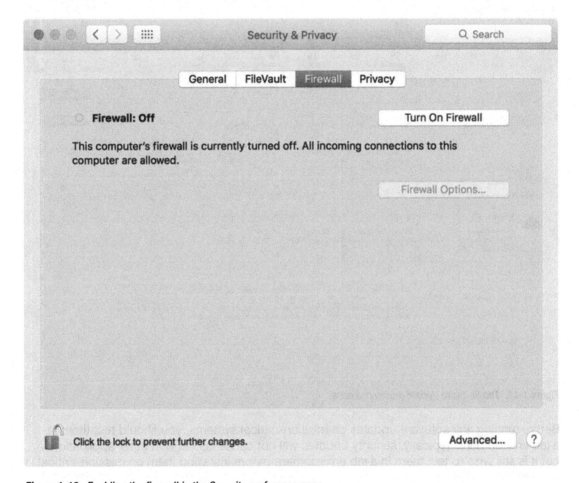

Figure 1-10. Enabling the firewall in the Security preference pane

Once it is enabled, click the Firewall Options button for more granular settings, which are covered in further detail in Chapter 11.

Software Update

You can use the App Store to keep your system updated quickly and easily with the latest Apple updates and security patches. You will be prompted with a notification when updates are available. You can also manually check by opening the App Store and then clicking Updates in the row of icons along the top of the screen.

As you can see in Figure 1-11, you can click the Update All button to install any updates for the operating system and all apps installed, or use the Update button for a given patch to run only that one.

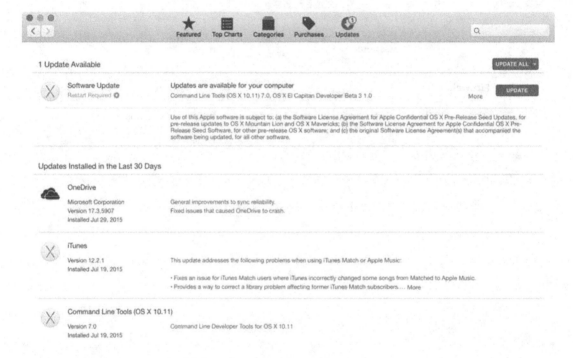

Figure 1-11. The Software Update preference pane

Before running any software updates on mission-critical systems, you should test them in a lab environment. Typically, security updates will not cause issues with other applications, but it is still wise to test them in a lab environment before installing them on mission-critical machines.

For many, using the Mac App Store will be adequate to keep your computer updated. However, if you have multiple systems on your network that need updating, you can quickly bottleneck your Internet pipe if multiple users are downloading updates all at the same time. You will most likely want to deploy a solution to help you conserve your bandwidth by managing these updates. The Software Update Server feature or the Caching Service in OS X Server are great solutions for controlling Apple software updates. However, this is not going to be the right solution for everyone because it requires an OS X Server to use.

Note   There are ways to run the Software Update Server feature without having it run on a Mac, if you don't mind deploying Open Source software in your environment.

Security updates should always be taken seriously and be run when possible. One unique aspect of the Apple security updates is that they are always deployed independently from other updates. Security updates rarely force a restart of the computer, and they almost invariably provide a comprehensive description explaining what they fix and why they were written, with links to descriptions of the vulnerabilities they fix.

Bluetooth Security

Bluetooth is a globally unlicensed short-range radio frequency for wireless networks, also known as IEEE 802.15.1. It is a wireless technology that provides a way to connect and exchange information between devices such as mobile phones (such as the iPhone), laptops, PCs, printers, headphones, speakers, and digital cameras. The Apple Bluetooth keyboard and mouse are popular Bluetooth devices in Apple environments.

Bluetooth works by pairing two devices. While two devices are paired, they are able to freely exchange data. To pair a device with an Apple computer, you will need your computer to be *discoverable*, or awaiting a pairing. You are also required to accept the pairing in most cases. However, there are a variety of attacks that can force a pairing if your system is set to be discoverable without using a password. Once a connection is established, files can be shared over Bluetooth, creating a security vulnerability; to prevent it, you need to disable Bluetooth.

Bluetooth is enabled and discoverable by default. If you don't have a need for Bluetooth on your system, you should disable it. To do this, open System Preferences and select the Bluetooth preference pane. Once you have this pane open, click the Off button to disable Bluetooth on your system (see Figure 1-12).

Figure 1-12. The Bluetooth preference pane

The left side of the pane shows the various devices that have been paired with your Mac. Here, you will be able to configure each device with its appropriate settings.

The Advanced button allows you to change some settings associated with Bluetooth (see Figure 1-13):

- Open Bluetooth Setup Assistant at startup if no keyboard is detected: Prompts a user if a keyboard is not detected at boot. Irrelevant on a laptop but a good idea on a desktop.

- Open Bluetooth Setup Assistant at startup if no mouse or trackpad is detected: Prompts a user if a mouse is not detected at boot. Irrelevant on a laptop but a good idea on a desktop.

- Allow Bluetooth devices to wake this computer: Allows a Bluetooth device to wake the computer from sleep. If you require a password to unlock the computer, this causes little security risk.

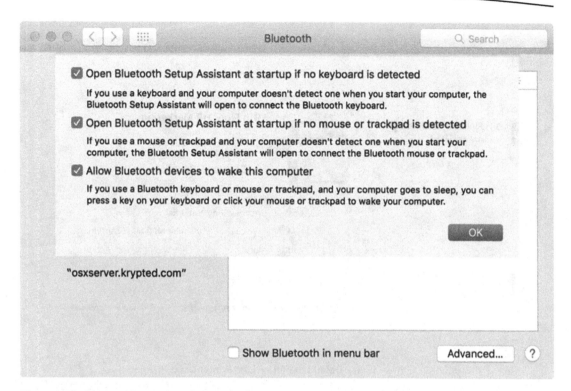

Figure 1-13. Advanced Bluetooth settings

Printer Security

The Printers & Scanners preference pane in System Preferences offers a few options for configuring access to shared printers and faxes. Only printers that multiple users need access to should be shared. Allowing a user to print to a printer that they shouldn't be using can cause confidentiality issues if the documents they are printing land in the wrong hands. To disable printers not in use, uncheck "Share this printer on the network" for each printer (see Figure 1-14).

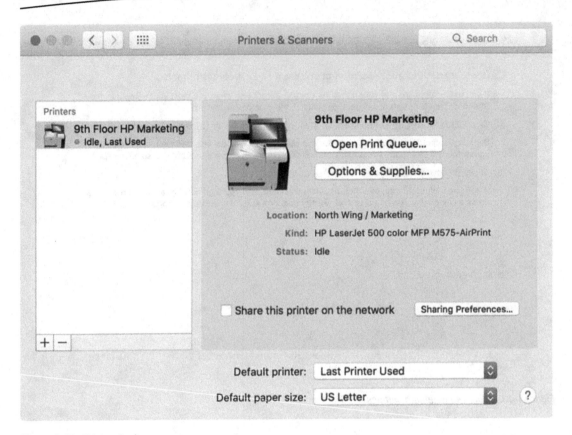

Figure 1-14. Printer sharing

By default, all users will have access to shared printers. Click the Sharing Preferences button to bring up the Sharing System Preference pane, where you can change the Everyone setting to a smaller subset of users or even a single user. For example, in Figure 1-15, we set the Everyone group to No Access (Everyone cannot be removed from the list). Single users will have the ability to print.

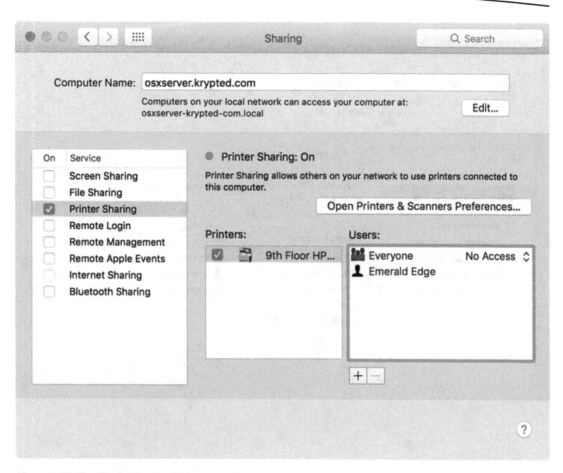

Figure 1-15. The Sharing System Preference pane

Sharing Services

We have already shared printers. But what about everything else? If you are not sharing a resource on your computer, use this Sharing System Preference pane to disable any sharing services that aren't necessary. To do this, open the Sharing preference pane, and review the items on the Services window on the left that are being used to share resources (see Figure 1-16). If you are sharing files, use the Shared Folders window to show you which folders you're sharing out on your computer and which users are able to access them under the list of Users. It's a nice feature for us security folks who would like to see at a glance which folders are being shared.

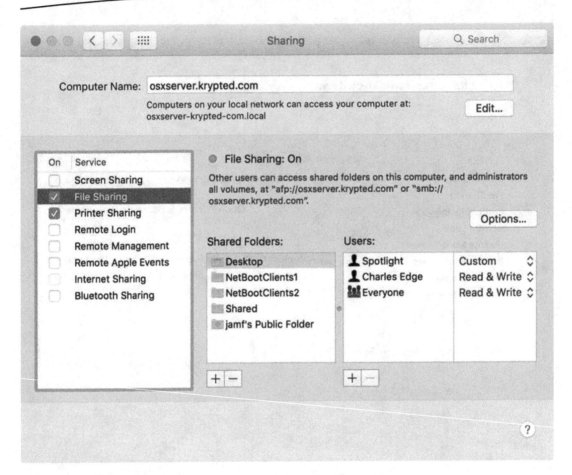

Figure 1-16. Sharing preferences

> **Tip**   Disable all services that are not needed by the user for whom you are configuring access. These services are more comprehensively discussed in Chapter 13, Chapter 14, Chapter 15, and Chapter 16 for OS X Server Services.

Erasing Disks

When you delete a file from a hard drive, the file is marked for deletion but is often kept by the file system until the system needs to free up space for new files. Reformatting a hard drive should provide additional assurance that data is erased. To ensure that data isn't accessed by malicious users, always erase a disk before disposing of it or repurposing the drive.

To erase a disk, open Disk Utility, and click the drive in the left column. Next, click the Erase button (see Figure 1-17).

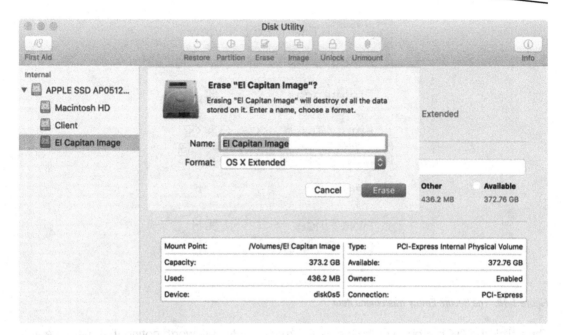

Figure 1-17. The Erase feature of Disk Utility

> **Note** Make sure there is no data that is needed on the disk you're securely erasing. Once you
> have erased data securely, the cost of retrieving the data will be great, if it's even possible.

Using Secure Empty Trash

The Secure Empty Trash feature works much the same way as the Secure Erase feature.
This is more secure than simply emptying the trash in that it also overwrites the location on
the hard drive where the data in the trash was stored with random data. This will cause the
data to be much harder to recover if it were to fall into the wrong hands. To empty the trash
securely, in Finder click Secure Empty Trash (see Figure 1-18).

Figure 1-18. The Secure Empty Trash menu item

Then click the OK button to make the files unrecoverable. It is worth noting that there are a variety of popular applications to help undelete files. As Figure 1-19 warns, once you click OK to securely erase your trash, you will not be able to recover the files at a later date, even with these data recovery applications.

Figure 1-19. The Secure Empty Trash confirmation prompt

Using Encrypted Disk Images

Encrypted disk images offer you a place to keep files in an encrypted form. Let's say that for speed or compatibility reasons you don't want to keep your entire home folder encrypted, as you would by using FileVault, but you do want to keep certain folders encrypted. You can use encrypted disk images, which are much like ZIP files that compress a bunch of files into one file. Anyone attempting to access the data within them will need a password to do so.

To create an encrypted disk image, open Disk Utility and click the File menu, selecting Blank Image in the Image section of the menu. The resulting screen (see Figure 1-20) will have a wide variety of options. The Volume Size and Encryption settings are the most important to consider when creating the disk image. The volume size determines the size limit of the disk image. The encryption type can be 128-bit or (for more security) 256-bit; 256-bit images are harder to crack, but they are slower to create and to open when created. They will also take up more disk space than 128-bit. It's important to consider whether 256-bit encryption is worth the performance hit and disk space increase you will experience from using it.

> **Tip**   If you are unsure what the size of your disk image should be and are not worried about limiting its size, choose Sparse Disk Image from the Image Format options, and the image will automatically grow as it requires more space (such as when you add files to it).

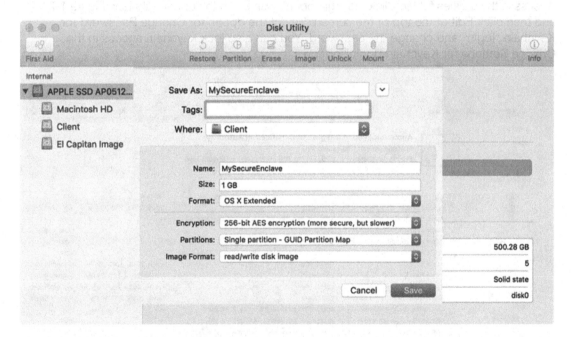

Figure 1-20. Encrypted Disk Image options

When you choose an encryption type, you will be asked for a password. Next you will click the Save button, and OS X will create a file using the encryption parameters you have selected. Once you have created an encrypted disk image, you will need the password anytime you need to access the image.

Securing Your Keychains

OS X uses encrypted keychains to keep track of commonly used passwords and certificates that are accessed regularly. You can also securely store notes in Keychains. Keychains are meant to make your life easier by automating the manual re-entry of this information every time you need to access it. One keychain password can be used to unlock a number of passwords, allowing your computer to keep track of credentials; this both saves you time and spares you from keeping track of them yourself. Another benefit is that it allows a single service to maintain a centralized database of passwords, rather than having each application ask for passwords.

The result is a substantially secure way of caching passwords for future use. But it's really only as secure as the complexity of the password used to access it. When setting the keychain password, make sure to use one that is both difficult to crack and unique from all the other passwords on the machine. To change the keychain password, open Keychain Access in the Utilities folder. Click the login open padlock on the upper right (see Figure 1-21) and then click Edit at the top of the screen. Select the option for Change Password for Keychain "login" and change the password. You can also lock keychain access in the Change Settings for Keychain "login" option.

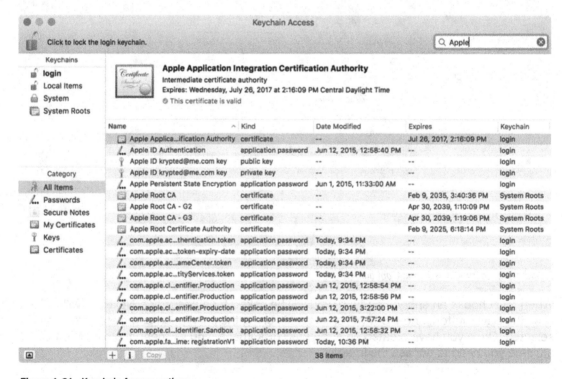

Figure 1-21. Keychain Access options

There are always multiple keychains on OS X computers. They include the system keychain and the user keychains, which appear as Login for each user (by default). With multiple users on a machine, there are inevitably multiple user keychains as well. Each user has a default keychain stored in their home folder. These can be managed using Keychain Access (at /Applications/Utilities/Keychain Access), which can help further secure multiple keychains. To access Keychain Access, from your Finder choose Go and then click Utilities. Locate the Keychain Access folder within the Utilities folder, open it and then locate the top left panel, labeled Keychains. The Keychains panel displays all the keychains on the system known to the user. From here you can lock and unlock keychains by clicking them and clicking the lock icon at the top of the screen (see Figure 1-21). This will require a password every time an application or service attempts to access the keychain.

You can create new keychains by clicking Open Keychain Access and clicking the + sign on the next screen. This essentially creates an encrypted file containing other information that needs to be secured, such as cached passwords to web sites. This is similar to an encrypted disk image. The password assigned to each keychain will decrypt the keychain file, thereby unlocking the keychain. Each keychain can and should have a different password.

Finally, each time a keychain item is created, you will be prompted for a password to allow the computer to access the stored repository and write a new object into it.

Best Practices

Here is a quick "cheat sheet" of important practices you should employ in keeping your Mac secure, followed by the chapter numbers that explore these security practices further:

- Install antivirus software (see Chapter 8).
- Always install Apple's security updates (as discussed in this chapter).
- Open files only from known sources (see Chapter 9).
- Use a standard account for everyday work (see Chapter 3).
- Disable automatic login, and assign a password for every user (as discussed in this chapter).
- Lock your screen when you step away, and require a password to unlock it (as discussed in this chapter).
- Give your keychain its own password, and lock it when it is not in use (as discussed in this chapter).
- Use a firewall (see Chapter 11).
- Encrypt important files (see Chapter 9).
- Protect your wireless network with WPA, and use VPNs when using public wireless (see Chapter 12).
- Protect sensitive e-mail from prying eyes using encryption (see Chapter 7).
- Practice private surfing (see Chapter 7).
- Encrypt your chat sessions (see Chapter 7).

## Chapter 2

Services, Daemons, and Processes

A computer is never entirely at rest unless it's shut down. Even when you move to another room to watch television and your computer's display has gone to sleep, there might be a dozen or more things at work in the background that you can't immediately see happening. The services, daemons, and processes responsible for all of this activity keep your system running smoothly and able to handle regular chores such as backups, checking mail, and listening for incoming web clients.

This chapter helps you understand how these services, daemons, and processes provide the backbone of your operating system and how they function. By understanding what these essential elements are and how they interoperate, you will be best equipped to protect yourself from intruders attempting to turn these otherwise helpful programs against you.

Introduction to Services, Daemons, and Processes

The terms *service*, *daemon*, and *process* are frequently used interchangeably. However, each has a slightly different meaning, and understanding the difference between them is essential to properly securing and troubleshooting your system. Some of the terms defined in this section might seem a bit basic, but we feel it's important to review them to provide the proper context for understanding how they all fit together.

A Mac's hard drive contains hundreds of computer programs, or *applications*. These programs are written in a variety of programming languages, some of which are compiled into binaries, or source code that has been translated from the program's originating programming language, such as Objective-C or C++. Others are in noncompiled languages (often referred to as *scripting languages*) that remain as they are, such as PHP and Perl; these are typically considered *scripts*. You can usually read the source code of a script, but not a program (unless it is based on a scripting language, such as AppleScript).

When you manually start a program or script (or the computer starts the program, because it's been configured to do so), you're launching a *process*, which is any running application that takes up resources on the system. That process may consist of a single entity or a collection of entities, all working together in what are called *threads*. A thread is a stream of instructions that the computer can perform in sequence. A process can also have other processes that it invokes, known as *child processes*. Because you cannot have children without parents, the originating process is called the *parent process*.

Most modern operating systems, such as Mac OS X, can run multiple processes simultaneously, because they are multithreaded operating systems.

If the process is running in the background and isn't directly under your control, it's often referred to as a *daemon*. Common daemons running on an OS X system include cupsd (for printing), syslogd (for logging), and blued (for interfacing with Bluetooth). Although the daemons running on your system often may have names ending in the letter d, they don't always. Daemons interact more often with other programs than they do with the user, and they sometimes have additional controller programs (in Mac OS X, many of them rely on scripts) that are used to provide various instructions to the daemon.

> **Note** Whether an item is a daemon or a process can be a complicated topic. Many daemons can be run in nondaemon modes (interactively). You can take most programs or scripts and convert them to daemons to have them run in the background.

The definitions we've provided here for processes and daemons work with most of the Unix family of operating systems (Linux, OS X, Solaris, and so on). A *service*, however, is specific to Mac OS X. The Mac Developer Connection's *Mac OS X Reference Library's Services Implementation Guide* states that services in Mac OS X are "features exported by your application for the benefit of other applications." This means that services allow applications to communicate with one another by passing information through a shared pasteboard (not shared memory). You may have seen Services in your menu options in each application's main menu. Each application that offers a service advertises what operations its services can apply to data. It's these advertisements that make up the contents of your Services menus.

Putting it all together, it's easier to think of the three this way: a process can be a daemon if it's running in the background; and a daemon can be a service if its purpose is to act as a helper tool to interchange data between other programs. If you do not directly invoke a process, then it's typically considered a daemon. Apple recommends that daemons not use AppKit, so they're unlikely to be services. But not all developers are in tune with Apple's best practices, and this is not a recommendation that is always respected.

The final aspect of these core operating system underpinnings to review is the *application bundle*. Applications appear to be single files, but in fact, they're more than that. An application bundle is a collection of programs and supporting files for those programs that are displayed as a single application to the end user. A good example of an application bundle native to the Mac operating systems with Tiger and above is Automator. If you were to navigate to your Applications folder, control-click the Automator icon, and click Show Package Contents (or cd into it from the command line), you would discover that it's actually a directory of files. Inside this directory are a number of files and binaries. To run Automator from within the directory structure, you would need to navigate to the Contents folder and then into the MacOS folder to run the Automator binary. You will typically find binaries in the MacOS folder, and within the Resources you will find the supporting graphics, icon files, and compiled nib files that make up the application.

Viewing What's Currently Running

There are a number of ways to view what's currently running on your Mac, both from the command line and using graphical tools. We'll start with the handy GUI utility Activity Monitor, and then show you how to view things programmatically for those times when you feel like getting your geek on with the commands ps and top from the command line.

> **Note** Before you can ps and top, you'll need to open a Terminal window (/Applications/Utilities/Terminal.app).

The Activity Monitor

To view the processes running on your Mac (along with other information related to those processes), go to Applications, select Utilities, and open the Activity Monitor application, as shown in Figure 2-1. Activity Monitor will display a variety of resources in use on your system in real time. Activity Monitor has many uses. From disk activity to memory utilization, Activity Monitor provides a dashboard of sorts into what is going on in your computer. Our focus here, though, is specifically on which processes are running on the computer and learning a bit of information about each.

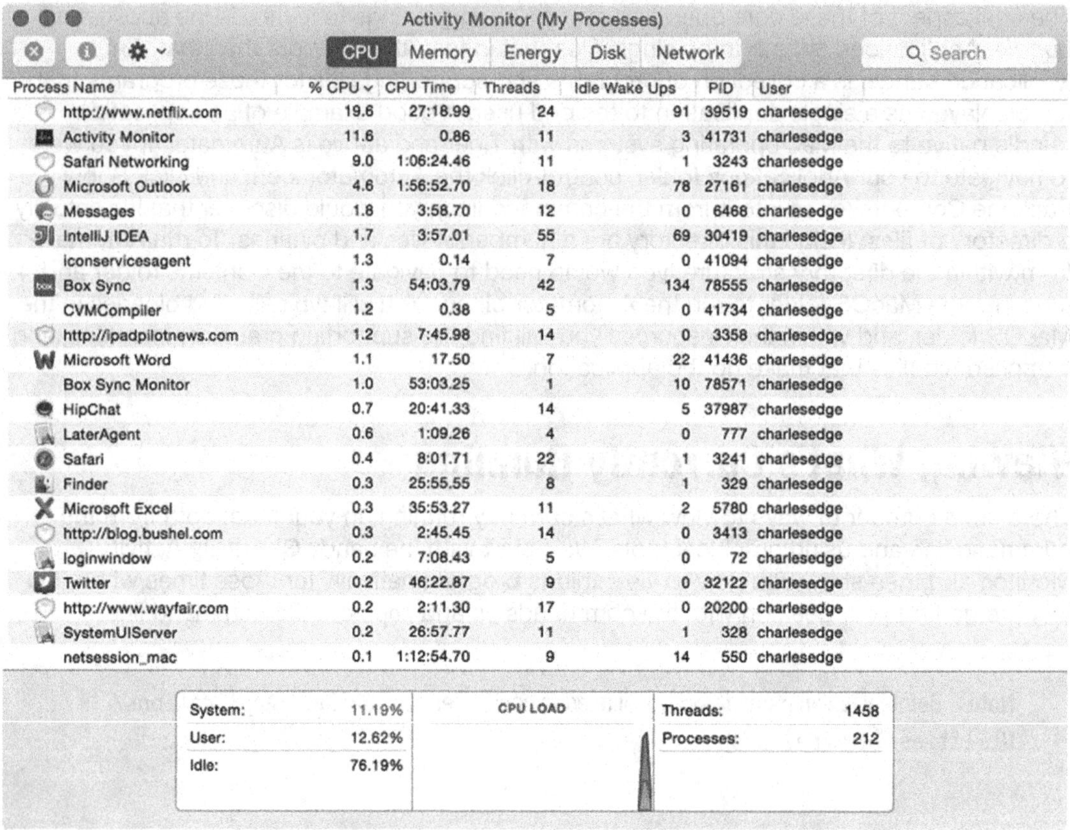

Activity Monitor (My Processes)

CPU | Memory | Energy | Disk | Network | Search

Process Name	% CPU	CPU Time	Threads	Idle Wake Ups	PID	User
http://www.netflix.com	19.6	27:18.99	24	91	39519	charlesedge
Activity Monitor	11.6	0.86	11	3	41731	charlesedge
Safari Networking	9.0	1:06:24.46	11	1	3243	charlesedge
Microsoft Outlook	4.6	1:56:52.70	18	78	27161	charlesedge
Messages	1.8	3:58.70	12	0	6468	charlesedge
IntelliJ IDEA	1.7	3:57.01	55	69	30419	charlesedge
iconservicesagent	1.3	0.14	7	0	41094	charlesedge
Box Sync	1.3	54:03.79	42	134	78555	charlesedge
CVMCompiler	1.2	0.38	5	0	41734	charlesedge
http://ipadpilotnews.com	1.2	7:45.98	14	0	3358	charlesedge
Microsoft Word	1.1	17.50	7	22	41436	charlesedge
Box Sync Monitor	1.0	53:03.25	1	10	78571	charlesedge
HipChat	0.7	20:41.33	14	5	37987	charlesedge
LaterAgent	0.6	1:09.26	4	0	777	charlesedge
Safari	0.4	8:01.71	22	1	3241	charlesedge
Finder	0.3	25:55.55	8	1	329	charlesedge
Microsoft Excel	0.3	35:53.27	11	2	5780	charlesedge
http://blog.bushel.com	0.3	2:45.45	14	0	3413	charlesedge
loginwindow	0.2	7:08.43	5	0	72	charlesedge
Twitter	0.2	46:22.87	9	0	32122	charlesedge
http://www.wayfair.com	0.2	2:11.30	17	0	20200	charlesedge
SystemUIServer	0.2	26:57.77	11	1	328	charlesedge
netsession_mac	0.1	1:12:54.70	9	14	550	charlesedge

System:	11.19%	CPU LOAD	Threads:	1458
User:	12.62%		Processes:	212
Idle:	76.19%			

Figure 2-1. *The Mac OS X Activity Monitor*

By default, you'll only see what you're running under the account with which you're logged in. If you know the name of a given process, you can click in the Search field and type the name of the process to constrain the view. You can also control which processes appear by going to the View menu (see Figure 2-2). You can stop each of these processes, however, if you need to stop one that is owned by a user other than yourself. You'll need to provide an administrative password to do so. This is because each process is started by a user, and it only has access to the files and folders to which the user who started the process has access. When analyzing system processes, remember that processes should be run by the user with the least privileges possible.

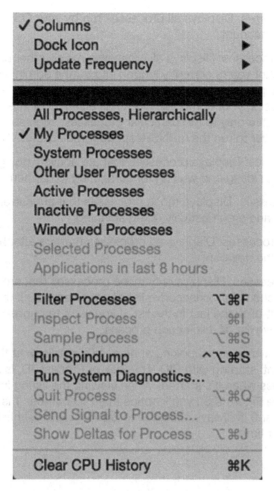

Figure 2-2. The Activity Monitor's Show list

Activity Monitor's View menu breaks down as follows:

■ All Processes: Displays every process running on the system.

■ All Processes, Hierarchically: Displays every process running on the system in a tree format, where child processes appear beneath their parent processes.

■ My Processes: Displays processes running under the account with which you're logged in.

- System Processes: Displays all processes run by your OS X administrator account.

- Other User Processes: Displays all processes run by other user accounts (not the account you're currently logged into, or the administrator). Expect to see processes running in this section even if you're the only person using your computer. OS X has a variety of internal users that were created only to run particular processes, such as the user _mdnsresponder to run the mDNSResponder multicast DNS service.

- Active Processes: Displays processes that are actively doing things rather than just idling and waiting for something to happen.

- Inactive Processes: Displays those processes that are currently in a waiting state and aren't actively doing anything.

- Windowed Processes: Displays all processes that are attached to windows on the desktop.

- Selected Processes: Displays only those processes that are currently selected. To choose a consecutive list of processes, click the first, and then Shift-click the last in the list. If you want to choose a nonconsecutive list, ⌘-click each process.

To help you understand what you're looking at here, let's also look at the process listing columns from left to right, starting with PID. The PID, or Process ID, is a unique number assigned to each process when it's started. When viewing the listing in the All Processes, Hierarchically mode (see Figure 2-3), you'll notice that PID number 1 is always assigned to launchd, and PID number 0 is always assigned to kernel_task, as this is the order in which they are invoked at boot time.

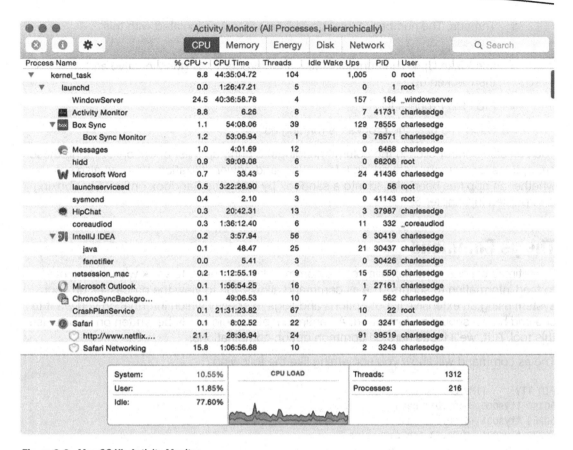

Process Name	% CPU ⌄	CPU Time	Threads	Idle Wake Ups	PID	User
▼ kernel_task	8.8	44:35:04.72	104	1,005	0	root
▼ launchd	0.0	1:26:47.21	5	0	1	root
WindowServer	24.5	40:36:58.78	4	157	164	_windowserver
Activity Monitor	8.8	6.26	8	7	41731	charlesedge
▼ Box Sync	1.1	54:08.06	39	129	78555	charlesedge
Box Sync Monitor	1.2	53:06.94	1	9	78571	charlesedge
Messages	1.0	4:01.69	12	0	6468	charlesedge
hidd	0.9	39:09.08	6	0	68206	root
Microsoft Word	0.7	33.43	5	24	41436	charlesedge
launchservicesd	0.5	3:22:28.90	5	0	56	root
sysmond	0.4	2.10	3	0	41143	root
HipChat	0.3	20:42.31	13	3	37987	charlesedge
coreaudiod	0.3	1:36:12.40	6	11	332	_coreaudiod
▼ IntelliJ IDEA	0.2	3:57.94	56	6	30419	charlesedge
java	0.1	48.47	25	21	30437	charlesedge
fsnotifier	0.0	5.41	3	0	30426	charlesedge
netsession_mac	0.2	1:12:55.19	9	15	550	charlesedge
Microsoft Outlook	0.1	1:56:54.25	16	1	27161	charlesedge
ChronoSyncBackgro...	0.1	49:06.53	10	7	562	charlesedge
CrashPlanService	0.1	21:31:23.82	67	10	22	root
▼ Safari	0.1	8:02.52	22	0	3241	charlesedge
http://www.netflix....	21.1	28:36.94	24	91	39519	charlesedge
Safari Networking	15.8	1:06:56.68	10	2	3243	charlesedge

System:	10.55%	CPU LOAD	Threads:	1312
User:	11.85%		Processes:	216
Idle:	77.60%			

Figure 2-3. Mac OS X's Activity Monitor

Note that launchd in OS X is similar to init in other Unix flavors (if you are familiar with other Unix-based operating systems). OS X also has its own form of the init process, mach_init.d, which is located in the /etc directory. The launchd daemon starts first as the system boots, and calls every other process to start. The kernel_task process is a memory manager for the OS X kernel (a kernel is the heart of any operating system).

> **Note** Except for launchd and kernel_task, PIDs will be assigned differently every time the machine is booted, and you can't typically assume that other processes will get the same PID every time.

Continuing with the Activity Monitor columns from left to right, we have

- Process Name: The name of the process associated with this PID.
- % CPU: The percentage of your CPU the process is currently using.
- CPU Time: The amount of time the process has been running.

- Threads: The number of threads (subprocesses) associated with this process.

- Idle Wake Ups: The number of times the process has gone inactive and then woken up.

- PID: The Process ID.

- User: The user the process is running as.

You can also control-click in the column headings to bring up a list of options. Among these are options for memory, networking information, and power utilization. You can also see whether an app has been placed into a sandbox by using the Sandbox option. Sandboxing is explained in Chapter 6.

The ps Command

Sometimes we crave the flexibility of the command line, or need to work with text output to feed information to scripts. The ps command allows you to view the processes on your system using an extensive list of options and flags to specify which information you want to see and how it should be formatted. An entire chapter could easily be written on how to use this tool. But, we'll focus here on common option combinations.

The ps command will show you something like the following:

```
PID TTY      TIME CMD
60250 ttys000  0:00.01 -bash
60263 ttys001  0:00.01 -bash
60272 ttys001  0:00.03 ssh catherine
```

Let's analyze what we're looking at here:

- PID: This is the same information we discovered in the Activity Monitor.

- TTY: This is the terminal controlling the process. A full list of available TTYs appears in the /dev directory, with all of the file names beginning with tty (for example, /dev/ttyp0).

- TIME: How much CPU time the process has used.

- CMD: Which command launched this process.

Used by itself, the ps command doesn't give you a lot of information. To see more information about the processes, you will want to invoke other options. When running the ps command, the following options are the most frequently used:

- a: Show all users.

- u: Can show user names instead of user IDs. (If you do not see the user name, try the –f option).

- x: Show processes that don't have a controlling terminal.

Here is an example of the output of running all of these options together, as ps aux, formatted and with the command paths truncated for easier reading:

```
USER  PID % CPU %MEM  VSZ       RSS    TT  STAT  STARTED      TIME COMMAND
dee   37783     40.8  16.1  1382764 676328  ?? R   Fri02PM  1784:51.31 /Applications/...
root     21      2.7   3.7   951712 157036  ?? Ss  30Oct09    37:39.45 /System/Library/...
dee   86042      2.5   1.3   543076  54328  ?? S   13Nov09    85:57.91 /Applications/
                                                                       iTunes.app/...
```

> **Tip** When using ps aux, it's a good idea to resize the Terminal window to as wide as you can manage. Many of the program paths are quite long, and the output can be visually confusing with all of the line wrapping.

The %MEM column shows you the percent of your RAM being used by this process. In STAT, you'll find the state this process is in, which is typically one of the following:

- I: Idle
- R: Runnable
- S: Sleeping for less than 20 seconds
- T: Stopped
- U: In an uninterruptible wait
- Z: A zombie, (the walking dead)

> **Note** There are additional characters that can appear as well. For example, notice that the second process in the code listing above is in the state Ss, meaning that it's sleeping and a session leader. See the ps man page for more information about this and other identifiers.

Because the output of ps aux tends to scroll off of the screen due to the number of processes running, most command-line aficionados use the following command to view the output one screen at a time:

```
ps aux | less
```

The top Output

While we could say the top program is a simplified version of the Activity Monitor, it's really more accurate to say that the Activity Monitor is a fancier version of top. Open a terminal session and type top to take a look (when you're done with top, press q to stop the program).

If you're used to top from other flavors of Unix, you'll find that OS X's top output is slightly different than you'll find elsewhere. As shown in Figure 2-4, top's output is divided into two major sections: the upper portion of the screen shows a variety of system state information, while the lower part shows processes.

```
●  ●  ●                            ⌂ charlesedge — top — 128×24
Processes: 225 total, 2 running, 10 stuck, 213 sleeping, 1372 threads                                                    23:44:35
Load Avg: 2.05, 2.48, 2.40  CPU usage: 9.9% user, 8.61% sys, 82.29% idle      SharedLibs: 14M resident, 15M data, 0B linkedit.
MemRegions: 133770 total, 1721M resident, 47M private, 492M shared. PhysMem: 8169M used (2738M wired), 21M unused.
VM: 600G vsize, 1063M framework vsize, 41020275(64) swapins, 46027562(0) swapouts.
Networks: packets: 269275547/292G in, 172821475/72G out. Disks: 75830581/1014G read, 50666463/1367G written.

PID    COMMAND      %CPU TIME       #TH   #WQ  #PORT MEM    PURG CMPRS  PGRP  PPID  STATE      BOOSTS           %CPU_ME %CPU_OTHRS
96462  com.apple.We 0.0  00:24.72 11    0    263   3408K  0B   61M    96462 1     sleeping *0[7249]       0.00000 0.00000
96457  Mail         0.0  06:11.69 14    0    1401  48M    0B   101M   96457 1     sleeping *176[2027]     0.00000 0.00000
87692  DiskArbitrat 0.0  00:00.21 2     1    39    4096B  0B   1148M  87692 1     sleeping *0[1]          0.00000 0.00000
78571  Box Sync Mon 1.0  53:11.54 1     0    9     216K   0B   196K   78555 78555 sleeping *0[1]          0.00000 0.00000
78555  Box Sync     0.9  54:13.45 39    0    273   29M    0B   165M   78555 1     sleeping *0[2586]       0.00000 0.00000
76539- jamfAgent    0.0  02:08:30 3     1    60    14M    0B   15M    76539 1     sleeping *0[1]          0.00000 0.00000
76520- jamf         0.0  22:07.04 5     0    182   5200K  0B   74M    76520 1     sleeping *0[1]          0.00000 0.00000
76328  ntpd         0.0  01:12.98 2     0    29    208K   0B   596K   76328 1     sleeping *0[1]          0.00000 0.00000
74990  com.apple.sp 0.0  00:01.49 2     0    41    4096B  0B   11M    74990 1     sleeping *0[1]          0.00000 0.00000
73697  DashboardCli 0.0  01:00.08 10    0    192   1932K  0B   19M    327   327   sleeping *0[5250]       0.00000 0.00000
72984  com.apple.We 0.0  03:37.63 14    0    258   2204K  0B   135M   72984 1     sleeping *0[8369]       0.00000 0.00000
71981  rtcreporting 0.0  00:09.52 4     0    69    1028K  0B   3276K  71981 1     sleeping *0[1]          0.00000 0.00000
68206  hidd         1.1  39:13.77 7     2    98    1048K  0B   4424K  68206 1     sleeping *0[1]          0.00000 0.00000
60995  nsurlstorage 0.0  23:18.40 4     2    219   9728K  0B   36M    60995 1     sleeping *1[142684]     0.00000 0.00000
54222  ssh-agent    0.0  00:14.89 3     0    45    736K   0B   2980K  54222 1     sleeping *0[1]          0.00000 0.00000
42811  helpd        0.0  00:00.67 2     0    37    4096B  0B   1184K  42811 1     sleeping 0[2]           0.00000 0.00000
41935  screencaptur 0.0  00:00.03 7     5    55+   2072K+ 20K+ 0B     328   328   sleeping *0[12+]        0.00000 0.00000
```

Figure 2-4. The top *program in Terminal*

The first line in the upper portion shows us a summary of how many processes are running and in what states. The lower portion's columns contain information that you're mostly familiar with: PID, COMMAND, %CPU, TIME, and #TH (number of threads). Items you might not recognize include the following:

- #PRTS: The number of Mach ports (secure pipes used for interprocess communication) in use by this process.

- #MREGS: The number of memory regions in use by this process.

- RPRVT: The amount of resident private memory in use by the process.

- RSHRD: The amount of resident shared memory in use by this process.

The top command has many flags and options available for controlling what information is displayed and how it appears in the window. Of particular interest is the ability to change what information top is using to sort its output. To sort on a column, press o and then enter the keyword for the information you're interested in. Most users will sort one of the following:

- cpu: Sort on what percentage of your CPU power the process is using.

- pid: Sort on process ID.

- vsize: Sort on how much virtual memory (swap) the process is using.

- time: Sort on how much CPU time the process is using.

- uid: Sort on the user ID associated with the process.

- username: Sort on the user name associated with the process.

See the top man page for more information on sorting top columns.

Viewing Which Daemons Are Running

You can view which daemons are running by looking at processes. Most daemons are processes that end in *d*; however, you can't trust that every process that ends in a *d* is a daemon, or that every daemon's process name ends in a *d*. One place to find those daemon-related tasks that are enabled and share data over your network is the Sharing section of your System Preferences, as shown in Figure 2-5.

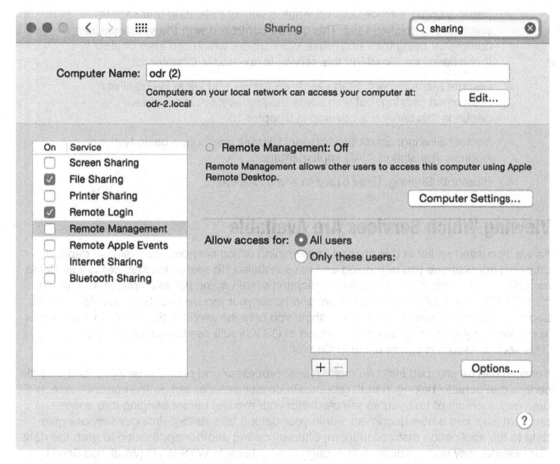

Figure 2-5. Turning daemons on or off in the Sharing system preferences pane

The Services listed here (not to be confused with the services discussed in the next section) each correspond to a daemon or set of daemons that run a specific type of sharing; only that which is critical should be enabled. Some of these services include the following:

- Screen Sharing: Enabling this option starts RFBRegisterMDNS, VNCPrivilegeProxy, and AppleVNCServer, with VNC being the main back end solution that allows for screen sharing. Securing this service is covered in Chapter 15.

- File Sharing: Consists of three types of sharing. When FTP is enabled, ftpd is invoked through launchproxy. When AFP is enabled, /System/ Library/CoreServices/AppleFileServer.app/Contents/MacOS/ AppleFileServer is invoked, which listens for network traffic on port 548. Securing this service is covered in Chapter 13.

- Printer Sharing: The cups process is running all the time but is altered when sharing printers.

- Remote Login: Remote login is Apple's way of indicating that sash is enabled and invokes sshd. This can be controlled with the systemsetup command, using the -setremote login option, which can start or stop these daemons. Securing this service is covered in Chapter 15.

- Remote Management: Starts AppleVNCServer and VNCPrivilegeProxy like Screen Sharing, but also starts the AppleVNCServer process. Securing this service is covered in Chapter 15.

- Internet Sharing: Starts the InternetSharing daemon, a basic Network Address Translation (NAT) implementation.

- Bluetooth Sharing: Uses blued to share Bluetooth.

Viewing Which Services Are Available

As we discussed earlier in this chapter, determining which services are available depends on which applications you're running and have installed. To see which services are available for a particular application, select the application's main menu (for example, in iCal, you'd click the iCal icon next to the Apple icon) and hover your mouse over Services. As of Snow Leopard, this menu was streamlined to show you only the services that apply to a particular application. If you're using an earlier version of OS X, you'll see the full list of services. (This section assumes you're using El Capitan.)

Services can be grouped into two major types: *processor* and *provider services*, and a single service can actually belong in both groups. Processor services act on the currently selected data (say, a chunk of text you've selected with your mouse) before sending it to another program (say, into a new document within your default text editor). Provider services give data to the application that called them, often by calling another application to grab the data. For example, say you're editing a web page in your favorite WYSIWYG (What You See Is What You Get) HTML editor and want to copy and paste a screenshot of your desktop. If your editor supports the services you need, you might go to the application's main menu at the top of the screen and click Services. Then, if you click Grab (or its equivalent) and then Timed Desktop to take a screenshot, you would then open your favorite HTML editor and paste the image into a location in the menu.

> **Tip** You can create new services through Automator.

The first thing you'll notice if you start looking at various programs' Services menus is that many programs don't support any services at all. When this is the case, the Services menu displays a notice that No Services Apply, and also offers you the Services Preferences menu, which we'll discuss later in this chapter.

> **Note**   One notable exception to the built-in services in Mac OS X is Microsoft Office. If you notice, Office has no Services advertised. Microsoft's developers have decided not to leverage these options that Apple has made available to developers.

For an example of an application that does support services, check out the humble Finder. There, you'll see a Services menu containing what's shown in Figure 2-6. As you can see, many of the related services revolve around image handling in this case.

Figure 2-6. *The Finder Services menu in El Capitan*

Stopping Services, Daemons, and Processes

Imagine that each of the running services, daemons, or processes on your system has its own door. Some of the doors are well secured, made of steel with a complex system of locks that only a true master could finesse their way through. Others are made of flimsy gauze and might as well have big flashing lights that say, "Waltz on in!"

Notice that neither extreme refers to a 100% safe door. There's no such thing. The reality is that most of the services, daemons, and processes fall somewhere between the two extremes, where each running item presents a risk that a script kiddy, hacker, malware-writer, phisher, spammer, scammer, thief, or other type of malcontent will jimmy a specific door open. When that happens, they're one step closer to having full access to your system.

The more concerned with security you are, the more work you should put into identifying everything running or listening on your computer. If you discover something you don't need, stop or disable it. When there's no door, there's no way in. Let's apply what we learned in the previous sections to start to control these processes.

> **Caution**   It's easy to damage your system seriously by stopping the wrong process. For example, if you stop launchd, that's it; you've stopped the daemon that rules them all. Be sure you understand what each item does before changing it, or make careful backups so that you can revert to a stable state if something goes horribly wrong.

Stopping Processes

It's happened to all of us: we're working in Microsoft Word or some other program, and all of a sudden it stops responding. We click around on a menu and just can't get it to do anything. Usually this happens to the authors when we try to put a joke into one of our chapters (guess it just does not compute). If you have a program that becomes unresponsive and will not quit, then you may need to *force quit* it.

There are two ways to do this. The first is to simply click the icon for an application that is in use in your dock until you get a menu that will give you the option to Force Quit (if Mac OS X has determined that the application is hung), or simply Quit (if Mac OS X has not determined that it is hung). The second is to use the ⌘-Option-Escape key combination to bring up the Force Quit Applications screen, which you can see in Figure 2-7. If Mac OS X considers the application to be hung, the title for the application will appear in the list in red. You will then be able to click the application and then the Force Quit button, whether the application is hung or not. The one exception is the Finder. If the Finder needs to be Force Quit, because it is your interface to the computer, it will give you a button to Relaunch, which you can click and after a time, the Finder will likely lower.

> **Caution**   If you Force Quit an application, you will not have the opportunity to save data for that
> application.

Figure 2-7. Force Quit Applications

Not all processes will appear in the Force Quit dialog box, but the applications that you interface with graphically should. For those that are not in the list, you can use the Quit Process button in Activity Monitor, which we covered earlier in this chapter.

You can also use the process ID to terminate a process from the command line. This is most commonly done using the kill command, which terminates a process. To use the kill command, look up the process ID using one of the methods mentioned throughout this chapter. Once you know the process ID, simply run kill followed by the process ID. For example, if Safari would not stop using the Force Quit Applications screen and it had a process ID of 57072, then you would run the following command to stop it:

```
kill 57072
```

Once you attempt to kill the process, it should terminate. If you continue to see the process running, then you can run kill more forcefully by sending different signals to the processes. For more information on those, see the man page for kill.

In addition to kill, you can also use killall. The killall command will terminate processes based on the name of the process. This can be a fairly dangerous step, considering that many processes can have multiple instances of the process running. The killall command works similarly to kill; simply place the killall command in the line followed by the string that you would like to match. To continue with the Safari example, you could use this:

```
killall safari
```

Stopping Daemons

While kill and killall are very useful for stopping some services, others will start right back up. This may be because they are launchd items and were told by the property list (.plist) that launched them to restart. Launchd is the first process started in Mac OS X, and it starts a process that starts every process in Mac OS X. The most common way to manage (and troubleshoot) launchd is using the launchctl command.

A fairly simple example of using launchctl to troubleshoot and manage a daemon can be seen with something as seemingly innocuous as the clipboard. com.apple.pboard is the process that makes up the clipboard (or the pasteboard). If you unload the pboard entry using launchctl you will no longer be able to cut, copy, and paste. pboard relies the user that initiated pboard (such as root, if root is enabled) having access to the /tmp folder. Therefore, pboard will not work correctly without /tmp, and without pboard you won't be able to paste things. When troubleshooting cut, copy, and paste issues, first verify that /tmp exists and then verify that pboard is running by using the following command:

```
launchctl list | grep com.apple.pboard
```

And if it isn't running, start it with

```
launctl start com.apple.pboard
```

There are other, more complicated processes in Mac OS X whose process names end up being dynamically generated. The diskarbitrationd is the process that handles mounting disks when they are inserted into the computer (such as FireWire, USB, and the like). Diskarbitrationd runs in the background, is always on (by default), and is started by `launchd`. New disks inserted into the computer are automatically mounted with `diskarbitrationd`; however, you might not want this and will want to disable it for any of a number of reasons (you might be forensically imaging a system, investigating malware on a device, attempting to fix corruption, or simply trying to keep users that don't know how to manually mount a disk from accessing one, just to name a few).

There are a number of ways to stop `diskarbitrationd`. One of the easiest (and least intrusive, because it doesn't require a restart) is using `launchctl`. First, run `launchctl list` to obtain a list of currently running `launchd`-initiated processes; however, that command alone is going to output a few too many processes, so let's constrain our search to those that include the string `diskarbitrationd`:

```
launchctl list | grep diskarbitrationd
```

You'll now see a PID and the name of the process. You'll notice that it has an alphanumeric string in front of it, appearing similar to `0x10abe0.diskarbitrationd`. You may also notice `com.apple.diskarbitrationd`, but if you see the alphanumeric string then `launchd` should not be managing the process. Next we will go ahead and stop this process, again using `launchctl`, but this time with the `stop` option:

```
launchctl stop 0x10abe0.diskarbitrationd
```

Once it is stopped, let's verify that `diskarbitration` is no longer running, by using ps aux. Once you have completed your tasks and want to re-enable disk arbitration, you can restart it using the `start` option in `launchctl`:

```
launchctl start 0x10abe0.diskarbitrationd
```

Finally, this process is not persistent across reboots. If you will be rebooting the system you are mounting the disk on, you might want to unload `diskarbitrationd` and then move the plist from `/System/Library/LaunchDaemons/com.apple.diskarbitrationd.plist`. For example, to move it to the desktop, use the following command:

```
mv /System/Library/LaunchDaemons/com.apple.diskarbitrationd.plist ~/Desktop/com.apple.
diskarbitrationd.plist
```

Types of launchd Services

Now that we've looked at programmatically managing `launchd`, let's look at the two types of services that `launchd` manages: LaunchAgents and LaunchDaemons.

LaunchAgents run on behalf of a user and therefore need the user to be logged in to run. LaunchAgent configuration plist files are stored in the `/System/Library/LaunchAgents` and `/Library/LaunchAgents` folders. User launch agents are installed in the `~/Library/LaunchAgents` folder.

LaunchDaemons can run without a user logged in. Launch daemons cannot display information using the GUI. Much like LaunchAgents, LaunchDaemon configuration plist files are stored in the `/System/Library/LaunchDaemons` folder (for those provided by Apple et al) and `/Library/LaunchDaemons` (for the rest).

GUI Tools for Managing launchd

There is also a simple tool called Lingon on the Mac App Store that can be used to manage launchd. Lingon, shown in Figure 2-8, provides users and administrators with the ability to interface graphically with launchd items not installed by Apple.

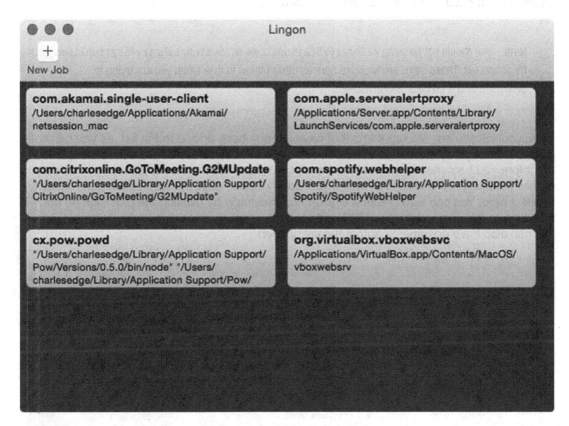

Figure 2-8. *Using Lingon to manage Launchd*

Changing What Runs at Login

Launchd manages processes. However, there are other tools that traditional Unix or Mac engineers may look to for managing processes. These are all, in fact, going to be started by launchd. For example, SystemStarter is a tool that can automatically start items stored in /Library/StartupItems and /System/Library/StartupItems. As Mac OS X continues to transition much of the previous functionality of other facilities, such as the cron daemon, into launchd, development has also reduced the reliance on StartupItems (also known as SystemStarter, an older technology that has arguably been around since before Mac OS X 10.0). Even though many third-party applications still use StartupItems, Apple development prefers the launchd facility and will continue to rely more heavily on it in 10.11 and beyond.

One of the easiest ways to set up a startup item is by dropping items (or shortcuts to items) into those traditional folders that Apple computers have been using for some time (such as /Library/StartupItems or /System/Library/StartupItems). But in addition, you can also create startup items for each user in the Users & Groups System Preference pane. To do so, open the System Preferences and click Users & Groups. Click the user you would like to create a startup item for and click the Login Items tab.

> **Note**   You should not be using /Library/StartupItems or /System/Library/StartupItems for processes. Those paths are included here as other places to look when you are trying to determine how a process was invoked.

Here, you will see any startup items that have already been added to the list, as you can see in the list of Login Items in Figure 2-9. If you find startup items here, take a look at what they do before you become alarmed. A number of third-party tools create a startup item as part of their installation process. However, if you don't need to start the application automatically, delete it here. You can also create a startup item manually by clicking the plus sign (+) and browsing to the item to be added. While Applications are most commonly launched at login, you can also have documents automatically opened.

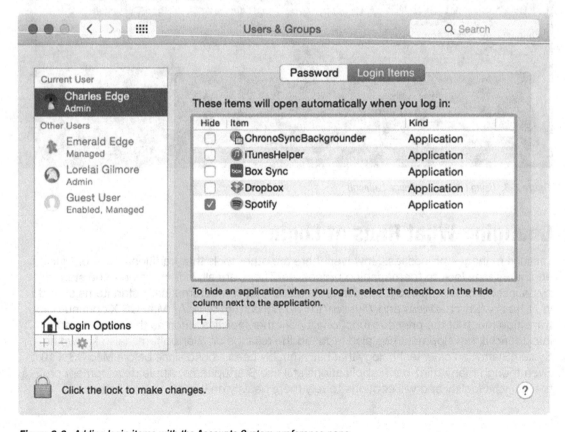

Figure 2-9. Adding login items with the Accounts System preference pane

Validating the Authenticity of Applications and Services

We've spent much of this chapter describing how to categorize processes, how to identify information about a process, and how to interact with processes. Finally, it's important to look at which processes should and should not be running on your systems. Every process should be reviewed for merit, either by running a quick search through sites you trust on the Internet or consulting trusted publications for validation. If a process is found not worthy it should be removed. Those processes that are worthy should also be authentic.

What do we mean by authentic? Virtually any application or service can be plucked from an operating system, altered, and then put back into the OS and run. And it would appear to be a valid service or application if you were to only look at the name of the service. But if a file has been edited, then usually the date and time of creation and/or last modification will change. To add insult to injury, date and time stamps can also be faked. So another good place to look for changes is in its default file size. These are two quick and easy ways to tell if a file has been altered, but they can both be faked (although it is rare that both would be faked at the same time). Therefore, a better method was devised to determine whether an application or service is authentic, by having it signed by a Certificate Authority. The signatures of files and folders cannot be faked, and therefore the application becomes signed using PKI. That signature then becomes a means to determine that the application is therefore authentic.

Leveraging application signing allows the operating system itself to then validate the authenticity of applications. Because the applications come from vendors, the packages that install applications and the applications themselves should be able to be validated with PKI as well. For more on application signing, see Chapter 6.

Summary

Throughout this chapter, we have looked at how services, daemons, and processes are started in OS X. Each of these will take up resources on a computer and depending on which account invokes them, they can each be dangerous. In order to mitigate some of the damage that can be done by a process, we will now turn our attention to managing these users in Chapter 3.

## Chapter 3

Securing User Accounts

Over the years, Apple has gone to great lengths to make OS X strong by hardening its user security. *Hardening* means strengthening a component in a system to make it more secure. User accounts can be hardened in OS X by limiting the resources that users can access. You can accomplish this two ways: by using the built-in GUI tools, or by using the command line. In this chapter, we will go deeper into securing the Mac by focusing first on restricting user access and then on more advanced command-line security that can be used to harden user accounts.

Introducing Identification, Authentication, and Authorization

Identification is determining who a user is, or what something is. *Authentication* is an operating system's attempt to verify the digital identity of someone or something attempting to communicate with the computer, such as a request to log in to the system. The sender attempting to be authenticated might be an actual person using a computer, a computer itself attempting to authenticate, or a computer program looking to run software on the machine. For example, if you are attempting to install software, authentication is the act of your Mac asking for your username and password and verifying that you are who you say you are.

> **Note** Because authentication is the act of establishing or confirming something as authentic, a key security component of authentication is to protect authentication attempts, such as passwords or key pairs in transit.

Authorization is a process that determines whether a user has access to a given resource. All modern multiuser operating systems include an authorization process. This gives the operating system the ability to identify users and then verify whether they have the appropriate credentials to access a resource. Permissions are generally defined by a system administrator, either on the computer itself or in a networked environment. On OS X, the authorization process starts with the /etc/authorization file, which contains rules used when authorizing users.

Authorization can also be made extensible using pluggable authentication modules (PAMs), which were initially developed by Sun Microsystems. A PAM allows multiple authentication schemes to be integrated with new software so that programs that rely on authentication can be written independently of the underlying authentication scheme.

Verifying that the person sending you information is really who they say they are is obviously desirable at all times. Authentication, however, is time-consuming and can inconvenience users while resulting in overhead on the authentication services. To make situations like this more convenient and efficient, many systems use a method of *identification*, a procedure that verifies that the person or entity authenticating is the same one it communicated with when they last authenticated. The means of identification can be established through the use of a ticket or token issued when authentication is complete. This saves the user from being required to authenticate on each communication with the server.

WHEN IS SECURE TOO SECURE?

One example of a situation where security and usability often collide is in the deployment of one-time passwords. A one-time password is one that must be changed each time you log in to your computer. This effectively makes any intercepted password good for only the brief interval of time before the legitimate user logs in the next time. This way, if someone intercepts a password, it is probably already expired or will be on the verge of expiration within a matter of hours.

For nearly every situation, this is too much security and impacts the ability of users to remember passwords. In our experience, when one-time passwords are deployed, it typically means that users are writing passwords down. Anytime your password policy causes users to have to write down their passwords, it is a good idea to review whether you are being too strict with password policies. For example, if passwords are too complicated to remember, people will invariably write them down. This is how the kid in the movie *War Games* got into his school computer, thus sparking an entire generation of hackers.

Managing User Accounts

OS X is a multiuser operating system, and therefore every file on the system is owned by a user, and every process is run by a user. One great way to analyze the processes in use on your system, along with the names of the users running them, is to view them using the Activity Monitor, accessible via the Utilities folder. As you can see in Figure 3-1, a variety of accounts are listed in the User column, each running separate processes. Activity Monitor has permissions to manage processes that the user can access. Therefore, processes are restricted from accessing data they should not be able to access. This security extends to files and other system resources on your computer.

Process Name		% CPU	CPU Time	Threads	Idle Wake Ups	PID	User
▼	kernel_task	2.6	8:25.31	113	764	0	root
▼	launchd	0.1	21.31	5	1	1	root
	WirelessRadioManagerd	0.0	0.18	2	0	492	root
	wirelessproxd	0.0	0.22	2	0	88	root
	WindowServer	7.1	4:46.91	6	29	184	_windowserver
	Wi-Fi	0.0	0.19	4	0	1190	jamf
	wdhelper	0.0	0.04	2	0	84	root
	watchdogd	0.0	0.07	4	0	329	root
	warmd	0.0	0.30	4	1	74	root
	ViewBridgeAuxiliary	0.0	1.54	2	0	3196	jamf
	usernoted	0.0	1.67	2	0	466	jamf
	UserEventAgent	0.0	2.33	6	0	53	root
	UserEventAgent	0.0	4.04	6	0	415	jamf
	useractivityd	0.0	0.25	2	0	631	jamf
	ushmuxd	0.0	0.10	3	0	93	ushmuxd

System:	3.74%	CPU LOAD	Threads	1090
User:	18.42%		Processes:	358
Idle:	77.83%			

Figure 3-1. Activity Monitor

Key to being able to secure an operating system is understanding what actions each user account can perform on the operating system. Next, we will discuss the types of accounts available within OS X.

Introducing the OS X Account Types

Limiting the capabilities of users in a standard operating environment is one of the first and most important steps in securing a system or a network, no matter which operating system you're running. There are six types of accounts in OS X: standard, managed, administrative, sharing, guest, and root.

The first and default user of a system is an *administrative* user; this user has almost unlimited access to the system. Administrative users can use many of the configuration utilities and change permissions of files to gain access to other users' folders if need be.

With all the power that an administrative user has, it is easy to damage the operating system accidentally. Best practices for operating in a secure environment dictate that once a Mac is set up, the administrative account should not be used for everyday use, and a *standard* account should be used instead. When the system needs more privileges than a standard account allows, such as installing applications or making system preferences changes, you will be prompted to authenticate as an administrator. Standard users can operate basic applications, access their own files, and change some of their settings. They cannot make global configuration changes or changes to other accounts. The reasoning behind this is that it is easy to accidentally perform inappropriate actions on the system as an administrator without asking for authentication to confirm the action. For example, you can accidentally delete critical system data when logged in as an administrator, or use the rm command to remove the wrong data without being prompted if you've elevated your privileges.

For a standard user, the likelihood of malware activity and misconfiguration on the system is almost nonexistent.

Sharing accounts were added to give other users access to log into shared resources over the network on your computer without giving them physical access to the machine locally.

To set up a sharing account, follow these steps:

1. Open System Preferences from the Apple menu.

2. Click Accounts to open the Accounts preference pane, and authenticate if needed by clicking the lock icon.

3. Click the plus (+) sign on the lower-left side of the pane.

4. Select Standard in the Type field (see Figure 3-2).

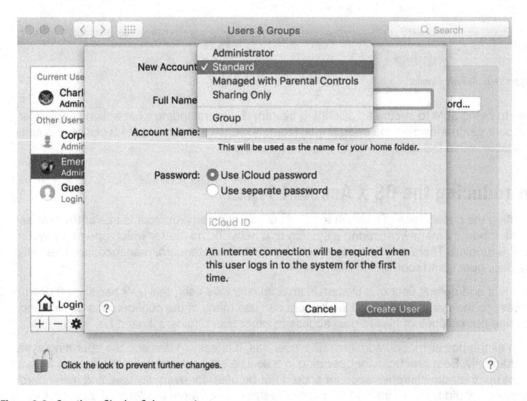

Figure 3-2. Creating a Sharing Only account

5. Enter a name for the account in the Name field. This is the full name of the user who will be logging in.

6. Enter a short name for the account in the Short Name field (keep in mind that this will be difficult to change at a later date).

7. Enter a password for the account.

8. Enter the password again in the Verify field.

9. Enter a hint for a password reminder.

10. Click the Create Account button.

Guest accounts allow users to perform basic functions such as surfing the Internet and checking email. Once the guest user logs off, their account's settings are deleted. If you need to give someone access to your computer but would like to keep your data private, enabling a guest account is a quick-and-dirty way to give them access without going through the trouble of setting up another user account on the machine.

> **Note**   Selecting the guest account will allow you to enable the "Allow guests to connect to shared folders" option, which should only be used in extremely rare cases where you want to allow users without passwords to connect to your computer.

Root accounts, or *superusers*, are powerful user accounts that have full access to the entire filesystem on a Mac. More on root accounts in a bit.

Adding Users to Groups

You can grant access to resources based on group memberships. In Leopard and Snow Leopard, Apple has introduced a new account type to the GUI of Mac OS X, called a *group*. Groups contain users who are created on the Accounts preference pane. To create a group, follow these steps:

1. Open System Preferences from the Apple menu.

2. Open the Accounts preference pane by double-clicking Accounts.

3. Click the plus (+) sign on the lower-left side of the pane.

4. Change the account type to Group.

5. Give the group a name (see Figure 3-3).

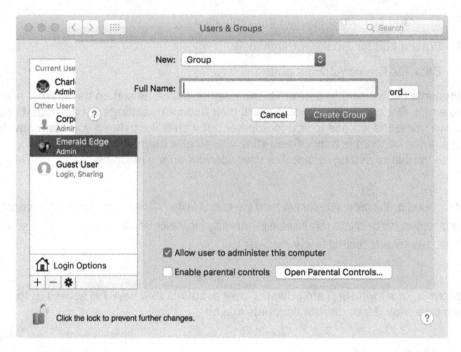

Figure 3-3. *Creating a group*

6. Add users to the group by selecting the check boxes for each user you want to include as a member (Figure 3-4).

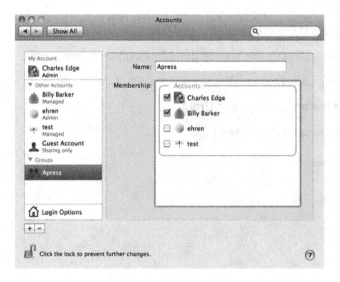

Figure 3-4. *Adding users to a group*

7. Close the window to save the group settings.

Enabling the Superuser Account

Some items in this book will require the *superuser*, often referred to as the *root user*, to be enabled. The root account is disabled by default (for a reason) and has unlimited access to everything on the computer. This level of access is different from the level an administrative user has. For example, while logged in as a root user, one can incorrectly type commands that can erase important files in the operating system. Root is rarely required as a permanently accessible user account. Unless you are using the root account for specific tasks, such as running Carbon Copy Cloner, disable it for the majority of the time.

To enable the root account, follow these steps:

1. Open the Directory Utility located in the /System/Library/ CoreServices/ folder.

2. Click the lock icon to authenticate as an administrator.

3. Click the Edit menu, and select Enable Root User from the menu (see Figure 3-5).

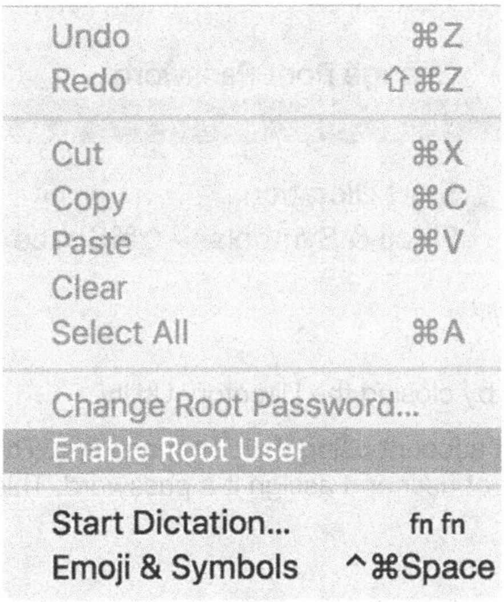

Undo	⌘Z
Redo	⇧⌘Z
Cut	⌘X
Copy	⌘C
Paste	⌘V
Clear	
Select All	⌘A
Change Root Password...	
Enable Root User	
Start Dictation...	fn fn
Emoji & Symbols	^⌘Space

Figure 3-5. Enabling root

4. Once you've enabled root, make sure to change the root password by clicking Change Root Password in the same menu.

5. Save the settings by closing the Directory Utility.

To disable the root account, follow these steps:

1. Open the Directory Utility by following the previous procedure.

2. Click the lock icon to authenticate as an administrator.

3. Click the Edit menu, and select Disable Root User in the menu (see Figure 3-6).

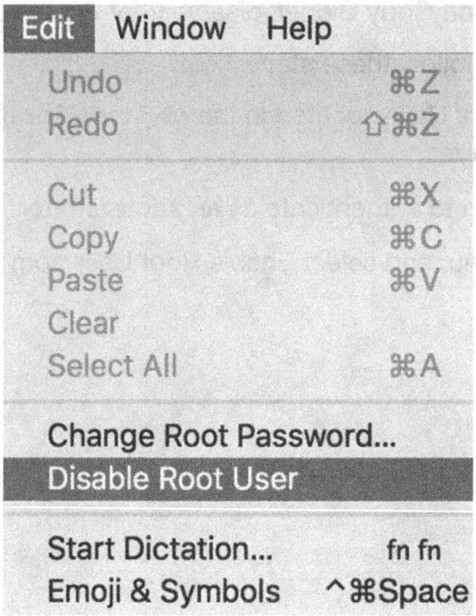

Figure 3-6. *Disabling the root account*

4. Save the settings by closing the Directory Utility.

You can also enable the root account using the command line. The dsenableroot command can be used to enable the root user and assign it a password. This command enables root:

```
Dsenableroot
```

First you will be prompted for the current user password; this user must be an administrative account. You will then be prompted twice for a password to assign the root account and then to verify the password. If you were successful, you'll see the following success code:

```
dsenableroot:: ***Successfully enabled root user.
```

To then disable the root account:

```
dsenableroot -d
```

> **Tip**   For security reasons, it is best to leave the root account disabled when you do not need it. If you do enable it, then do so temporarily. You can also use the sudoers file and sudo to manage which users can elevate privileges and how they are able to do so. We will cover sudoers later in this chapter.

Setting Up Parental Controls

Apple provides a rich set of ways to limit user access on a Mac. Included under the umbrella of empowering parents with the ability to limit their children's access, Parental Controls also give administrators the ability to fine-tune their users' access to resources. Using the Parental Controls system preference pane, you can configure controls for any user with the account type of Managed and have control over what they can do with Mail.app, iChat, and web browsing with Safari.

To use Parental Controls, open OS X's System Preferences and click the Parental Controls preference pane. Here, if it's the first time you're opening Parental Controls, you will be prompted with two options: "Create a new user account with parental controls" and "Convert this account to a parental controls account" (see Figure 3-7). You can easily create a new account that is managed here.

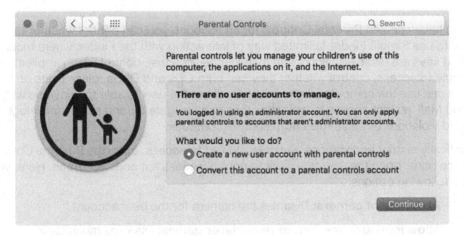

Figure 3-7. Enabling the Parental Controls feature

You can also enable Parental Controls for a user by clicking a user account and then the option to "Enable parental controls." Then click Open Parental Controls, as shown in Figure 3-8.

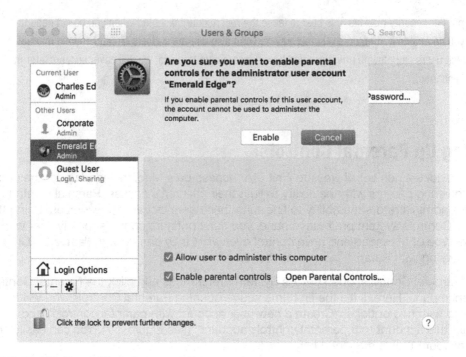

Figure 3-8. Enabling Parental Controls on preexisting accounts

Once you have enabled Parental Controls for an account, you can control whether the user is forced to use Simple Finder (a limited way of interacting with the Finder, where most of the command keys are disabled, along with many Finder options), control which applications a user is able to access, control whether they can burn CDs and DVDs, place limits on how long they can use the computer, limit access to whom the user is able to converse with over iChat and Mail, restrict access to web sites they can navigate to, and even review logs of attempted violations of these rules from another computer.

To specifically restrict applications a user is allowed to access, open the Parental Controls preference pane, open the user you want to control access for, and click Apps. Here, you have the following options:

- **Allow use of camera:** Disables the camera for the user account.

- **Allow joining Game Center multiplayer games:** Disables multiplayer games in Game Center.

- **Allow adding Game Center friends:** Disables adding new friends in the Game Center application

- **Limit Mail to allowed contacts:** Allows you to limit whom a user can communicate with. Click the Manage button to add new users that people can communicate with.

- **Limit Applications on this Mac:** This is the important part of this section. Here, you can use the checkboxes to disable which apps the highlighted user can check or uncheck, as you can see in Figure 3-9.

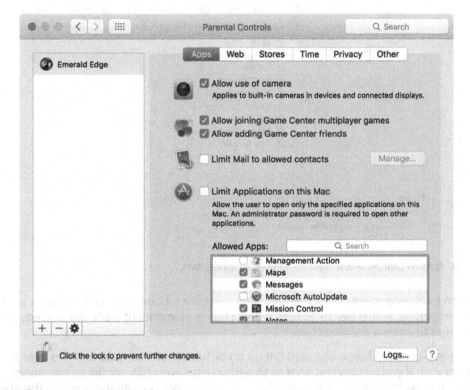

Figure 3-9. Managing apps in Parental Controls

Then go through the list of applications and place a check mark next to each application the user should be able to access. Once you've got a solid list of what a user should and should not be able to open, click the Web tab. Here, there are three options to limit access to web sites, as you can see in Figure 3-10:

- **Allow unrestricted access to websites:** Allows the user to visit any web site that they'd like to.

- **Try to limit access to adult websites:** Lets the computer guess at which sites should be accessed and which shouldn't. Click the Customize button to whitelist or blacklist web sites. Sites that are whitelisted are allowed, even if the computer guesses that the site is bad. Sites that are blacklisted are blocked.

- **Allow access to only these websites:** Allows access only to sites for which you explicitly enable access.

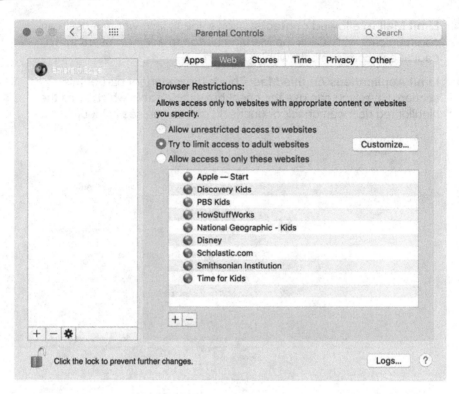

Figure 3-10. Parental Controls, allowing access to selected applications

The option to allow access only to certain sites can be a bit challenging. Each time your child, or employee, would like to access a new site, or elements of a site are loaded, you will be prompted to enter a password.

As shown in Figure 3-11, you can also set up an opt-in list of web sites that the user is allowed to visit. If you are limiting access to certain sites, you can configure the whitelists or blacklists. If a user with this control enabled attempts to go to a site that's not in the allowed list, they will have to enter an administrative password to be allowed to visit the site. You can also add sites to the "Never allow these sites" section. Sites listed in this section will not ask for an administrator password when requested, and access to the sites in this list will be denied whether or not they are allowed by the adult content filter.

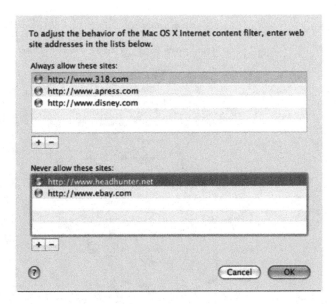

To adjust the behavior of the Mac OS X Internet content filter, enter web site addresses in the lists below.

Always allow these sites:

- http://www.318.com
- http://www.apress.com
- http://www.disney.com

+ −

Never allow these sites:

- http://www.headhunter.net
- http://www.ebay.com

+ −

?   Cancel   OK

Figure 3-11. *Parental Controls, allowed and disabled web sites*

Click the Stores tab (Figure 3-12). Here you can limit various forms of access to certain aspects of the iTunes Store. You have the following options:

- **Disable iTunes Store:** Disables the ability to buy music and movies using iTunes.

- **Disable iTunes U:** Disables the ability to access content in iTunes U.

- **Disable iBooks Store:** Disables the ability to purchase items in the iBooks Store.

- **Restrict Music with explicit content:** If you leave the iTunes Store enabled, this option will prevent access to content marked E for explicit.

- **Restrict movies to:** Disables the ability to watch movies of a certain rating (and above).

- **Restrict TV shows to:** Disables the ability to watch televisions of a certain rating (and above).

- **Restrict Apps to:** Disables the ability to access apps that are a certain rating (or above).

- **Restrict Books with explicit sexual content:** Restrict access to books on the iBooks Store that are marked with the explicit sexual content option.

Note   If you would like more features for limiting access to sites for children, definitely consider a product such as NetNanny if an opt-in list will not work for you. NetNanny can be found at www.netnanny.com/mac.

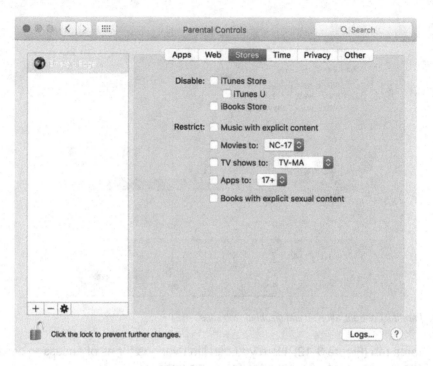

Figure 3-12. Parental Controls, limiting content from the iTunes Store

Click the Time tab (see Figure 3-13). Here, you can configure when users will be able to access the computer. Use the following checkboxes to configure when computers are usable:

- **Limit weekday use to:** Provide a number of hours that a computer can be used by the user account during weekdays.

- **Limit weekend use to:** Provide a number of hours that a computer can be used by the user account during weekend days.

- **Bedtime School nights:** Enter the hours that bedtime begins and ends, respectively, for nights before a school day.

- **Bedtime Weekend:** Enter the hours that bedtime begins and ends, respectively, for nights that are not school days.

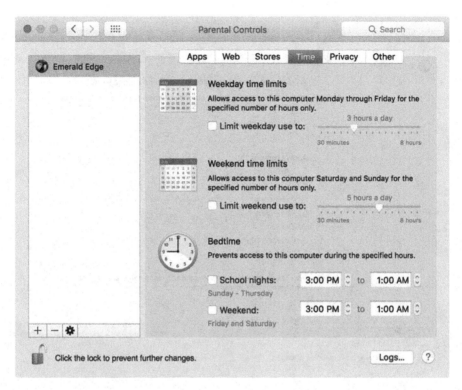

Figure 3-13. *Parental Controls, setting time limits*

Click the Privacy tab. Here you can restrict items that users can edit for themselves. As you can see in Figure 3-14, uncheck each box to restrict making changes to Contacts, Calendars, Reminders, Twitter, Facebook or Diagnostics.

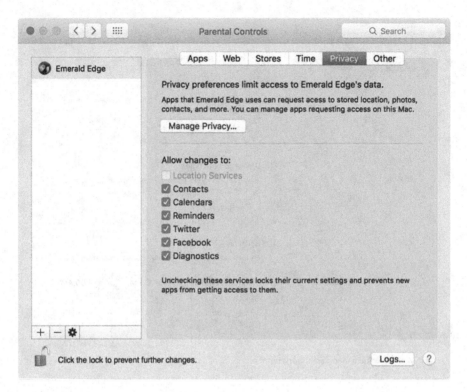

Figure 3-14. Restricting changed in Privacy tab

Click the Other tab. Here are a few miscellaneous options (see Figure 3-15), which include the following:

- **Turn off Dictation:** Disables the dictation entry in the Dictation & Speech System Preferences pane.

- **Disable editing of printers and scanners:** Restricts users from altering their printer settings. This includes adding or removing printers.

- **Block CD and DVD burning in the Finder:** Restricts users from burning new optical media.

- **Restrict explicit language in Dictionary:** Disables accessing any entries in the Dictionary or Thesaurus that contain explicit content.

- **Prevent the Dock from being modified:** Prevents a user from accessing the Dock on their computer.

- **Use Simple Finder:** Forces the use of Simple Finder, which is a simple operating environment.

Figure 3-15. Miscellaneous Options

Managing the Rules Put in Place

Once you have set the controls for your managed users, you will be able to review logs on traffic, allowing you to find users attempting to breach the rules you have put in place. You can do this using the Logs tab of the Parental Controls preference pane.

You can also copy Parental Controls settings from one user to another. This makes it easy to set up multiple accounts on a system and quickly assign the same settings to new accounts. To do this, click the account with the settings you would like to copy, click the cogwheel icon at the bottom left of the screen, and choose the Copy Settings for "<Username>" option (see Figure 3-16).

Figure 3-16. Copying user settings in Parental Controls

Then select the user to whom you would like to copy the settings, select the Paste Settings option, and verify that the settings have been applied (see Figure 3-17).

Figure 3-17. Pasting settings to another user

The Parental Controls system is not just for parents to control access to resources for their children. Although Parental Controls existed in Tiger, it has been expanded to include the options in the new sandbox system and provide a more granular control of managed settings in Leopard. Sandbox represents a giant step forward from the options in Tiger, and as such, it's a powerful new feature in Leopard that can be used in the workplace to limit what managed users can access, be it web sites or contacts used for iChat. It can even limit when a computer can be accessed, and in a manner that is not easily circumvented.

Profiles on OS X Server are a powerful way to provide administrators with more granular control of user access to resources. For example, with profiles, you can limit access on systems to global settings such as other System Preferences, Bluetooth, Fast User Switching, and Login Items. (For more on profiles, see Chapter 16). Parental Controls used in conjunction with Open Directory or a Mobile Device Management solution can push out these granular settings to many systems concurrently. It is an extremely attractive option to use these technologies together in schools or large corporations that have hundreds or even thousands of workstations.

The new Parental Controls system is missing some features that we would like to see, such as an online database that is updated with acceptable sites, but overall it is a big step in the right direction for limiting access to local resources. You can expect that Apple will continue to build on Parental Controls in the future.

Advanced Settings in System Preferences

You can also edit some slightly more advanced settings from within the Accounts System preference pane. These are accessible by Ctrl-clicking the account name and then clicking Advanced Options. This will bring up a screen similar to that shown in Figure 3-18. Here you can change a number of values for various attributes of the accounts, including Account name, UID, default group, path to the home folder, default shell, and the GeneratedID for the account. You can also add aliases using the plus (+) sign. This will allow the same account to authenticate using multiple names in the authentication dialogs throughout the operating system. We will discuss these attributes later in the chapter.

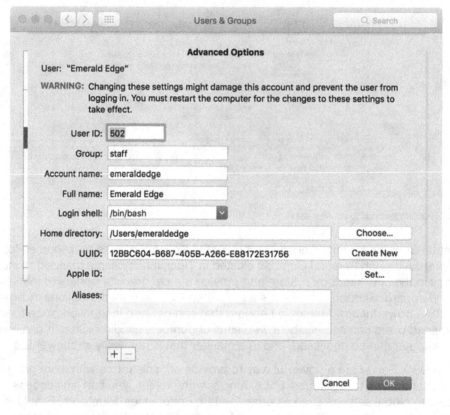

Figure 3-18. Advanced account options

Working with Local Directory Services

Accounts in OS X client can come from a variety of locations. But by default, they all reside in what is known as a local directory service. The local directory data resides primarily in the folder found at /private/var/db/dslocal. This folder, which will require elevated privileges to access, contains numerous files pertaining to the computer's directory service configuration. For instance, accounts for Users and Groups are stored in flat property list (.plist) files nested in the /private/var/db/dslocal/nodes/Default directory. Users are stored in property lists located in /private/var/db/dslocal/nodes/Default/users, while groups are stored property lists in /private/var/db/dslocal/nodes/Default/groups. Every local user and group account has a corresponding .plist file found in these directories. Accounts that begin with an underscore (_) are hidden service users and groups. For example, the web server uses the _www account, which obtains user settings from the _www.plist file. The _www user account does not have the ability to log into the machine, because it has no terminal access, nor does it have a password. Creating a new user in the /private/var/db/dslocal/nodes/Default/users directory will create a .plist file with a name that corresponds to the new user's short name.

Inside a .plist file are a number of attributes containing data about a given user or group. Readers with a Microsoft Windows background will notice that files in the local directory node more closely resemble registry keys for local accounts. Examine the .plist file for the user created earlier and look for the key named authentication_authority:

```
<key>authentication_authority</key>
    <array>
        <string>;ShadowHash;</string>
    </array>
```

This authentication key specifies the service that will be utilized to authenticate the user. Notice that it mentions ShadowHash, which indicates that the system will utilize a local file called a *hash* file to authenticate the user. OS X password hash files contain copies of a user's password in multiple formats. This allows different services to authenticate a user each with its own native password encryption type. The name ShadowHash means that passwords are stored outside the directory service, in another location (one that "shadows" the directory). Going back to the concepts introduced earlier in this chapter, identification is done through the directory; authentication to the account is done through the shadow.

> **Note** In OS X, users by default also have a Kerberos v5 authentication authority with a generated principal on the local KDC; accounts can be authenticated against the KDC or the shadow hash.

In the user's .plist file, you will also see a generateduid key. This key is used to track the user account, even if the short name is changed. Generated UIDs are based on a standard called the Universally Unique IDentifier (UUID), which is a complex programmatically generated string of characters that are never duplicated. A UUID is unique across time and space for all users.

Unless full disk encryption is being used on the local boot volume of the computer, once you know a user's GeneratedUID it is possible, in single-user mode, to swap password files with another user and log in to their account. To guard against this, you can require a password to enter single user mode. To do so, open /etc/ttys and then find the line that reads as follows:

```
console "/System/Library/CoreServices/loginwindow.app/Contents/MacOS/loginwindow"↵
 vt100 on insecure onoption="/usr/libexec/getty std.9600"
```

Next, change the line to read as follows:

```
console "/System/Library/CoreServices/loginwindow.app/Contents/MacOS/loginwindow"↵
 vt100 on secure onoption="/usr/libexec/getty std.9600"
```

Once this code is saved, attempting to boot into single user mode will require a password.

If you were to look in the /private/var/db/shadow/hash directory, you would find a file that is named using the value of this key. This means that even in the event of a user account's username changing, their password would still be tied to their account. This also prevents the collection of stale password files that would accumulate if they were based on the short name.

In this example, the authentication_authority record, which has a value of ;ShadowHash;, tells the local directory service to consult the user's local hash file when the user attempts to authenticate. This hash file will contain at least an sha-1 salted hash for the user, which is a secure unrecoverable password type. If Windows file-sharing services are enabled for the user, it will also contain the respective NTLM hash for that user, which is used by Windows file-sharing components. Over the years, Apple has struggled to balance security and functionality as it pertains to password hashes. Although hashes for Windows file sharing require NTLM, the NTLM hash type is more susceptible to common password attacks, which makes its recoverability more feasible. To solve this, Apple only enables the NTLM hash when windows file sharing users are specifically configured for SMB/Windows sharing access in the sharing pane of the system preferences. Storing a password in a hash file allows for a consistent password file location with flexible extensibility for other password hashes such as NTLM.

The data from the account plists can be managed by altering the text files directly. For example, if you preferred to change a user's image for their profile pic without using System Preferences, then you would simply alter the picture key. However, editing property lists directly can be pretty cumbersome, and so Apple has provided a plethora of commands that can be used to manage and query data from the local directory node and other directory services plug-ins without needing to read raw XML-style property list data. Some have GUI equivalents while others do not. These commands include the following (you can learn more about these commands using their manuals; that is, by entering man '*command*'):

- dscacheutil: Looks up information stored in directory services cache and flushes various caches.

- dscl: Interactive command used to edit and browse directory services settings, such as user accounts, group accounts, and search policies (the order with which Mac OS X looks up account information in each directory service). The closest GUI equivalent would be twofold: the Accounts System Preference pane and the Directory Utility. This command is covered in more depth in the next section.

- dseditgroup: Used to edit, create, and delete groups, or to add or remove group members.

- dsenableroot: Controls the root user account (enable, disable, and reset the root password). The GUI equivalent would be the "Change root password", "Enable root user" or "Disable root user" options in the Edit menu of the Directory Utility. (This command was covered earlier in this chapter.)

- dserr: Prints a description of directory services-related errors, example "dserr 14090." Once you have the error code, you can then use the man page for DirectoryService to look up the meaning of each error (or search Google for more information on the specific errors; if there is a minus sign in front of the number, put quotation marks around the errors).

- dsexport: Exports directory services data. Similar functionality is available using the Export feature of Workgroup Manager, a tool distributed as part of Mac OS X Server.

- dsimport: Imports directory services data. Similar functionality is available using the Import feature of Workgroup Manager.

- dsmemberutil: Looks up UUIDs and group information and flushes group cache (example: dsmemberutil flushcache).

- dsperfmonitor: Runs performance monitors of the directory services plug-in, useful with debugging operations (example: dsperfmonitor -dump).

- id: Looks up a user identity, including the group memberships (example: id cedge).

When administrators from other platforms migrate to using OS X directory services, one of the first things they notice is that, by default, domain administrators from a directory service are not administrators of local Mac OS X client. To mimic this functionality, it is possible to nest a network directory service group inside the local administrators group, thereby propagating local administrator rights to all network members of that group. This is very handy in large environments where administrator access to specific resources may need to be limited to subsets of administrators.

Many still choose to maintain a dedicated local administrative account on Mac OS X systems; this is useful for desktop support, automated patch management, and other administrative tasks. There are three ways to go about creating those local administrative accounts. The first is using the Setup Assistant or the Accounts System preference pane, common in monolithic imaging environments but not entirely scalable in large deployments. The second is by taking the .plist and the password hash files that comprise an account and dropping them into the default directory domain's hierarchy (as explained previously). The third way is by creating a script to automate the account creation. Scripting account creation is beyond the scope of this chapter, but there are many resources available on the Internet and in other books in this series that describe this process.

Creating a Second Local Directory Node

Now that we have a better understanding of how the local directory service works, let's look at how to create a second instance of that local directory service database. This is useful for hiding administrative accounts and, if you have a rogue account running on your system, it can also be useful for finding the source of that account. To create another directory node, first make a copy of the local directory services information store that we've been working on throughout this chapter. For this example, we're going to copy it into the same nodes folder that Mac OS X uses by default, but rather than call our node Default, we're just going to call it NEW:

```
sudo cp -prnv /var/db/dslocal/nodes/Default /var/db/dslocal/nodes/NEW
```

When it is started, the accountsd daemon will look in the nodes directory for any newly created nodes, as we want it to do. Let's restart the daemon with the following:

```
sudo killall accountsd
```

Now go ahead and open up the Directory Utility (as described previously in this chapter) and click the Search Policy tab. Authenticate using the lock in the lower-left corner of the screen, and then change the Search field to Custom path.

External Accounts

External accounts are similar to mobile accounts (which we will cover in more depth in Chapter 16). With an external account, you can store the user profile, password, and account information on removable media, making it portable across computers without a network. To do this, we're going to do some crafty manipulation of the createmobileaccount command, which is located in the /System/Library/Coreservices/ManagedClient.app/ Contents/Resources directory. This command is normally used when a Mobile Account logs into the computer. Rather than let the operating system decide whether it wants to invoke the createmobileaccount dialog at the login window, we're going to force it to run the dialog manually now. The -n, -p, and -h flags define the username, password, and home directory of the account. Assuming your USB drive is named JUMPDRIVE, the following code will set up your external account on the removable media (by the way, this is not in your default path, which means you must always type the full path to the command or modify your shell preferences to make it your default path):

```
./createmobileaccount -n mobileadmin -p 'MYSECRETPASSWORD' -h↵
/Volumes/JUMPDRIVE/Users/mobileadmin
```

That's about all there is to it. If we wanted to, we could also enable FileVault by using the -e flag and/or run the command verbosely (a great option for troubleshooting issues during account creation) by using the -v flag. Next, use ls -al to verify that your new external account can write to the volume.

Restricting Access with the Command Line: sudoers

By editing the sudoers file, you can take a much more granular approach to securing users' access to resources. *Sudo* stands for "su do," and *su* stands for "substitute user." sudo is a command-line utility in Unix, Linux, and Mac OS X that allows users to run programs as though they were another, more powerful user. By default, sudo will run as a system's superuser, or root account (although this can be changed using the runas_default setting in the sudoers file). The syntax sudo will run *one* command as another user. The syntax su will run *all* commands that follow it as the administrative user who is invoked. su and sudo are useful tools, but they are also very powerful and can be used to accomplish almost anything once invoked, so take precautions. You should use su and sudo in as limited a fashion as possible. In fact, you should use su with even more caution than sudo, because it maintains the elevated permissions for the duration of a Terminal session, and its use is generally not recommended.

> **Note**   sudo keeps a record of every command executed through it, while su (and sudo -s, sudo /bin/sh, and so on) let users evade auditing once they have elevated.

As stated earlier, by default the root, or superuser, account is disabled in Mac OS X but can be enabled using the Directory Utility. In Mac OS X Server (as opposed to Client), the root account is enabled by default and automatically is given the password of the first administrative user who is created during installation (more about root access in Mac OS X Server in Chapter 16).

> **Note**   By default, any administrative user can use the sudo command.

The sudoers file is located at /private/etc/sudoers. Editing the sudoers file is a direct way to add or remove the ability of users and groups to run certain commands and perform certain tasks from the system without having to use the GUI. Before editing the sudoers file, you should always back up the file. The following code is the default content of the sudoers file on a system (the lines that start with # are inactive):

```
# sudoers file.
#
# This file MUST be edited with the 'visudo' command as root.
#
# See the sudoers man page for the details on how to write a sudoers file.
#
# Host alias specification
# User alias specification
# Cmnd alias specification
# Defaults specification
Defaults   env_reset
Defaults   env_keep += "BLOCKSIZE"
```

```
Defaults  env_keep += "COLORFGBG COLORTERM"
Defaults  env_keep += "__CF_USER_TEXT_ENCODING"
Defaults  env_keep += "CHARSET LANG LANGUAGE LC_ALL LC_COLLATE LC_CTYPE"
Defaults  env_keep += "LC_MESSAGES LC_MONETARY LC_NUMERIC LC_TIME"
Defaults  env_keep += "LINES COLUMNS"
Defaults  env_keep += "LSCOLORS"
Defaults  env_keep += "SSH_AUTH_SOCK"
Defaults  env_keep += "TZ"
Defaults  env_keep += "DISPLAY XAUTHORIZATION XAUTHORITY"
Defaults  env_keep += "EDITOR VISUAL"
# Runas alias specification
# User privilege specification
root  ALL=(ALL) ALL
%admin  ALL=(ALL) ALL
# Uncomment to allow people in group wheel to run all commands
# %wheel  ALL=(ALL)  ALL
# Same thing without a password
# %wheel  ALL=(ALL)  NOPASSWD: ALL
# Samples
# %users ALL=/sbin/mount /cdrom,/sbin/umount /cdrom
# %users localhost=/sbin/shutdown -h now
```

In the following lines (part of the original file), root and users in the admin group are given access to a Host_Alias of ALL to Runas_Alias for all users and run Cmnd_Alias of ALL. This is unlimited access to the system, and it is what makes root the powerful account that it is. If you want to reduce the access that administrative users (users defined as administrators in the Accounts preference pane) are given, you can edit this setting. Let's take a look at the following two lines in the default sudoers file:

```
root  ALL=(ALL) ALL
%admin ALL=(ALL) ALL
```

> **Note**   In a Unix file, when you see an item with % in front of it, you are typically looking at a variable. Thus, %admin is the administrators group. If you create a new group named pirates on the Accounts preference pane, you would refer to it as %pirates here.

Table 3-1 lists some of the flags that you can use to define privileges in the sudoers file.

Table 3-1. sudoers *Flags*

Flag	Description
mail_always	Sends mail to the mailto user for every sudo event.
mail_badpass	Sends mail to the mailto user if the password is entered incorrectly.
mail_no_user	Sends mail to the mailto user if the user is not in the sudoers file.
mail_no_host	Sends mail to the mailto user if the host disallows the user.
mail_no_perms	Sends mail to the mailto user if a disabled command is run.
tty_tickets	Specifies that users must authenticate per shell instance.
authenticate	Specifies that users must authenticate before running commands.
root_sudo	Disables users from invoking a shell using sudo.
log_host	Adds the hostname to logs.
log_year	Adds the year to logs.
set_home	Sets the HOME variable (~) to the target user's home.
always_set_home	Always sets the HOME variable (~) to the target user's home.
path_info	Disables prompts warning that a command is not in a user's path.
fqdn	Puts fully qualified hostnames in the sudoers file.
insults	Insults users when they enter incorrect passwords.
requiretty	Disables running visudo unless a Terminal session is present.
env_editor	Allows other text editors to edit the sudoers file. This is useful if limiting to pico or vi.
rootpw	Prompts for root password versus invoking a user's password.
runaspw	Prompts for the password of the user defined by runas_default.
targetpw	Prompts for the password of the user specified with -u.
set_logname	Logs sudo events using the invoking user's name.
stay_setuid	Runs sudo as the real UID of the invoking user (same as set_logname).

To edit the sudoers file, you will use the visudo command. This command will lock the file so that it cannot be written to by multiple programs. It will also verify that the file is complete with all its necessary parts and will check the file for syntax errors before allowing you to save it. Because the visudo command uses the vi text editor to edit the sudoers file, you will likely want to become familiar with vi before editing your sudoers file. For more on using the vi command, see the man page by entering the following from a command prompt (/Applications/Utilities/Terminal):

```
man vi
```

> **Tip**   Before editing the file, it is also a good idea to read the man page for `visudo` by entering man `visudo` at the command line. man will go into full detail on the uses and syntax for the program as well as any other command you're curious about.

If the file is not edited properly, `visudo` should not allow you to save it when you are finished editing. You can use the `-c` option with `visudo` to run a check of the file's syntax and ensure that it is able to parse properly. The `-c` stands for "check mode." You can run the command by entering the following:

```
visudo -c
```

This should return with the following line, provided that the file parses correctly:

```
/private/etc/sudoers file parsed OK
```

Now that you know how to check the file, let's take a look at the `-f` option, which is used to specify an alternate `sudoers` file in a different location, leaving the live `sudoers` file untouched. There are a variety of reasons for wanting to work with a file in a separate location, such as transferring the file to another system or changing its configuration, with the reconfiguration planned to go live at a later date. For example, you can use the following command to create a temporary `sudoers` file named `sudoers.inprogress`:

```
visudo -f /etc/sudoers.inprogress
```

You can use aliases in the `sudoers` file to indicate a variable that contains a user, multiple users, a group, or multiple groups. When working with multiple users or groups on a system, it is always a good idea to create aliases on the system to apply attributes to multiple users or groups at once. If you need to apply the same access rights to a group of users, you can do that by using an alias membership rather than by applying permissions for each user individually. When referencing an alias or group of users in `sudoers`, you will notice that % will be placed in front of the group name. To be clear, the % character is not used to signify the name of a new group, but is used to reference groups. For example, by adding the following line to the `sudoers` file, you could create an alias named `powerusers` that contains members of a group named `admin`, the user named `cedge`, and a user named `MyCompany`. We will also create an entry that simply lists those who the webmasters are:

```
User_Alias    powerusers = %admin, cedge, MyCompany
User_Alias    webusers = mark, joel, michael
```

Setting up a `Runas_Alias` for a user or group will define the user or system daemon that a user or alias can run as when using the `sudo` command. In the following line, we will tell the system that the `webusers` defined previously are able to run commands as the `apache` system user:

```
Runas_Alias    webusers = apache
```

The Host_Alias command allows you to define a group of computers, also called *hosts*. You can reference hosts by name, by IP, or by a range of either. When defining a range, rather than specify every element within the range, it's preferable to use wildcards as catchalls. Wildcards that can be used are similar to those available in shell scripting, as shown in Table 3-2.

Table 3-2. Wildcards

Wildcard	Description
?	Matches a single character.
*	Matches multiple characters.
[...]	Matches a character in a range.
[!...]	Matches a character that is not in the range, except in a regular expression, which uses the syntax [^...].
\x	Escapes characters, similar to regular expressions.

> **Note** When using wildcards, you cannot grant access to commands in subfolders of those you define. You will need to specify those separately.

For example, if you want to create an alias list of all your servers, which are named afpserver1, afpserver2, odserver1, odserver2, adserver1, and adserver2, then you could use *server? for the Host_Alias. Additionally, you can use specific IP addresses or IP addresses with a subnet defined. Host_Alias comes in handy when you are pushing out a sudoers file to a large number of machines and want to have different options for different hosts. An example of a Host_Alias configuration might include the following:

```
Host_Alias  Servers = *server?, 10.0.1.0/255.255.255.0
Host_Alias  Workstations = 10.0.2.0/255.255.255.0
```

The next portion of the sudoers file defines the commands that aliases or users can access. Cmnd_Alias is used to set them. For example, if you want to give a user access to run all the commands in the /usr/sbin directory and all the commands located in the /usr/bin folder, you would use the following line:

```
Cmnd_Alias = /usr/sbin/*, /usr/bin/*
```

The final portion of the sudoers file is where access to resources is granted to users or aliases. In previous sections of the sudoers file, we defined lists of groups, computers, and commands. Now you can take all of this and put it together by listing the group of users that has access to run specified commands on specified machines. The basic syntax of the sudoers file would read like this:

```
<User_Alias>  <Host_Alias> = (<Runas_Alias>) <Cmnd_Alias>
```

To put this into a real-world example, you can look at allowing the web scripters who were defined earlier to access the `/private/etc/httpd` program on servers. Here you will also introduce `NOPASSWD` and `PASSWD` into the `sudoers` file. This tells the system whether to prompt a user for a password when they are attempting to `sudo` the command that is being called. Keep in mind that when using the `NOPASSWD` tag, you will not be prompted for a password. Once you've written in a section and you're committing a password to authenticate, it's a good idea to give it a once-over to catch any errors with the line before submitting the password to the system.

The section of the `sudoers` file for `webscripters` is as follows:

```
User_Alias  webscripters = mark, joel, michael
Runas_Alias webscripters = apache
Host_Alias  Servers = *server?, 10.0.1.0/255.255.255.0
Cmnd_Alias  web = /private/etc/httpd
Webscripters Servers = (webscripters) NOPASSWD: web
```

Once you have written a good `sudoers` file, you can push it to other users on your network. You can do this a variety of ways; most notably through ARD, radmind, the Casper Suite, or SSH. These technologies are a bit beyond the scope of this book, but they're definitely worth researching for their administrative abilities. You can find more information on ARD at `www.apple.com/remotedesktop`. You can find more information on radmind at `http://rsug.itd.umich.edu/software/radmind`. You can find more information on the Casper Suite at `www.jamfsoftware.com/products/casper5.php`.

> **Note**   If rules in `sudoers` conflict, the last rule applied will be activated.

Securing Mount Points

Navigating the file system through the Finder or through Terminal on a mounted drive is one of the most common tasks a user will do on their computer. It is also one of the most common things an attacker looking for information will do. You never want your system to be compromised, but when it does happen, you want to limit the access that an unauthorized user will have. Restricting access to disks, volumes, and RAIDs using mount options is one way to accomplish this.

> **Note**   Each disk in a computer has a collection of disks that are mounted. This can be seen and controlled easily in the Disk Utility application. However, you will often need more granular controls, such as mounting a volume in verbose mode.

Once a disk is mounted, it is typically considered a *volume*. Running the `df` command, which is used exclusively for mounting disks, shows you all the volumes mounted on the system. Another command, `mount`, also displays mounted disks but can further be used to mount disks with different options, giving administrators a higher level of control over those disks.

Until a disk is mounted, it remains listed in /dev/diskname (disks are often listed sequentially, as disk0s2, disk0s3, and so on). The mount command will be active only until the first reboot.

Common options for the mount command include the following:

- ■ -t Specifies the file system type.

- ■ -r Mounts the file system as read-only.

- ■ -f Forces the file system into a read-only state.

- ■ -a Mounts all the file systems available in the fstab file.

- ■ -d Uses all the options in a dry run.

- ■ -v Uses verbose mode with the mount command.

Administrators can mount drives that have disabled the ability to write to them or enabled other access options by mounting a disk using the -o flag in the command. The proper syntax for this command is to put the option in front of the o, such as -fo or -do. One example of using the option with the mount command is using -ro to make a disk read-only (or more specifically revoke-write access), often used when forensics are being performed on a system.

It is also possible to stop Mac OS X from automatically registering and mounting drives that are inserted, by disabling diskarbitrationd, the system process that polls for new disks. There are multiple methods for doing this, which will force users to use the mount command in order to register a new disk with the operating system. One way is to kill the process and then remove the /usr/sbin/diskarbitrationd file, completely removing the daemon. Another is to move the /System/Library/LaunchDaemons/com.apple.diskarbitrationd.plist file to another location, such as the Desktop. Removing or renaming the property list (plist) file is typically the best choice. You can also control the mounting and unmounting of disks using the Disk Utility or the Terminal diskutil framework.

SUID Applications: Getting into the Nitty-Gritty

There are a variety of applications running on your system, and not all run as your user. When you open Activity Monitor from /Applications/Utilities and change the filter option to Administrator Processes, you will see all the processes running on the system as root. Applications that are running as root often have the SUID bit set, causing them to be run as the owner of the file, which for many of these applications is root. To view whether a file has the SUID bit set, you can run an ls -l command in a given directory to look for any file with a listing that has an s listed rather than an execute bit in the permissions line for owners of the file. For example:

```
-r-s--x--x  1 root root 19809 Jan 14 14:05 ps
```

Binary files (executables) that are not written well can cause SUID bits to allow for privilege escalation to an administrative user. Although you might not want to allow SUID files on your system, it's not realistic to remove the SUID bit from all files, because some applications will require certain files to be SUID, such as login. Most SUID applications exist specifically to let users perform privileged operations or gain access to resources that require root privileges when they are not logged in as the root user. Therefore, the root user owns most SUID applications.

Many applications that are not written specifically to allow manual privilege escalation actually provide a way for users to execute a command. vi allows users to run commands from within the interactive text editor. Many other commands, such as less and more, allow commands to be executed by pressing the ! key while viewing a file that takes up more than one page of content. Knowing whether each SUID application is dangerous requires knowing the usage details of these applications, and whether a shell command can be run from within the command or some binary file can be invoked receiving root access. To find all SUID applications, use the following command for a listing of all SUID or SGID files:

```
sudo find / -type f \( -perm -04000 -or -perm 02000 \) -ls
```

> **Note**   Mac OS X allowed SUID shell scripts until the 10.3.9 software update, so if you are running an operating system prior to Tiger 10.4, consider SUID shell scripts when auditing your system, as they are too dangerous to allow on the system.

To fix the SUID scenario, set the UID for a user. In our example, the user will be test. If the file is executed, it will now run with the rights of the user invoking the file and not with the rights of the user who runs it:

```
chmod u+s test
```

If you are in an SGID (group SUIDs) scenario rather than an SUID scenario, set the GID for test. If executed, the file will now run with the rights of the group of the file and not with the rights of the group that runs it:

```
chmod g+s test
```

If an SGID is set on a directory, all newly created files inside this folder won't inherit the main group ID of the creator. Instead, they will be created with the group ID of the folder. For example, the SGID is set for the test folder folder1, and it has the group ID for www. Now, if the root user creates a file inside folder1, the group ID for this file will not be root but www. SUID and SGID can be set at the same time.

Creating Files with Permissions

By default, when creating a new file, the default permissions of that file are determined by the umask variable. You can work with the umask to edit the default permissions of new files. You can configure the umask setting by using the umask command. Of course, we advise that you only perform the following commands if you have a pretty good idea of what you're doing here. Fixing disk permission mistakes can be a time-consuming and costly endeavor.

First, run the command umask from a Terminal screen by typing **umask** at a command prompt. When you do this, you will get a number as your response. The umask variable is subtracted from the total permissions number possible for securing Unix files, 777. This leads to a umask of 0022, creating new files on a hard drive with permissions of 755.

> **Note** For more information on POSIX permissions, see Chapter 4.

If you enter **umask 0002** at the command line, you will be telling the system to create new files with permissions of 775. However, if you use a umask of 077, you will cause all new files to be readable only by the user who creates and subsequently owns the files.

Using the umask command to set default file permissions only applies to the umask setting for your session. This means the next time you restart your system, this setting will be lost. To permanently reset the permissions for new files, you will need to edit the globalpreferences.plist file on a per-user basis by inserting an NSUmask override setting in the file ~/Library/Preferences/.GlobalPreferences.plist. Insert these lines using your favorite plist file editor or using the defaults command:

```
<key>NSUmask</key>
<integer>0</integer>
```

Replace the 0 with the decimal conversion of the octal umask you want to set. A decimal NSumask of 0 gives the octal umask value of 007, meaning that we allow only owners and users in a files group access to newly created files. The recommendation from Apple is to use /etc/launchd-user.conf, with a line containing umask nnn. However, users can then set their own umasks using ~/.launchd.conf. The umask can also be defined in /etc/launchd. conf, but that sets it for all processes, including system daemons, which can potentially cause unexpected results.

> **Note** To edit this globally, insert the same setting into the file /Library/Preferences/. GlobalPreferences.plist.

Summary

We started this chapter with securing accounts using graphical tools such as the Accounts system preferences. Once we looked at the options available through graphical means, we switched gears and started looking at those available only from the command line (such as visudo). You'll notice that the granularity of control over accounts goes far beyond that which has been provided in those preference panes. Once we moved through the options in the preferences, we then correlated them with how those options reflect some of the changes in the property list files that make up the local directory service. By the way, there are other locations where accounts can reside, and so in Chapter 16, we will look at how Open Directory impacts accounts.

In Chapter 4 we cover permissions, one of the most important aspects of securing Mac OS X, a concept that builds on the concepts explained throughout this chapter!

## Chapter 4

File System Permissions

File system permissions are your data's first line of defense in a multiuser environment. A well-managed permission scheme ensures that your data is accessible and modifiable only by the proper people. The file system, after all, is the gateway to your data. An ineffective permission scheme is the equivalent of handing your data out to anyone who would express interest in it, or even worse, allowing them to destroy it. Furthermore, poorly implemented permissions can serve a different evil, preventing honest, hardworking Joe from accessing either his own documents or documents created by his collaborators.

Thus, file system permissions cover the triad of information security: *confidentiality* (ensuring that your sensitive data isn't viewed by the wrong eyes), *integrity* (ensuring that data isn't manipulated by unwanted parties), and *accessibility* (ensuring that the right parties can access data consistently and reliably). This is no light matter: a small change to permissions on a directory toward the top of your file system hierarchy can have wide-sweeping effects in all three areas. Suddenly, that chmod -R 777 command that you read about online and are about to run might not seem like a good idea, and it probably isn't (if you don't understand what this means, don't worry, you will by the end of this chapter). Too many environments take a lax view on file system permissions simply because it's easier not to have to deal with them. Unfortunately, many people don't realize the importance of data security until they have to reassemble the damage caused by poorly managed permissions on vulnerable data.

This chapter covers the ins and outs of file system discretionary access controls provided by OS X version 10.11. Specifically, we will explore techniques utilizing all of El Capitan's tools (graphical and command line) to help ensure that your data is accessible by those who need to access it and safe from manipulation by those who don't.

In this chapter we will also examine the impact of file system permissions on the security of an operating system itself. Permissions problems can lead not only to exposed or vulnerable data, but also to the complete compromise of your system.

Mac File Permissions: A Brief History of Time

For many Mac users, the concept of file system permissions is both relatively new and oft misunderstood. First introduced in OS X, file system permissions were a drastic departure from Mac OS 9's largely unprotected system, a trait reflecting the earlier system's single-user nature.

With OS X came a true multiuser OS, born of Unix roots and as such, a POSIX-compliant (Portable Operating System Interface) file system permissions implementation. If you're scratching your head right now, don't worry; the term POSIX simply refers to a series of standards covering a number of OS conventions, of which the most relevant to this chapter are those covering file system permissions. Outside of Windows, the POSIX permissions standard has been the primary permissions model used by every relevant operating system on the market today. Realistically, this boils down to all of the various Unix and Linux distributions out there. Windows does itself provide a POSIX-compliant file system in NTFS, though its primary permissions model is based on Access Control Lists (ACLs), which we will get to in a bit.

The basic premise found in a POSIX-compliant permissions scheme is that each file system object, say a file or directory, has associated controls that determine the level of access a user is granted to that object. In such a scheme there are three access levels (referred to as *modes*) that can be defined for an object: *read*, *write*, and *execute*. These three levels can be applied for each file or folder at three distinct targets: the file's owner, the file's group, and everyone else. With POSIX, a file system object can have only one owner or group; so at first glance, this may seem somewhat limiting, and it certainly can be. However, you can actually establish quite complex and workable permission schemes using POSIX alone.

ACLs were introduced to OS X in version 10.4 and provided a new approach to permission access to files. While the POSIX standard does have a working draft for ACL permissions in the form of the POSIX1.e proposed standard, the status of the standard is very much in limbo, to say the least. Apple instead chose to implement an ACL system based on the NFSv4 standard as defined in RFC 3010. This standard is implemented in a way that makes it compatible with ACL implementations utilized by Windows systems beginning with Windows NT. Other systems that include support for NFSv4 ACLs include Solaris and FreeBSD9. Most Linux systems adopt the POSIX1e ACLs, which support only a subset of access controls provided by the NFSv4 system.

With The OS X ACL implementation, each file system object contains a single access control list table, which contains multiple access control entries (ACEs). Each ACE defines a subject and a set of specific access rights. In OS X, the subject can be a user or a group, and there are up to 17 different access rights that can be explicitly allowed or denied for any file system object (access control rights are discussed in detail later in this chapter). On top of this, a particular file's access control list is completely extensible, which means that an arbitrary number of ACEs can be assigned to any particular file system object. Basically what this means is that ACL-based file system permissions allow for extremely granular and flexible management.

In early OS X incarnations, permissions problems were common among long-time Mac users, and to a degree they still are. However, any permissions problems that persist in a 10.11 environment are, plain and simple, due to poor administration (which isn't to say that we don't hear a lot of people still blaming all of their problems on there being something wrong with ACLs or their being too complicated). The truth is that in the earlier days of OS X, permissions problems were abundant, and they were due not only to user inexperience but also to significant limits of OS X's permissions implementation. Although OS X has always had a basic POSIX permission system, in the early days there were fairly significant limitations to its implementations that made it difficult to properly harness. Luckily, the OS X permission system has continuously improved throughout the life of OS X, and since 10.6 we have had a combination of basic POSIX permissions and ACLs that provides for rock-solid, flexible file system permission structures.

POSIX Permissions

As previously mentioned, basic POSIX permissions have been with OS X since its inception. Using POSIX, you can apply access restrictions to three different classes: that of the owner, of the group, and of everyone else. A file references its owner or group based on an ID that is stored directly with the file. In order to determine the actual owner or group of a file, the OS cross-references the file's user and group IDs against its Directory Services database.

For instance, every OS X system out of the box has a local user admin, created with user ID 501, and the default group staff, which has an ID of 20. Therefore, any file that is owned by the user ID 501 and the group ID 20 is owned by the user admin and the group staff, respectively. The third class is implicit for anyone that is not user admin or a member of group staff. When qualifying for access to a file or directory, OS X will first check to see if the requested file or directory is owned by the effective owner or group of the currently running process. If the system determines that the user is the owner, the user will receive effective permissions assigned to the owner class. All other classes will be ignored. If the user is a member of the group associated with the file or directory, and is not the owner, then the user will receive effective permissions assigned to the group class. If the user is neither the owner nor a member of the file/folder's group, then the user will receive effective permissions of the "everyone" class.

> **Note**   If the user is the owner of the file, and the file's class does not have write permission, then the user will not have write privileges to the file regardless of "group" or "everyone" class permissions.

Modes in Detail

Each class has three possible access capabilities, represented by three modes:

Read: The read mode, when set on a file, allows a user to read its contents. For a directory, the read mode grants the ability to list its contents.

Write: The write mode allows a user to modify a file's contents. When set on a directory, the write mode grants the ability to create subfolders or files. It also allows the user to rename or delete files it directly contains, even if the user does not have write privileges on the file she is attempting to rename or delete. If a user does not have write privileges to a directory, she will be unable to rename, move, or delete any items directly residing in it, even if she has write privileges to the item itself.

Execute: The execute mode grants the ability for a file to execute in the system. This is not the same as opening a file. Execution implies that the file contains either compiled executable binary data or scripting text, which references an interpreter via a hash-bang (#!) statement, such as a shell script. For instance, if we were to write a basic bash shell script named "Click Here For Cool Stuff," save the file, and then grant ourselves execution privileges to that file, we could simply double-click it for it to execute. If this script were malicious in intent, for example if it provided instructions to delete all data that the user can access, then that malice is only a double-click away for any user that has access to the file, and it has a fairly intriguing name that many of your users would likely freely click. (Who doesn't want to see cool stuff?) If that malcontent script does not have execution privileges assigned, then it's largely relegated to a text or binary data file. Once execution is granted, it becomes a significant and warranted threat to your user base. This is not to say that the data is completely harmless without execution rights, but removing the executable bit means that the code will not be a double-click away from execution.

When applied to a directory, the execute mode grants the ability to traverse a directory. Essentially, this mode controls the ability to access any resources that exist in this directory. When applied to a directory, the execute mode is nondiscriminating and absolute; without execute permission on a directory, you will not be able to access any items inside that directory regardless of permissions or the depth of any of its containing items.

> **Note**   When set on a directory, the write mode grants the ability to rename its direct descendants, even if the user does not have write privileges on the subfolder or file they are attempting to rename. This has significant security ramifications: any directory that contains directly executable code or referenced code that will operate under the root user, or otherwise in system automations or routine maintenance, should be closely scrutinized. It is a possible vector for attack; a malicious user can rename the executable or referenced code and inject his own routines, thereby compromising your system in full or part.

As an exercise, if we were to remove the execute permissions from the root directory of our volume, /, then a significant number of critical processes, including our own user environment, would fail to operate properly due to lack of resources. By eliminating execute privileges on the root directory, we essentially cut off access to all data on the drive. Denying execute privileges is a good way to completely block users from accessing data at the perimeter of a directory structure, thus allowing you to continue to use owner, group, and everyone management on subdirectories with impunity from users that don't meet criteria further up the tree.

Contrast this to the read mode: if we were to simply remove read permissions from root, the ramifications would be far less drastic. We would not be able to view the contents directly of the root directory, but once we traversed into a subfolder, such as /Applications (possible because it is executable), we would be subject to the permissions of the Application's folders, and subsequently the permissions on any of the individual files in that subdirectory. Now, because we don't have read access to list the contents of the root volume, we wouldn't be able to traverse into a subfolder unless we knew that it existed and what it was named. But this type of security through obscurity can also be bypassed. What we want to emphasize here is that denying users read privileges on a directory will not prevent them from traversing into its subdirectories, where they'll have any access granted at the applicable owner, group, or everyone classes, a potentially less secure environment.

Modes are established on a file through the use of a bit-flag system. To truly understand this system, look at it from the command line (we will cover GUI permissions shortly).

For example, consider the list of files and directories in the /Users folder that the command `ls -al /Users` produces, shown in Figure 4-1.

```
bash-3.2# ls -al
total 0
drwxr-xr-x    8 root            admin    272 Jul  5 21:28 .
drwxr-xr-x   32 root            wheel   1156 Jul  6 01:46 ..
-rw-r--r--    1 root            wheel      0 May  9 22:22 .localized
drwxrwxrwt   14 root            wheel    476 Jul  3 19:46 Shared
drwxr-xr-x+  12 emeraldedge     staff    408 Jul  4 14:37 emeraldedge
drwxr-xr-x+  19 jamf            staff    646 Jul  3 21:49 jamf
drwxr-xr-x+  12 nicoleedge      staff    408 Jul  5 21:29 nicoleedge
drwxr-xr-x+  11 emeraldedge     staff    374 Jun 12 19:18 test (Deleted)
bash-3.2# 
```

Figure 4-1. Output of command `ls -al /Users` with permissions, owner, group, and folder name identified

As illustrated in the figure, in every line of the output, the first field (the one containing combinations of dashes and the letters *d*, *r*, *t*, *w*, and *x*) reports the POSIX permissions. For clarity, let's look at the emeraldedge folder:

```
drwxr-xr-x+ 20 emeraldedge   staff  1870 Jul 8 00:56 emeraldedge
```

Here, the string drwxr-xr-x defines the POSIX permissions. In an ls -al output, the first digit, d, specifies the file system type, and in this case, a directory. Other common entries include a dash (–) for a file and l for a symbolic link. The next three characters, rwx (read, write, and execute), represent the mode for the owner, who in this example is emeraldedge. Thus, user emeraldedge has read, write, and execute privileges for this folder. The next three digits represent group privileges: Staff has read and execute privileges. The final three characters represent permissions for everyone else: in this case, only read and execute privileges.

On a lower level, POSIX uses bit flags to represent modes. This means that permissions are represented by a unique numerical value. The read, write, and execute modes are each represented by three bits. The easiest way to illustrate this is by comparing it to our previous ls output.

```
drwxr-xr-x
d111101101
```

As explained earlier, the first three characters after the d designate permissions for the owner. In this case, rwx is represented in binary as 111, which has a decimal value of 7. The group also has rwx privileges, which is also a decimal value of 7. The everyone class has only read and execute permissions, r-x, which is 101 in binary and a decimal value of 5. Thus, these permissions translate to 775 in their decimal form, a common type of notation called octal notation. See Table 4-1 for a better representation of the permissions layout.

Table 4-1. Permissions Represented in Alpha, Binary, and Octal Format

Permission	String Notation (ls –l)	Binary Notation	Octal Notation
Read	r--	100	4
Write	-w-	010	2
Execute	--x	001	1
Read & Write	rw-	110	6
Read & Execute	r-x	101	5
Read, Write, & Execute	rwx	111	7

You don't really need to be able to do binary math in your head to manage POSIX permissions, but knowing the numeric values of each mode can be important, as they are commonly used when managing permissions from the command-line interface, as discussed later in this chapter.

Inheritance

Another aspect to understanding POSIX permissions in OS X is inheritance, or how the system deals with group assignment on newly created files and directories. Apple is compliant with Single Unix Standard, version 3 (SUS3), which dictates that the group established for the new file will be inherited based on group ownership of the parent directory. This system allows you to use group permissions on directories to establish group-specific collaboration areas. For instance, imagine that user jdoe creates a file in the Workgroup1 folder, which has the group workgroup1 assigned to it. The file will be owned by user jdoe and will have a group of workgroup1 regardless of the primary group assigned to jdoe's user account. The user can then browse into the Workgroup2 folder, and create a file under that folder. The second file will have a primary group of workgroup2.

There are a few potential wrinkles in this plan. First, if it's not planned properly, the new behavior of group inheritance on files and folders may have some unexpected side effects. For instance, if you are using file system quotas, it is important to note that when establishing group ownership on a directory to a group that has quota limitations, any new files in that folder will count against the group quota. Thus, if you are using quotas, you need to take this consideration into account when structuring your hierarchy. The second problem is that, by default, OS X ships with a umask value of 022. The umask is a value that is used to determine default permissions on newly created files. When a user creates a file, its established permissions are determined by taking the default mode of 666 (777 for new folders), and then filtering that value by the user's umask value (022). To determine ultimate privileges, you simply subtract the number representing the umask from that of the privileges. So in this case, newly created file system objects will have a mode of 644 (666 minus 022), or rw-r--r--.). It would be an extremely bad idea for all new files to be executable, so their default mode is 666. On the other hand, if folders don't have execute permissions, then no one will be able to navigate into them. Thus, folders have a default mode of 777. The umask is then used to determine final permissions for any new files or folders.

The main problem with a file that has rw-r--r-- (644) permissions is that the middle octal, the group octal (r--), assigns read (r) permissions, but no write (w) capabilities. This is a very important thing to understand: by default in OS X, newly created files are *not* group-writable. This means that when a user creates a new file in OS X, by default, only the creating user has the ability to modify (write) that file. Although this is the most secure configuration, it immediately becomes a problem when more than one person needs to modify that file. Failing to recognize this leads to serious permissions problems when using POSIX permissions in a collaborative environment. Luckily, you can change the user's umask. To do this, we must first calculate our desired umask. In most cases, we want new files to be writable by both the creating user and the group owner of the file, which is represented as rw-rw-r-x visually or as 664 using octet representation. To determine the umask that we want to use, we subtract our desired mode for new files (664) from the default file mode (666). 666-664 is 002, thus our desired umask is 002.

To apply this umask in OS X 10.5 or later, simply run the umask command with the desired mode /usr/bin/umask 002.

Unfortunately, executing umask may not affect all running processes, and the result won't persist across reboots. To remedy the situation, we recommend using the `launchd-user.conf` file found at `/private/etc/launchd-user.conf`. To set this, simply run

```
echo "umask 002" >> /private/etc/launchd-user.conf
```

as root. That's it. Reboot and you're done. From now on, whenever your machine boots up, it will read this file and set the desired umask value for any user `sessions.launchd.conf` at the root of their home directory.

If you're running OS X 10.4 or earlier (not likely, but it could happen), the process for changing the umask is slightly different and a lot more complex. We recommend installing the program Umask Doctor and setting it to launch at login if you do not wish to do this programmatically. This utility specifically performs this duty, and it works out pretty well. Alternatively, you can simply make the change via the `defaults` command, run with root/sudo privileges:

```
defaults write /Library/Preferences/.GlobalPreferences NSUmask 2
```

Note, however, that the *NSUmask* value is actually a decimal value of the octal umask, so you'll have to do a conversion. In other words, instead of viewing the number 777 as three different values of 7 (owner), 7 (group), and 7 (other), it instead views it as a single number: 777.

The approach to determining the decimal umask for this command is to convert the binary representation of the umask octal to decimal, so a little knowledge of binary is required.

For example, let's examine a umask of 022. If we convert each of these octets (0,2,2) into binary, the values are 000 (0), 010 (2), and 010 (2) (when doing this conversion, it's important to always use three significant digits). After converting each octet into binary, the next step is to concatenate the values. In this case, 000, 010, and 010 become 000010010. This value, when converted to decimal is 18 ($0 \times 2^0 + 1 \times 2^1 + 0 \times 2^2 + 0 \times 2^3 + 1 \times 2^4 = 18$). This decimal value is then the number to substitute for the *NSUmask* value. One other note: the programs that honor the NSUmask will typically operate in an OS X GUI environment, as it is a function of the Cocoa framework. Technically, command-line applications can support this property, but typically command-line apps will utilize the more traditional POSIX/umask model. Not all third-party Cocoa programs support this value, but generally the major players do.

Once you have set the umask, simply restart the computer. From then on, that computer will freely interact in collaborative folders, and other group members will be able to modify files that its users create without having to file a help desk ticket. Neat.

> **Note**   Fortunately, if you don't know binary, the OS X Calculator app has a programmer mode that does all the mental work for you. To access this function, open up the Calculator application, found in `/Applications`, and then select Programmer in the View menu (or use the keyboard shortcut +3).

The Sticky Bit

For day-to-day management of POSIX permissions, the three modes we previously discussed (read, write, and execute) will be your primary weapons against those pesky permissions issues. But you do have a few more tools at your disposal. In a previous `ls` output we showed, you may have noticed some special permissions on the directory `/Users/Shared`. Here's the line again:

```
drwxrwxrwt 13 root    wheel   442 Jun 29 23:54 Shared
```

Under the "everyone" digits (the letters in **bold**), instead of the expected *x* (execute), we have a *t*. This is referred to as the *sticky bit*. This bit has no effect on files in OS X, but when enabled on a directory, it prevents deletion or renaming of files inside of that directory by anyone other than the file's owner. Thus, if Jimbob creates a file and then gives everyone read and write privileges (or if you modified the umask), Geraldine will be able to edit its content, but not delete it or rename the file. Only Jimbob can delete the file. It's worth noting, though, that with write privileges, nothing stops Gerry from simply deleting all of the file's contents. The sticky bit simply disables the user from completely deleting it.

To assign the sticky bit to a directory, you simply use a fourth octal number, which has a value of 001. Thus, the Shared folder in the previous example line has a mode of 1777, with the 1 (001 binary) being the "sticky" directory. To apply this mode to a file, use the `chmod` command. Run it as root if you're the owner of the targeted directory:

```
chmod 1777 /Users/Shared
chmod -R 777 /Users/Shared/*
```

The second line specifies the –R flag, which will apply the mode 777 to all items in the /Users/Shared/ directory. Thus, all files in the directory will be editable by anyone, but because of the first command that was run, only the owner can delete a file.

The suid/sguid Bits

The fourth octet has two modes in addition to sticky: *set-group-ID-on-execution,* which has a value of 010, and *set-user-ID-on-execution bit,* which has a value of 100. If either of these modes is set on an executable, whenever that file runs, it will do so in the context of the owner and group assigned to it. Thus, if a program is owned by root and has setuid on, whoever runs that program will have root access (within the confines of that program). This is a bit of a scary thought, so use this capability with great care. Many a local privileged-escalation exploit has been born from the setuid bit. In the early days of OS X, it was possible to set the suid bit on shell scripts as well as other interpreted scripting languages (Python, Perl, Ruby, and the like). Shell scripts have numerous attack vectors, and Apple considered this to be a large security risk. Thus this is no longer applicable. The suid and guid bits will now only be honored on precompiled binary executable files. Additionally, regardless of what the man page for chmod claims, the suid and sguid bits have no effect on directories in OS X. They are simply ignored. In general, use of the suid bits should be extremely limited and rare. OS X is one of the worst offenders of this principle, as OS X has historically had a large number of suid programs in a default number. Thankfully, the number of programs that ship with this privilege is reduced with each iteration of OS X. It is important to note that the setuid and setgid bits are not honored on removable file systems. This is important, as it provides protection against a rogue program that is introduced from a foreign (and potentially contaminated) file system, such as a Thunderbolt, Firewire, USB, or optical drive. This prevents a malicious user from being able to introduce setuid and setgid programs into the environment.

> **Note**   You may want to occasionally audit which executables in your system have the setuid and setgid bits set, as any executables with such privileges are potential attack vectors by local users. To see a list of all such files on your system, you can use this command:
>
> ```
> find / -type f \( -perm -4000  -o -perm -2000 \) -ls
> ```

POSIX in Practice

So that is POSIX permissions in a nutshell. The system may seem somewhat limited; but really, you're limited only by your own ingenuity and the speed at which your fingers type. In a POSIX environment, groups and nested hierarchies are your friend in creating collaborative environments, though it is also important to pay attention to file-level permissions as well to ensure data confidentiality and integrity. To illustrate this, we'll walk through some complex permissions scenarios and discuss strategies for deploying POSIX permissions.

One environment where complex POSIX hierarchies are crucial is education. Consider the various levels of accessibility that servers in an educational institution would need configured. Education environments have needs for private file-sharing collaboration areas among faculty. Such a file share needs to have facilities to provide documents to students, facilities for students to collaborate (share files with each other), and finally it is necessary for students to provide teachers privately with documents that cannot be viewed by other students (hand-in assignments).

To fulfill these various needs, you must first examine how you want to structure your data. Do you need to isolate faculty data from student data? Should it be on a different server altogether, or is it OK to store on the same volume as the rest of the student data? What kind of faculty data should be stored on a server with student data? Will faculty be storing only class-relevant data on this data store, therefore making it okay to group faculty data along with student data? This illustrates a very important point: securing your permissions on your file system is only part of your solution. It is important that you, as the admin, educate your end users on acceptable use policy, data security policies, and practices. For instance, it would be a very bad idea for your teachers to place personal information about students, such as social security numbers, medical information, and so on, in a public location. This may seem like simple common sense, but as an administrator it is your duty to ensure that your users are educated and in line with company/organization security best practices and policies.

So, with all considerations in mind, we have devised an appropriate permissions hierarchy to allow students and teachers to utilize their file storage securely. There is a top-level folder MySchoolShare that contains course-specific subdirectories: Comm101, English101, and Sci101. Each of these contains a folder template that is meant to securely address our access requirements. Let's take a look at an ls -al output for the folder Comm101:

```
drwxr-x---    7    root    comm101        238 Jan 24 14:37 .
drwxr-xr-x    6    root    staff          204 Jan 24 14:44 ..
drwxrwxr-x    2    root    comm101staff    68 Jan 24 14:20 Course Files
drwxrwx-wx    2    root    comm101staff    68 Jan 24 14:20 Hand-ins
drwxrwx---    2    root    comm101         68 Jan 24 14:20 Public
drwxrwx---    2    root    comm101staff    68 Jan 24 14:19 Staff
```

In this template, to even be able to access the directory, the user must be a member of thecomm101 group (as is seen on the "." entry). In this case, the comm101 group would contain members from both the comm101staff group and the comm101students group; thus we have a group that qualifies either set of users. The Comm101 folder itself allows only for read and execute permissions to the comm101 group, which means that users will not be able to add any top-level subdirectories or files and prevents them from renaming any existing items. This allows the administrator to define a folder template structure and ensure that users, whether faculty or students, adhere to it.

The Course Files folder is used by instructors to provide course-specific files and templates to students, and so write privileges are limited to the comm101staff group. All users have the ability to read files from this directory, as they qualify for the "everyone" class. In this case, the "everyone" class is guaranteed to contain only members of the comm101 group that are not also in the group comm101staff. We know this because of the permissions on the Comm101 folder itself:

```
drwxr-x---    7    root    comm101    238 Jan 24 14:37 .
```

These permissions indicate that any items inside of this folder are accessible only by members of group comm101. Therefore, the "everyone" class on any subfolders or files is effectively restricted to the comm101 group, or a subset of it.

The Hand-Ins folder is used by students as a drop-box: a folder where they can add their own files but cannot read any files it contains. This allows a place for users to provide teachers with their homework assignments and not have to worry about other students viewing those files. Because the Hand-Ins folder provides all members of the group Comm101staff with read, write, and execute privileges, any members of that group can access and view files provided by students for review. A drop box is created by allowing users write and execute permissions on a directory, and is indicated by the special drop-box icon, shown in Figure 4-2.

Figure 4-2. A Finder drop-box folder

The Public folder in the example hierarchy provides a place for all users of the comm101 group to collaborate. This means that both students and faculty will have the ability to modify, add, or remove files from the directory. It's a bit of the wild, wild west permission-wise, but it allows a place for everyone to collaborate, which is often desirable in a classroom setting. We make the folder public by ensuring that it is owned by the more global comm101 group, and that all members of the group have read and write capabilities, as shown in the trimmed ls output:

```
drwxrwx---      2      root      comm101         68  Jan 24 14:20 Public
```

In this case, we may want to set the sticky bit on this folder to ensure that users can delete only their own files from this folder. Last but not least, we have the Staff folder, which is a folder where teachers/instructors can privately share files outside the purview of students. This can be handy for substitutes, multi-instructor classes, or for professors who have to collaborate during the teaching process. To facilitate this, the comm101staff group is set as the primary group and given full read and write access. Students, who will receive effective permissions of the "everyone" class, will then have no access to any items in this directory, as made evident by the permissions on the folder:

```
drwxrwx---      2      root      comm101staff   68 Jan 24 14:19 Staff
```

> **Caution**   A good permissions hierarchy is only a partial solution. As an administrator, it is important that you take precautions to protect your data on a social level by educating your users. If they are not aware of the consequences of placing a sensitive file in a potentially public area (such as a folder named "Public"), you will likely have a security breach due simply to user ignorance.

Access Control Lists

Mac OS X 10.4 saw the introduction of ACLs, and Apple has continually refined them through the various iterations of OS X since then, providing a mature and robust access control system in 10.11. For a traditional Windows system administrator, ACLs are likely easier to work with than POSIX. ACLs match the permission options almost identically. In fact, as we mentioned earlier, the OS X NFSv4 ACL format is compatible with Windows ACLs.

A file's access control list is completely extensible, allowing you to assign very granular permissions to specific users and groups. It frees you from the constraints of the POSIX user/group/everyone paradigm, which greatly simplifies permissions management. On top of their extensibility, ACLs also define numerous access levels and inheritance capabilities, which allows for especially effective permission hierarchies.

Access Control Entries

There are 17 access rights that the ACL system allows you to apply to a file or directory. An access control entry, or ACE, is simply a specification that includes either a user or a group combined with an allow or deny directive, and a comma-separated list of one or more rights. These rights can be grouped into four categories: Administration, Read Permissions, Write Permissions, and Inheritance.

Administration

The Administration category includes two permissions capabilities:

Change Permissions: Users with this right can manage privileges on a file via POSIX or ACLs. They may also delete any ACLs on the file or folder, so assign this permission with caution. When using chmod to manage ACLs (as discussed later), you grant the change permissions with the writesecurity privilege.

Change Ownership: Enabling this for a user allows that individual user to assume ownership of a file. However, that person can't transfer ownership to anyone else. To do so, a user must have root access. You can grant the Assume Ownership privilege with the chown permission when using the chmod utility, which we'll discuss a bit later in this section.

Read Permissions

The Read category includes five specific permissions:

Read: The read privilege behaves similarly on both files and directories, letting users view the content of both. If you're working with ACLs from the command line, you grant this right using read for files and list for directories.

Execute/Search: The execute and search bits behave similarly to the execute bit in the POSIX model, though they are now given differentiating descriptions to more clearly define the delineation between the *execution* capability that the attribute provides when applied to a file and the *list/ traverse* behavior when it is applied to a folder. From the command line, you grant this privilege using the execute permission for files and the search permission for folders, although the terms can be used interchangeably when applying to either.

Read Attribute: This permission is granted, using the readattr privilege, to let a user view the data describing a file's characteristics, such as its size, ownership, mode, inode number, and file creation, modification, and access times. You enable this permission with the readattr privilege.

Read Ext Attribute: This permission allows a user to read a file's extended-attribute data: file attributes commonly utilized by the OS, such as information about the OS X quarantine system, Time Machine, disk-image checksums, and third-party software for metadata purposes. Extended attributes are also responsible for the data found under the More Info tab when you get information on a file. Use the readextattr permission to grant this right.

Read Permissions: Given this privilege, a user can view security information, such as ACLs or POSIX permissions, as well as ownership of a file or folder. To assign this right, use the readsecurity privilege.

Write Permissions

The write-permissions category allows users to create and modify file data, including file metadata stored via extended attributes. There are six specific write permissions:

Write Attributes: This permission allows a user to change a file's attribute data.

Write Ext Attributes: Granting this right lets a user edit files' and folders' extended attribute data (extra information about a file's traits) as well as create new entries in that data. You'll rarely want to make such data user accessible, though. Software behind the scenes usually manipulates this data.

Write/Add Files: The Write and Add File privileges are analogous when applied to a file or directory. Like search/execute, the two terms exist solely to illustrate the functional difference when applied to a directory versus a file. When applied to a directory, the add_file privilege serves as a subset of the POSIX directory write capability. The key difference is that, unlike the POSIX write capability, the add_file permission does not grant the ability to delete a file or create a new directory. These abilities are now bestowed by delete and append, respectively. When the privilege is applied to a file, the user will have the ability to modify the contents of the file. When applying ACLs via the command line, you can use write on both directories and files, but on directories, it's ultimately interpreted as the add_file permission.

Delete: This capability is a subset of the POSIX write capability. With ACLs, we now have a specific right granting a user the ability to delete files or directories. This right is defined by the privilege delete.

Append/Add Directories: This capability is also a subset of the POSIX write capability. When applied to a directory, it allows users to create new subdirectories. When applied to an existing file, it allows the user to modify the file. Note that to create new files, a user must have write privileges. Using chmod from the command line, you assign the append/add directories privilege using append. The flag is interpreted as add_subdirectory.

Delete Child: This permission, which applies solely to directories, lets a user delete any file directly residing inside the directory, regardless of ownership on the item. In the case of subdirectories residing in this directory, the subdirectory can only be removed if the user also has the ability to delete any files it contains. The delete_child flag assigns the right.

Inheritance

This category applies solely to directories. You would use inheritance to customize how permissions are inherited by a directory's children. For example, if you apply ACL inheritance to just the first level of subfolders and files, new folders that users create will inherit their parents' permissions, but items created inside the new folders will not. Likewise, by using the inherit_only flag, you can assign ACLs specifically for inheritance, but not have them apply to the parent object, which can be very useful. You control inheritance with the four separate rights in the following list:

Apply to This Folder: When this is selected, the ACL will apply to this folder. Otherwise, the folder will have only_inherit permission, and the ACL will be active only on children that inherit the ACL.

Apply to Child Folders: When you activate this option, newly created child folders of the directory will inherit the ACL. Use the directory_inherit permission to grant this privilege.

Apply to Child Files: When enabled, this privilege will cause new files created in the directory to inherit the ACL. You use the file_inherit permission to grant this right.

Apply to All Descendants: If you activate this option, the inheritance properties of the directory will pass on to newly created directories; allowing for automated propagation of ACLs as users create additional directories and files. Otherwise, the directory you're currently attending to will have the limit_inherit privilege.

The specificity of the various access rights allows you to more pointedly prescribe access. You can now differentiate between modification and deletion as well as differentiate various rights to files and folders. More importantly, ACLs provide multiple options to define inheritance, which can be very handy in establishing complex permissions hierarchies, such as those in education.

Caution   If no Access Control Entries are applicable for a particular user on a file, ensure that your baseline POSIX permissions are structured in a manner to prevent unauthorized access. In some instances, it may be desirable to utilize explicit deny ACLs to ensure that access is unconditionally restricted.

Effective Permissions

One major limitation of ACLs can be found in protocol support. In order to utilize ACLs, a protocol must be built to support it. Apple has mitigated this issue by building ACL support into its first-party file systems and network protocols: HFS+ (Hierarchical File System, the OS X native file system), Xsan (Apple's cluster file system based on Quantum/ADIC's StorNext file system), and AFP (Apple Filing Protocol, Apple's native file sharing protocol). Thanks to its NFSv4 ACL implementation and the Samba open source project, OS X also includes support for ACLs via the CIFS protocol, which is used for connecting to and serving files to Windows clients.

So what about services that do not include support for ACLs? How do they handle permissions provided via ACLs? Luckily, on a standard OS X server this list is pretty short. The most notable offenders are FTP and NFS, but certainly that is not an exhaustive list. The fact that the OS X NFS daemon doesn't support ACLs might have you raising an eyebrow. After all, the ACL model utilized by Apple is based on the NFSv4, right? Unfortunately, Apple's NFS implementation supports only versions 2 and 3 of the standard, which don't yet have ACL support. Even if this wasn't an issue, there are definitely scenarios where you'll be providing file services over a nonstandard protocol that most likely does not include native support for ACLs. In any of these scenarios, the protocol in question will operate under what is referred to as "effective permissions." Essentially, permissions as defined by the ACLs will be flattened into equivalent POSIX permissions. This means that if you have an ACL that prevents append access to user jdoe on folder folder1, then when user jdoe connects to folder1 over FTP (which does not support ACLs) and attempts to create a new subfolder, the action will fail. The same is true of NFS shares; exported NFS shares will boil down to effective permissions. The NFS implementation in OS X doesn't support ACLs, but it does honor them via effective permissions: if a user is granted read/write via an ACL, they *will* have read/write access via NFS. However, there are a few things to note here. First and foremost, granular ACLs won't translate completely. Second, although you might have effective write privileges via ACLs, if you don't have write privileges via POSIX, it will *seem* as if you don't have privileges when you run ls on the mounted NFS volume; however, if you try to read or write a file, it will work without issue. Poorly written third-party software might inspect the POSIX permissions and determine that you don't have access to an asset when you really do. However, most software will attempt to read/write an asset and will only report errors when encountered (as it should).

Also, for cases such as this, ACL inheritance *is* honored. For instance, an ACE on a folder ensuring that all created subfiles have write permissions will in fact appropriately apply the inherited entry to files uploaded via FTP or created via an NFS mount. You won't be able to view the ACL strictly across the FTP connection or the NFS mount; but on the back end, if you check the file on the server, you will see that inheritance is in fact applied to new files.

> **Note**   If you are using a third-party file service that runs as root and implements its own abstracted permission system, effective ACL permissions will *not* apply.

ACLs in Practice

We have now covered all of the various rights provided by the ACL system, but how can we use the system in practice? Well, the granular and specific nature of ACLs makes the system a little less difficult to wrap your head around than a POSIX permissions structure. With basic POSIX permissions, you have to be somewhat clever with your folder hierarchies and group structures to create a workable system. With ACLs, the approach is much more clear and direct. Let's consider the example that we discussed earlier in this chapter, in the section "POSIX in Practice," in which we discussed a permissions hierarchy for a school that seeks to provide collaborative file sharing environments for its Comm101, Science101, and English101 classes. Although we were able to accommodate the schools requirements solely with POSIX permissions, what if there were more requirements attached to that problem? For instance, let's say there is a Comm101 teacher's aide who needs access to the Staff folder for collaboration, but is not permitted access to student's final work delivered to the Hand-Ins folder. Likewise, this teacher's aide needs to be able to add files and directories to the Course Files folder, as well as modify existing assets in that folder. To accomplish this task in POSIX, it would be necessary to create an additional group in our Directory Service, such that we could assign privileges as follows:

```
drwxr-x---    7    root    comm101             238 Jan 24 14:37 .
drwxr-xr-x    6    root    staff               204 Jan 24 14:44 ..
drwxrwxr-x    2    root    comm101contributers  68 Jan 24 14:20 Course Files
drwxrwx-wx    2    root    comm101staff         68 Jan 24 14:20 Hand-ins
drwxrwx---    2    root    comm101              68 Jan 24 14:20 Public
drwxrwx---    2    root    comm101contributors  68 Jan 24 14:19 Staff
```

To accommodate the request, we have created a special group named comm101contributors, which now has access to the Course Files as well as the Staff folders. In order to access via the comm101staff group, that group has been added to the comm101contributors group, along with the teacher's aide user.

This solution will surely meet the need, but it's not long before you reach the practical limit of POSIX: what if the teacher's aide is to be provisioned read-only access to the Staff folder? In order to accommodate that request and ensure that other students do not have access, you will need to create a subfolder that differentiates between comm101staff and comm101contributors. This is highly impractical. Instead, let's revert to our original POSIX structure before creating the comm101contributors group, and approach the situation with ACLs in mind. The first thing to do is analyze the situation and determine whether the need to provide additional use is an edge case, or if it will become a common use-case scenario. If this will prove to be a common case, then we should create a comm101contributors group to manage access. Access would then be provisioned in Directory Services, thereby minimizing the need to change permissions on the file system.

> **Tip**   In general, it is best to avoid provisioning ACEs to specific users. The larger your file structure and the larger your user base, the more management overhead will be needed as you provision specific user access. Moreover, the more often changes are made to a file system's permissions structure, the more likely that human error will result in unwarranted exposure of data. Instead, it is best to define specific groups for any common access patterns that you expect to be needed by members of your organization.

In this case, we have determined that this is a very specific edge case, and so we will go ahead and provision our access to our teacher's aide, who has a user account of comm101aid. To provide the necessary access rights, we will assign ACLs as demonstrated by the command ls -ael, which is run against our Comm101 folder.

```
drwxrwxr-x      7      root    comm101staff    238 Jan 24 14:37 .
drwxr-xr-x      6      root    staff           204 Jan 24 14:44 ..
-rw-rw-r--@     1      root    comm101staff   6148 Jan 24 15:05 .DS_Store
drwxrwxr-x+     2      root    comm101staff     68 Jan 24 14:20 Course Files
 0: user:comm101aid allow list,add_file,search,add_subdirectory,delete_child,readattr, ↩
writeattr,readextattr,writeextattr,readsecurity,file_inherit,directory_inherit
drwxrwx-wx      2      root    comm101staff     68 Jan 24 14:20 Hand-ins
drwxrwxr-x      2      root    comm101staff     68 Jan 24 14:20 Public
drwxrwx---+     2      root    comm101staff     68 Jan 24 14:19 Staff
 0: user:comm101aid allow list,add_file,search,add_subdirectory,delete_child,readattr,↩
   writeattr,readextattr,writeextattr,readsecurity,file_inherit,directory_inherit
```

There are a few things to note about this ls -ael output. First, if we examine the POSIX permissions of a particular folder's output, we will see that on some folders, there is a trailing + at the end. For instance, the Staff folder looks like this:

```
drwxrwx---+     2 root    comm101staff    68 Jan 24 14:19 Staff
 0: user:testaid allow list,add_file,search,add_subdirectory,delete_child,readattr, ↩
writeattr,readextattr,writeextattr,readsecurity,file_inherit,directory_inherit
```

The + character means that the file has one or more access control entries. When passed the –e flag, ls also outputs each files' ACL, as seen on the Course Files and Staff folders. In each case, the user testaid has been allowed access permissions, which effectively provide Read and Write permissions in POSIX terms. The user testaid can read existing files and their metadata (list, readattr, readextattr), can traverse into the directory (search), add new files and directories (add_file, add_subdirectory), modify and rename existing files or directories (delete_child), and can modify file attributes and extended attributes (writeattr, writeextattr). On top of this, these permissions will be inherited by any newly created files or subdirectories (file_inherit, directory_inherit). This common combination of Read and Write privileges is utilized by a number of Apple's administration toolsets. For a detailed table of Apple's primary access groups Read and Write, Read Only, and Write Only (Drop Box), see the next section, "Administering Permissions."

Through the use of ACLs we can easily adapt to various permissions needs. For instance, if the aide was only to have read permissions on the staff folder, we could apply the following ACL:

```
drwxrwx---+    2 root   comm101staff  68 Jan 24 14:19 Staff
 0: user:comm101aid allow list,search,readattr,readextattr,↵
file_inherit,directory_inherit
```

This ACE would allow the user testaid read only access to the Staff folder, and any newly created items. Keep in mind that our POSIX permissions are still playing a role in this scenario, as the "everyone" group has no capabilities. This goes to illustrate the need to ensure properly planned POSIX permissions in addition to ACLs. It is not enough to rely on only one system. If necessary, we could apply an explicit deny ACL, which would override any set POSIX permissions:

```
drwxrwxrwx+    2 root   comm101staff   68 Jan 24 14:19 Staff
 0: user:comm101aid deny add_file,add_subdirectory
 1: user:comm101aid allow list,search,readattr,readextattr,↵
file_inherit,directory_inherit
```

In this model, even though the user has the ability to create files or directories via POSIX permissions, they will be unable to do so, because of the explicit deny applied to the directory. Another important characteristic to note is how the ACL system resolves conflicting ACEs. In the event of two conflicting access privileges, the first entry found in the system will be applied. So in the previous example, if our allow rule (rule index #1) had an add_file flag, the user would still be unable to add a file because of the higher-precedence (though lower-index) deny rule.

Administering Permissions

You have a number of tools at your disposal for administering permissions. If you prefer the command line, you can use the commands chmod and chown. We must warn you though, because of the verbosity of access control entries, using chmod to apply ACEs can be a bit hairy.

The easiest way to manage ACLs on an OS X server is via the Server application. Then click the name of the server and then the Storage tab, as shown in Figure 4-3.

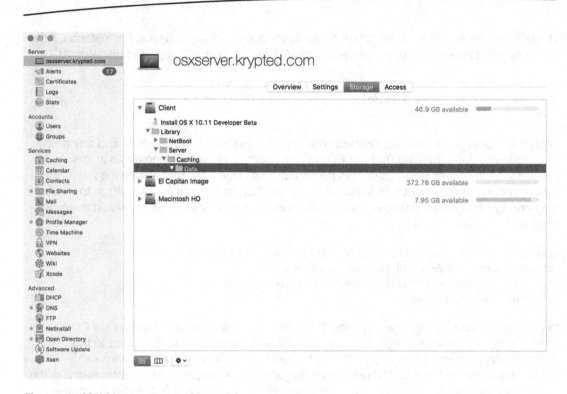

Figure 4-3. OS X Server app screen: Storage tab

You can find the Server application inside the /Applications directory on any OS X server box, or any client onto which you've installed the Server app tools (available on the downloads section of Apple's support web site). Once you have the application open, you can get to the File Sharing interface by highlighting the server container in the ServerList, and then clicking File Sharing. Here, you can browse your file systems or share points and assign both POSIX and ACL permissions. The Server app is a pretty good tool for modifying POSIX permissions, but it has no direct concept of execution. There is no way to set the execution bit exclusively using this tool; if you assign read privileges to a folder, it will include execution. When assigned to a file, the read permission includes only read, not execution. This probably isn't a bad thing, as the number of scenarios where execution privileges need to be applied to files should be pretty rare, and the likelihood for human error would be high. Thus, the added consideration required to fire up a command line tool to grant execution rights to specific files isn't necessarily a bad thing.

You can modify POSIX owners and groups by dragging them into the respective slots and then choosing the appropriate level of permission for each. To create ACLs for users and groups, drag them into the ACL list and apply appropriate permissions. Apple has several basic presets for you to use: *Full Control*, *Read & Write*, *Read Only*, *Write Only*, and *Custom*.

Table 4-2 illustrates these privilege mappings when applied to files and directories.

Table 4-2. ACE Permissions Mapping

Permission	File System Object	Rights
Full Control	Directory	list, add_file, search, delete, add_subdirectory, delete_child, readattr, writeattr, readextattr, writeextattr, readsecurity, writesecurity, chown, file_inherit, directory_inherit
Full Control	File	read, write, execute, delete, append, readattr, writeattr, readextattr, writeextattr, readsecurity, writesecurity, chown
Read & Write	Directory	list, add_file, search, add_subdirectory, delete_child, readattr, writeattr, readextattr, writeextattr, readsecurity, file_inherit, directory_inherit
Read & Write	File	read, write, execute, delete, append, readattr, writeattr, readextattr, writeextattr, readsecurity
Read Only	Directory	list, search, readattr, readextattr, readsecurity, file_inherit, directory_inherit
Read Only	File	read, execute, readattr, readextattr, readsecurity
Write Only	Directory	add_file, delete, add_subdirectory, delete_child, writeattr, writeextattr, file_inherit, directory_inherit
Write Only	File	write, delete, append, writeattr, writeextattr

The Server app allows you to define custom privilege sets, which allow you to assign rights based up four main categories, *Administration*, *Read*, *Write*, and *Inheritance*, which we discussed in the earlier section "Access Control Entries." To modify these permissions, highlight the object in the Server app and then click the cog wheel icon and click Edit Permissions. This will bring up a utility window, as shown in Figure 4-4.

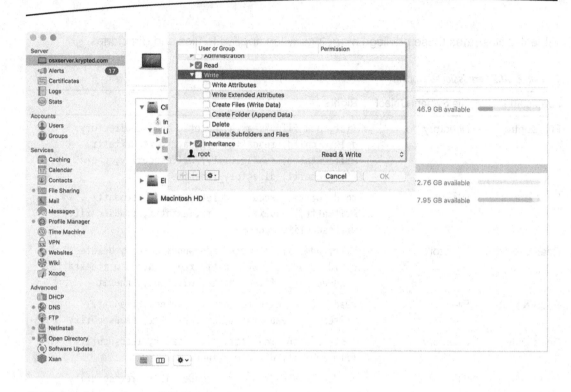

Figure 4-4. Server's Custom ACE rights

Once you have established permissions on a directory, it is important to note that they only affect that directory. If you establish an ACE that has inheritance properties, those properties will only be inherited on newly created objects. To establish your permissions on existing files and folders, you will likely want to propagate those permissions to existing files and directories. To do so, with the desired parent folder selected, click the widget menu and select Propagate Permissions. You will then be presented with a sheet allowing you to select which permissions to propagate. Choices include owner name, group name, owner privileges, group privileges, everyone privileges, and Access Control Lists.

On a collaborative sharepoint, there will be few cases where we would recommend propagating an owner name (migrating a user's home directory is the primary use-case for that option). All other options can prove to be extremely useful when establishing permissions hierarchies. When propagating ACLs, all subfolders and files will contain an "inherited" ACL, an implicit ACL that it received based upon the directory in which it was contained. If you have propagated an ACL to a particular directory and you would like to change an ACE that was propagated, you must first make the ACE explicit. You can do this by selecting the directory in question, clicking the widget, and then selecting Make Inherited Entries Explicit. Once you have done so, you can modify or delete the inherited entries, and then further propagate those changes using the propagation tool.

Last but not least is the Server app's Effective Permissions tool. This very useful utility allows you to examine permissions that can be effected to an individual user. To access the utility, select a directory in the Server app File Browser, by once again clicking the widget menu and selecting Show Effective Permissions Inspector. This will bring up the Effective

Permissions window. To check a specific user's access rights, just drag the appropriate user from the Users and Groups pane. As shown in Figure 4-5, the tool will define exactly which rights that user has to the specified directory.

Figure 4-5. Server's effective permissions tool

Using the Finder to Manage Permissions

It is also possible to manage permissions using the Finder's Info pane, shown in Figure 4-6. However, this interface is fairly pared down, and the POSIX/ACL system is abstracted a bit. One major limitation is that it is not possible to change the POSIX owner or group. It is possible to change the mode for owner, group, and everyone class, but outside of that, you can only manage ACLs. For ACEs, the Finder uses the Read & Write, Read Only, and Write Only presets used by the Server app with one crucial change: they do not set any of the inheritance properties. It is possible to propagate permissions to enclosing items using the Finder (once again found under a similar widget menu), but the propagation still doesn't set any inheritance properties. This means that newly created subdirectories or files will not inherit any ACEs that you establish through this procedure. This is a fairly significant limitation. If you are attempting to manage ACEs on an OS X client machine and wish for propagation, you'll need to set the inheritance rights yourself using the command line.

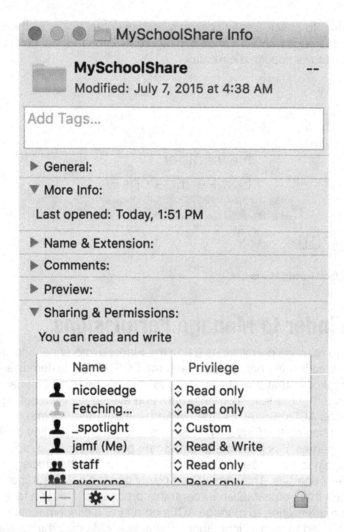

Figure 4-6. The Finder's Sharing & Permissions window

Using chown and chmod to Manage Permissions

You may often find yourself managing permissions from the command line. There are a few primary command-line apps that you will use to do this: chown, chgrp, and chmod. To change POSIX ownership of a file or folder, you use the chown utility. Its syntax is fairly straightforward:

```
chown owner[:group] /path to file
```

If all you're doing is changing ownership, you can omit the *:group* (the colon followed by the actual value for *group*). Alternatively, you can use the chgrp command, which has similar syntax, but you instead provide the desired group name in the place of a user. OS X won't let just anyone change the owner of a file. To change ownership, you must either have been granted the chown ACL right or be running as root. However, even if you have been granted the chown ACL right, you will only be able to assume ownership of a file yourself. Only the root user can change the owner to a user other than itself. For example, the following command changes the owner of file /tmp/myfile.txt to emeraldedge:

```
chown emeraldedge /tmp/myfile.txt
```

If we also want to change the group owner of the file, we can use the following command, which assigns admin as the group owner. As with ownership, a user can only change the group owner to a group that the user is a member of.

```
chown emeraldedge:admin /tmp/myfile.txt
```

> **Tip** You can use the command chflags hidden /MyFolder to make a file or directory invisible. When you run it, the folder will no longer be displayed in the Finder, though it will still be visible from command-line tools such as ls. To make these items invisible also from the command line, you can deny the readattr right.

You can use chmod to manage both POSIX and ACL permissions. Understand, however, that managing ACLs from the command line can be a bit hairy. It's not for the faint of heart. Having said that, let's walk through some of the basics.

As discussed a bit earlier, you can use chmod to modify POSIX permissions. The syntax is

```
chmod [-R] mode /path to file
```

The -R option, if used on a directory, applies the mode recursively to all descendants. To modify or create an ACE using chmod, you would use the +a, and -a flags. For instance, to grant full control of the file test.txt to the user emeraldedge, run the command:

```
chmod +a "emeraldedge allow read,write,execute,delete,append,readattr,writeattr,↵
readextattr,writeextattr,readsecurity,writesecurity,chown" test.txt
```

Subsequently, as discussed earlier, you can view the ACLs on that file by passing the -e flag to ls as follows:

```
ls -ael test.txt
-rw-r--r--+ 1 emeraldedge staff 0 Jul 9 00:56 test.txt
0: user:emeraldedge allow read,write,execute,delete,append,readattr,writeattr,↵
readextattr,writeextattr,readsecurity,writesecurity,chown
```

Likewise, if you want to grant full control of a directory, run this command:

```
chmod +a "emeraldedge allow list,add_file,search,delete,add_subdirectory,delete_child,↵
readattr,writeattr,readextattr,writeextattr,readsecurity,writesecurity,chown,↵
limit_inherit,only_inherit" testfolder
```

To remove an entire ACE, you can use the –a# flag followed by an index number, as shown in the first example next. Or, if you wish, you can remove only specific attributes as shown in the second command, which removes only delete privileges, leaving the others in place.

```
chmod –a# 0 test.txt
chmod –a "emeraldedge allow delete"
```

When first applying ACLs or when making changes, you'll likely want to propagate these changes to existing files and folders, because inheritance rules apply only at file- or folder-creation time. You can apply permissions recursively via the chmod –R +a command, but we'd recommend that you do this in the Server app via the Propagate Permissions menu item, which you can find by clicking the widget, shown previously in Figure 4-6 directly to the right of the pencil icon, a bit above the bottom of the screen. With this method, descendant file system objects will receive inherited, rather than explicit permissions.

When a large portion of your file system contains explicit permissions, management becomes harder. In addition, explicit permissions override implicit permissions, so you might end up with unexpected results. More care must be taken when managing such a model.

You can create inherited ACEs with chmod as well, which can be very useful. You do so by using the +ai flag instead of the +a flag. For example, the following commands will set a noninherited ACE on /MyAwesomeFolder, but will then recursively copy inherited ACEs to all descendants:

```
chmod +a "emeraldedge allow read,write,execute,delete,append,readattr,writeattr,↵
readextattr,writeextattr,readsecurity,writesecurity,chown" /MyAwesomeFolder
chmod –R +ai "emeraldedge allow read,write,execute,delete,append,readattr,writeattr,↵
readextattr,writeextattr,readsecurity,writesecurity,chown" /MyAwesomeFolder/*
```

> **Tip** Because of the way the chmod utility parses the ACE, using the traditional syntax for chmod ACLs does not work correctly when used with user or group names that contain spaces in the short name. This is primarily an issue in Active Directory environments, where user and group names routinely contain spaces. Fortunately, to get around this issue, you can use the colon as the user and rights delimiter. So, to assign an ACL for the group MYCO\Mac Server Admins, the following syntax can be used:
>
> ```
> chmod +a 'MYCO\Mac ServerAdmins:allow:read,write, execute' /MyAwesomeFolder
> ```

If you do a lot of ACL management from the command line, you may wish to save the common access rights as a shell variable so that you don't have to type them out every time. To do this using The OS X default bash shell, you can simply add the following lines to your .bash_profile file, found directly inside your home directory:

```
export ACEFULLCONTROL="read,write,execute,delete,append,readattr,writeattr,↵
readextattr,writeextattr,readsecurity,writesecurity,chown,file_inherit,↵
directory_inherit"
```

```
export ACEREADWRITE="read,write,execute,delete,append,readattr,writeattr,↵
readextattr,writeextattr,readsecurity,file_inherit,directory_inherit"
export ACEWRITEONLY="write,delete,append,writeattr,writeextattr,file_inherit,↵
directory_inherit"
```

Once you have saved this file, open up a new shell or reprocess your .bash_profile (run the command . ~/.bash_profile) file to establish the new variables. Once that is done, you can establish various ACE controls with the following example commands:

```
chmod +a "user:professorbrown allow $ACEFULLCONTROL" Hand-Ins
chmod +a "group:comm101students deny $ACEWRITEONLY" Course\ Files
chmod +a "group:comm101students allow $ACEREADANDWRITE" Public
```

You can also remove all of a file or directory's ACEs via the chmod –N syntax. Combined with –R, you can use chmod to recurse through directories and remove all ACLs. For instance, to remove all ACEs on the Public folder, as well as nested items, the command syntax is chmod –RN Public.

The Hard Link Dilemma

One common issue faced with file system security is related to a low-level file system capability known as *hard links*. A hard link in generic terms is a legal occurrence of the same file on a file system in multiple directories. When created, a hard link serves simply as a reference to an existing file, and the link maintains the exact same attributes as its source file. Thus, if ownership, mode, or even the containing data is changed on a link, those exact same changes will be realized on the source file. In OS X, and indeed most POSIX-compliant systems supporting hard links, a user can create a hard link to any file to which they have read access, as long as they have write access to the destination that they specify, and that destination resides on the same file system as the source file. Because in most default OS X environments a user will have at least some file system path to which they have write access, this can present a fairly significant security issue.

For instance, consider a user who logs into a system and has a local home directory on that system. Next, consider all of the various system configuration files, which have world-readable access (hint: take a look at /etc/). Through the use of hard linking, a user with a shell account and a home directory can potentially exploit any of these world-readable files. To do so, they simply create a hard link to the file in their own home directory, using the ln command as shown here:

```
ln /etc/crontab ~/Public/Drop\ Box/crontab
```

In this particular case, the user is creating a hardlink on the file /etc/crontab in their Dropbox folder. This folder is chosen specifically because it has historically proven to be handled insecurely by system administrators who do not fully understand how to manage POSIX or ACL permissions. In some cases, to promote collaboration, administrators will run scheduled scripts to change ownership on a directory. After all, user Leroy needs to be able to modify all files in his drop box, so why not just routinely make him the owner of everything added to this folder? Well, as we can see if we have a hard link in that folder, suddenly that routine script isn't quite so innocuous: with the linked file present in this directory, it, too, will be affected by the ownership change. Because, as we learned, hard link files share all file attributes, the net result is that the crontab file at /etc/crontab will now have the ownership changes applied to it as well. Suddenly this user has the ability to modify our crontab files, which means they have the ability to create schedule tasks that can operate under any user of their choosing, including root. Combine the privilege change with the fact that corn does no ownership checks on the file, and the net result is that the user now has complete access to the system—a major compromise.

> **Note**   Although typical OS X command-line tools do not allow for creating hard links of directories, the OS does support it, and thus users can use lower-level tools such as Python or Perl to create hard links to attack entire directories in a similar fashion.

How do we defend against such an attack? Well, one key thing to know is that hard links can only be created when the source and the destination reside on the same volume. Thus, a very easy measure to ensure system stability against hard link attacks is to ensure the separation of system data and user data via separate file systems. That is, if a user's directory does not reside on the same file system as system data, they will be unable to create a hard link to a system configuration file. Separation of user and system data in such a matter is a security and operational fundamental that should be routinely honored.

If you employ a network home directory model, then you are already provided some protections here, as the user's home directory will not reside on the same file system as any system data. The problem, though, is still present when used in a collaborative environment. In such a case, a user may have read-only access to a particular file. By hard-linking the file to their home directory, they may be able to take advantage of any administrative tasks that deploy file system privilege modifications (whether manual or automated) to ultimately gain write access to the file. Fortunately, when a user creates a hard link, the attributes of the source file will be directly inherited from the source: any POSIX or ACL inheritance that would normally be applied to a new file will not be applied to a linked file. The security of the file remains intact: the user will have no access capabilities to the linked file that they don't have to the original. Thus, hard linking in itself is not dangerous. The danger comes if any administrative routines are applied to the link, and thereby the source.

So how do we protect against this? Well the truth of the matter is that there isn't a great way to protect against all possible misuses of hard links. The most approachable solution is to present access to collaboration data via protocols that do not support hard linking. For instance, neither the SMB nor the AFP protocol support hard links in default OS X configurations. Thus, any collaborative shares presented via these protocols are immune to such hard link attacks. Presenting collaborative data via a network protocol isn't always an option, however, as sometimes collaboration will need to reside on a local volume. This might be, for example, an Xsan volume. In such a case, your best form of protection is to first avoid running administrative scripts that globally grant write provisions to files: lay down your file system hierarchy and a good inheritance model from the get-go, and you can avoid having to run such routines against the data. This certainly isn't a complete answer, though. Another step would be to restrict the user from utilizing tools that can be used create links. At an extreme level, this would include preventing the user from accessing a shell altogether, as well as access to AppleScript capabilities. If the user must absolutely have shell access, an alternative approach would be to utilize OS X sandboxing to restrict access to certain CLI utilities: most notably /bin/ls, but also interpreted runtimes such as Python, Perl, PHP, or Ruby. Utilizing sandbox technology to protect an OS X environment is covered in detail in Chapter 6.

Using mtree to Audit File System Permissions

If you are reading this book we assume you have sensitive data to protect, and if so, you might want to consider routinely auditing your file system permissions. Earlier in this chapter, we learned of the risks that can be incurred when permissions are poorly applied. An inadvertent write mode granted to a directory containing executables means that a malicious user can inject her own executables, thereby granting her the ability to further exploit your system. The suid bit, when granted to an insecure program, can lead to a user subverting the program and gaining complete control of your box. If an executable must be suid to function, then there's not much you can do with POSIX or ACL permissions to prevent damage. To protect against such a scenario, consider sandboxing your program, as discussed in Chapter 6.

However, one thing we can do is make sure that our intended permission structures maintain integrity. To do this, we can routinely audit our hierarchies to ensure that there are no unknown changes, and that even the files themselves have not changed. This can be used to ensure, for instance, that someone has not hijacked a program in your path and injected their own version. Fortunately, OS X includes by default a powerful tool for performing such an audit: mtree. Located at /usr/sbin/mtree, this command can be used to generate a *specification* file that contains information about the provided file system hierarchy. This specification can then be later referenced for comparison against the live file system. Any changes to the current structure from the specification will be reported. mtree provides the user the ability to specify the attributes to query and compare when running. Keywords can be specified to control exactly which statistics are saved to the specification and then which stats to compare with on the live file system. Though it is not an exhaustive list of mtree's keywords, we should make note of the following important attributes:

> *gid, gnam*: The file group as a numeric value.

> *md5digest*: The MD5 message digest of the file. Specifying this keyword will ensure that an md5digest of each file is written to the specification. If the file is modified, it will modify the file's digest, and therefore our routine audits will notify us of changes in the file. Because of potential weaknesses found in the MD5 algorithm, use of the sha1digest isn't a bad idea.

> *sha1digest*: The SHA-1 message digest of the file. This is more secure but also more CPU-intensive than md5digest.

> *mode*: The current file's permissions as a numeric (octal) or symbolic value. Monitoring this attribute will help detect any changes to POSIX permissions on the file.

uid, uname: The file owner as a numeric value and as a username, respectively. Monitoring these values can help to detect changes in directory services that might otherwise affect access.

size: The size, in bytes, of the file. Monitoring this value can help detect if any changes are made to the file itself.

link: The path that the symbolic link references. A symbolic link can be exploited by linking to a malicious program. Monitoring this keyword can help to detect such problems.

time: The last modification time of the file.

type: The type of the file. This keyword detects the type of object that is at a given path, such as a file, directory, a disk or network mount.

> **Note** mtree as of version 10.6 does not support ACLs or other extended attributes. Changes made to either will not be detected when performing mtree audits. Depending upon your scenario, you may want to write a custom script to audit or apply appropriate permissions.

With these keywords in mind, let's venture into creating a specification file for comparison. To generate a spec file, we simply call mtree with the –c flag, and then point it to a path to reference for the specification with the –p flag. We use the –k flag to specify our desired keywords. And thus, the following command is born:

```
/usr/sbin/mtree -c -k 'gid gname -K sha1digest mode uid uname link ↵
type time' -p /usr/bin > /Volumes/mtree_spec_files/myFreshSpec.txt
```

In this command, we specify our desired keywords and then create a specification based on the path /usr/bin. When it is run, mtree writes the specification to stdout. We capture this and redirect it to the file at path /Volumes/mtree_spec_files/myFreshSpec.txt. Preferably, once the file is written, it is then placed into a read-only state, safe from alteration or subterfuge. Once this specification file is in a secure place, preferably a read-only network mount, we can then reference it to audit the active environment. To do this, we call mtree with the following syntax:

```
/usr/sbin/mtree -f /Volumes/mtree_spec_files/myFreshSpec.txt -k 'gid gname ↵
sha1digest mode uid uname link type time '-p /usr/bin
        modification time expected Mon Jan 25 00:29:27 2015 found Mon Jan 25 01:16:14
tar changed
        modification time expected Mon Jan 25 00:29:27 2015 found Mon Jan 25 01:16:14
        link_ref expected bsdtar found /tmp/XEOSUHEJOUE/t4Rpwn4g3
```

When run with this syntax, mtree will output any detected change made since the specification file was generated. In this case, we see that the object at path /usr/bin/tar has been relinked to a suspicious file located at /tmp/XEOSUHEJOUE/t4Rpwn4g3. Armed with this knowledge, we can repair the compromised link and begin to investigate the seriousness of the breach and the vector of the exploit.

> **Tip**   In highly sensitive environments, it may be desirable to compile a custom copy of mtree to run from read-only media. This ensures that your auditing tool itself cannot be compromised.

Consider scheduling routine checks against critical directories on your system to warn you of any issues. The default system path is a good place to start here: /usr/bin:/bin:/usr/sbin:/sbin. If you have installed programs at /usr/local, you may also want to monitor that hierarchy. The /etc/ folder also contains important configuration files that you may want to monitor for modification.

If your systems contain valuable or sensitive data, then it is always a good idea to audit your system's security. Through the mtree binary, OS X provides a built-in tool that does a pretty good job of accomplishing this. The mtree tool certainly isn't as extensive as tools such as Tripwire, but it does its job well and is fairly easy to use.

Summary

In this chapter, we discussed the various tools and facilities that are provided in OS 10.11 to allow for the management and provisioning of data access provided through the file system. You should have a good fundamental understanding of both POSIX and ACL permission schemes, and you should have enough knowledge to apply them for use in your collaborative environment. We also discussed using the mtree tool for auditing file system permissions and structures to help guarantee system integrity and peace-of-mind.

In the next chapter, we will discuss various logging facilities that can be used for tracking historic data, useful in forensics and nonrepudiation.

## Chapter 5

Reviewing Logs and Monitoring

Whether you're dealing with a car or a computer, poor maintenance habits lead to the same consequence: disaster. You're on the freeway, carefully driving at the posted speed limit, and your engine suddenly dies. You go to the mechanic, who roots out the cause: your timing belt broke. You would have replaced your timing belt, had you kept to the maintenance schedule and taken your car in for service at 60,000 miles. Airline maintenance crews who stick to a steadfast and detailed maintenance schedule rarely have this happen to them, mainly because they know precisely on what date the plane was maintained, at what time, and what maintenance was performed.

This is how many seasoned network administrators treat security. They proactively manage their systems. They log when they perform maintenance on the machine and notice when anomalies occur. They review their logs regularly. But logs often go unnoticed and unread, which is unfortunate, as they can be a great source of insight into securing your systems. Even when security has been compromised, many administrators don't think to check the logs to see what happened.

Why is this? It's simple. Logs can be complicated to the untrained eye, and some administrators just don't understand what the logs are telling them.

In this chapter, we will show you where to look for log files on the Mac (and Windows machines as well, because they can tell you a lot about security with respect to a Mac) and show you what they mean. We hope that once you realize what kind of information is stored in logs, you'll start using them a lot more effectively.

What Exactly Gets Logged?

It may seem weird to think that much of what you do on your computer gets logged. Imagine if every move you made was written down, and you could review every step you made over the course of the day. Although we may never know whether the National Security Agency (or AT&T) is actually recording our every move, logging every move on a computer is commonplace.

What gets logged can be determined by the application or by the operating system. This differs for each program, and what gets logged can be configured manually. The act of escalating your privileges is typically logged, as are failed attempts to do so. Many items are logged for the purposes of troubleshooting, but when it comes to security, any item that elevates privileges, references a password entry, or indicates the occurrence of an application failure should be logged.

A log entry can be as simple as one line indicating the deletion of a file, or as detailed as each file created during an installation or process. The following shows a portion of the output of the install.log file during the installation of the Mac OS X Server Admin tools. The install log shows each file created during the process as well as the corresponding date, time, and system on which each was created (or touched).

```
Oct 23 14:03:03 Gene-Sullivans-MacBook installd[137]: PackageKit: Registered bundle⏎
 file://localhost/Applications/Server/Xgrid%20Admin.app/
Oct 23 14:03:03 Gene-Sullivans-MacBook installd[137]: PackageKit: Registered bundle⏎
 file://localhost/System/Library/CoreServices/Server%20Assistant.app/
Oct 23 14:03:03 Gene-Sullivans-MacBook installd[137]: PackageKit: Registered bundle⏎
 file://localhost/Applications/Server/Server%20Monitor.app/
Oct 23 14:03:03 Gene-Sullivans-MacBook installd[137]: PackageKit: Registered bundle⏎
 file://localhost/Applications/Server/Server%20Admin.app/
Oct 23 14:03:03 Gene-Sullivans-MacBook installd[137]: PackageKit: Registered bundle⏎
 file://localhost/Applications/Server/Workgroup%20Manager.app/
Oct 23 14:03:03 Gene-Sullivans-MacBook installd[137]: PackageKit: Registered bundle⏎
 file://localhost/Applications/Server/Server%20Admin.app/Contents/Resources/⏎
ServerAdminLauncher.app/
Oct 23 14:03:03 Gene-Sullivans-MacBook installd[137]: PackageKit: Registered bundle⏎
 file://localhost/Applications/Server/iCal%20Server%20Utility.app/
Oct 23 14:03:03 Gene-Sullivans-MacBook installd[137]: PackageKit: Registered bundle⏎
 file://localhost/Applications/Server/System%20Image%20Utility.app/
Oct 23 14:03:03 Gene-Sullivans-MacBook installd[137]: PackageKit: Registered bundle⏎
 file://localhost/Applications/Server/Server%20Preferences.app/Contents/Resources/⏎
ServerPrefsLauncher.app/
Oct 23 14:03:03 Gene-Sullivans-MacBook installd[137]: PackageKit: Registered bundle⏎
 file://localhost/Applications/Server/Server%20Preferences.app/
Oct 23 14:03:03 Gene-Sullivans-MacBook installd[137]: PackageKit: Registered bundle⏎
 file://localhost/Applications/Server/Podcast%20Composer.app/
Oct 23 14:03:03 Gene-Sullivans-MacBook installd[137]: PackageKit: Registered bundle⏎
 file://localhost/Applications/Server/System%20Image%20Utility.app/Contents/⏎
Library/Automator/Create%20Image.action/Contents/MacOS/AutoPartition.app/
Oct 23 14:03:03 Gene-Sullivans-MacBook installd[137]: PackageKit: Registered bundle⏎
 file://localhost/Applications/QuickTime%20Broadcaster.app/
Oct 23 14:03:04 Gene-Sullivans-MacBook installd[137]: Installed "Server⏎
 Administration Software" ()
Oct 23 14:03:04 Gene-Sullivans-MacBook installd[137]: PackageKit:⏎
 ----- End install -----
Oct 23 14:03:05 Gene-Sullivans-MacBook Installer[127]: Running install actions
Oct 23 14:03:05 Gene-Sullivans-MacBook Installer[127]: Removing temporary directory⏎
"/var/folders/cm/cmSii-8XGFiRvFh+UL8r3U+++TI/-Tmp-//Install.127IGw3rb"
Oct 23 14:03:05 Gene-Sullivans-MacBook Installer[127]: Finalize disk "Snow Leopard"
Oct 23 14:03:05 Gene-Sullivans-MacBook Installer[127]: Notifying system of updated⏎
 components
```

Multiple processes can be logged simultaneously, because they use such little processing power. Logging software writes entries to log files while you're performing many of the common tasks you do every day and when routine tasks are running on your system in the background. This may be some of those pesky items that cause the computer to run slowly at various times of the day, such as right around 3:15 AM (this is when the normal daily periodic Unix scripts run).

When looking at logs, try to keep in mind that reading every single line of every log file can become tedious. Rather than doing this, look for strange entries in the files. For example, if the previous log also had included a line that indicated the installation of something called keystrokelogger, that would be something to be concerned about.

These strange entries are also called anomalies, or one-offs. They are entries that can appear odd or unexplainable or can be indications of something going wrong, or a process or an account doing something that it should not be doing.

Of course, looking for strange entries and anomalies assumes that you already know what the patterns are in your logs and that you can then tell when a strange entry or an anomaly turns up. Which really means that you should be looking at your log files regularly so that reading them becomes second nature. Also, when you do these regular reviews you should be practicing your searching so that when the time comes for you to search for that anomalous needle in your log entry haystack you will have little problem constructing a good search and then narrowing it down.

Using Console

In general, log files are text files that can be read with any text editor. (One exception to this rule are the BSM logs, which are addressed later in this chapter.) But trying to find and read all the system logs in a text editor can be a daunting endeavor. With OS X, Apple has simplified and streamlined this by giving you a handy tool in the /Applications/Utilities folder called Console. In this section we'll cover how to use Console to view and mark logs.

Viewing Logs

You can use Console to review logs quickly without having to open and read each file independently. When you open Console, you are immediately viewing Console Messages. Clicking the Show Log List button gives you a listing of all the logs that Console is aware of, divided into three sections (see Figure 5-1). The Files section is a list of plain text log files, laid out according to where they're located in the file system. Any other log files you open for viewing with Console will appear in this section.

The top two sections don't show the contents of text files, but rather information drawn from the Apple System Logger database. ASL is a new logging facility that Apple introduced with Leopard, which consists of syslogd and aslmanager. The *de facto* standard for logging messages on Unix system is syslogd. It is historically used by the kernel to write messages to the system log, and is also used by daemons and programs such as Apache and Postfix. Since Snow Leopard, messages logged by the syslogd server are stored in a binary database located in /private/var/log/asl/. The files in that directory are managed by aslmanager. For compatibility with the many other systems that use syslogd, many of the

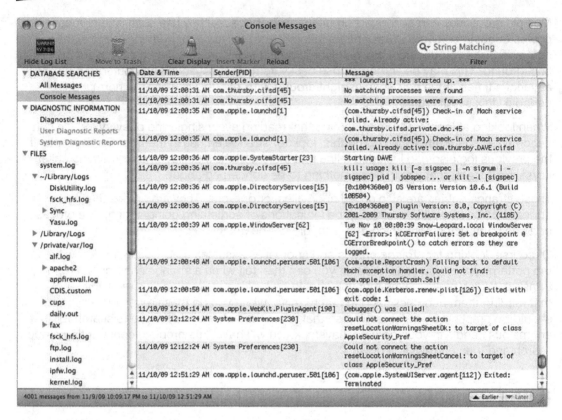

Figure 5-1. Using Console

messages are elso echoed to /private/var/log/system.log.

Console was designed to give you an easy one-stop shop for reviewing system logs. Although this is helpful, Console doesn't show you every log on your computer. Each application logs information a little bit differently, and it would be impossible to cover every aspect of every log file ever created. Happily, many of the apps made for Mac OS X follow a fairly standard method that Apple established with its own logs. We'll point out the ones to check for most security purposes. You can then apply this knowledge to other network-aware applications in order to check their logs for issues. Before we delve into what these logs can tell you, we'll discuss how you can interact with the logs.

Though the log files use .log as their file type designator, they are mostly text files. As such this means they can be opened, read and searched by text editors such as vi or vim (built into the Mac), TextEdit, or advanced text editors such as BBedit. Console has good search functionality, but if you prefer to work in another editor and use something like regular expressions for more powerful pattern recognition and search capabilities you can do that.

Marking Logs

It is sometimes helpful to mark a spot in a log, while you are reviewing them, much like using a sticky note or highlighter to mark a passage in a book. To do so, select the log in the

Logs window of Console and click the Insert Marker button. It's important to note that these markers are not inserted into the log itself, but into your view of the log in Console. Clicking the Reload button, choosing another log, or quitting Console will cause those markers to disappear.

Another way to insert a marker into system.log and the ASL database is to use the logger utility, which provides an interface to syslogd. All entries you write will be prefaced with the date and time, and will include whatever message you send to it.

```
logger Marker
```

This command will insert the following line in system.log:

```
Nov  8 22:12:32 Snow-Leopard gene[1421]: Marker
```

Console also makes it easy to copy data out of the logs. When you click a log in Console, you can highlight text and copy it to TextEdit, Word, or any other program that supports pasting. To copy, you can either use Cmd-C key or select Edit ä Copy. Notice that you cannot cut text; Console does not let you modify logs.

For performance and simplicity, when you view the logs in the Database Searches section of Console, it will show you only the most recent 4,000 lines of data in the log. If there is more data in a log than Console can show, the Earlier and Later buttons on Console's status bar will become active. When viewing any of the other logs, Console will only show the most recent 16MB of messages. When a log is larger than this, the Earlier and Later buttons will allow you to view the rest of the log.

> **Note**   When viewing very large log files, such as Console.log, you might have to wait for a long time if the log size is bigger than a few megabytes.

Searching Logs

If you're looking for a specific item in a log, the Filter box in Console's Toolbar will filter the log you're currently viewing, showing you only the lines containing the text you're seeking. If you're looking for successful and failed ssh attempts, you could enter sshd in the Filter box. As you type, the messages will be filtered until you're only viewing messages containing sshd. This can be very useful for simple searches, but it can be difficult to put the results in context.

You can also search within a log by going to Edit ä Find (or pressing Cmd-F) and entering a search term. The first matching instance will be highlighted, and you can see what you're looking for while still seeing what else was being logged around that time. It's also possible to find terms within a filtered log.

Console also allows you to create saved Database Searches that will appear at the top of the Log List alongside All Messages and Console Messages. Go to File ä New Database Search (or press Cmd-Option-N), and you will be presented with the Database Search editor (see Figure 5-2).

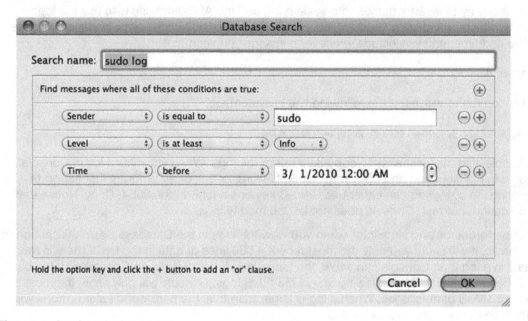

Figure 5-2. Creating a database search

Give your search a name and select your search criteria. You can search by the contents of the message (as with filtering, explained previously), by Sender (the name of the process sending the message), by Facility (a legacy designation of the part of the system sending the message), or by Level (the severity of the message). It's possible to create very granular searches that will be a big help in keeping an eye on your system.

Finding Logs

The /private/var/log directory is where OS X stores most of its important log files. If you write an application or script that builds its own log file, then you can write these logs to /private/var/log and they will automatically appear in Console under /private/var/log. Many developers put their logs here because the /private/var directory is used in most Unix distributions (flavors) to house logs that are not user-specific. This includes logs for open source software that has been installed by Apple such as the firewall (ipfw), the Windows sharing component (samba), the web server (apache), and many other items.

The Finder is intentionally designed to not make these folders easily accessible. To get to the /private/var folder, you need to use the Terminal application and access it through the command line, or you can use the Cmd-Shift-G keystroke and type **/private/var** (or just **/var**, which is a symbolic link) in the "Go to the Folder" field. This is a fairly standard way of accessing many of the logs we will be discussing in this chapter.

Generally you can configure third-party applications to log to wherever you want. For example, Rumpus, the popular FTP server, stores its logs by default in the /usr/local/ Rumpus/Logs directory. However, you can customize this using the Log Folder field (as shown in Figure 5-3). Additionally, with third-party applications, you can usually customize the frequency with which logs are trimmed and the amount of data that is written to the logs.

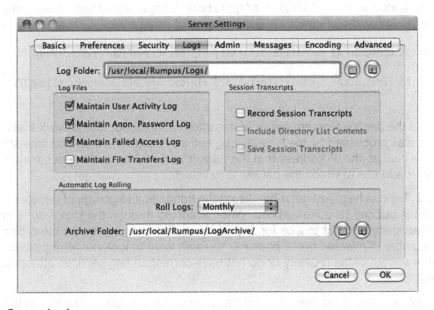

Figure 5-3. Rumpus logging

> **Note**   To access the /usr/local folder, you need to use the Cmd-Shift-G keystroke and type **/usr/local**.

Because logs are compressed and stored for a short period of time before being deleted, if you are doing deep forensics on a system you may need to go into the backups to do a more extensive search. It's not uncommon to go back months or even years in the backups to search older log files to find what you are looking for or to find a pattern.

What Happened to the Secure.log??

The secure.log file had its last hurrah in Snow Leopard, 10.6. With 10.7 and up through 10.11 the security events that were captured in secure.log are captured in the system log. Some of the security events can be captured by other logs. Some enterprise environments may install third party software that facilitates and enhances authentication to Active Directory. In this case that software may have its own logs – and you may find the login event information not on the Mac but in the Active Directory logs. However, those events go through the kernel too, so if you have the Basic Security Module enabled for certain security events (including but not limited to logins and logouts) you can refer to the BSM audit logs. For more on BSM and auditing see that section later in this chapter.

appfirewall.logThe built-in firewall (covered in greater detail in Chapter 11) is a feature-rich application layer firewall that is capable of logging massive amounts of data. `appfwloggerd` is a program built specifically for the purpose of logging firewall events to the `appfirewall.log` file. This file located at `/private/var/log/appfirewall.log`. `appfwloggerd` logs only those events that the Application Firewall determines are not acceptable.

```
Jul 16 15:10:18 dimac.local socketfilterfw[182] <Info>: CrashPlanService: Deny TCP CONNECT
(in:25 out:0)
Jul 16 15:10:18 dimac.local socketfilterfw[182] <Info>: AppleFileServer: Allow TCP CONNECT
(in:12 out:0)
```

The format of the previous log entries indicates information about the network traffic, or packet, that was processed by the firewall. Log entries include the date and time stamp the source of the packet (the IP address that the packet came from), and the destination of the packet (the IP address to which the packet is traveling).

appfirewall.log can help you get a handle on the comings and goings of network traffic on your computer, but can be quite verbose. When scanning through the logs, your goal should not be to read every line, but to look for any information that seems out of the ordinary, such as a large number of rejected traffic packets. You also want to look out for repeated attempts on ports that are out of the ordinary or do not have corresponding services attached to your system.

In the example above I discovered that my backup service was being blocked at the firewall. This is a good reminder to check your logs.

> **Note**   Date and time stamps are a common theme in logs. They're invaluable correlating log entries with real-world events, or tracking a user's activities across one system or many. Some log aggregators will place the log events on a timeline so they are more intuitive to view, and will also reformat the log entries so they are easier to read. If you have to read logs frequently it may be worth your time to look into using a log aggregator.

Reviewing User-Specific Logs

Many user-specific operating-system components and third-party applications, such as 1Password, Carbon Copy Cloner, ClamXav, and Yasu, log data into files inside each user's home directory. These logs are stored in the ~/Library/Logs folder. Because they are kept inside each user's folder, the logs are accessible only to that user (or anyone who has access to the account). This is good for the privacy of each user, but it can make troubleshooting difficult. Keep in mind that logs stored in a user's home directory are owned by that account, and could easily be modified by a proficient user. Any information gleaned from these logs should be taken with a grain of salt.

> **Note**   You can get around the multiuser issues with logs. Logging in with the root account will allow you to view the logs for other users.

One log of note in the ~/Library/Logs folder is DiskUtility.log. This log file stores all the activities run by the Disk Utility application, including fixing permissions, fixing the disk, and formatting and partitioning. The Disk Utility logs do not get *rotated*, or cleared out on a routine basis, which makes them particularly useful if you are investigating suspicious behavior on the system. Let's say you suspect that a hard drive was reformatted. By reviewing DiskUtility.log for each user on a system, you will find who reformatted a hard drive as well as any settings that were customized during the reformat process. The following is a sample Disk Utility log:

```
**********
2015-06-12 23:05:51 -0400: Preparing to erase : "8GB_xinuos"
2015-06-12 23:05:51 -0400:     Partition Scheme: GUID Partition Table
2015-06-12 23:05:51 -0400:     1 volume will be created
2015-06-12 23:05:51 -0400:        Name          : "8GB_xinuos"
2015-06-12 23:05:51 -0400:        Size          : 8.02 GB
2015-06-12 23:05:51 -0400:        File system   : Mac OS Extended (Journaled)

2015-06-12 23:05:51 -0400: Unmounting disk
2015-06-12 23:05:53 -0400: Creating the partition map
2015-06-12 23:05:56 -0400: Waiting for the disks to reappear
2015-06-12 23:05:56 -0400: Formatting disk3s2 as Mac OS Extended (Journaled) with name 8GB_xinuos
2015-06-12 23:06:06 -0400: Initialized /dev/rdisk3s2 as a 7 GB case-insensitive HFS Plus
volume with a 8192k journal

2015-06-12 23:06:06 -0400: Mounting disk
2015-06-12 23:06:20 -0400: Erase complete.
2015-06-12 23:06:20 -0400:
```

Another log of note is the ClamXav-scan.log, which records all the results from an antivirus scan, and then summarizes the findings.

```
/Users/dano/Sites/surfcam_files/.DS_Store: OK
/Users/dano/Sites/surfcam_files/index.html: OK
/Users/dano/Sites/surfcam_files/jwplayer.js: OK
/Users/dano/Sites/surfcam_files/player.swf: OK
/Users/dano/Sites/surfcam_files/SurfCams.html: OK
/Users/dano/Sites/surfcam_files/swfobject.js: OK
/Users/dano/Sites/surfcam_files.zip: OK
----------- SCAN SUMMARY -----------
Known viruses: 3731269
Engine version: 0.98.5
Scanned directories: 73406
Scanned files: 544600
Infected files: 4
Total errors: 11
```

```
Data scanned: 144820.95 MB
Data read: 481779.80 MB (ratio 0.30:1)
Time: 18750.559 sec (312 m 30 s)
Mar 28 12:19:34 dimac04-2 newsyslog[10265]: logfile turned over due to size>5120K
```

Whether you believe in the efficacy of antivirus scans of OS X or not, it may be a requirement in an enterprise environment.

Launchd, the process that controls scheduled activities, also has the ability to log data. When you suspect a root kit (discussed further in Chapter 8) has infected your system as one user but isn't active for all users, take a look at the launchd logs for your user account to see whether any events are occurring that you should be concerned about. Things to be concerned about include non-Apple services being initiated. The log level for launchd is set with the launchctl command. launchctl log mask notice will configure launchd to log events with every severity between Emergency and Notice.

User logs can be helpful in determining what was done while logged into your account. When used in conjunction with the other logs mentioned, you can get a fairly specific idea of what was performed on the system recently.

Some other user-specific logs to be aware of for forensics or information are: 1Password, appstore.log, the directory with Diagnostic Reports, FaceTime, the FlashPlayerInstallManager.log (especially this, since Flash must be kept up to date), GoogleSoftwareUpdateAgent.log, LittleSnitch (if you run it), gpg logs (if you use that personal privacy application), the VMware Fusion logs, and more.

Reviewing Command-Line Logs

DiskUtility.log lets you know if somebody burned a disk with Disk utility, but it won't show whether someone ran a reformat or repair operation from the command line. For command-line information, it is often best to look into the command-line history for each user. This information is stored in the history file. The history file is different for each shell in which a user is operating. For example, the history file for the default shell, bash, is .bash_history. It is located in the root of each user's home folder. The history files do not get automatically rotated by OS X subsystems and, by default will only keep 150 commands. As new commands are entered, old commands will expire. You can view history by using the history command (no arguments are needed), and you can clear the history by using history -c. Although the history file can be difficult to correlate events to when unaltered, it is one of the most important items to review as most will not alter this file.

When you use the su command, you are substituting your identity for that of root, the system's built-in administrative user, or another user if you indicate another user during that process. Any commands that are run as the user you have switched to using the command line would be captured in the root user's history, not your own. This means you need to log in to each account in order to review the account's history. Reviewing the history file can be fairly difficult if you are looking to correlate history events with other logs. Unfortunately, there are no date and time stamps available in the history file to indicate when commands were run. However, provided a user has not rotated their logs, you know which commands were run, and in which order, and sometimes you can correlate this with system events from log files. Some of these commands may be recorded in the BSM log file, so that can help to correlate events on a timeline. However, BSM has to be configured appropriately to capture these events. To complicate matters even further, different users like to use different shells (a shell is just a different way to interface with the command line). Most users use bash (which is the default on Mac OS X), but others might use tcsh or ksh. Each shell has a different history file, and some, by default, don't log history at all. If you switch to the bourne shell, your history will be stored in .sh_history. This gives you a lot of places to look for information if you have multiple shells running in Terminal. Luckily, bash is the most commonly used shell.

The last command will show a listing of the last users who logged into the computer and how long the login sessions were open. The format of the output of a last command is the username followed by the Terminal type, then the date logged in, and finally the start and stop time of the Terminal session. ttys001 indicates the first Terminal window opened. If a second is opened, it is ttys002, the third is ttys003, and so on. This goes back to mainframe days when each terminal station had a unique identifier. This can give you a good log of recent login activity for a specific machine.

```
gene      ttys001              Tue Nov  3 23:09 - 23:15  (00:05)
gene      ttys001              Tue Nov  3 23:04 - 23:04  (00:00)
gene      ttys000              Tue Nov  3 22:35   still logged in
gene      console              Tue Nov  3 22:23   still logged in
```

Reviewing Library Logs

If you've ever helped a friend move, and that friend was a fairly efficient mover, he probably assigned someone to stay in the moving truck to arrange everything so that the maximum amount of stuff could fit. This lets everyone else maximize efficiency by moving stuff from the house to the truck without worrying about how it's packed. This idea can be translated into the ways in which software applications are programmed to work in an operating system. It often makes sense to use a shared library of items that many different applications can access. This allows more features to be written with less programming, which means greater efficiency, much like the guy in the truck allows the people moving furniture from the house to do so more efficiently.

Because the /Library folder keeps many shared application libraries (think of these as mini-applications), the types of logs stored here tend to be those generated by components that are shared across multiple applications. This includes CrashReporter, which writes application crash information into logs, and also server and directory service logs. Many application programmers also choose /Library/Logs as their log destination. This, for instance, would explain the random Timbuktu log you might notice in there.

Many applications and shared libraries communicate using data that might not make much sense to the untrained eye. In the crash logs, you will typically see hexadecimal memory segments listed, followed by the library that wrote the alert and then the path to the library. For example:

```
0x96e15000 - 0x96e2ffff libPng.dylib
/System/Library/Frameworks/ApplicationServices.framework/
Versions/A/Frameworks/ImageIO.framework/Versions/
A/Resources/libPng.dylib
```

These hexadecimal sequences in the logs can help decipher why a crash occurred if foul play is suspected. Nine times out of ten, rather than confirm irregular activity, you will instead find that there is actually a technical problem that caused the crash.

Breaking Down Maintenance Logs

Chances are you see your doctor at regular intervals. The dentist you'll see every six months, and the family physician you'll see every year. Just as your body needs to be maintained in regular intervals, so must your computer. Maintenance scripts run at scheduled times, and if one is missed, much like a doctor's appointment, it is usually scheduled for the next available time. Maintenance scripts need to be run because they log what devices were plugged into a system, they back up the user database, and they do much more. Machines can be left off at night, laptops can get closed, and power outages can disable a system, helping to explain the disparity in time stamps you may see when viewing your maintenance scripts and why you may occasionally skip the execution of a maintenance script.

One thing that maintenance scripts do is rotate and archive certain log files, which can get really big. Try to imagine how large a log file would get if it logged every step, turn, and move you made. When archiving, the log files are usually archived into compressed files using the bzip format, a compression technique commonly used to reduce the size of single files. Once archived, the file will be renamed and cleared and become ready to begin writing new data. Some people refer to archiving a log as "rotating it."

Those logs that are not rotated by the periodic scripts are maintained by newsyslog, which is run every 30 minutes by launchd. The configuration files for newsyslog are located in /private/etc/ and /private/etc/newsyslog.d. Newsyslog.conf covers the rotation of files written by syslogd, and the files in newsyslog.d cover the rotation of files written by other processes.

The important option to configure in newsyslog.conf is count, which determines how many archive files to keep. By default, seven old versions of system.log will be kept, but only five old versions of secure.log will stick around. If you're interested in greater retention of files, change count to 10 (or even 15). Take care, though, as keeping more logs will take up more space than you might imagine.

> **Note**   Console will uncompress files when they are accessed. This can be time-consuming on larger files, which is why Console will, by default, show you only the first 128K of a log file.

In addition to archiving logs, maintenance scripts also perform other functions. These include removing temporary files, performing backups, reviewing drive capacity, checking how long you've been logged into your computer, and checking network statistics.

Mac OS X uses three main maintenance scripts that log data into separate files. These are known as *periodic scripts*. They include daily, weekly, and monthly. You can manually run these periodic scripts by using the periodic command. For example, to run the daily periodic script, use the following command:

```
sudo periodic daily
```

You can configure the periodic scripts to log more data than they do with the default settings. You can configure the manner with which `periodic` runs the daily scripts using the `periodic.conf` file located at `/private/etc/defaults`. You should make some minor adjustments to the `periodic.conf` file to increase the logging of events. These include the following:

- Change the NO in the lines for `weekly_show_badconfig="NO"` and `monthly_show_badconfig="NO"` to YES to have a periodic report of when there is bad configuration data found by the `monthly.out` file.

- Change the NO in the line containing the `daily_clean_logs_verbose="NO"` option to YES to have `periodic` show the files as they are being deleted.

daily.out

The `daily.out` file is an output file created by the daily maintenance scripts that run on your system. Like many of the maintenance logs, `daily.out` begins with a time stamp to provide you with the context of when it ran. Next, the `daily.out` log shows which old logs the daily script removed. For example:

```
Sun Nov  8 19:41:40 PST 2009

Removing old log files:

Removing old temporary files:

Cleaning out old system announcements:

Removing stale files from /var/rwho:

Removing scratch fax files

Disk status:
Filesystem      Size  Used  Avail Capacity  Mounted on
/dev/disk0s3    118Gi 50Gi  68Gi    43%     /

Network interface status:
Name  Mtu   Network      Address          Ipkts Ierrs   Opkts Oerrs  Coll
lo0   16384 <Link#1>                         82     0      82     0     0
lo0   16384 localhost    ::1                 82     -      82     -     -
lo0   16384 localhost    fe80:1::1           82     -      82     -     -
lo0   16384 127          localhost          82      -      82     -     -
gif0* 1280  <Link#2>                          0     0       0     0     0
stf0* 1280  <Link#3>                          0     0       0     0     0
en1   1500  <Link#4>     00:1e:c2:ab:d7:9f 4536     0    4271     0     0
en1   1500  localhost    fe80:4::21e:c2ff: 4536     -    4271     -     -
en1   1500  192.168.11   192.168.11.5      4536     -    4271     -     -
en0   1500  <Link#5>     00:1e:c2:19:fd:b0    0     0       0     0     0
fw0   2030  <Link#6>     00:1f:5b:ff:fe:2d:89:c0  0  0       0     0     0
```

```
Local system status:
19:41  up 44 mins, 4 users, load averages: 0.02 0.05 0.01

-- End of daily output --
```

The big thing to look out for here is that the `Ipkts` field is greater than the others. The `Name` field refers to the name of the interface that the MAC address and the other statistics will be relevant for. The `Network` field is similar to the `Name` field but states the network that the interface can run on. The `MTU` field is the maximum transmission unit, which means the largest "packet" size that can be transferred in one physical frame on a network. `Ipkts` refers to the incoming packets, and `Opkts` refers to outgoing packets. The `Ipkts` field should always be higher than the `Opkts` field. If anything here looks like it is out of the ordinary, such as the `Opkts` field being higher than the `Ipkts` field, it often means you need to reinstall the drivers for your network interface. Another item to look out for is high numbers of collisions (the `Col` column). If your collisions are more than 10 percent of the `Ipkts` field, then you might have issues with your network.

> **Note**   If the same network interface is listed multiple times, it is nothing to be alarmed about.

The final action of the daily maintenance script is to rotate the `system.log` file. The `system.log` file is often the largest log file on the system. This is discussed in further detail later in this chapter. The daily script is scheduled to run at 3:15 AM every day.

> **Note**   People often ask whether they should leave their computers on at night. If they have a good battery backup system, we usually tell them to do so. This allows the daily script to run when it is supposed to run.

Yasu

Yasu is a nice little free application that will run maintenance scripts if they are missed because the computer was turned off during their regular schedules (see Figure 5-4). Not only is it important to run the periodic maintenance scripts in order to view their output logs for errors, but it is equally important to run them in order to manage the size of the various log files that get archived with this script. To do this, simply open Yasu, make sure only the daily, monthly, and weekly cron script boxes are checked, and then click OK.

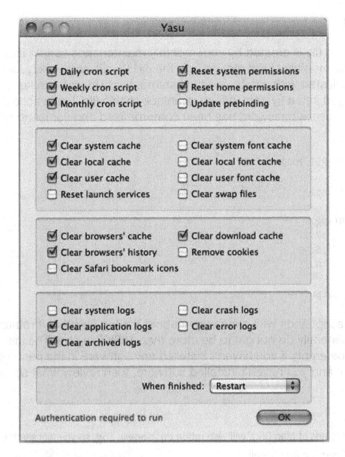

Figure 5-4. Running maintenance scripts with Yasu

Caution   If you leave the check boxes at the bottom of the Yasu screen checked, then you will erase many of the log files that you might need to review!

Weekly.out

The weekly `periodic` script runs at 3:15 AM on Saturdays. It updates the "whatis" database (used for the `whatis` command, which searches through man pages for words you provide), and little else.

```
Sun Nov  8 19:42:20 PST 2009

Rebuilding whatis database:

-- End of weekly output --
```

Monthly.out

The monthly.out log file is created by your monthly maintenance scripts and can be used to display what the monthly script did. As with the daily.out and weekly.out files, the monthly.out file will start with a date and time stamp. Monthly.out can keep track of how long a user is logged into a system, a feature unique to this file. Login accounting is useful if you suspect that a user's password has been compromised and someone is illegally logging into a machine.

```
Sun Nov  8 19:58:15 PST 2009

Rotating fax log files:

Doing login accounting:
        total       17.11
        gene        16.99
        root         0.11

-- End of monthly output --
```

The monthly.out script ends with a statement about the log files that it rotated. Logs that are rotated monthly generally do not get to be more than 150KB in size. The install log, for example, should be empty if you haven't installed any software in the past month. If you do see data in this file and you haven't installed software, then review what software it is and check it.

> **Note**   Older versions of Mac OS X will also rotate cu.modem.log, so you will see this noted in your monthly.out log file as well.

The monthly script is scheduled to run on the first of the month at 5:30 AM local time.

What to Worry About

Los Angeles can be a strange place to live. If we ducked for cover every time we heard sirens, we wouldn't get a wink of sleep or any writing done, and you wouldn't be reading this book. To some extent, much of what could be considered worrisome simply becomes normal in a big city because of all of the "white noise" to which we're exposed.

The same goes for log files. There is a lot of information in your log files, and not everything is important. This can be overwhelming for anyone, even the most senior systems administrators. We'll now cover some of the items to be on the lookout for when reviewing your logs and some of the ways to reduce the amount of "white noise" in the logs.

One way to do this is by using keywords. The words `failed`, `error`, and `incorrect` are usually important to look out for. Read the content surrounding these for more information, or use an automated analysis tool. Sorting through a log file can also be automated by using a log analyzer to help keep track of events on user systems. An excellent open source option is Swatch, which has been used by Unix systems administrators for a long time. It has been ported to Mac OS X, and can monitor just about any type of log you'll find. Other open source options are logsentry (formerly known as logcheck), a component of a security suite called Sentry Tools, and logwatch, both of which are available through MacPorts. There are also commercial options such as Sawmill, an analysis tool that can analyze hundreds of different log file formats, Graylog, an open source log aggregation tool, and Splunk, a monitoring and reporting tool that consolidates logs (as well as data from many other sources) into a searchable database.

Activity Monitor

In order to more easily identify some of what you see in your logs it is helpful to have an idea of what is going on in your machine. By this we mean you ought to have an idea of what processes are running behind the scenes. A good way to look at this is with the Activity Monitor. You can find the Activity Monitor in /Applications/Utilities.

Virtual Machine and Bootcamp Logs

It's hard to imagine that discussing the methods that Windows uses to log events would ever factor into a book about the Mac. Who knew ten years ago that two competing technologies would ever converge? But converging they are. And if your computer is running VMWare Fusion, Parallels, or Bootcamp with Windows, then security is going to be one of your top concerns. As we've discussed throughout this chapter, logs can give you a wealth of information about how secure your system is. Windows has its own tools that can help you to secure a Windows environment on the Mac.

Event Viewer

The Event Viewer is similar to the Console application on a Mac. It provides an administrator with one place to go to find information about service-oriented errors on the system itself. Microsoft changed the structure and event codes after Windows XP. While Windows 7 and Server 2008 have much more detail in their event logging, the concepts are the same.

The Event Viewer is split into three parts (see Figure 5-5) in Windows 7. Windows XP and the different versions of Windows Server may look different, but for the sake of discussion in this book, we will concentrate on Windows 7. On the left is a list of Event categories, similar to the Log List in Console.

- Application contains events that are logged by programs. This includes database, Microsoft Exchange, SharePoint, and other applications that write data into logs that are not part of the core operating system.

- Security contains information about security events that have occurred when logging onto the computer. If you have enabled audit trails on file access, then this can be a verbose log. Otherwise, it is usually a very small log. Look out for anything with the word *failure* in the log because this can signify a failure with a security process.

- System shows you the events that get logged by the operating system. This includes drivers and other system components that could produce an error.

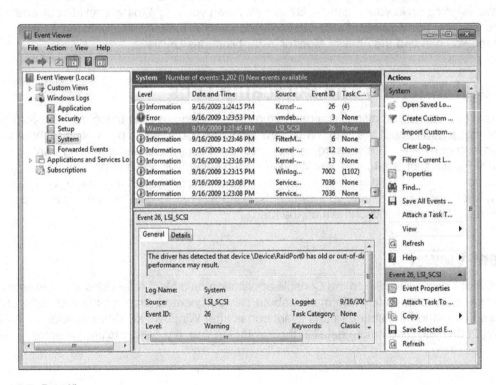

Figure 5-5. Event Viewer

There is a plethora of Microsoft event IDs in the Event Viewer. Microsoft has made it fairly simple to sift through these event IDs to find the errors by using color-coding. Blue means no action is necessary, yellow indicates that an item should at least be looked at, and red indicates a failure. By researching the contents of each of these entries, you will get a good handle on what Windows is having any problems with, including many events directly related to the security of your system. Windows Event logs are rather easier to read than OS X' raw logs, but the readability of both is vastly improved by using an audit log aggregator.

Although it may seem daunting at first, you should know what every warning and error message means. The Microsoft Web site is a good place to research information about these events. Another good reference to Windows event logs is Ultimate Windows Security.[1]

> **Note**   In response to the need for a more comprehensive listing of event information, EventID.net publishes information about Windows events and links to Microsoft Knowledge Base articles and third-party web sites to find more information on fixing issues you may find here. Searching for the event message, enclosed in quotation marks, on Google is also a good bet.

Task Manager

The Event Viewer is helpful for researching events that have already occurred on your system. But it doesn't go into detail about all the processes currently running on your system. The Task Manager in Windows is similar to the Activity Monitor on a Mac, and will provide you with the ability to look at what processes are currently running (see Figure 5-6).

---

[1]Randy Franklin Smith's Ultimate Windows Security: `https://www.ultimatewindowssecurity.com/securitylog/quickref/Default.aspx`

Figure 5-6. Task Manager

To see the Task Manager, press the Ctrl-Alt-Del keys on your keyboard, and choose Start Task Manager. Here you will see a few tabs. The first is Applications, which contains applications currently running under your account. The second is Processes, which contains the applications you have launched and any background processes that might be running, as well as the user who started the process and the CPU and memory being taken up by that application. You can use the Performance tab to check memory and processor utilization and get a chart that shows this.

To stop a process that is running, you can right-click it and click End Process. To find out more about a process, consider using Google or the Microsoft Knowledge Base at www.microsoft.com/support to research what each process is doing on the system.

Note You can use the Networking tab to view the network traffic running on your network interfaces.

Performance Alerts

You can use the Performance Monitor Management Console Snap-In (see Figure 5-7) to customize the amount of information that is being logged and to provide you with extremely detailed information about nearly every aspect of how your system is running. This tool is far more advanced than those available on the Mac platform for tracking down bottlenecks in speed, levels of inbound traffic, and other items that could introduce security issues. A comprehensive discussion about this tool is beyond the scope of this book, but should definitely be consulted when trying to troubleshoot why the Windows environment on your computer is running poorly.

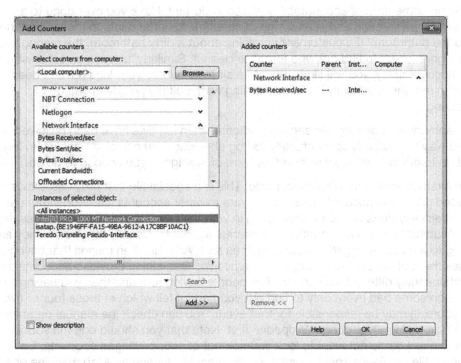

Figure 5-7. Performance counters

While it is possible (maybe even common) for many Windows admins to know just one operating system, many Mac admins need to know at least one OS in addition to OS X. While this is usually Windows, it does not hurt and can be quite helpful to learn to work with linux and perhaps even a BSD variant (most likely FreeBSD). In an enterprise security environment it's common to use one of these unix-like operating systems in security appliances or dedicated systems. (For example, your penetration testing system will probably be Kali Linux.) With the added functionality of virtual machines in VMware Fusion or Parallels, these highly useful systems can be installed for free.

Review Regularly, Review Often

Reviewing logs is an integral aspect of security, and you should review them routinely. If you are the only person responsible for looking at logs, set up a recurring event in your calendar program to remind you to do this. This might be daily, weekly, or monthly, according to how concerned your organization is about the health and security of your system coupled with how complex your environment is.

Accountability

Establishing some form of accountability is also important. Have you ever gone to a bathroom in a gas station and seen a sign-in sheet for the attendants to mark when they've cleaned the bathroom? If a customer complains about a dirty bathroom, the manager can use the sign-in sheet to find out who forgot to clean it. Similarly, unless you establish some form of accountability, you will likely run into a situation where your logs haven't been checked in months, especially if you are dealing with multiple people in charge of log checking.

Using a spreadsheet or a sign-in sheet to indicate when log files have been reviewed is an excellent way to establish accountability for log checking. You can also track when logs are backed up to optical media (or some other form of storage) if you choose to do so.

Another alternative is to use the sudoers file. This is a special file that provides allows designated users and account access to elevate to other accounts, i.e. "substitute user". What it effectively does is force a user to log in with their own account and then use the sudo or "substitute user do" command to change accounts. Usually this means they are switching to a more privileged account, such as root. And this then means that anybody who uses the root account must log in as themselves first, which provides accountability. It is fundamentally different from four or five people having root and then you having to do forensics on some bad event only to find out you cannot tell which of those four or five (minus yourself) may be responsible for that event. You can check the manual page for sudoers (`man sudoers`), or check Wikipedia[2] first. Note that you should edit the sudoers file with caution as you do not want to lock yourself out of your privileged accounts. Editing the sudoers file requires a special syntax so you should practice on a lab machine or a lab test virtual machine before you edit the sudoers files on production computers. This is particularly useful if you have to track down an APT event or an outside intruder who has captured a login from one of your privileged users and done something untoward in one or some of your machines. The sudoers files is located at /etc/sudoers.

---

[2]Wikipedia on sudoers: `https://en.wikipedia.org/wiki/Sudo`

The following are the items to include in your regularly scheduled log reviews:

- When were the `periodic` maintenance scripts (daily, weekly, and monthly) last run? You can easily find this using `ls -l /var/log/*.out` to see when their log files were last updated. Was there anything out of the ordinary in those logs?

- Were there bad password attempts? Look for repeated bad password attempts in the log for any service that accepts a network connection, such as the `smb.log` (if there are Windows computers on your network) or `ftp.log` (if you are sharing files through FTP).

- Look for any bad password attempts, and check for privilege escalations.

- Do you know who your privileged users are? Do you know when they log into your system? Set up the sudoers file and give explicit access only to those privileged users who need it.

- Review the `history` command to check for strange commands and the `last` command to look for weird user logins.

- If you're running Parallels or Bootcamp, check your Windows Event Viewer.

- The `access.log` file in the `/private/var/log /cups/access_log` folder shows all the CUPS activity on your print server.

- The logs located in the `/private/var/log/samba` directory deal with access attempts from Windows computers.

Incident Response

Smart homeowners have a disaster plan in place for what to do if their home is affected by a natural disaster or burglary. They post the phone number to the local police or fire department next to their phone. In California, earthquake country, they keep gallons of water and canned foods stored in their pantries. Whether they know it or not, they are developing an *incident response plan*.

If, in your searching through regular log files, you find something that concerns you, then you will want to also have an incident response plan for how you are going to handle these incidents. Incident response plans don't have to be very complicated, but the more people who are involved in the operations of your information systems, the more involved the incident response plan will be; therefore, the more complex the infrastructure, the more thought out the incident response plan should be.

The incident response plans can vary from location to location. For example, if you are troubleshooting your security logs at home, a typical incident response to a suspicious item in a log might be to spend an hour trying to discover what occurred. After that initial hour, if you haven't managed to discover the culprit, you will immediately reformat your hard drive and restore your data from backup. (You do have backups, right?) But at the office, you might decide that if a security event occurs and you cannot figure out what the problem is, you will open a ticket with AppleCare immediately, down the system, make a check-summed clone of it, install a new hard drive, install OS X on the new hard drive, and migrate data. Home incident response plans are typically easy to compile and really just offer you a task list of what to do in the case of a security incident. Office incident response plans are typically more comprehensive, and need to go through committees or IT groups for approval, especially because they could contain some mission-critical systems with guaranteed uptimes that need to be maintained.

We cannot stress enough the importance of implementing an incident response system. Intellectual property theft is on the rise. Companies have lost billions of dollars in revenue over the years because of stolen intellectual property. When it occurs, it is usually not a sudden occurrence; it happens over time. More often than not, the logs were giving clues to breaches in the security framework long before the actual theft occurred. Some companies have been put out of business because of security breaches. An incident response plan coupled with a tested, reliable backup plan spares everyone the heartache and devastation of stolen intellectual property and financial information.

Incident response plans can become fairly complex if you consider some of the possibilities such as a disaffected insider doing damage or data theft, or an intruder who has gained privileged access and you have to determine the extent of the damage and their access. Your incident response plan should have policies as well as technical measures.

BSM – Auditing with the Basic Security Module

During the early production period of OS X 10.3 (Panther) Apple quietly contracted with McAfee Research Labs to develop a system of internal monitoring and logging of a large number of diverse actions that occurred outside the normal logging environment. The purpose of this was to achieve Common Criteria certification for the operating system, as well as to enhance the security posture of the OS. This security subsystem allows auditing of many processes, and it is auditing that enhances the security and is one of the major factions in Common Criteria certification.

Since OS X is derived from FreeBSD, which is more similar to Solaris than many operating systems, the choice was made to create this security subsystem for both FreeBSD and OS X, and to model it after BSM that is built into Solaris. In late 2004 OS X 10.3.6 was released with BSM as an option that could be installed into the system, and would be operational with some additional configurations.

(The audit subsystem was part of Common Criteria Tools.[3] From 10.6 to the present 10.11.x the audit subsystem is built into the operating system so you do not have to install it. In fact you should not attempt to install it as doing so will break your system. There is an Administrator's Guide (see the link in the footnote below) that includes a guide to using the audit system and interpreting its output.)

---

[3]Apple's Common Criteria Tools for 10.3.6 (to the end of 10.3.x), 10.4 and 10.5, https://support.apple.com/downloads/Common_Criteria_Tools

Over the ensuing years this BSM was developed so that it quickly became a native part of the OS (not optional) and no special configuration was required for it to work. Also, this version of OS X was granted Common Criteria certification,[4] which validated it for some high security uses such as the US Government. In the ensuing years BSM was developed further for both FreeBSD and OS X, and is now commonly known as OpenBSM to distinguish it from BSM in Solaris.

Currently Apple has documentation about the OpenBSM system in its Open Source Projects description tree here[5] and here,[6] and in the Developers guide.[7]

The OpenBSM subsystem also creates log files, but this log environment is completely separate and different from the Apple System Logs (ASL) and the other log files that are described above. While the OpenBSM system could have an entire chapter devoted just to it, let's take a look at its basic functions, configurations, and uses of auditing.

If you boot a Mac while holding down the Command-V keys you will set the machine to boot into *verbose mode*. This will send to the display a line for every process that starts, and many configurations. This will amount to hundreds of lines, and is sometimes a useful tool in troubleshooting. If you watch the first few lines you will see the BSM system start up. That is, the Basis Security Modules is one of the very first processes to start in the operating system. This is important in tracking everything that the system does, or that any process or user does as well.

[illustration of the top of the boot screen]

The OpenBSM process is one that is owned and managed by the kernel. This means that – unlike nearly all the other log files – it can only be accessed by the superuser or root. Consequently this also means that both configuring the system and reading its output requires that an administrator account in the OS must elevate to root in order to get at the OpenBSM system.

One of the first places to look for information about OpenBSM is in the man pages. Here you will find information about *auditd*, the audit daemon, as well as the commands and configuration files that are available to you, the system administrator and/or auditor.

Fortunately for us, there are actually few commands to learn. However, the configurations files are somewhat more complex, and the output files are actually very complex and can require considerable time, study and practice to learn to work with and understand.

---

[4]Common Criteria certification, https://en.wikipedia.org/wiki/Common_Criteria
[5]Open Source Projects, http://www.apple.com/opensource/
[6]the OpenBSM project files, http://www.opensource.apple.com/source/OpenBSM/OpenBSM-21/
[7]Apple Developer, https://developer.apple.com

The Audit Daemon and Audit Commands

The audit daemon is controlled by the kernel, so you will not touch *auditd* directly. However, you have access to several commands that tell the audit daemon what to do: The audit command allows you to restart and resynchronize the audit daemon to a new configuration of audit settings, or to simply close the currently open audit file (also known as an audit trail file, or simply audit trail) and to open a new audit trail. There are a few other flags available to you in the audit command, but these two are most commonly used.

The two other important commands in the audit system are *auditreduce* and *praudit*. (The command auditpipe also exists, but it is used much less than the first three.)

The *auditreduce* command allows the auditor to filter out data that is not important to the audit search when looking through the existing audit trails. For example, you may configure the audit system to capture when a user logs in or out, when a user opens and closes files either successfully or unsuccessfully, and when either a user or the operating system starts and closes processes. But you may want to do a search through these audit trails that only returns the action of when a specific user logs in. Or you may want to restrict that even further, to when a specific user logged in on a certain day and between certain times. The *auditreduce* command allows you to do this.

The *praudit* command is when you want to convert those audit trails, whether they are reduced or whole, from the native binary format into text files.

This is another facet of the security that the OpenBSM system provides. That is, the audit trail files that are generated by the kernel are stored in binary encoded form that is similar to encryption, and they can only be read after being decoded by the kernel upon your command to "print" the audit trail files. This prevents any user who does not have access to root from reading the files. In addition the directories (or folders) that these audit trail files are stored in are owned by root and no other user on the system has access to write to or read from these directories.

Of course if a user already has access to the machine and knows enough about OS X to know of the existence of the audit files then they may be knowledgeable enough to figure a workaround and access the files anyway. For this reason, in an environment where the integrity of these security files is important we recommend that you or your system administrator move the files to a remote server that is inaccessible to most general users. (This is one advantage to using a log aggregator.)

The praudit command has only a few modifiers. You can change the style in which the audit trail records are displayed so that all records are on a single line, or that the components of each new record (called tokens) are themselves each printed to a new line. The latter setting is the default and this is probably the configuration you will most commonly choose to print to.

You can also choose to print a short, long, or raw version of the audit trail.

One of the more useful options in the *praudit* command allows you to choose whether to view the user ID (UID) as a number or as a user name.

Finally, another useful option in praudit is to print the decoded audit trail files into XML format. This can be useful if you need to view the audits in a browser or if you are converting them to a format that is ultimately going into a log aggregator such as Splunk or Graylog.

Configuring the Audit System

The audit system is installed in a default configuration that is probably sufficient for home use, but in an enterprise environment you probably want to collect more information about the dynamic security of the host machines. These primary configuration settings are in the audit configuration file, named audit_config, which is located at /etc/security/audit_config.

There are five configuration files located in /etc/security and as root you can modify all of them, but in practice you will probably only change audit_control. These five config files are: *audit_class*, *audit_control*, *audit_event*, *audit_user*, and *audit_warn*.

The illustrations below show three different configurations of the audit_control file. The first configuration is the default configuration for all versions of OS X since (about) 10.6.

Default Audit Settings

```
                        audit_control

  T,   □   File Path ▼ : /private/etc/security/audit_control

           ◄  ►  □ audit_control  ↕

    1     #
    2     # $P4: //depot/projects/trustedbsd/openbsm/etc/audit_control#8 $
    3     #
    4     dir:/var/audit
    5     flags:lo,aa
    6     minfree:5
    7     naflags:lo,aa
    8     policy:cnt,argv
    9     filesz:2M
   10     expire-after:10M
   11     superuser-set-sflags-mask:has_authenticated,has_console_access
   12     superuser-clear-sflags-mask:has_authenticated,has_console_access
   13     member-set-sflags-mask:
   14     member-clear-sflags-mask:has_authenticated
   15
```

[illustration of audit_control.orig]

The default settings and flags in /etc/audit_control

Let's look at some of the settings in this configuration. The first line is preceded by the # symbol, so it is commented out of the actual configuration. However, it is a good reference to the OpenBSM project.[8] The most relevant settings are lines 4-10.

---

[8]Security Event Auditing in the FreeBSD manual, http://www.freebsd.org/doc/en_US.ISO8859-1/books/handbook/audit.html

Line 4: The default configuration of "dir:" directs the system to store the audit trail files in /var/audit. It's best to leave this configuration in place unless you really need to place the files somewhere else. And if you do need to change the default audit trail store location remember that this directory has special access controls that you may need to apply to the new location.

Line 5: The audit "flags" tell the kernel which actions it should monitor. In the default configuration it tracks only logins and logouts with the "lo" flag, and the "aa" flag, which records authentication and authorization events. These two flags are basic requirements for any enterprise, but there are other flags that add more richness to a host security profile.

Line 6: The "minfree" setting determines the minimum free space on the storage volume that is required before the audit daemon will stop the entire system from operating. In this case if the boot drive gets down to 5% of its total storage volume then the audit system will cause the OS to stop functioning. This can be a dramatic event for the user, but it is not drastic for the administrator. If the drive fills up to this point then somebody – probably the administrator – needs to clear some of the files. But you might ask how does that happen if the OS is no longer functioning? Actually, the OS will continue to function, it just will not get to a login screen. The seasoned administrator will have to log into the system in single-user mode and then clear files to create adequate storage availability so the OS can return to normal function on reboot.

In these days of very large hard drives this may seem like a trivial consideration. But in fact the audit daemon itself can generate extremely large volumes of audit trail files if it is configured to capture too much information. Consider this a cautionary note as you modify the "flags" and "naflags" in the audit_control file. It is possible to generate gigabytes of audit data in minutes or even seconds. At this rate it is possible to fill up multiple terabytes of data within hours.

Line 7: Certain actions can be considered as non-attributable to a specific user or process, and these actions are captured by "naflags". Consider a scenario where an intruder attempts to log into a Mac. Before completing an authenticated login the intruder's actions are not attributable to any user or process on the machine, and his (or her) attempts will be captured by these flags. And just as in the settings for "flags", lo and aa stand for login/logout and authentication and authorization. Less data will be captured, but there are processes that can run without attribution and these will be monitored by this na-flag setting.

Line 8: You can set certain policies for the audit daemon. The default case of "policy:cnt,argv" tells the system to, with 'cnt', continue auditing even if there is a failure in the audit subsystem, and with 'argv' to audit commands issued in the Terminal. If 'argv' is not entered as a policy, then a user could bypass the audit subsystem by working from the command line.

Line 9: The setting "filesz" tells the audit daemon how big a file should be allowed to become before it is closed and a new audit file is started. This is equivalent to how the Apple System Logs are rolled over when they reach a certain size.

Line 10: The audit trails will continue to collect indefinitely in /var/audit without a configuration setting telling the system when to discard files. Setting "expire-after:10M" tells the system that the audit directory should be maintained at no more than 10 megabytes, with a policy of first-in-first-out. This should be sufficient for you to capture the audit trails in a log aggregator or an audit log server before they are automatically deleted by the system. However, in these days of very large boot drives you are probably safe in changing this setting to something somewhat larger. I often set this to 100M if I have to manage the audit trails manually, as this gives me some extra time to get to the files.

Now that we have examined the default settings, let's look at some examples of settings that provide more functionality.

Naming of the Audit Trail Files

Like all the other log files the audit trail files are named automatically. In a localized environment such as a home user or even a small office it may not be important to distinguish the audit trail files, but in an enterprise environment where the audit trails are being collected and indexed for later analysis.

The audit trail files have a naming convention that is very different from any of the conventional log files. By default the audit files are named with the date and time that the file was created, then a dot for separation, followed by the date and time that the file was closed. A shorthand notation for this format would look like: yyyymmddhhmmss. yyyymmddhhmmss. For example, an audit trail file that was created on September 30, 2015 at 8 AM (Pacific Daylight Time) and then closed exactly 24 hours and 1 minute later would be named: 2015093015000.2015100115001. Note that there is no indication of the hostname of the machine that produced this file, and unlike the conventional log files there is not always a solid indication of the host source inside the audit trail files. To rectify this problem the programmers have built in a setting that allows the system administrator to tell the kernel how to name the files.

Setting the Hostname in Audit Trails

```
                            audit_control

T.  []   File Path ▾ : /private/etc/security/audit_control

         ◀  ▶  []  audit_control  ↕

  1    #
  2    # $P4: //depot/projects/trustedbsd/openbsm/etc/audit_control#8 $
  3    #
  4    dir:/var/audit
  5    host:rincon
  6    flags:lo,aa
  7    minfree:5
  8    naflags:lo,aa
  9    policy:cnt,argv
 10    filesz:2M
 11    expire-after:10M
 12    superuser-set-sflags-mask:has_authenticated,has_console_access
 13    superuser-clear-sflags-mask:has_authenticated,has_console_access
 14    member-set-sflags-mask:
 15    member-clear-sflags-mask:has_authenticated
 16
```

[illustration of audit_control mod 1, hostname added]

In the illustration above I inserted a new Line 5, with the entry "hostname:rincon". This tells the kernel to append a dot followed by the name to the end of each new audit trail file. This is particularly helpful when using a log aggregator where all the audit trail files can appear to be identical. Also note that this feature is not identified in the man pages (yet), so you will need to remember it when doing your configurations or when making and following up on images for distribution.

Audit Trail Configurations for High Security Environments

```
                              audit_control

T.        File Path▼ : /private/etc/security/audit_control

              ◄  ►      audit_control   ▲▼

    1    #
    2    # $P4: //depot/projects/trustedbsd/openbsm/etc/audit_control#8 $
    3    # Modified with hostname addition and NISPOM Ch.8 flag configs
    4    dir:/var/audit
    5    host:rincon
    6    flags:lo,aa,ad,-fr,-fw,-fc,-fd,-fm,-cl
    7    minfree:5
    8    naflags:lo,aa
    9    policy:cnt,argv
   10    filesz:2M
   11    expire-after:10M
   12    superuser-set-sflags-mask:has_authenticated,has_console_access
   13    superuser-clear-sflags-mask:has_authenticated,has_console_access
   14    member-set-sflags-mask:
   15    member-clear-sflags-mask:has_authenticated
   16
```

[illustration of audit_control mod 2, Ch.8 config added]

In some cases you may need a more complex audit_control configuration to provide more detailed auditing. The reason for this might be because the systems operate under stringent regulations or because you need to have better insight into what a particular user or process is doing. (An excellent example of using audit trails to follow the behavior of processes can be found in a 2012 research paper by Todd Heberlein, MSCS.[9] In this study he tracks how Google's Software Update mechanism works in a Mac.)

In this revised audit_control configuration file I have further modified the flags so that the audit daemon also watches for the following:

> *ad* – administrative events, either succeeded or failed,

> -fr – failed attempts to read a file

> -fw – failed attempts to write to a file

> -fc - failed attempts to create a file

> -fd - failed attempts to delete a file

> -fm - failed attempts to modify the metadata of a file such as a creation date

> -cl - failed attempts to close a file

---

[9]"The APT You Have: Google Chrome", Todd Heberlein, 2012, http://www.netsq.com/Documents_html/GoogleAPT/

In line 3 you'll see that I have also added a comment about the addition of the hostname and these new audit flags. These audit flags are the minimum requirement for a US government security regulation found in the National Industrial Security Program Operations Manual for Protection Level 1 (PL1).

If the config file for this computer was required to meet PL2, then I would remove all the dashes in front of the flags so that the audit subsystem would collect both failed and successful instances for each of the operations.

More On Audit Trails

These nine audit config flags above are actually settings for classes of events rather than for individual events. These nine are just about half of all the available classes, and each one of the nine contains numerous individual event types. For example the ad or administrative event class alone watches for and will record the details of more than 80 individual event types. And though ad is one of the larger event classes it is not unusual to have this many events in a classes.

The other classes that are available are as follows (from the FreeBSD manual[10]):

Class Name	Description	Action
all	all	Match all event classes.
aa	authentication and authorization	
ad	administrative	Administrative actions performed on the system
ap	Application	Application defined actions.
cl	File close	"close" system events
ex	exec	Audit program execution
fa	file attribute access	Audit access to file attributes.
fc	file create	Audit when a file is created.
fd	file delete	Audit when a file is deleted.
fm	file attribute modify	Audit when metadata about a file is modified.
fr	file read	Audit when data is read or a file is opened for reading.
fw	file write	Audit events when data is written or files are written or modified.
io	ioctl	Audit when use of the ioctl call is used.
lp	ipc	Audit when inter-process communication occurs.
lo	login_logout	Audit when login or logout events occur.

(continued)

---

[10]FreeBSD Manual, 16.3.1, Event Selection Expressions, http://www.freebsd.org/doc/en_US.ISO8859-1/books/handbook/audit-config.html

Class Name	Description	Action
na	non attributable	Audit when non-attributable events occur.
no	invalid class	Match no audit events.
nt	network	Audit when events related to network actions occur.
ot	other	Audit for miscellaneous events.
pc	pc	Audit process operations.

With these 20 classes there are over 160 actual events.

Viewing Audit Trails

The audit trails are stored by the kernel in /var/audit and they are owned by the kernel. Because these files are owned by the kernel, in order to access them in any way you will have to elevate to root. I commonly use the sudo su command to temporarily operate as the super user.

After elevating to the super user you can cd into /var/audit and ls to view all the files. Use ls –al to view the metadata of the files.

Since our configuration file says these files should rotate every 2MB we should see no files bigger than that. Also, the config file is set to expire old files to keep the aggregate file volume no larger than 10MB. These are the default configurations and you may find that you prefer to keep an expiration size somewhat large. This is especially useful if you set the flags and non-attributable flags to be more than the default. I commonly use the PL1 configuration so I set my expire setting to be 100MB. (And in these days of terabyte hard drives you can probably afford to keep your audit files stored locally for a longer time period.)

Since these files are stored in binary code they will not be viewable in their native form in any text viewer. This is different from most other files that have been discussed earlier in this chapter. To view these files you will have to work within the audit system and use the commands auditreduce and praudit. The use of these commands is addressed above in the section The Audit Daemon and Audit Commands.

Output and Interpretation of Audit Trails

For an example of how to deconstruct and interpret an audit trail file I scrubbed through a few files using auditreduce to look for an example of a login or logout. To do this I used the following command to 1) search for and extract an lo record, then piped that record to praudit, then told praudit to print that result to a text file.

```
auditreduce -c lo 20151022043941.20151022044928.dimac | praudit >
20151022043941.20151022044928.dimac.txt
```

This resulted in the following record. Note that the record consists of four lines. Each of these lines is referred to as a token, and each token has comma-separated values which are known as fields. In this example of a login, there are four tokens – header, subject, return, trailer.

```
header,72,11,loginwindow login,0,Wed Oct 21 21:46:27 2015, + 366 msec
subject_ex,dano,root,wheel,dano,staff,276,100007,50331650,0.0.0.0
return,success,0
trailer,72
```

Header Token Fields	Subject Token Fields	Return Token Fields	Trailer Token Fields
Token ID (type of token)	Token ID	Token ID	Token ID
Record length in bytes, including both header and trailer token	User audit ID	System call error status	Number marking end of record (invisible)
Audit record structure version	Effective user ID	System call return value	Number of audit record characters including both header and trailer
Event ID for type of audit event	Effective group ID		
Event ID modifier with description	Real user ID		
Date and time stamp	Real group ID		
	Process ID		
	Session ID		
	Terminal ID		

Every record will have a header and a trailer, so you can expect to see those formatted in the structure above. All other records will have different tokens for different events, and those tokens can and do have different structures depending on the kind of audit event information they contain.

For more information about the various events and their respective token structures see the Apple Common Criteria Configuration Guide, Security Event Auditing in the FreeBSD Manual, and the Sun Basic Security Module Guide.

Summary

In this chapter we looked at the various logs and logging facilities built into Mac OS X. These logs provide insight into what is happening on the inside of your computer. They can be used to guide you in troubleshooting efforts and to act as an early warning sign, even when you don't have a symptom you are looking to troubleshoot.

The logs in Mac OS X can also be used to obtain critical security information. Using the steps we laid out, you can centralize logs, or run scripts to aggregate information routinely. Those aggregated logs can enable you to see what is going on throughout an enterprise with very little work from savvy systems administrators.

Now that we have looked at logs, we'll move on to one of the aspects of Mac OS X that can place information in those logs, applications. In Chapter 6 we will jump into securing applications, with a focus on leveraging Apple's sandbox facility and rich application signing framework.

## Part II

Securing the Ecosystem

## Chapter 6

Application Signing and Sandbox

This chapter discusses two critical security features in OS X: application signing and the App Sandbox. These technologies were both introduced with Mac OS 10.5 and provide facilities that improve the overall security of the platform. Incidentally, both technologies are also heavily leveraged by iOS, the underlying operating system on the iPhone, iPad, iPod Touch, and AppleTV.

Application Signing

Application signing is technology included in OS X that addresses the issue of application identity and integrity. Application signing provides protection to the operating system so that it can both uniquely identify an application and also determine whether the contents of the application have been modified. This includes integrity checks to both the application payload (the main function of the application) and the metadata about the application: its bundle identifier, version information, and the like. Once an application is signed, if any of this information changes for it, OS X can detect that such a change has been made and keep the application from opening.

Signing an application addresses two areas of security: authentication and integrity. By implementing these protections, Apple has created a very good system to allow developers to provide a means for end users to verify the integrity of their applications, and thereby provide a method for nonrepudiation. That is, when a vendor signs an application, an end user can confidently operate with knowledge that the code has not been otherwise altered by a party other than the original vendor. The concept of nonrepudiation predates that of any computer system by a long shot, and seeks to provide a means for one entity to uniquely validate a piece of information.

In fact, nonrepudiation has been around for centuries in one form or another. Perhaps the earliest form was the use of scarab seals, which date back as far as the Egyptian Middle Kingdom (around 2080–1640 BCE). These seals were small ornaments made of stone or clay and shaped in the form of a scarab (dung beetle). Each seal was engraved with a unique design and thus could be used to authenticate documents. Another early form can be found in the Imperial Seal of China, a jade seal first used by the first Emperor of China around 221 BCE. In a traditional noncomputer context, consider signing a legal contract. By providing your signature to a contract, you are providing a means for the parties involved in that contract to certify that you are a participant. Once you've signed a (printed) contract, the other party can't change the wording without printing out another version, which doesn't contain your signature. However, if you only sign the last page, the other party is free to change the content of any other page, and insert or delete pages: you can repudiate the agreement to the original terms. Thus, to legally enforce nonrepudiation of a contact, every page must be signed. Certainly as the world progresses, the efficacy of various nonrepudiation methods has proven to be flawed. In some cases this has been due simply to the need for better standards, and in others it is due to the advancements and proliferation of technology. But with that progression come new methods for nonrepudiation, with each successor becoming more and more secure.

With today's digital world, we have achieved a new level of nonrepudiation, with systems that are orders of magnitude more capable than anything achievable previously. In the old days, seals and stamps could be forged, signatures could be lifted, and all of them provided rudimentary protection over the associated data as well; none of these methods provided concrete assurance that the contents or associated data had not been tampered with or manipulated.

By utilizing modern cryptography, it is possible to both identify an object uniquely and verify its contents, even when compared against millions or even billions of other entities. Such technology has seen widespread adoption in our digital age: S/MIME and PGP signatures allow a user to uniquely sign an e-mail, and they allow the recipient to accept confidently that the e-mail is a valid communication and that its contents are presented exactly as they were at the date of signing (the time the e-mail was sent). If at any time the e-mail's contents are manipulated by a third party, the e-mail's signature won't reflect the change, and the recipient will be able to see that the content is malformed. Conversely, the third party is also unable to generate a signature that is valid for the original sender's identity. This precludes an attacker from either modifying existing content or generating new content. As we will discuss in detail throughout this section, Apple's digital signing functionality utilizes this very system. Not only does it provide a very strong method for authentication, which allows developers to put what is in effect their own personal signature on their wares, it also provides a secure way to certify the content of the application.

You may be asking why this is important for an application. First and foremost, as a computer professional, you may have come to the realization that the biggest security vulnerability on many systems is that of the PEBKAC variety. That is, the Problem Exists Between the Keyboard And Chair. In the history of OS X, the majority of publicized exploits for the platform involved the use of a Trojan horse. Akin to the historic tale of *The Aeniad*, in computer terminology a Trojan horse is a piece of malicious software disguised as something innocuous that, when run, takes over your computer (malware is discussed in depth in Chapter 8). As a seasoned veteran, you know that an e-mail offering you an MS

Word update available on the site `www.pwningucinz2002.ru` probably isn't a good thing to download and run, but your end user might not. Even after that, being the good Samaritan that your end user is, she might even offer it up to her coworkers. After all, it's a good idea to apply updates, right? Well, the concept of application authentication can be used to mitigate the damage this threat poses. Without a proper digital signature, malware can never truly masquerade as another company's product.

In this chapter we will discuss Apple's digital signing implementation. We'll delve into the nuts and bolts of the technology utilized by the system, explore its potential, and have an overview of system facilities currently utilized in OS X 10.11, El Capitan.

Application Authentication

Historically, the Mac OS has had only rudimentary facilities for application identification, and really no methods for application authentication. That is, an application could identify itself, but there was no way for it to *prove* its identity absolutely. With the original Mac OS, application identification was stored primarily in an application's resource fork in the form of a four-byte string called the *creator code*. This creator code was then used by the operating system to associate data files with their respective applications, and thus there was no need for the standard three-letter extension used by other operating systems (.exe, .doc, .txt). At first, this actually worked out very well, and it is one of the reasons that in the early days the Mac had been considered a more user-friendly platform.

Unfortunately, the system just didn't hold up, for a number of reasons. Four bytes of data equate to four characters, and certainly the possibility for collisions (two applications with the same creator code) is fairly high. To address this issue, in OS X, Apple provided a registration system and database that ensured that all Mac OS developers' applications had unique identifiers. It was cumbersome, but it worked, and developers could reasonably assume that their application's identifier was unique.

The other problem with creator codes as a means of application identification is that there is absolutely no way to prevent your creator code from being hijacked: if an unscrupulous party wants to create an application using your creator code, there is nothing to stop them from doing so. Once that application hits the system, there is a chance that when a user double-clicks on a file meant for your application, it will, instead, open in the malicious application. There was never a great way for guaranteeing the association of data with a specific application in such an event; the Mac OS contained a database, called the Desktop Database, that maintained a list of all files, applications, and creator code associations. When an application saved a file, that file would be associated with your application, and the association would be saved in the Desktop Database. Such files would continue to open in your application.

The problem here is that when any files were introduced to your system from a third party (file server, e-mail, and so on), that association would not already exist, and the system would automatically try to associate the file with the appropriate application. In the event that there are two applications with this creator code (yours and the bad guy's, let's say), Apple had a custom algorithm that considered a number of factors for determining which application to associate with. First it would consult all running applications. Next it would look for a qualifying application on the system volume, followed by a search of other local volumes. Finally it would check against remote volumes. The first qualifying application found for that file would then be launched and utilized, and it might very well not be yours.

With the introduction of OS X, Apple introduced a new way for an application to identify itself: the bundle identifier. A bundle identifier is a carryover from the NeXT system, upon which OS X was built, and is an application- and organization-unique string that allows for very specific application identification. Referred to as *reverse-domain notation*, the format of this string is essentially identical to that used by the Internet's Domain Name System, but reversed (as you may have assumed). For instance, the bundle identifier used by Apple's Text Edit application is `com.apple.textedit`, but for Microsoft Word it's `com.microsoft.Word`. Like DNS, the system is very scalable and allows an application developer to identify their wares uniquely, and this alone proves advantageous over creator codes. It did not replace creator codes altogether, however, as creator codes were utilized in OS X for backward compatibility until version 10.6, which controversially killed support. If bundle identifiers are better than creator codes, then why the controversy? The controversy primarily surrounded the ability that creator codes allowed applications to associate files with themselves. That conversation is for another time, though; the reality is that for application identification in OS X, the creator code as an identifying mechanism has been replaced by the bundle identifier, and the data file/application association provided by the creator code has now been usurped by the UTI mechanism, which is a new system that uses bundle identifiers and inheritance to define association (and the primary focal point of all the creator code removal controversy). The Desktop Database as it applied to data file/application storage has been long replaced by OS X's LaunchServices database.

An inherent problem with the bundle identifier, as with creator codes, was that there were no provisions to actually protect it. It was no longer a four-byte string (which is a good thing), but it could still be manipulated or spoofed, and malicious parties could still create their own application with your organization's bundle identifier. As such, the concept of application authentication was still pretty weak in OS X: we had identification, but authentication was still a complete no-show. Unauthenticated identification is akin to an airport TSA screener asking you for your name and country of origin and simply taking your word from it, rather than checking your documentation. Because of this, any application restrictions that were deployed on a system were suspect: even Apple's Parental Control system, or its bigger brother, MCX (Managed Client for OS X) weren't safe. Each of these systems could be trivially bypassed through the manipulation of process file names and bundle identifiers; there was no great way as a system administrator to truly restrict application usage on OS X. A disallowed application could simply mimic the identifier of an allowed application, and any access restrictions are thereby avoided.

The situation changed with the introduction of application signing in OS X 10.5, which allowed a developer or administrator to place their own stamp on an application, certifying that it was their own creation (provided they use an identity signed by a trusted authority). For applications that aren't signed directly by the first-party company (Firefox for example), an administrator can sign it themselves using their own signing identity (for more information about signing applications, see the later section "Signing and Verifying Applications"). When an administrator signs such an application, he is placing his own digital signature on the application. It's a different signature than that which would have been provided by the developer, so there is no way to certify it against the exact code that the developer shipped, but it still provides a secure way for an admin to identify *and authenticate* an application. When a signed application is provisioned to a user via parental controls or MCX, that access control is effectively incapable of manipulation: it contains a cryptographic signature of the application's bundle identifier, along with the contents of the application's executable, and it can be used to protect application resources. It provides full detection capabilities for any applications posing under the same bundle identifier and application name. If any such coercion exists, the MCX system will prevent the application from running.

In the end, Apple's implementation provides a very good way for a developer to implement concrete authentication for any of their applications. Likewise, it provides a way for the operating system to legitimize applications. In doing so, it opens the door for a number of powerful and very beneficial security protections that can be provided for users and administrators.

Application Integrity

Historically, the Mac OS had absolutely no ability to ensure application integrity. In the early days of personal computing, there wasn't much thought given to the possibility of malfeasance or sabotage; and as such, the concept of even needing to verify integrity wasn't a great concern in the mind of early OS designers. The fact that it could be done was known, but it wasn't thought of as a security issue (probably because no one was thinking much of information security issues at all back then). Well, things have changed in today's modern world, and the need to verify an application's integrity is now very apparent. As we've learned, the ability to identify an application is not always enough: identities can be stolen, mimicked, and spoofed. They are fallible. In order to truly establish nonrepudiation we need to be able to verify both the application's identity (authenticate) *and* verify the integrity of its data. If the identity is not directly associated with the data, then the system's nonrepudiation factor is pretty weak.

Consider a standard computer virus, spreading mercilessly across infected computers and networks. A very common technique that viruses use for replication is referred to as *binary data injection*; a malicious piece of software, generally referred to as a *loader* (such as a Trojan horse) modifies an existing application to inject malicious code. Once an infection occurs, whenever this familiar application is launched, the malicious code is executed. This code may contain further viral function, which means that the application may spread the infection to other existing applications on the system; or even worse, the malicious code may serve as a backdoor into your computer by listening over the network for inbound connections. Suddenly any application on your computer can serve as a vector for exploitation. What an attacker can do with this is limited solely by the privileges of the executing user. If this user is an admin user, then the potential for damage is pretty high; the system will be compromised. Sadly, code signing in OS X doesn't currently prevent such an attack. It detects the attack, which permits quick reaction on the part of whoever notices the detection. Detection and reaction are important—though often overlooked—factors of a good security posture. Novel attacks are always being found, or you may have just overlooked an important risk: the only way you'll find out is if you have some detection in place.

Application signing can potentially be used to defend against such occurrences with its ability to confidently validate integrity. When an application is signed, that signature uniquely identifies the executable code of the application, providing a unique fingerprint. If the application's code is altered, that fingerprint changes unequivocally, and the digital signature will have been broken.

Code signing provides an additional benefit for application integrity: when an application runs, its contents are copied to memory and then executed. In the traditional sense, code signing provides the ability for an operating system to detect on-disk modifications to an application. But in actuality, it goes even further than that. Apple's code signing system actually provides the functionality to verify dynamically the validity of code running in a given process. This facility helps to verify integrity of the application on the disk and while running. Even if an application loads new code such as a plug-in after it has started, code signing can detect that and update its view of the application's integrity.

Gatekeeper: Signature Enforcement in OS X

Although application signing is utilized exclusively in iOS, its implementation in Mac OS X is a little less prolific. Gatekeeper is a tool built into OS X that, by default, allows only applications signed by the Mac App Store to be opened. Gatekeeper can also be configured to allow only signed apps or apps that aren't signed at all. Obviously, the option to allow unsigned apps should only be used in the rarest of cases. However, it is not every environment that is able to leverage only apps available on the Mac App Store.

Digitally signing applications is an excellent foundation for enforcing extremely tight controls in the OS. When we view iOS, for instance, we find a system that is 100% reliant on application signing. In such a case, Apple serves as the root authority, and as such has complete control over all applications that are allowed to run on the platform. This has proven to be a very effective system, providing a near-ironclad guard against malware on the platform. Interestingly enough, the act of *jail-breaking* an iPhone involves circumventing and ultimately disabling the signing system. This is done not by attacking the signing system itself, but by penetrating the OS through some other means to disable the signing system altogether. Also interesting to note is that the early iOS malware—the iKee and Duh worms—targeted jail-broken devices.

Apple has slowly enforced more and more application signing requirements into the system over the six versions since it was introduced, starting with access to the OS X keychain, perhaps the juiciest (if not the best-protected) target on any user's system. Additional uses, as mentioned earlier, include the OS X application firewall, the parental control mechanisms, and the MCX system. In this section we will delve into each and discuss exactly how the system utilizes signing to protect end users.

Keychain Access

The *keychain* is a prevalent and critical component of OS X. It is also significantly misunderstood. Its function lies much in its name: it serves a digital keychain for all of your digital keys (including actual PKI keys, passwords, and now even secure notes). These keys can be a number of things, from the password of an e-mail account configured with Mail.app or Microsoft Outlook to saved credentials from your banking web page. By default, a user has only one keychain, the login keychain. This keychain has the same password as their OS X account. When a user logs into OS X, the default login keychain is unlocked, and trusted applications can access their respective entities without user interaction or notification. The key word here is *trusted* applications, and in OS X, all applications have an inherited distrust when first attempting to access the keychain. When an application first attempts to access a keychain item, the user will be prompted to trust the application. Figure 6-1 shows the contents of a keychain item.

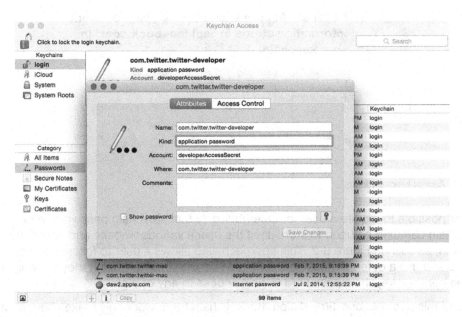

Figure 6-1. Providing keychain access to an application

Unsigned applications prompt users with text to warn that their authenticity could not be verified, while the signed application simply requests access. The difference between the notices is so subtle and minimized that it's doubtful that anyone but the most experienced users will ever notice it, which is unfortunate. On top of that, there is no indication as to *who* signed the application. If an application from a vendor isn't signed, some other party may very well have injected all kinds of badness before signing it. Certainly more attention could be paid to show that an application is trusted and signed by a trusted Root Authority.

As shown in Figure 6-2, users can select different options when allowing applications access to a keychain item. If a user selects to Allow, an application will be granted one-time access to the keychain item. If Always Allow is selected, the application will have the ability to access the unlocked keychain without ever prompting the user. If the keychain becomes locked, the user will be prompted to enter his or her keychain password when any application seeks to access it.

Figure 6-2. *Access keychain items*

Thus it is possible to require a user to remember only their keychain password, and the keychain can then be used to store all of the user's various website and application passwords, as seen in Figure 6-2. This approach also allows a user to follow good security practices and use a different password for every website they go to; yet they will only have to remember their keychain password to gain access to any of them.

Outside of this possible one-time dialog, the keychain framework only makes benefit of application signing for one user-visible feature. Without application signing, whenever an application is updated (for example, a new version is released and installed), a dialog is presented to the user. If the application is signed, a developer can release updates to the software, and as long as they are signed with the same identity, you will never be prompted again to allow access to the keychain.

The OS X Application Firewall

With OS X 10.5, Apple replaced the lower-level IPFW firewall used by previous versions of OS X with a new Application Layer Firewall (ALF). The IPFW firewall (which can still be used) operates at the network layer and allows users to provide access provisions to specific ports and IP addresses for access. All of these provisions were global across the system; that is, they were not associated with a particular application. The new application firewall, as its name implies, operates at a much higher level. The primary implication here is that instead of defining specific access to ports and IP addresses, restrictions are applied to specific applications. Once an application has been trusted, it is provisioned full access to any port that the application might seek to open, as long as the application is allowed to access that network resource via the sandbox profile associated with the application. Application firewalling is a much more user-friendly implementation, and considering the skill level of the vast majority of the Mac computer-using public, it is effectually more secure. On top of this, traditional firewalls can't react to Trojan horse attacks, because they allow any application access to the permitted ports.

There's much to be said for the conception that as the complexity of a software implementation increases, so also do the odds of the software being misconfigured or misused by the user. So instead of requiring a user to open up ports 24000–36000TCP and 1408TCP/UDP to host their favorite game online, with ALP the user only has to provide access to the application itself. What the user doesn't see is that when they allow network access to their game, if that game is not already signed, it will be signed by the system using an ad-hoc authority and will be provided access to the network. That application's digital signature then serves effectively as the key to the firewall; as long as the signature for that application is verifiable by the system, it will be granted access to the firewall. If the application is in violation of the policy, the firewall will no longer provide access to the application without user approval.

The firewall is simple to manage, as can be seen in Figures 6-3 and 6-4. Found hiding under the Security & Privacy preference pane, the primary interface provided for the application firewall consists simply of buttons to turn it on or off, as shown in Figure 6-3.

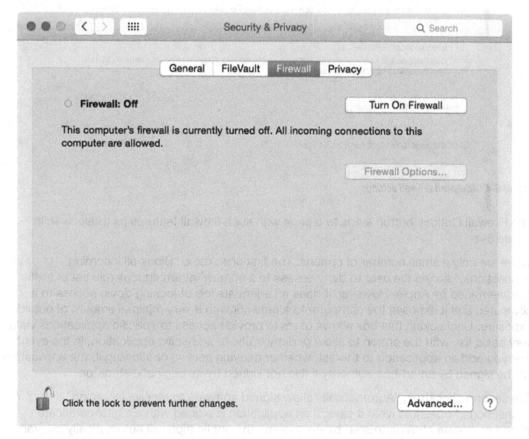

Figure 6-3. Turning on the application firewall

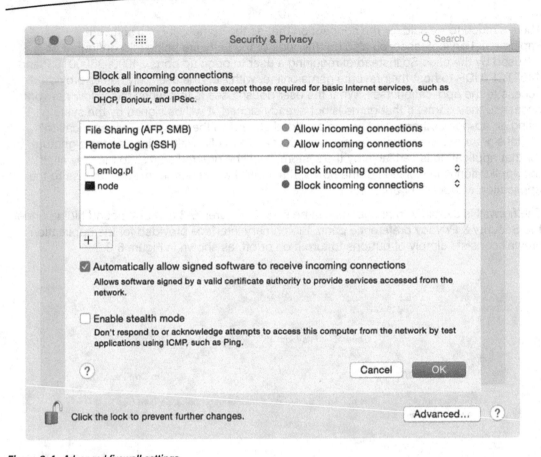

Figure 6-4. Advanced firewall settings

The Firewall Options button leads to a page with such firewall features as those seen in Figure 6-4.

There are only a small number of options. The first checkbox, "Block all incoming connections," allows the user to deny access to a somewhat ambiguous rule set of traffic, predetermined by Apple. However, it does an adequate job of locking down access to a computer, and it exposes the computer to a network with a very minimal amount of outside exposure. Unchecking this box allows users to provide access to specific applications via a very basic list, with the option to allow or deny traffic to a specific application. In the event that you add an application to this list, whether denying access or allowing it, the application will be signed by an ad-hoc authority if it is not signed by its original distributor.

The second checkbox, "Automatically allow signed software to receive incoming connections," does just what it says: if an application is signed with a digital certificate whose certificate chain is trusted by the system, the application will automatically be granted access to the network. Checking this box is equivalent to inherently trusting any application signed by a legitimate certificate authority (CA).

> **Note**   The fact that an application has been signed by a certificate whose chain leads to a CA does not mean that the application is legitimate or trustworthy. Obtaining a certificate from a major CA does involve a considerable amount of paperwork and vetting, but it does not absolutely guarantee the legitimacy of a company or its wares. Alternatively, the application could be perfectly legitimate but do something you don't want, like a commercial key scanner. The general point is that while a signed application carries proof of its integrity, it carries no proof of its purpose (or its fitness for that purpose). You can sign buggy applications.

The last option, "Enable stealth mode," doesn't deal with application signing but is worth a brief mention; enabling it configures the client to not respond to pings, and it prevents Bonjour messages from being sent out. It's a pretty good way to make your computer silent on a network. For more extensive discussion of setting up the Mac OS X Firewall, including accessing the command-line options to facilitate mass deployment, see Chapter 11.

Client Management: Profiles, MCX, and Parental Controls

Managed preferences in Mac OS X provide administrators (and parents!) with a valuable tool set for managing many aspects of the Mac OS X computing environment. Referred to as MCX, or Managed Client in OS X, the tool set has fairly expansive capabilities, providing many functions such as managing individual user and application settings, applying user restrictions to inserted/removable media, managing message capabilities, and most relevant to the topic at hand, controlling application access.

OS X has two primary facilities for working with MCX. The first that we'll talk about is more relevant perhaps to the enterprise Mac administrator. Directory services can be used to deploy managed preferences. However, in 10.10 and later, Apple has been moving administrators from deploying MCX using a directory service to deploying it using custom profiles or a mobile device management solution, a similar method with the added benefit of enabling admins to change settings and policies on clients dynamically using a centralized server or service.

Applications are restricted with MCX on an *explicit allow* basis. That is, once you choose to restrict applications for a user, an implicit deny will be applied to all applications that are not in the allowed applications list. Because of this, it is important to have a good understanding of the applications that will be used in the managed environment prior to embarking on this endeavor. If restrictions are not properly planned, you will be flooded with support requests from users, saying that they can't access their applications. However, when implemented using application signing, the system proves to be extremely resilient to various hacks that might be used to subvert it.

To restrict applications using profiles, begin by opening Profile Manager and selecting a device, user, group or group of devices. From here, click the Edit button for the object you will restrict apps on and then locate Restrictions in the list of settings that can be managed in the sidebar. Then click the Apps tab and use the "Restrict which apps are allowed to launch" check box to enable application restrictions. There are three sections, shown in Figure 6-5:

- Allow Apps: Select which apps are allowed to be opened. This produces a list of apps installed on the Profile Manager server (rather than a client computer accessing the server.

- Allow Folders: Select folders that contain apps that can be opened. The most common folder is going to be the `Applications` folder.

- Disallow Folders: Select specific folders that contain apps that are not allowed to be opened; for example, the Utilities folder.

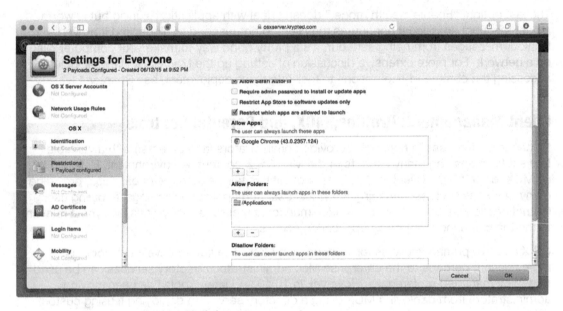

Figure 6-5. Configuring application whitelisting

Click the plus sign (+) to bring up a dialog box to select an app, as shown in Figure 6-6. Apps will contain versions. New versions of apps specifically defined will need to be added as well, as each has a different signature.

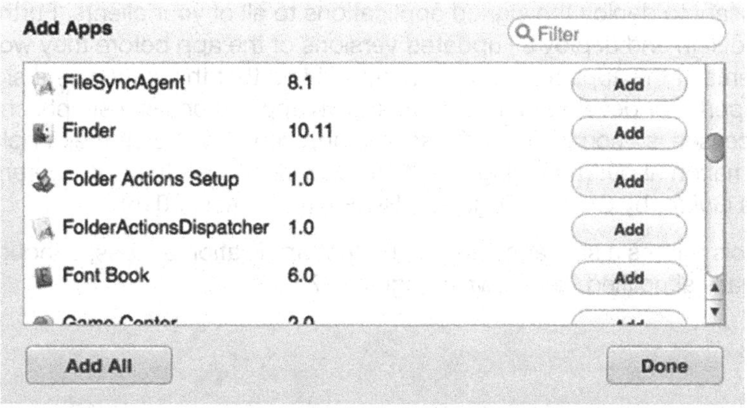

Figure 6-6. Adding an application

Using this interface, you can allow a specific application, or you can specify a *whitelisted* folder, wherein any application that resides within it is always trusted. Specifying broad access based on folder paths is not inherently secure, and it doesn't utilize digital signing protections. To utilize application restrictions to their fullest, you will want to allow specific applications in-use by your organization. This allows for fine-grained targeting of applications without the need to worry about whether file system restrictions have been bypassed or not. Using application signing provides the system with a very secure way to ensure that only intended applications can be launched. If a provisioned application is modified, it will no longer match our signature and will therefore be treated as a foreign entity.

> **Note**   When adding an application to an allowed applications list, you must first specify the application from the client machine running Profile Manager. If the application that you wish to allow is not resident on this computer, you will not be able to select it from the list, and thus will not be able to provision access to the app.

Likewise, when you add an unsigned application to the allowed applications list, you will be greeted with an option to either sign the application or add it to the list without signing it. If you choose the latter, the application will be allowed to launch, but it will be possible to utilize this inclusion for exploitative purposes. Because the application is not signed, it is possible to alter any arbitrary application to impersonate the application, and thereby bypass any restrictions that would otherwise be applied. As such, if any allowed application is unsigned, it represents the ability for the user to launch any application, provided they have the skills to do so.

You can also sign applications using the codesign tool. There are some ramifications for signing an application when adding via Profile Manager as well. Most notably, when you sign the application with codesign, you are only signing the local copy of that application. As such, all those hundreds of copies of that application in the field remain unsigned, and therefore restricted from launching. So in order to fulfill a securely restricted environment, it will be necessary to deploy the signed applications to all of your clients. Furthermore, you will need to sign and deploy all updated versions of the app before they work on the client systems. If the apps auto-update, you will find that this becomes a significant burden on support. For developers to sign their own applications is a simple change to their build processes, so complain loudly at your app vendors to sign their applications. For more information about managing the MCX system, consult the book *Enterprise Mac Administrator's Guide*, by Charles Edge and Bill Smith (Apress, 2015).

Parental Controls utilizes a similar system to restrict application access, although its interface is greatly simplified, as shown in Figure 6-7.

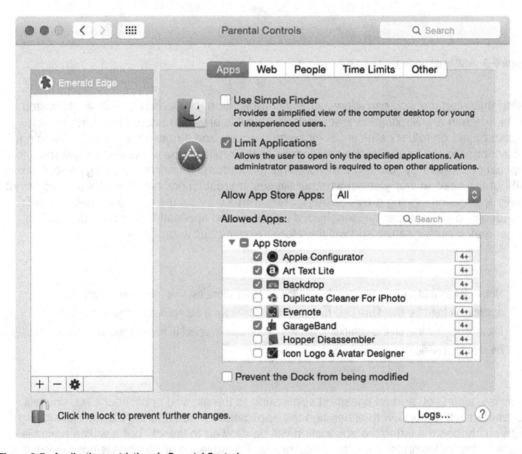

Figure 6-7. Application restrictions in Parental Controls

One very notable aspect of Parental Controls: while the system can utilize application signing, the GUI does not provide facilities to sign unsigned applications themselves. Therefore, any allowed application that is not signed represents a potential hole for a user to exploit in the system; it is possible for any program to then pose as that unsigned application, and then all kinds of unscrupulous shenanigans can occur. If you intend to use application restrictions through Parental Controls, consider signing any unsigned applications yourself. We'll discuss how to do so in the next section.

> **Note**   For more information about setting up Parental Controls, see Chapter 3.

Signing and Verifying Applications

We've already discussed all the benefits of signing, and how OS X actually enforces its provisions. So let's get our hands dirty dabbling with it. To understand how signing works, it's first important to understand a little bit about the system. If you've ever used SSL, you'll have some familiarity here. Apple's implementation, like other code signing implementations, uses Public Key Infrastructure (PKI) to get the job done. Signing an application is achieved through the use of a private key and its associated digital signing certificate. The private key, as its name implies, is to be forever protected by the organization that is performing the signing, whether it's Microsoft signing MS Word, or you, the admin, signing an application. If your private key is exposed, then the entire system is compromised. Fortunately, it is possible to revoke an identity and thereby invalidate it, but that is not a fun process and should be avoided.

The digital certificate contains less sensitive, but nonetheless important information. It includes organizational information, such as the company name and address. It also includes information vital to decoding the signature; this includes the signature algorithm (typically the SHA-1 hash in modern-day certificates), and it includes information about the public key, the key itself, and the algorithm that is used. This certificate may itself be signed by a greater entity. In many cases, this will be a legitimate CA, such as VeriSign or Thawte. These are private CA organizations that establish a root chain of trust for certificates. Apple itself is a public CA of sorts, though not in the traditional sense as they only provide signing services specifically for code-signing identities to be used for iPhone applications.

In order to get an application to run on the iPhone (which relies heavily on application signing), your application must be signed by a certificate that is part of Apple's certificate chain. It is this certificate chaining that ultimately provides the basis for nonrepudiation with digital certificates. That being said, it is not a requirement that your signing identity is signed by a chain leading to a trusted Root CA. Considering this, even a signed application could contain malware as there is no burden of evidence; the application is signed, but signed by an unknown (and potentially suspect) authority. This is not to say that an application signed by a trusted certificate cannot contain malware; it certainly can, provided either deliberately or accidentally (and either knowingly or unwittingly) by the distributor before signing. The certificate chain of an identity gives you *some* assurance about the identity of the signer, but none regarding the content of the product. On the iPhone, this is a show-stopper, thanks to Apple's aggressive enforcement of code signing on that platform. In OS X, the application is simply considered untrustworthy, and the user will be prompted if the application attempts to access any security features that utilize signing protections, such as access to a keychain entity or traversing the application firewall. Once the user trusts the application through this dialog, the digital signature is considered trusted from then on.

In the previous section, we discussed how to utilize GUI tools to sign applications indirectly: when an application is allowed or denied access to the application firewall, the utility will sign any unsigned application so that the OS can properly identify it. Likewise, if you add an application to the MCX system, any unsigned application will warrant a prompt asking if you would like to sign it. Each of these systems provides fairly easy methods to sign an application, and both use Apple-provided certificates to do the signing. If you want to sign applications with your own signing identity, you must use the command-line utility codesign. Preferably, such a signing certificate would come from a trusted CA; however, it is possible to create your own. To do so, you can utilize the Keychain Access application found at /Applications/Utilities. With this application open, under the Keychain Access menu, select Certificate Assistant, and then select Create a Certificate. As shown in Figure 6-8, you will be presented with the option to specify a certificate name. In this example, we use MyCo Signing Certificate, but naturally, the name of this certificate will depend on your own organization. In this first screen, you will also want to ensure that the option "Let me override defaults" is checked and that the certificate type is Code Signing. In this example, we are using a self-signed root identity type. You can also specify a leaf type, which you can sign by your own internal CA. In the upper-right corner, you will be prompted for organizational information. For all other screens during this process, the default settings will be adequate.

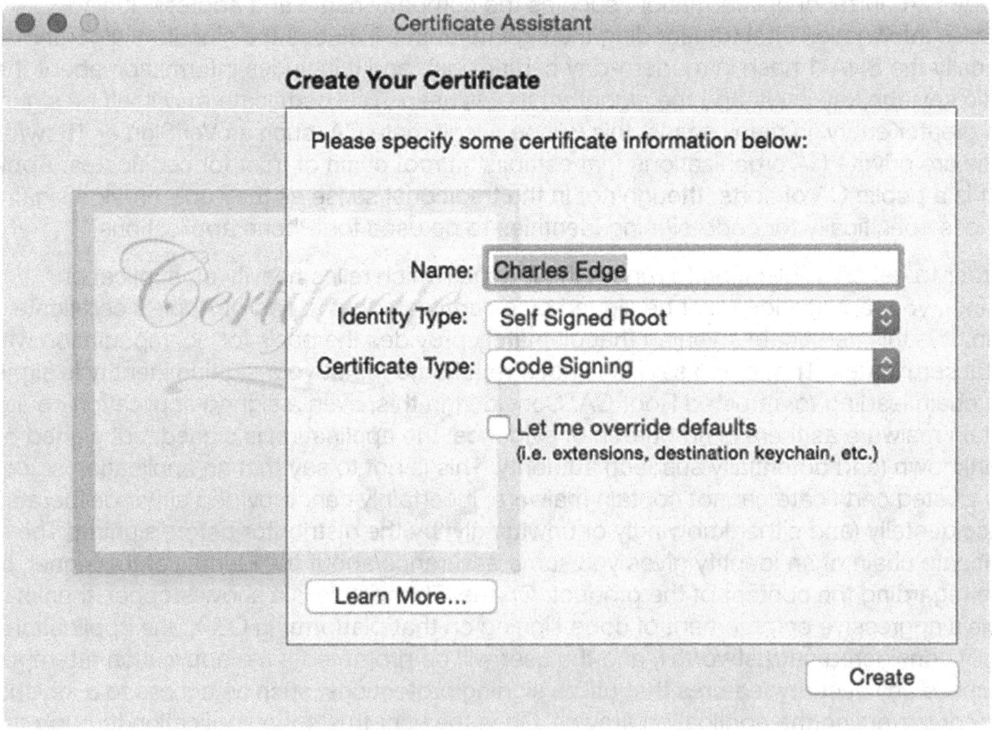

Figure 6-8. Creating a self-signed signing certificate

Once the signing identity has been created, it will be present in the Keychain Access utility. In this case, the certificate root has been imported into the system keychain and has also been trusted (by default it is not trusted). To trust the certificate by the system, double-click the certificate, and under the Trust pulldown ensure that Always Trust is selected for the option "When using this certificate." Once the certificate is in place, you can then sign the application from the command line using the aforementioned codesign application using the following syntax:

```
codesign -s 'MyCo Signing Certificate' /Applications/Firefox.app
```

Upon executing this command, you will be prompted to insert credentials to access the System keychain. Upon successful authentication, the stored private key and signature will be used to sign the application.

It is also possible to use the codesign tool to verify the state of the application. To do so, we can run it with the following syntax, against the same application that we just signed (Firefox), as in this example:

```
krypted:~ cedge$ codesign --verify -v /Applications/Firefox.app
/Applications/Firefox.app: valid on disk
/Applications/Firefox.app: satisfies its Designated Requirement
```

It is also possible to display more information that has been signed into the application, as shown here:

```
krypted:~ cedge$ codesign -dvvvv /Applications/Firefox.app
Executable=/Applications/Firefox.app/Contents/MacOS/firefox-bin
Identifier=org.mozilla.firefox
Format=bundle with Mach-O universal (i386 ppc)
CodeDirectory v=20100 size=228 flags=0x0(none) hashes=5+3 location=embedded
CDHash=3928da04d4ce2480a5a077e7fe37c41750d138f0
Signature size=1566
Authority=MyCo Signing Certificate
Signed Time=Mar 4, 2010 2:33:39 AM
Info.plist entries=15
Sealed Resources rules=4 files=4
Internal requirements count=1 size=152
```

As we can see, this copy of Firefox has now been signed by an organization and deployed throughout. The signature contains information pertaining to the application. In this case, we can verify the application identifier, org.mozilla.firefox, as well as the authority that signed it, MyCo Signing Certificate. From here on, if the application is altered in any way, its signature will fail and the user will be informed. If the application has no signature, the codesign operation will so state:

```
krypted:~ cedge$ codesign -dvvvv /Applications/Camino.app
/Applications/Camino.app: code object is not signed
```

Users are not warned if they launch an application whose contents have been modified! The honest truth is that users commonly identify applications based upon their filename, or even their icon. Anything that happens beyond the screen is simply magic: they click the blue W and expect to see a word processor. The issue here is that with the state of the system, OS X simply doesn't have the enforcement facilities to truly protect users like this.

OS X ships with all of the default applications signed by Apple. Third-party developers can do the same. Users can rest assured that if they have their application firewall employed, provisioned applications won't freely be granted network if they have been modified. Likewise, system administrators who deploy signed applications have a very good system for restricting application usage on their managed networks; MCX is no longer a system easily subverted. However, the lack of communication that OS X maintains with end users minimizes the impact that all of these features have on the security situation for everyday OS X users.

Apple is no doubt treading lightly here; iOS has complete enforcement of application signing. In fact, it's not even possible to run an unsigned application on an iPhone unless you jail-break it (which completely disables application signing enforcement). Apple was able to introduce this extreme right off the bat with OS X and does by default. Things aren't so cut and dry with a desktop-class OS like OS X, where dependencies on third-party vendors are more of an issue. Apple certainly wants to avoid a Windows-like experience where security alerts are so common that users dismiss them altogether as an annoyance. As such, it's difficult to foresee a future where OS X warns users of unsigned applications. However, there's no reason why a user shouldn't be warned if a signed application is altered. Hopefully with OS X we'll see more user exposure and utilization of this powerful security feature.

Sandboxing

In OS X, access control restrictions support a limited security model referred to as *Discretionary Access Controls (DAC)*. The most visible form of DAC in OS X is in its implementation of the POSIX file-system security model, which Chapter 4 discussed in detail . The POSIX model establishes identity-based restrictions on an object in the form of a subject's user or group membership. Additionally, Access Control Lists are a form of discretionary control, though as we learned they are far more extensible and discrete than the POSIX model. In such models, newly created objects or processes inherit their access rights based upon those of the creating subject, so that any spawned objects are not granted access rights beyond those of their parent. The key idea behind the DAC model is that the security of an object is left to the discretion of the object's owner, who has the ability to assign varying levels of access control to that object within the confines of the DAC implementation.

For decades, the DAC model has been a staple in the management of both object/process creation and access across all mainstream computer systems thanks to its user-centric nature. However, there is a persistent caveat in these implementations; in all mainstream implementations of such models, there exists a superuser which has the capabilities to completely bypass access restrictions placed on objects. In POSIX-based operating systems such as Unix, Linux, or OS X, this superuser exists in the form of the root user. The existence of such a loophole presents a bit of a paradox. On one hand, it introduces several obvious security ramifications by providing capabilities to bypass the DAC model altogether.

Any processes that are invoked by the superuser inherit the "god mode" access controls; they have free rein over the entire system. At the same time, the existence of the superuser account becomes a vital tool for the practical administration of data objects and system resources. In a perfect world, this wouldn't necessarily be a bad thing. Unfortunately, that's not the world we live in; and it is not uncommon to hear about processes being hijacked by malice. There have been no small number of exploits that take advantage of vulnerable daemons running as the superuser. Once such a daemon is compromised, so is the entirety of your system. Likewise, environmental or binary poisoning can be used to subvert a system's integrity.

The moral of the story is that if your system has a piece of software that must run as the root user, there is an inherent insecurity built-in; your system is only as secure as your least secure piece of software that runs with such permissions. The unfortunate reality is that there are many software implementations that need superuser access. Fortunately, such occurrences are largely relegated to the server-model, where daemonized software is much more common.

Apple has a low-level access control model, dubbed the seatbelt, in OS X. The seatbelt's implementation is based on the mandatory access control (MAC) model. Conceptually, the MAC system implements restrictions based upon actors, objects, and actions. In such a system, the actor typically assumes the form of a process, thread, or socket. The object can be any type of resource, such as a file, directory, socket, or even a TCP/UDP network port, among others. The action is simply the request of the actor to be applied to the respective object, and it varies depending on the type of object involved in the request. Referring back to the file system model, the actor would be a word processor application, the object would be a .txt flat file, and the action would be a call to either read from or write to that text file. When the actor requests access to the object, the MAC authorization system evaluates security policies and decides whether the request can proceed, or if it should be prohibited. The main lesson to draw from this is that in a MAC model, ownership of object or process is not generally a consideration; individual users do not have the ability to override defined policy. This applies to the superuser as well; policies are applied without discrimination.

Leopard implements the MAC model via a framework architected from TrustedBSD's MAC framework, which is designed to support US Federal government "Trusted Computing" security requirements. This framework introduces *sandboxing* access control capabilities that allow a developer or user to apply access control policies to a process, restricting privileges to various specified system resources. The restrictions are generally enforced upon acquisition, so any active file descriptors (open files) would not be immediately affected by any policy changes, however, any new open() operations would be subject to the new restrictions. In a fashion similar to the DAC model, new processes and forks will inherit the access restrictions of their parent. The scope and breadth of possible control points has grown; new actions include, but are not limited to, the following:

- Filesystem access
- File/directory read/write
- File metadata read/write
- File/Directory Extended Attributes read/write
- System sockets

- Network access
- Inbound/outbound control
- IP-specific controls
- Port-specific controls
- Process execution
- Forking
- Subprocess execution
- IPC (inter-process communication)
- Process signaling
- Mach-O messaging
- Shared Memory
- Low-level OS functions
- `sysctl` read/write
- `ioctl` (device/tty access)
- `fsctl` (file-system control: mounting/unmounting)

Sandbox policies can be precompiled into any given program, or they can be applied to any executable at runtime. The majority of this section will focus on applying sandbox profiles with the `sandbox-exec` command, which employs the latter strategy, although we will also cover implementing sandbox calls directly into an application. After reading this section you will be familiar with using sandboxing to help secure your Mac.

Sandbox Profiles

The App Sandbox enables you to apply mandatory restrictions via sandbox profiles. *Profiles* are text configuration files defining access provisions to various system facilities. If we consider the previously discussed paradigm, in which the MAC framework consists of actors, actions, and objects, a sandbox profile defines and associates actions and objects via allow or deny declarations. An individual sandbox profile contains a number of these declarations, which ultimately define the allowed behavior of an application. When a sandbox profile is applied to a process, that process will be ultimately restricted in its function to the actions provisioned in the profile. Any attempts to access resources outside those defined in the applied sandbox will be rejected, regardless of the operating user.

Sandbox profiles are applied at runtime to an executed process via the executable /usr/bin/sandbox-exec. By passing this command the -f key, you can specify the path to a sandbox profile to apply to an executable. The last argument passed to `sandbox-exec` should be the path to the executable binary. For example, the following command launches TextEdit with the sandbox profile found at /usr/share/sandbox/lockdown.sb:

```
cedge$ sandbox-exec -f /usr/share/sandbox/lockdown.sb⏎
 /Applications/TextEdit.app/Contents/MacOS/TextEdit &
```

Notice that, when launching an .app-based application bundle, such as TextEdit, you must supply the full path to the binary executable program, rather than the path to the .app bundle itself. Once this command is executed, TextEdit will open and operate normally. However, until the user quits TextEdit, it will be restricted only to actions defined in the `lockdown` profile. If the user launches it again by clicking it from `Applications`, it will no longer have the sandbox profile applied and will operate under normal conditions. So, it's a little harder to control access to GUI-launched user-initiated applications. That being said, sandboxing serves as a great tool for performing forensics: if you're running for the first time a suspicious application, it might not be a bad idea to launch it in a sandboxed environment just in case. In conjunction with the seatbelt's logging facilities (which we'll get to in a bit), it becomes very apparent to see exactly what resources the application is trying to access. Or maybe it's not the application that you don't trust, but rather the data that it is trying to process. If we wrap Preview.app in a sandbox prior to opening a suspect PDF, then should the PDF contain some payload, its effect can be largely mitigated: in such a case Preview could be restricted from writing to any file system location, as well as from spawning processes, initiating network connections, Mach-O messaging, or other process signaling. Once we remove such abilities from Preview, any exploitive code executed in its guise is subject to the same restrictions.

> **Tip**   The directory `/usr/share/sandbox` is a built-in constant. Any profiles that reside in this directory can be called with `sandbox-exec` by passing the `-n` argument and specifying solely the profile name, without the `.sb` extension. Thus, `sandbox-exec -f /usr/share/sandbox/lockdown.sb` is equivalent to `sandbox-exec -n lockdown`.

OS X ships with a number of sandbox profiles installed by default, found in the folder `/usr/share/sandbox`. These default profiles provide a glimpse into the various interfaces provided by the sandbox system. Sandbox profiles are included for system components such as Bonjour, Quicklook, Spotlight, Kerberos, ntp (Network Time), serialnumberd, syslog, and xgrid. In the purview of OS X services, this is still a pretty small number, but it's a good improvement, and it's nice to see that many of the behind-the-scenes daemons are becoming sandboxed. For instance, Bonjour has relatively recently had an exploit that allowed for remote code execution (CERT VU#221876 www.kb.cert.org/vuls/id/221876). Bonjour functionality is provided by the mDNSResponder daemon, which runs under the user root (superuser), making this a particularly dangerous exploit. Luckily, the exploit has long-since been patched, but it serves as a reminder that OS X is not impervious to attack. If such an exploit were to be found and attacked, the defined sandbox profile would help to mitigate (if not eliminate) the damage.

Apple also provides some built-in profiles that can be used by running processes. These profiles are fairly broad in their implementation, so in many cases, it will most likely be desirable to create your own precisely defined sandbox profiles. That being said, it is certainly good to know about the built-in profiles. Here they are:

- Nointernet: Disables all TCP/IP networking.
- Nonet: Disables all socket-based networking.

- ▓ Nowrite: Disables write access to all file system objects.

- ▓ write-tmp-only: Disables write access to file system objects except /var/tmp and the environmental variable $DARWIN_USER_TEMP_DIR.

- ▓ pure-computation: All OS services are restricted

Each of these profiles is invoked with the -n flag. For example, the following command launches TextEdit with the nowrite sandbox applied; as a result, the application will not be able to make any file system writes:

```
sandbox-exec -n nowrite /Applications/TextEdit.app/Contents/MacOS/TextEdit
```

This command will launch TextEdit, but the program will have read-only access to any asset it can open.

> **Note** When launching a non-Mach-O, Carbon-based application, such as Microsoft Office 2004, you must previously launch the LaunchCFM application found at path /System/Library/Frameworks/Carbon.framework/Versions/A/Support/LaunchCFMApp. Thus, to open Microsoft Word with an attached profile, you would use the following syntax:
>
> ```
> "sandbox-exec -n nointernet /System/Library/Frameworks/Carbon.framework/
> Versions/A/Support/ LaunchCFMApp /Applications/Microsoft\ Office\ 2015/
> Microsoft\ Word
> ```

Current access control definitions used by sandbox profiles are designated as System Private Interface and are therefore subject to change. That's not to say they don't work; they do. Apple uses them, and so can you. The main implication here is that if you have problems with your sandbox profile, or problems caused by its implementation, if you call Apple support they will not be able to help you troubleshoot this. Likewise, as Apple makes updates available, it is possible that they will change the way profiles work without warning. In such an event, users relying on the behavior or file format (and books that document it) will be in trouble. That being said, if you believe your organization has a security need that can be fulfilled by applying a sandbox profile, the technology is robust and stable enough to warrant consideration for implementation.

The worst thing that happens when applying a too-restrictive profile is that the application cannot access necessary resources and therefore fails to run. In such an event it is possible to monitor logging to determine necessary resources and ensure that access is provisioned to the application in question. Once all resource needs are properly provisioned, the application should function inside the sandbox without adverse affect. That being said, test, test, test. If you plan on deploying a sandbox to a business-critical service, make sure that you have thoroughly tested all use-cases of the application under the sandbox before going live.

The Anatomy of a Profile

So, without further adieu, let's take a look at the makeup of a profile. To facilitate this, we'll walk through the creation of the previously mentioned lockdown sandbox profile one declaration at a time. But first, let's discuss a few basics. The first thing to know is that all declarations in a sandbox profile are encased in parentheses ( ). Next, the semicolon (;) denotes an inline comment; any text to the right of a semicolon will be treated as a comment and will not be processed. Finally, the sandbox has an enforcement model such that the last declaration wins. That is, if you have two potentially conflicting access provisions, one denying access to a resource and the other allowing access, whichever declaration appears latest in the profile wins. Armed with this knowledge, let's take a look at the first line of our lockdown profile:

```
(version 1)
```

Here we are declaring the version of our profile. This is a pretty easy line as there is only one version at this point. Next, we declare our logging behavior:

```
(debug deny)
```

In this declaration, we are telling the Sandbox system to debug only "deny" activity (that is, whenever an executable attempts to perform an action that is disallowed). Alternatively, (debug all) can be specified, in which case any activity tested against the Sandbox, whether allowed or denied, will be logged. These logs are sent to /var/log/system.log. An example "deny" log entry can be seen here:

```
Mar 7 23:18:38 krypted sandboxd[73914]: vim(73913) deny file-write*↵
  /Users/cedge/Desktop/test.txt
```

In this example, we can see the process (vim), the result of the action (deny), the requested action (file-write), and the requested file (/Users/cedge/Desktop/test.txt). Logging can be immensely helpful for determining the activity of a program. It can then be used to construct a sandbox profile for any particular program. By employing a (debug all) setting, you can start out with a very basic profile and then narrow it down based upon logged activity. After observing that no deny log entries are hitting after fully vetting your program, you can switch to a (debug deny) status and then monitor the file for any disallowed behavior. In such a case, you will need to investigate any deny log entries observed to determine whether they are a result of valid process activity that should be provisioned or are occurring for other reasons.

> **Tip** Once you have your sandbox profiles honed and deployed, it may be desirable to deploy monitoring software to alert you in the event of any syslog deny entries. This will allow you to respond promptly to any unexpected behavior.

We have now declared our profile version and logging (debug) behavior. At this point, we begin with our restriction declarations. Although it's not always necessary, it is often desirable to first declare our default behavior. To clarify, we must declare whether we allow or deny any activity that is not explicitly defined in our file. In this case, our profile is meant to prohibit all activity that we don't explicitly define as okay. Thus, our default behavior will be to deny access (this is a lockdown profile after all):

```
(deny default)
```

If this were the end of our profile, we wouldn't get very far. Although this is a perfectly valid sandbox profile, we have only defined default access, and we are denying access at that. So at this point, any applicable activity that our program attempts will be met with failure. To that end, we must now define explicitly what a locked-down process can do. First and foremost, we need to give it process execution capabilities. Typically this profile will be used for a very specific purpose, so we can give execution privileges to that program specifically. In this case, our 'lockdown' profile is a generic profile that can be applied to multiple processes. As such, we will allow all process execution:

```
(allow process-exec)
```

If we wanted to define this to a particular executable, so that only that executable could be used, we would do the following:

```
(allow process-exec (literal "/Applications/TextEdit.app/Contents/MacOS/TextEdit"))
```

In this case, this profile would really only work with TextEdit. We have introduced a few new concepts here that merit further explanation. First, we declare a basic global allow rule for the process-exec action. If we want to define specific criteria for this action, such as explicitly defining the TextEdit binary, we do so by referencing the path in another nested set of parentheses. When defining these criteria, we are explicitly provisioning access based on the file path; no digital signing or application verification is done. This isn't ideal, as it means that an external process that is not sandboxed could still alter behavior of a sandboxed process, but there's unfortunately not much we can do at that point.

In any case, here we are defining a literal path of /Applications/TextEdit.app/Contents/MacOS/TextEdit. In the previous case, we were a bit extreme in granting execution capabilities on all process, but in this example, we are restricting it exclusively to the TextEdit binary. Luckily the flexibility of sandbox profiles allow us to find a compromise. Considering the following declaration:

```
(allow process-exec
    (subpath "/Applications")
    (regex "^(/usr)?/(s)?bin/.*")
    (subpath "/tmp/SandboxedApps")
)
```

In this example, we have a number of file paths assigned to our allow process-exec right, each enclosed in its own parentheses. In this case, we separated each declaration onto its own line; however, they can all exist on a single line as well. In this case, we are introducing two new path-testing capabilities. The subpath test evaluates to True for any executable found in a subdirectory of the /Applications folder; this includes all subitems, so programs in the utilities folder will also apply. We are also applying a regular expression match against the file system, in this case using the regular expression string: "^(/usr)?/(s)?bin/.*". Boiled down to simple terms, this regular expression evaluates to True for directories

`/usr`,`/usr/bin`,`/usr/sbin`,`/bin`, and `/sbin`. Thus any executables found in this directory will properly execute given the sandbox entry just shown. Last but not least, we are provisioning access to the `/tmp/SandboxedApps` directory. In real-world situations, you will certainly want to avoid granting executable access to the `/tmp` directory. In fact, this is quite possibly the worst directory to allow this type of access, because it is globally writable. In this case, however, we will always be manually applying the lockdown profile to GUI apps for forensic purposes, so that's less of a concern. With this configuration, if you want to sandbox the application for testing, just copy it to `/tmp/SandboxedApps` and call it with `sandbox-exec`.

Next, because we're planning to use this sandbox to launch Cocoa applications, we must allow for Mach lookups. Mach is the microkernel that runs OS X at its lowest level, and it provides for interprocess communication, known as IPC. Mach IPC is used for a large number of basic behaviors, such as allowing processes to communicate with the WindowServer process to draw GUI elements, such as a window. Or, for example, allowing an application to communicate with the PasteBoard server in order to use Copy and Paste. IPC is also used in utilizing System services, such as looking up a contact in your address book, looking up directory services information, and even printing. Its use is prolific throughout applications that run in OS X, and its existence is something developers have come to expect. As such, when it is unavailable, some applications will simply cease to function. For the purposes of a lockdown profile, we'll want to protect against these calls: just because a program doesn't directly access the network or modify contents on disk doesn't mean it can't do damage. For instance, consider an application that uses Mach IPC to query your contact list, and then sends that information to a process that does have network access and can relay the data. If the target program allows remote calls to send external messages, this program functions as an open relay for outbound network communications, and it can thereby be exploited as a means to compromise confidentiality. To allow Mach IPC to flow without restrictions, we can use the following declaration:

```
(allow mach-lookup)
```

However, we want to provide more protection than that in this particular profile, so we will derive a basic set of allowances:

```
(allow mach-lookup
    (global-name "com.apple.CoreServices.coreservicesd")
    (global-name "com.apple.SecurityServer")
    (global-name "com.apple.dock.server")
    (global-name "com.apple.FontServer")
    (global-name "com.apple.FontObjectsServer")
    (global-name "com.apple.distributed_notifications.2")
    (global-name "com.apple.system.notification_center")
    (global-name "com.apple.windowserver.active")
    (global-name "com.apple.windowserver.session")
    (global-name "com.apple.tsm.uiserver")
    (global-name "Multilingual (Apple)_OpenStep")
    (global-name "en (Apple)_OpenStep")
    (global-name "com.apple.pasteboard.1")
)
```

These provisions allow for basic Mach IPC functions that are used by most GUI applications: the security server to lookup access provisions, the Font server for fonts, the window server so that the process can attach to the GUI, and the Clipboard, to name a few. The list just shown is *not* comprehensive, and will certainly be too restrictive for some applications. That being said, it provides a good base for forensics work. Launch the application with this profile, and then simply monitor the console log for `sandboxd-deny` log entries.

Lastly, we may want to provision some basic file system access. Remember that, thanks to our default deny rule, the application won't be able to make any file system writes. Depending on the application, this may or may not be a problem. Some programs do require the ability to write out support files to operate properly. In this case we will provision access to some explicitly defined directories:

```
(allow file-read-data file-read-metadata (regex "^/.*"))
(allow file-write*
    (regex "^/Users/.*/Library/Preferences/.*")
    (regex "^/Users/.*/Library/Application Support/.*")
    (regex "^(/private)?/tmp/")
    (regex "^(/private)?/var/folders/.*")
)
```

In this example, we are allowing the program to read any files on the file system. In this case, we are applying the restriction via a regular expression: `regex "^/.*"`, but the end result would be the same as `subpath "/"`.

> **Note**   One stipulation of the `subpath` expression is that it cannot end with a solidus (/); as such, `subpath` "/" is an illegal declaration (`regex` "^/.*" must be used instead).

We also have a couple of `file-write*` provisions. In this case we are using regular expressions to allow the process to write to a user's Preferences folder and their Application Support folder, in addition to the `/tmp` folder. This provision allows the app to write out its preference file if needed. Keep in mind that these provisions do not usurp standard discretionary access controls; even if a process is allowed access via seatbelt, in order for it to alter a file the user responsible for running the process will need to have write access to the file as well. With the file system declarations just shown we are introducing yet another new concept through the use of a wildcard on our file-write action. Here, `file-write*` actually denotes several access provisions: `file-write-data`, `file-write-metadata`, and `file-write-xattr`, which allow for modification of a file's contents, metadata, and extended attributes, respectively.

For many OS X applications, these provisions would be sufficient for operation. However, there are a number of low-level functions that certain applications may need to function properly. Such functions may include access to shared libraries, dynamic libraries, shared memory, Mach-O messaging, and so on (all those things that make GUI apps powerful). Many applications will have their usefulness (or stability) significantly diminished without access to these facilities. Thankfully, Apple has provided a basic profile, `bsd.sb`, that provisions access to many of these low-level functions. Sandbox profiles can be imported from one profile to another, so it's extremely easy to build on existing profiles. In this case, we want to import the provisions specified in bsd.sb into our current lockdown profile. We can accomplish this task with the following declaration:

```
(import "bsd.sb")
```

We place this include at the end of the file to ensure that any allow declarations that it provides are not overridden by any resource denials specified in our file. And that completes our lockdown file, as shown in full here:

```
(version 1)
(debug all)
(deny default)
(allow mach-lookup
    (global-name "com.apple.CoreServices.coreservicesd")
    (global-name "com.apple.SecurityServer")
    (global-name "com.apple.dock.server")
    (global-name "com.apple.FontServer")
    (global-name "com.apple.FontObjectsServer")
    (global-name "com.apple.distributed_notifications.2")
    (global-name "com.apple.system.notification_center")
    (global-name "com.apple.windowserver.active")
    (global-name "com.apple.windowserver.session")
    (global-name "com.apple.tsm.uiserver")
    (global-name "Multilingual (Apple)_OpenStep")
    (global-name "en (Apple)_OpenStep")
    (global-name "com.apple.pasteboard.1")
)
(allow process-exec
    (subpath "/Applications")
    (regex "^(/usr)?/(s)?bin/.*")
    (subpath "/tmp/SandboxedApps")
)
(allow file-read-data file-read-metadata (regex "^/.*"))
(allow file-write*
    (regex "^/Users/.*/Library/Preferences/.*")
    (regex "^/Users/.*/Library/Application Support/.*")
    (regex "^(/private)?/tmp/")
)
(import "bsd.sb")
```

This profile is a bit too generic to deploy on a daemonized program. In such a case, we would want to explicitly define all file system paths used by the process and allow only those. This profile is better served in a forensics role.

Sandbox Profiles in Action

So now we know what a sandbox profile looks like, but that is really only half of the picture. In the next section, we'll review some possible scenarios where sandboxing can be used to improve the security outlook dramatically. If you are an administrator who provides shell access to your users, if you deploy automations utilizing preshared keys for password-free authentication between machines, or if you are simply looking to provide a safety barrier from a root-run process, the following profiles will serve as a good primer toward implementing your own sandboxes.

Using the Sandbox to Secure User Shells

If you are an administrator who must provide shell accounts for your user base, you've probably already put a lot of thought into securing them. Even with only a default shell, a nonadministrative user has a significant amount of access. In environments where all users are trusted, this might not be a huge concern to administrators, but it probably the case that security in this respect is overlooked. In environments where the user base is unknown or cannot be trusted, the integrity of the system must be carefully protected from your users themselves. OS X, however, is known in the security community to have problems with local privilege-escalation vulnerabilities.

A *privilege-escalation vulnerability* is an exploit employed by a user to gain access to system resources outside of those that have been provisioned to that user. In many cases, this entails a standard user gaining root privileges and thereby having complete control of the system. In a perfect world this would never happen. Unfortunately, we don't live in a perfect world, and a quick Google search for the term "OS X local privilege escalation" reveals security advisories for many familiar applications: AppleScript, Apple Remote Desktop, Disk Utility, and System Preferences, to name a few. Even these legitimate applications have in the past provided avenues for users to subvert the system. Fortunately, Apple has addressed each of these specific vulnerabilities through various security updates. Even so, it's a bit naïve to think that there isn't still a vulnerability out there that could potentially be exploited. If you are an OS X administrator and need to provide shell access for your user base, consider sandboxing the user's shell to reduce the number of tools that they have access to and thereby reducing the surface area for attack.

Sandboxing doesn't only apply to user shell access, though. In OS X, the SFTP service is directly tied to SSH. In fact, both are provided by the same daemon. The main concern with using OS X as an SFTP platform is that the daemon is not *change-rooted* at all. What this means is that users could easily walk all over your file system. You cannot limit SFTP access for a user to the user's own home directory, for example. While that can certainly be their starting point, they have full access to go anywhere that standard users can go: your Applications folder, your /System folder, and portions of /etc are also exposed. While these resources should be impervious to damage from such users thanks to standard POSIX permissions, it still represents a security risk to the loss in confidentiality. Because of the blanket nature of the problem, traditional file system access control measures could not adequately address the issue. The workaround to this problem is to install an alternative SFTP service, whether that is a chrooted SSH-based solution or a different product altogether, such as Rumpus. This isn't always a step in the right direction, though. For example, Rumpus itself was vulnerable to a zero-day exploit that allowed for remote code execution. The Rumpus daemon runs as root, so administrators implementing this solution had exposed servers that could be fully compromised remotely. We're big fans of Rumpus and don't mean to call it out specifically. We just feel it's important to acknowledge that no software is immune to exploitation.

> **Note**   Again, no software is immune to exploitation. While it is certainly true that properly written software will be much harder to compromise than poorly written software, the general attitude that a security administrator must hold is that all software is vulnerable.

Fortunately, with the introduction of sandboxing, we have tools to adequately address these types of problems through the use of sandbox profiles, whether we're beefing up protections on Apple's solutions or implementing a sandbox around a third-party solution.

The following profiles, base.sb and shell.sb, were specifically designed to provide reasonably secure SFTP/shell services using OS X servers' built-in SSH daemon. We accomplish this by limiting available binaries to any user and limiting available utilities to those required for traditional shell functionality. It further provides protection by restricting read access to any directory or file that both falls outside our specified file system tree and also is not critical for the proper operation of a shell. Writes to /tmp are allowed for general compatibility.

base.sb

The base.sb profile provides minimal resources needed to establish a remote shell session. It contains two main privilege blocks, shell.dependencies and shell.whitelisted-apps. Privilege blocks are to sandbox profiles what functions are to programming and scripting; they allow for the definition of predefined behavior that can be easily referenced from other profiles. To create a privilege block, you define the block by specifying the name and then encapsulating all of your standard sandbox access provisions inside the (define) block, as shown here:

```
(define (userProcesses)
 (allow process-exec
  (subPath "/Applications")
  (subPath "/bin")
  (subPath "/usr/bin")
 )
)
```

In this example, we are creating a set of access provisions that allow the execution of programs found in /Applications, /bin, or /usr/bin. These provisions are defined but are not applied until the privilege block is referenced in the profile. This is done by enclosing the defined name on its own line enclosed in parentheses:

```
(userProcesses)
```

This same concept applies if this profile is imported from a different profile. To enable the access provisions provided in this shell (named userProcesses.sb), we would use the following text in our own profile:

```
(import "userProcesses.sb")
(userProcesses)
```

We note this because base.sb itself enforces only a small number of access provisions, but as mentioned primarily defines two privilege blocks, shell.dependencies and shell.whitelisted-apps, that can be utilized by other profiles. The former privilege block includes only resources necessary to the establishment of an interactive shell, and the latter includes innocuous support apps, such as man, pagers/editors, compression utilities, and basic file operands. None of the processes established under shell.whitelisted-apps are needed for basic shell access but are rather nice things to have in a shell environment.

This profile provides security by limiting available binaries to those installed in /bin, and a select number of applications residing in other system directories. Additionally, it restricts read access, in the traditional POSIX sense, to any directory or file that falls outside our specified fs trees and is not critical for the proper operation of a shell. Writes to /tmp are allowed for general compatibility. This profile is referenced for use by several of the previously mentioned profiles and can be included in others as a way to define minimal provisions needed for a shell account.

```
(version 1)
(debug deny)
(allow default signal sysctl* mach*)
;; our global denies
(deny file-write* file-read-data file-read-metadata (regex "^/.*"))
(deny file-write* (regex "^/.*"))
(deny process* network*)
;; import the bsd profile
(import "bsd.sb")
(define (shell.dependencies)
  ;; required processes for remote shell/sftp access
  (allow process-exec file-read-data file-read-metadata
    (regex "^/bin/.*")
    (literal "/usr/bin/which")
    (literal "/usr/libexec/sshd-keygen-wrapper")
    (literal "/usr/libexec/sftp-server"))
  (allow process-fork)
  ;; our fine-grained reads.
  (allow file-read-data file-read-metadata
    (regex "^(/usr)?/bin")
    (regex "^/dev")
    (literal "/usr/lib/charset.alias")
    (literal "/private/var/run/utmpx")
    (literal "/private/etc/csh.cshrc")
    (regex "^/usr/share/locale")
    (regex "^/usr/share/terminfo")
    (regex "^/usr/libexec")
  )
```

```
  ;; Basic write access to tty and temp directory
  (allow file-write* file-read-data file-read-metadata
    (regex "^/dev/tty")
    (regex "^(/private)?(/var)?/tmp"))
) ;; end shell.dependencies
(define (shell.whitelisted-apps)
;; define our basic apps. Nothing in this block is critical for shell/sftp
;; access. Edit any of these as you see fit
  (allow process-exec file-read-data file-read-metadata
    ;; man support
    (literal "/usr/bin/groff")
    (literal "/usr/bin/grotty")
    (literal "/usr/bin/less")
    (literal "/usr/bin/man")
    (literal "/usr/bin/more")
    (literal "/usr/bin/tbl")
    (literal "/usr/bin/troff")
    ;; compression apps
    (literal "/usr/bin/bunzip2")
    (regex "^/usr/bin/bz") ;; bunzip2 binaries
    (regex "^/usr/bin/z[^print]") ;; zip binaries
    (literal "/usr/bin/gunzip")
    (literal "/usr/bin/gzcat")
    (literal "/usr/bin/gzip")
    ;; editors/interpretors
    (literal "/usr/bin/awk")
    (literal "/usr/bin/vi")
    (literal "/usr/bin/vim")
    (literal "/usr/bin/egrep")
    (literal "/usr/bin/emacs")
    (literal "/usr/bin/grep")
    (literal "/usr/bin/nano")
    ;; file operations
    (literal "/usr/bin/ditto")
    (literal "/usr/bin/rsync")
    (literal "/usr/bin/tar")
    (literal "/usr/bin/srm")
    ;; misc
    (literal "/usr/bin/banner")
    (literal "/usr/bin/clear")
    (literal "/usr/bin/cksum")
    (literal "/usr/bin/cut")
    (literal "/usr/bin/dig")
    (literal "/usr/bin/du")
    (literal "/usr/bin/env")
    (literal "/usr/bin/getopts")
    (literal "/usr/bin/head")
    (literal "/usr/bin/id")
    (literal "/usr/bin/killall")
    (literal "/usr/bin/kinit")
    (literal "/usr/bin/klist")
    (literal "/usr/bin/kpasswd")
```

```
      (literal "/usr/bin/last")
      (literal "/usr/bin/passwd")
      (literal "/usr/bin/printf")
      (literal "/usr/bin/screen")
      (regex "^/usr/bin/svn")
      (literal "/usr/bin/top")
      (literal "/usr/bin/touch")
      (literal "/usr/bin/xargs")
   )
   ;; support files
   (allow file-read-data file-read-metadata
      ;; man support
      (literal "/private/etc/man.conf")
      (regex "^/usr/share/groff")
      (regex "^/usr/share/man")
      (regex "^/usr/X11/man")
      ;; other
      (literal "/Library/Preferences/edu.mit.kerberos")
   )
) ;; end shell.whitelisted-apps
```

shell.sb

The profile shell.sb is the primary profile that we will apply to a user's shell. It provides security by building on restrictions already applied through our base.sb profile, providing access to our user's home directories. When deploying this profile in your own environment, you'll want to update the following line in the file-write* block with the appropriate path. In this expression, we accept both local and automounted homes:

```
(regex "^(/Network/Servers(/.*)?/)?/Users/")
```

For most server environments, this default setting will likely work out pretty well. The regular expression used here allows access to both /Users and the standard network home directory location used in OS X, /Network/Servers/server.myco.com/Users. At these locations we will rely on POSIX and ACL-based access controls to ensure that users have access to only their own data. If we are providing solely sftp access to users, then we only care to import shell.dependencies from our base.sb profile. If we will be providing user shells as well, we can uncomment the line to allow applications defined by shell.whitelisted-apps also.

```
(version 1)
(debug deny)
(deny default)
;; import the base profile
(import "base.sb")
;; include our shell dependencies
(shell.dependencies)
;; and if we're not totally evil, uncomment this to our allow our app whitelist
;;(shell.whitelisted-apps)
;; specify the root of our rw branch, update this setting for your own environment
```

```
(allow file-write-data file-read-data file-read-metadata
 (regex "^(/Network/Servers(/.*)?)?/Users/.*")
)
;; The following is needed for sftp support
(allow file-read-metadata
    (regex "^/.*")
    (regex "^/etc")
)
(allow process-exec file-read-data file-read-metadata (literal↵
 "/usr/local/bin/sbshell"))
```

In this profile we apply a default deny policy, import our base.sb profile, import provisions from base.sb defined in shell.dependencies, and then provide access to our user home directories. But what about that last line:

```
(allow process-exec file-read-data file-read-metadata (literal↵
 "/usr/local/bin/sbshell"))
```

Well, remember that in order to apply a profile to an environment, we do so using the sandbox-exec command. In order to do this to a user's shell, we have to create a wrapper script that performs the function. In this case, the wrapper script is defined at /usr/local/bin/sbshell and is detailed next.

sbshell

As mentioned, to apply the sandbox profiles to our logged-in users, we'll need to create a wrapper script to accomplish our task. We can do this by creating a very basic shell script that executes the user's normal shell program within the confines of our desired sandbox profile. As can be seen in the following code, this shell simply calls the shell found at /bin/bash. That shell is passed through all parameters that were passed to the original shell (designated by $@) to function properly with any parameters passed to the shell (utilized by commands such as ssh and rsync).

```
#!/bin/bash
PATH="/bin:/usr/bin"
## basic shell wrapper to provide sandboxed rights control.
## requires userShell.sb and shell.sb sandbox profiles to
## be installed at /usr/share/sandbox/
declare -x myShell=/bin/bash
if [ -x "${myShell:?}" ]; then
    if [ -f /usr/share/sandbox/shell.sb ]; then
        sandbox-exec -n shell "$myShell" "$@"
    else
        echo "Sandbox profile not found, cannot continue!"
        exit 2
    fi
else
    echo "Illegal shell: $myShell, cannot continue!"
    exit 2
fi
```

With this simple shell script installed at /usr/local/bin/sbshell, the next step is to ensure that it is executable, with the command chmod:

```
chmod +x /usr/local/bin/sbshell
```

Once that is done, you can now configure the user's shell to reside at /usr/local/bin/sbshell. From here on, whenever the user logs in via SSH, SFTP, rsync, or any SSH-based connection, their environment will be restricted to the confines of the applied sandbox profile.

Carbon Copy Cloner

Carbon Copy Cloner is a popular backup-based directory written by Mike Bombich (www.bombich.com) and available on the Mac App Store. It has a strong group of followers because it is a reliable piece of software that performs basic backups with minimal configuration and hassle. It even has the option to back up over a network connection to facilitate offsite backups. The facility that it uses to perform this action utilizes password-free, key-based SSH authentication.

Unfortunately, there are some inherent insecurities introduced with the model. First and foremost, it creates password-free authentication to the root user on the remote machine. This means that the host machine unconditionally trusts the backup-client; if the client machine is compromised, so is the server. Carbon Copy Cloner attempts to mitigate this issue by implementing a public key system that works only with a predefined wrapper script. That is, the key can only be used to launch a specific script, which is located at /var/root/.ssh/rsync-wrapper.sh. When a remote connection is established with the preshared key, this script is executed. The script has some sanity checks in it to ensure that the only programs allowed to run are scp and /var/root/rsync. If neither of these commands is called, the shell will exit and the remote shell is closed. Theoretically, this provides us the protection that we need—only rsync and scp can use the key; and SSH isn't included, so a user can't initiate an SSH session, right?

Well, the problem is apparent when we consider the nature of the applications that are allowed, rsync and scp. Both applications are fully capable of modifying the file system, and there is nothing to prevent them from modifying the wrapper script itself. After all, the remote shell *is* granted root access; what's stopping the user from using rsync to copy a new wrapper and replace the existing wrapper that applies the restrictions? Well, in truth, nothing. Say that you have several laptops that use this function to back up to your server. Any user of these laptops could potentially take over your server if they had the malice or intent to do so. Constructing a basic, no-frills-no-restrictions SSH key wrapper is pretty easy and can be accomplished with the following script:

```
#!/bin/bash
$SSH_ORIGINAL_COMMAND
```

That's it, two lines, nice and simple. Once we have this code saved into a file and that file is made executable via chmod, we can then push the new file to the server and thereby override all access controls that have been put into place:

```
cd "/Applications/Carbon Copy Cloner.app"
cd "Contents/MacOS/ccc_helper.app/Contents/MacOS/"
./rsync -e "ssh -i /var/root/.ssh/ccc_dsa" -a --rsync-path=/private/var/root/rsync /tmp/my-
evil-rsync-wrapper.sh root@mybackupserver.myco.com:/var/root/.ssh/rsync-wrapper.sh
```

This command replaces the file /var/root/.ssh/rsync-wrapper.sh on the server with my own copy, located at /tmp/my-evil-rsync-wrapper.sh. Provided my rsync-wrapper contains the shell code mentioned here, we will now have full, unfettered access to the backup server.

Game over.

This, obviously, is a bad thing. However, we now have power to fight against this attack, using the profile defined next. In the following profile, we deny write access to our rsync wrapper, preventing that exploit from being accomplished, and we define a sandbox profile that allows for secure remote backups with CCC. In this profile, we specify a backup directory on the remote server at /Backups; you will probably want to change this to satisfy your environment.

```
(version 1)
(debug deny)
(allow default signal mach*)
(deny network-outbound)
;; change PathToBackupDir to the local target directory.
(allow file-write* file-read-data file-read-metadata
       (subpath "/Backups"))

;;; Static Entries, shouldn't have to mess with the below
(allow process-exec file-read-data file-read-metadata
   (regex "^(/private)?/var/root/\.ssh/rsync-wrapper\.sh$")
   (regex "^(/private)?/var/root/rsync$")
   (literal "/usr/bin/scp")
   (literal "/usr/bin/which")
   (regex "^/bin")
   (literal "/usr/libexec/sshd-keygen-wrapper"))
(allow process-fork)
(deny process*)
;; our global denies
(deny file-read-data file-read-metadata
       (regex "^/.*"))
(deny file-write*
   (regex "^/.*"))
;; our fine-grained allows.
(allow file-read-data file-read-metadata
       (regex "^(/private)?/var/root")
  (literal "/dev/autofs_nowait")
       (literal "/usr/lib/charset.alias"))
;; CCC seems to want to overwrite its copy of rsync
```

```
;; in root user's home on the server each time it runs,
;; the backup fails if the scp fails, so we add a rule.
(allow file-write* file-read-data file-read-metadata
       (regex "^(/private)?/var/root/rsync$")
       (literal "/Library/Logs/CCC.log")
  (regex "^(/private)?/tmp"))

;; import the bsd profile
(import "bsd.sb")
```

We now have our nice secure profile all written up, but we're missing a key piece: we still have to implement this profile (otherwise it's just another text file sitting idly on the server). To do that, we must modify the wrapper script that CCC uses during the remote rsync session stored at /var/root/.ssh/rsync-wrapper.sh. This wrapper is created by CCC and deploys checks to ensure that only rsync and scp applications can be used by its preshared key. To make the wrapper itself secure from being overwritten, we can modify a few lines in the file. Specifically, locate the following text, which appears twice in the file on its own line, as follows:

```
$SSH_ORIGINAL_COMMAND
```

Change both occurrences of this line to read:

```
/usr/bin/sandbox-exec -n ccc $SSH_ORIGINAL_COMMAND
```

From here on, all the CCC-based rsync will forever be sandboxed, and it will prevent the remote exploit from succeeding.

Securely Automating Remote rsync

While Carbon Copy Cloner is a popular Mac backup program, even more common is the old but trusted rsync utility. In fact, as we just discovered, Carbon Copy Cloner actually uses rsync on its back end to perform backups. While CCC is a great program, rsync is ubiquitous and powerful, and it's very handy for basic backups and data mirroring. If you're looking to automate rsync between machines, you're pretty much looking at exactly the same setup that CCC deploys: a public key, and preferably a wrapper script to provide at least some baseline security. To understand how to secure such a setup, we'll need to walk through the entire process.

The first thing that you need to establish to provide cross-machine automation is a password-free authentication scheme. GUI apps will often leverage the keychain for this, but that option isn't approachable from a command-line app like rsync. Password-free authentication works through public-key-encryption, which we discussed earlier in this chapter. More specifically, we set up password-free SSH authentication by using preshared keys: to deploy this solution, you must create a private and a public key, and then distribute the public key to the remote host that you want to log in to. To create this key, we run the following command on our client machine from the user account that we want to have password-free authentication from (this will commonly be root):

```
ssh-keygen -f ~/.ssh/id_dsa -N "" -t dsa
```

This command will create a private key named id_dsa in the .ssh folder found at the root of the running user's home directory. This file is automatically consulted by OS X's SSH client when initiating a remote connection to a server. This command will also create a public key, id_dsa.pub, which is the key that we distribute to our remote server. We can accomplish this by using a remote connection to the server, which for this first attempt will require you to enter your user credentials. When logging into the remote server, we specify the remote user (in this case cedge) that we want to establish remote automation for: the remote user does *not* need to have the same username as the local user. In these commands, we are first creating the .ssh folder in case it's not there:

```
## Create the remote .ssh directory (password required)
ssh cedge@remotehost.com "mkdir ~/.ssh"
## Establish appropriate permissions (password required)
ssh cedge@remotehost.com "chmod 700 ~/.ssh"
## Copy the new public key into the file "authorized_keys" on the remote host
## This file is consulted by default in OS X for ssh preshared key authentication
## (password required)
cat ~/.ssh/id_dsa.pub | ssh cedge@remotehost.com "cat - >> ~/.ssh/authorized_keys"
## Perform a remote folder listing (no password required)
ssh cedge@remotehost.com ls
Desktop
Documents
...
```

So, after initiating this command, we have verified through our last command that preshared key authentication is fully operational. If that command failed for you, consult log files /var/log/system.log and /var/log/secure.log for hints as to why (it typically has to do with overly lax POSIX permissions on a user's home directory or .ssh directory).

Now that we have this setup, we can then perform remote rsyncs to our heart's content without requiring authentication, as long as we run the command from the user account that created the keys in the previous step (notice that the remote user must also be the same as used previously):

```
rsync -av /MyAwesomeFiles/ cedge@remotehost.com:/Backups/MyAwesomeFiles/
```

All is well and good. Right? Well, not exactly. In this instance, the public key can be used to access *any* command, and there is no sandbox in place. How very wild, wild west of us. Well, we don't like to roll like that, so the first thing we do is put some restrictions on our preshared key, just as Carbon Copy Cloner does. To do this, we modify the authorized_keys file that we just copied over to the remote host. So, on this box we open up the file ~cedge/.ssh/authorized_keys, which will look similar to the following:

```
ssh-dss AAAAB3NzaC1kc3MAAACBAOYUR6cON9uiyfLvGNtYtmVKOOX2AOGXmer3PJgbwR/T9Lu8kDhKOEcE6g
NEZTWzeVFxWel6WqDRALs8bZnvPBVLLLp1yM5ntcVM3tXB9NkAQIfGghHZt/oeaayE8s9Mpq5rrndQJyg13RYpP9N
cMBgm5LYhptvQMTr3LGAWK35DAAAAFQDhsQpzMnYd3F4pqZ/m/m2pw3kHVwAAAIEAjo3+bTcWRfqISTuTu23EoOLF4n4
8aWD/rVFmgNPn7rTXd8rEOckZqY5kvL66vWBZO3ymMiN3TWf8zjR9aceLpc1MKuHZfghXOaiHNRrJgf9SVc7k78O5
fBXgex8xoppPOtXwblIO64gbTN4m66vwKzVkjppyHwOaOnIVOMAp7k4AAACBAMME9jrR2LhOAK+
5pCW7jt4m5HuxJOY8R+YbTkbRxoXtPt9OofS8xKvrQzfvb/5vZW8EDFOtnIvA6kax2h61II5ltStiEdT2T1/
N8yZdfBkftwODfRPOpphjgztjnmSgYfOHzzpz5ctT1PAPYw9pVzS4OXZMp77gb1MrcoDjHkDt cedge@krypted.lbc
```

It's hard to tell here, but all of that is actually on a single line of text. We can modify this file, specifically the line that contains our host's preshared key (in this case the host is krypted. lbc). To restrict this key to a specific command, we inject it at the beginning of the line, the end result looking like this:

```
command="/usr/local/bin/sshwrapper" ssh-dss AAAAB3NzaC1kc3MAAACBAOYUR6cON9uiyfLvGNtYtmVK
OOX2AOGXmer3PJgbwR/T9Lu8kDhKOEcE6gNEZTWzeVFxWel6WqDRALs8bZnvPBVLLLp1yM5ntcVM3tXB9NkA
QIfGghHZt/oeaayE8s9Mpq5rrndQJyg13RYpP9NcMBgm5LYhptvQMTr3LGAWK35DAAAAFQDhsQpzMnYd3F4pqZ/
m/m2pw3kHVwAAAIEAjo3+bTcWRfqISTuTu23EoOLF4n48aWD/rVFmgLPn7rTXd8rEOckZqY5kvL66vWBZO3ymWiN
3TWf8zjR9aceLpc1MKuHZfghXOaiHNRrJgf9SVc7k78O5fBXgex8xoppPOtXwblIO64gbTN4m66vwKzVkj
ppyHwOaOnIVOMAp7k4AAACBAMME9jrR2LhOAK+5pCW7jt4m5HuxJOY8R+YcTkbRxoXtPt9OofS8xKvrQzfvb/
5vZW8EDFOtnIvA6kax2h61II5ltStiEdT2T1/N8yZdfBkftwODfRPOpphjgztjnmSgYfOHzzpz5ctT1PAPYw9pVzS4
OXZMp77gb1MrcoDjHkDt cedge@krypted.lbc
```

Now, upon initiating a remote SSH session using this key all clients will be forced to call our sshwrapper script, /usr/local/bin/sshwrapper, rather than their default shell. This sshwrapper script, shown next, is the script that actually enforces which commands are authorized, and it also applies the appropriate sandbox.

```
#!/bin/bash
PATH="/bin:/usr/bin:/usr/sbin:/sbin"
#######################
##
## Basic ssh wrapper to restrict keyless authentication
## This script is meant to be called from a command declaration
## in ~/.ssh/authorized_keys
##
## All binaries are implicitly denied.
## tweak $allowedCommands to allow the execution of additional
## binaries.
##
##
#####################################
##########################


## a space separated list of absolute paths to allowed binaries
allowedCommands="/usr/bin/rsync,/usr/bin/scp,/usr/bin/true"
## Get our command's full path, if no command was specified
## then assume default shell
```

```
if [ -z "$SSH_ORIGINAL_COMMAND" ]; then
    cmd="$SHELL"
else
    fullCmd=`printf $SSH_ORIGINAL_COMMAND`
    cmd=${fullCmd[0]}
fi
declare -x cmdPath
if [ -x "$cmd" ]; then
    cmdPath="$cmd"
else
    cmdPath=`/usr/bin/which "$cmd"`
fi
## Iterate through our allowed commands, execute the command
## if it qualifies.
OLDIFS=$IFS
IFS=$','
for path in $allowedCommands;
do
    IFS=$OLDIFS
    if [ "$cmdPath" == "$path" ]; then
        sandbox-exec -n backup $SSH_ORIGINAL_COMMAND
        exit $?
    fi
done
## Here if the command wasn't in our allowedCommand
echo "sshwrapper.sh:: Access Denied for command:'$cmd' at path:'$cmdPath'"
exit 1
```

This script limits remote commands to those specified by the variable allowedCommands. We do a check against those absolute paths, and if the requested program matches that path, we allow the command to proceed. On top of this, we are applying the sandbox profile backup to the launched process, as seen in the line that actually does the execution:

```
sandbox-exec -n backup $SSH_ORIGINAL_COMMAND
```

$SSH_ORIGINAL_COMMAND is a special environmental variable set upon remote login; it contains the text in the requested command path (be it rsync, sftp, or a standard shell). Once we verify that this command is in our allowedCommands variable, we launch it in our sandboxed environment.

This particular script relies on our backup.sb profile, which is responsible for securing our preshared key environment. This means we need to restrict file system access to only directories that will be used by backups, so that the backup system itself can be used to overwrite any restrictions:

```
(version 1)
(debug deny)
(deny default)
(import "shell.sb")
(shell.dependencies)
;; specify any rw directories
(allow file-write* file-read-data file-read-metadata
```

```
    (subpath "/PathToBackupDir")
    (regex "^/var/log/backup.log$"))

;; add our allowed processes
(allow process-exec file-read-data file-read-metadata
  (literal "/usr/local/bin/sshwrapper")
  (literal "/usr/bin/rsync"))
(allow process-fork)
;; make sure we can read the user's home
(allow file-read-data file-read-metadata
    (regex "^(/private)?/var/root"))
```

As you can see, this profile uses our base profile and calls the shell.dependencies block. This profile also provisions access to the root user's home directory, so that the system can read the preshared key information. When utilizing this profile in your own environment, you'll want to change the subpath pattern matching PathToBackupDir to specify your backup target directory. Likewise, if a user other than root is the destination, you'll want to change the last class to point to the correct user's home directory.

BIND

OS X server and client both ship with the BIND DNS server. This is a very popular DNS server that is used by many Unix and Linux variants. BIND is yet another daemon that runs under the root user, and previous versions of BIND have been vulnerable to remote exploitation. Fortunately, the versions shipping with OS X 10.5 and 10.6 have proven to be both stable and secure in the context of data confidentiality, but it never hurts to add another layer of security. Apple actually ships a sandbox profile to be used to secure BIND, found on any recent OS X box at /usr/share/sandbox/named.sb. To enable this profile, we must modify the launchd plist that fires named (the name of the BIND daemon). This launchd plist can be found at /System/Library/LaunchDaemons/org.isc.named.plist. Helpfully, Apple has actually put some help text in this plist that explains how to enable the sandbox, so feel free to crack it open for an example. The gist of it is that we need to change our ProgramArguments declaration to include a call to sandbox-exec. Thus, the default ProgramArguments block for org.isc.named.plist:

```
<key>ProgramArguments</key>
<array>
 <string>/usr/sbin/named</string>
 <string>-f</string>
</array>
```

then becomes this:

```
<key>ProgramArguments</key>
<array>
 <string>/usr/bin/sandbox-exec</string>
 <string>-f</string>
 <string>/usr/share/sandbox/named.sb</string>
 <string>/usr/sbin/named</string>
 <string>-f</string>
</array>
```

These added calls to sandbox-exec ensure that named is launched with our appropriate sandbox restrictions applied.

> **Note** Apple assumes files in /System to be under their own control, so a future software update might revert the changes. It's probably a better idea to disable the DNS server in the Server Admin GUI and add your own launchd plist in /Library/LaunchDaemons.

I hope these profiles have given you a good primer about the different ways that the Sandbox can be utilized, whether running it ad hoc for forensics of an untrusted program or untrusted data, securing a background daemon, or locking down automations.

The Seatbelt Framework

As mentioned earlier, it is also possible to implement sandbox restrictions compiled directly into your application. This section discusses such an implementation. If you are not a developer, or are not interested in the lower-level functionality of the seatbelt, feel free to skip this section. To introduce sandboxing to be directly built into your application, Apple has offered their own Security Policy Module, dubbed the seatbelt, which is implemented as a KEXT installed at /System/Library/Extensions/seatbelt.kext. The only documented way to apply these controls in code is via the sandbox_init() function. Using this function provides a way for an application programmer to voluntarily restrict access privileges in a running program. sandbox_init() is very limited at this point, providing only five predefined constants, which are identical in function to the predefined constants available for sandbox-exec, which we discussed earlier:

```
kSBXProfileNoInternet - disables TCP/IP networking.
kSBXProfileNoNetwork - disables all sockets-based networking
kSBXProfileNoWrite - disables write access to all filesystem objects
kSBXProfileNoWriteExceptTemporary - disables write access to filesystem objects↩
 except /var/tmp and `getconf DARWIN_USER_TEMP_DIR`
kSBXProfilePureComputation - all OS services are restricted
```

An application can utilize one of these constants to restrict capabilities in spawned processes or threads, minimizing the potential damage that can occur in the event that the process is compromised. The following shows an example implementation of the kSBXProfileNoWrite profile in code:

```
#include <string.h>
#include <stdio.h>
#include <fcntl.h>
#include <sandbox.h>
int main() {
 int sb, fh;
 char **errbuf;
 char rtxt[255];
 char wtxt[255] = "Sandboxed you aren't\n\n";
```

```
// init our sandbox, if we don't return 0 then there's a problem
sb = sandbox_init(kSBXProfileNoWrite, SANDBOX_NAMED, errbuf);
if ( sb != 0 ) {
 printf("Sandbox failed\n");
 return sb;
};

// open our file with read-only access
fh = open("test.txt", O_RDONLY);
if ( fh == -1 ) {
  perror("Read failed");
} else {
  read(fh, rtxt, 255);
  close(fh);
  printf("FileContents:\n %s\n", rtxt);
};
// open the file with write access
fh = open("test.txt", O_RDWR | O_CREAT, 0000644);
if ( fh == -1 ) {
  perror("Write Failed");
} else {
  write(fh, wtxt, strlen(wtxt));
  close(fh);
  printf("Successfully wrote file!\n");
}
 return 0;
}
```

Compiling and running this code returns the following results:

```
$ ./sandBoxTest
FileContents:
 hello
Write Failed: Operation not permitted
```

So, even though our POSIX and ACL permissions allow for read/write access to the file, the sandbox prevents it, regardless of user. Running the program even with root privileges yields the same results:

```
$ sudo ./sandBoxTest
FileContents:
 hello
Write Failed: Operation not permitted
```

The key call in this code is the following, which initiates a sandbox using the standard kSBXProfileNoWrite profile, which eliminates all file system write access:

```
sb = sandbox_init(kSBXProfileNoWrite, SANDBOX_NAMED, errbuf);
```

Or, we can specify our own sandbox profile to apply more fine-grained, customized restrictions:

```
sb = sandbox_init("/usr/share/sandbox/myprofile.sb", SANDBOX_NAMED, errbuf);
```

> **Note**   Although providing `sandbox_init` with a file system path to a profile, it isn't a documented (and presumably therefore not a supported) use of `sandbox_init()`.

If you are a developer looking to sandbox your application and hit problems acquiring certain resources, such as shared libraries or the like, not all is lost. A key point to realize while coding is that the seatbelt's behavior does not affect already established resources. That is, any file descriptors, process executions, or other resource acquisitions that are performed prior to your call to `sandbox_init()` will not be restricted by the sandbox. Only resource requests after that call will be restricted. Thus, your program upon initializing can establish all of the necessary resources that it requires. At that point you can apply the appropriate restrictions and ensure that moving forward your program will have limited capabilities to acquire more resources. This ensures that if your program is hijacked, it will only be able to manipulate resources you have already allocated, which can greatly limit the impact of execution hijacking.

Considering the benefits in security that can be achieved through properly sandboxing your application, we believe it would be a mistake for a developer to shrug off seatbelting as a whole. Unfortunately, the amount of information and documentation provided by Apple on these technologies is minimal at best, so approaching the technology may be a little bit overwhelming. But now that you're armed with the information presented in this chapter, this technology is available for you to use as well. Whether you employ it to protect your valuable data or to run forensics on a suspect application, it can be a very useful security tool that merits consideration. The number of applications that run with root privileges these days is certainly on the decline, but they are still out there, and most likely even running on a server of yours. If that is the case for you, consider sandboxing the daemon to protect your system from its misuse.

Summary

In this chapter we discussed in detail two new security technologies in OS X. We discussed the implementation of application signing in Mac OS X from both technical and implementation perspectives. We also discussed OS X's Sandbox technology, which can be utilized to create a jailed environment around your application to limit its reach into the system. Both systems represent the future of security in OS X, as can be seen with their use (to the extreme) in iOS. Hopefully, as history progresses, Apple will find a happy medium between security and strict access measures. There's no doubt that their extensive and consistent use in iOS has helped contribute to the stability of the platform. That being said, such a model cannot simply be introduced as a replacement to an existing and established platform such as OS X. Eventually, we do foresee a model that more heavily enforces a signing requirement, and we hope such a system finds the middle ground of the two platforms, utilizing the security benefits that the technology provides without the totalitarian aspects of the iPhone model.

We also discussed application sandboxing extensively in this chapter and the ways that it can be used to mitigate damage from rogue applications. It, too, is utilized heavily by the iPhone, as each individual application resides in its own sandbox. As it's doing with application signing, Apple is taking a slow approach in implementing the technology in OS X. As time progresses, it's only inevitable that more and more processes will utilize this technology to provide a more secure system.

In the next chapter we will deal with security on more familiar ground: web browsing and e-mail. Read on to learn how best to protect yourself against the nefarious forces thriving on the Internet.

## Chapter 7

Securing Web Browsers and E-mail

Securing Web Browsers and E-mail

Identity theft is the fastest-growing crime in the world. According to the Federal Trade Commission (FTC), identity theft is the top concern of people contacting the agency, and has now passed drug trafficking as the number-one crime in the world. Nearly everyone I know has a friend that has had a run-in with some form of identity theft. And a likely spot to find plenty of information about someone, in order to masquerade as them, is their computer. And more specifically, the browser: the gateway people use to access the Internet. Threats to online privacy can be reduced by leveraging some very practical security with regards to our Internet browsers.

We commonly use computers to communicate with the outside world using cell phones, web browsers, instant messaging software, and e-mail; all technologies that rely on the Internet. Identity thieves know this, and use the Internet as their tool for stealing identities through the acquisition of credit card numbers and online banking information, as well as gaining access to e-mail and social networking web sites to masquerade as someone else online. Therefore, securing our messaging systems has become a high priority to protect us from identity theft.

For the purposes of this chapter, we will concentrate on the web browser and e-mail clients as common messaging and communications systems. As we explain in this chapter, each of the security features of these systems and what they do, you can apply the information to other browsers, chat programs, and mail programs that you may be using, and configure them for the same level of security. Although the actual terminology may change, the concepts remain constant across applications (and platforms, for that matter).

When discussing how to secure your web browser, we will be covering Safari and Firefox. There are other browsers out there, such as Opera and Google Chrome, but the security concepts for those browsers are similar to the ones we cover in Safari, even if the buttons are called different things and in some cases in different places. Likewise, there are a variety of e-mail clients out there. The two most common mail applications for the Mac are Microsoft Outlook and Apple Mail, so we will discuss these throughout the chapter as well.

> **Note**   We spend much of this chapter discussing how to fine-tune your browser for security purposes, but we should mention that downloading and installing software from questionable sources, such as BitTorrent web sites, for example, is dangerous, and could damage your computer. It's very hard to determine the origin of the software, and there is no guarantee the software won't perform nefarious tasks on your machine. Keep this in mind when downloading software from these unknown sources.

A Quick Note About Passwords

We've mentioned it before and we'll mention it again: if you take only one tip away from this book, take this one: *use good, complex passwords*! This is a mantra that we will use repeatedly throughout this book. We cannot overstate its importance.

> **Tip**   When we refer to complex passwords, we are referring to passwords that consist of eight or more characters of mixed case, contain a special character, and contain both letters and numbers where possible.

Your e-mail and online accounts are only as secure as the password you use to access them. And believe it or not, your e-mail account is quite valuable to a spammer. A resourceful spammer can make a small fortune by using insecure e-mail accounts to send spam. Because most web servers are fairly locked down with strong passwords, the spammer needs your e-mail account's password to use it. And even if they don't read your messages, they might end up getting your e-mail account disabled by your provider because of the high level of spam coming from your account. It can also be used to impersonate you to your friends and family, which can be very dangerous, especially when they ask for cash or private information. When this is used against high-profile individuals such as CEOs and celebrities, it's called *spear phishing*.

Encrypting the e-mail transport, as many e-mail servers claim to do, is good, but without a hard-to-guess password, encrypted e-mail transport is not enough. No matter how heavily you encrypt the password and its transport between client and server, if the password is too easy to guess, then you may as well have not encrypted it in the first place. A weak password can be quickly guessed, encrypted or not.

> **Note**   Not all providers allow the use of special characters in passwords. The characters that provide the most problems tend to be those that Unix reserves, such as `,`, `/`, `?`, and so on.

Securing Your Web Browser

A web browser is a tool used to view data that is hosted on a web server. The two most popular browsers in use on the Mac are Safari and Firefox. They are similar in security configurations; however, Firefox has more granular security controls.

When it comes to web browser security, privacy protection is the name of the game. We want to keep prying eyes away from your online purchase information, away from your passwords for web merchants, and away from the history of web sites you have visited. When securing a web browser, much of the security falls into two categories. The first is protecting your computer from the browser and any executables (such as cached scripts) that can run on the client; the second is securing the transport of data over the wire.

A NOTE ABOUT SECURE SOCKETS LAYER

The most notable form of protecting passwords and confidential information while in transit on the web and in e-mail is through the use of Secure Sockets Layer (SSL). SSL is a protocol developed by Netscape for transmitting private documents via the Internet. SSL works by using a shared session key to encrypt data that's transferred while en route to another system. Both Safari and Firefox support SSL, and many web sites use SSL to secure confidential user information, such as credit card numbers for transactions over the Internet. Most reputable banks and web sites with sensitive data require an SSL connection. You can easily tell when a web site is using an SSL connection as the URL will start with a `https`, not `http`.

Securing Safari

Safari is on every Mac by default. Thankfully, securing Safari can, for the most part, be done using the dedicated Security preference tab in Safari. On this tab, you can disable features of Safari that you don't need, block pop-ups, view and configure cookies, and tell the browser to prompt you before sending insecure data over the Internet. Out of the box, Safari disables pop-ups, but all of the other features are enabled; therefore, you should make a few minor adjustments to your Safari security configuration to maintain the highest level of security (based on your own security requirements), keeping in mind that changing many of these features might cause a more interrupted browsing experience.

Setting the Safari Security Preferences

By default, Safari is set to block pop-up windows. But sometimes you may need to access features of sites that cause pop-ups. You can find the option to enable and disable pop-ups by opening Safari in the top menu and selecting Preferences. Then, click on Security and uncheck the box for Block Pop-Up Windows (see Figure 7-1).

Figure 7-1. Blocking pop-up windows in Safari

Web browser attacks on the Mac (such as home page hijacking, infiltrating your file system through a web browser, or installing applications onto the workstation) are more likely than getting a virus on a Mac. Good security dictates that if there are features included in browsers that you do not use, you should typically disable them. Some features, such as Java-based plug-ins, can reconfigure your operating system. Therefore, Apple has seen fit to give you the ability to disable JavaScript within your browser using the Security preferences.

A *cookie* is a small text file of information that certain web sites attach to a user's hard drive while the user is browsing the site. A cookie can contain information that pertains to a specific web site such as the user ID, user preferences, shopping cart information, and any other setting that can be stored on a web site. For the longest time cookies got a bad rap, mainly because they were notorious for their security concerns. But most modern-day web browsers no longer store clear-text passwords in the cookies, do not allow access to cookies between multiple domains, and many cookies expire after a certain time frame, so they are at least manageable. The important thing to remember with cookies is that you should know where they come from. Some sneaky web sites will put cookies from ad servers in your browser that can track your Internet activity. Apple has included a Details… button in Safari's Privacy preferences so you can see the cookies on your machine. (See Figure 7-2.)

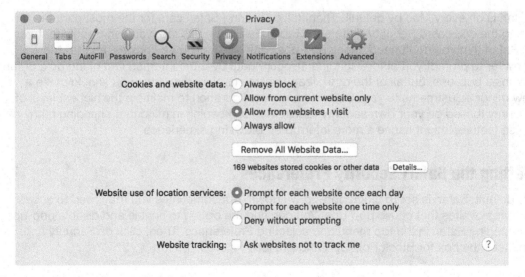

Figure 7-2. Privacy preferences for Safari

By default, Safari accepts cookies from every site that wants to give them to you. To configure Safari to accept cookies only from sites that you visit, while in Security preferences, choose "Only from websites I visit" in the "Cookies and website data" section. Safari gives the user the ability to limit cookies rather than disabling them, and for good reason: disabling cookies can cause annoying compatibility issues with more advanced web sites.

Windows has had a hard time with browser plug-ins. This is one area where your surfing can seem to come to a crippling halt in a Windows environment because of plug-ins that waste system resources, including those not related to browsing the Internet. For debatable reasons, browser plug-ins have not been a huge concern on the Mac platform. You can see which browser plug-ins have been installed in Safari by clicking Help and selecting Installed Plug-ins. If you take a look at the list that appears, you'll likely notice that nearly all the plug-ins are Apple-related (for example, related to QuickTime or iPhoto). If you notice a browser plug-in that you suspect is dangerous, navigate to the /Library/Internet Plug-Ins folder in your user folder and delete it.

> **Note**   Some older third party plug-ins, such as the Shockwave plug-in, are already integrated into Safari.

Safari can also protect against the installation of unwanted software. When you download new software through Safari and try to run it for the first time, you will receive a message alerting you that the software is an application downloaded from the Internet. You'll also be asked whether you're sure you want to open it. You can click Cancel here, which will stop the software from being opened. One of the most dangerous things you can do on your computer is to allow rogue software applications to be installed. Pay attention to this window, as this feature (only available on Leopard and Snow Leopard) will help you protect against unsolicited software being installed on your system. For more on Malware, see Chapter 8. You can also see our article at www.afp548.com/article.php?story=20090826235425679 for a little more information on the built-in malware safeguards in Mac OS X.

Privacy and Safari

Clearing out all of the caches, history, downloads, and cookies on your system keeps prying eyes from finding them. However, this can be annoying, because it may require you to re-enter passwords for some sites, which, if you're like the rest of us, you may have forgotten. These can be stored in iCloud Keychain, making them more persistent. But clearing this information will also reset the history information, thus clearing out your auto-complete functionality for recently visited and non-bookmarked web sites. You can reset Safari at any time by selecting the Clear History option in the Apple menu. You'll be presented with the timeframe to clear (see Figure 7-3).

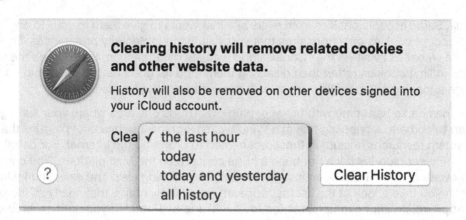

Figure 7-3. *Reset Safari options*

Securing Firefox

Firefox is a free, cross-platform, graphical web browser developed by the Mozilla Foundation with contributions from thousands of volunteers all over the world. Before its 1.0 release on November 9, 2004, Firefox had already garnered a great deal of acclaim from numerous media outlets, including *Forbes* and the *Wall Street Journal*. Firefox has now become more widely used than almost any other browser on the market, in large part because of the security features built into it (and because it isn't a hacker-targeted Microsoft product) and the cross-platform nature of the browser. For example, Figure 7-4 displays the rather powerful encryption features found in Firefox—features you're hard-pressed to find as easily configurable in other web browsers, easily located by entering about:config in the address bar of the browser.

Preference Name	Status	Type	Value
devtools.remote.tls-handshake-timeout	default	integer	10000
network.http.spdy.enforce-tls-profile	default	boolean	true
network.proxy.proxy_over_tls	default	boolean	true
security.tls.insecure_fallback_hosts	default	string	
security.tls.insecure_fallback_hosts.use_static_list	default	boolean	true
security.tls.unrestricted_rc4_fallback	default	boolean	true
security.tls.version.fallback-limit	default	integer	3
security.tls.version.max	default	integer	3
security.tls.version.min	default	integer	1
services.sync.prefs.sync.security.tls.version.max	default	boolean	true
services.sync.prefs.sync.security.tls.version.min	default	boolean	true

Search: tls

about:config

Firefox | about:config   Q Search

ℹ Firefox automatically sends some data to Mozilla so that we can improve your experience.   Choose What I Share ✕

Figure 7-4. *Firefox encryption features*

The about:config options provide access to hundreds of Firefox options.

Privacy and Firefox

One of the most compelling features of Firefox is its extensibility. There are numerous plug-ins available for Firefox. Luckily, the developers did not trade speed for security. Firefox gives users an impressive wide array of privacy options, allowing users to get pretty granular about configuring their privacy options. However, these options are not enabled by default. To enable them, click on the Privacy icon at the top of Firefox's preferences, and click on the drop-down menu next to "Firefox will." Select "Use custom settings for history" to change your browsing preferences.

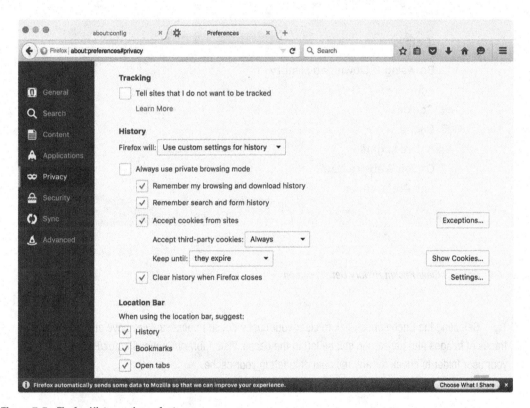

Figure 7-5. Firefox History privacy features

Clearing your recent history in Firefox works much like the Reset Safari feature, with the exception that it allows you to select which items will be reset, along with more fine-tuned control over what is reset. Remember, though, if you choose to reset your private data, you risk losing the information stored in the browser such as passwords, preferences, and auto-complete entries from previously viewed web sites, so make sure you choose these options carefully.

To clear private data in Firefox, click on the History menu and select the Clear Recent History option. This option opens the Clear Recent History screen (as shown in Figure 7-6). Click on the Details down-arrow to see a list of options for clearing data. You also have the option to select the range of time that you'd like your history deleted. This is especially useful for web sites with recent logins that you'd like to erase from the system. We recommend checking the following options: Browsing & Download History, Form & Search History, Cache and Active Logins.

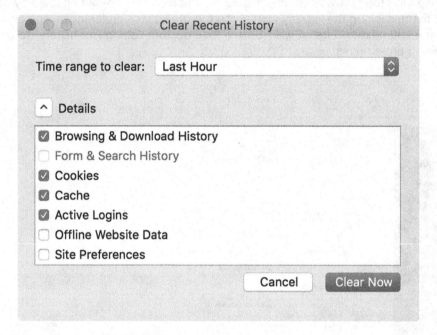

Figure 7-6. Firefox's Clear Recent History Details screen

Tip   Selecting the Cache check box to clear your cache doesn't necessarily remove all caches, and traces of images and pages can still be left in the cache. Visit /Library/Caches/Firefox/Profiles in your user folder to check for any residual data left in your cache.

Master Passwords in Firefox

If you allow Firefox to remember passwords for web sites and you share your computer with another user, you should set up a master password. Setting up a master password requires anyone visiting a web site on your computer to enter a master password every time a site tries to access your stored password information. A Firefox master password is not associated with any other program, creating a stand-alone secure environment within Firefox. This extra security layer will also keep your stored passwords safe in the event that someone else gains unauthorized access to your machine and visits web sites with highly sensitive information. If your user account is in any way compromised, your saved passwords within Firefox will not be revealed and the damage to your overall security footprint will be minimal. We highly recommend enabling this feature in your Security preferences. To do so, open Firefox's Preferences and select the Security tab. Then click the "Use a master password" check box. (See Figure 7-7).

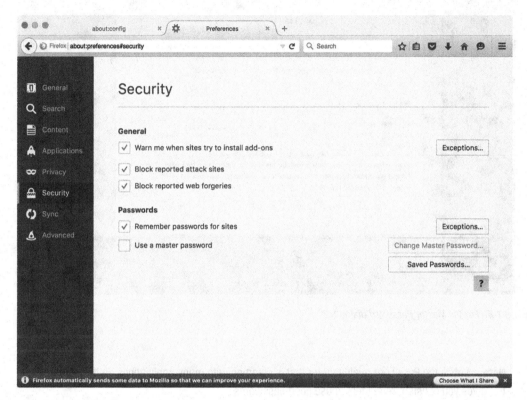

Figure 7-7. Firefox's Security preferences

You'll be presented with a dialog box asking for a new password and a confirmation of the new password (see Figure 7-8). Once you have set a password, you will be prompted for it the first time your system attempts to access the passwords stored by Firefox. This is similar to the keychain concept in Mac OS X, except that the password is contained within Firefox.

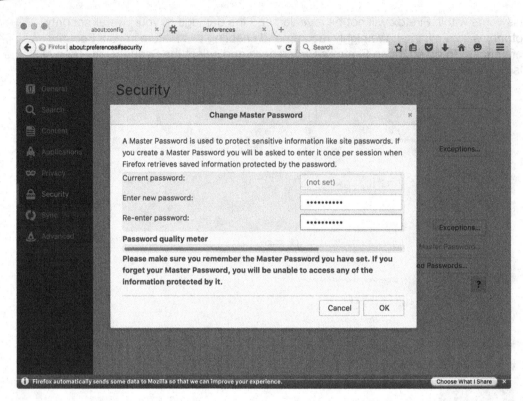

Figure 7-8. Firefox Master Password dialog box

> **Note**   Notice the Password quality meter that is common with many applications on this screen;
> this gives you constant reminders to use good passwords.

One of the dangers of Firefox is that passwords are stored rather insecurely by default if the master password option is not enabled. Firefox has the option to view saved passwords for web sites simply by opening Security preferences and clicking on the Saved Passwords button. Theoretically, it would be very easy for someone with access to your computer to open Password Manager, click a web site or fileserver for which they want to see the password, and then click the Show Passwords button to view it. Therefore, when you use the master password option, make the password a good one.

Thankfully, it is possible to stop Firefox from caching passwords for specific sites or fileservers. To do this, go to the Security preferences pane and click on the Saved Passwords button. Because you've entered a master password already, it will ask you for your master password. Once that's been entered, you'll be presented with a list of Firefox's cached information for web sites (see Figure 7-9). Then, click on the Show Passwords button at the bottom of the window to display the cached passwords.

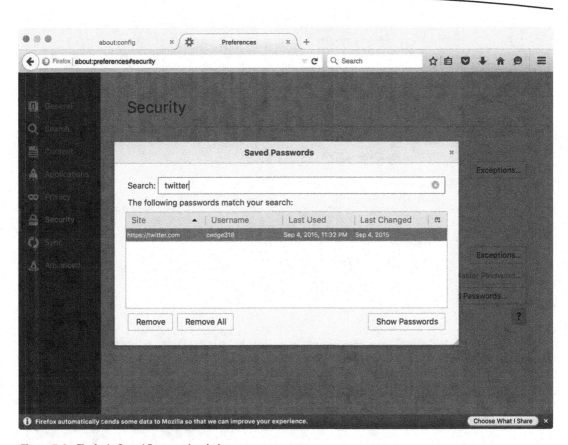

Figure 7-9. Firefox's Saved Passwords window

If you see a site in the list that you don't want Firefox to cache, you can remove it using the Remove button. The next time you visit that site, Firefox will ask again whether you want to cache that password for future access. You should click the Never button if you don't want Firefox to remember the password.

Once you are satisfied with Firefox's password security, let's move on to configuring other security features, such as pop-up windows. This is addressed on the Content option of the Firefox preferences (see Figure 7-10). Here, uncheck the box for Block Pop-up Windows setting to block pop-ups.

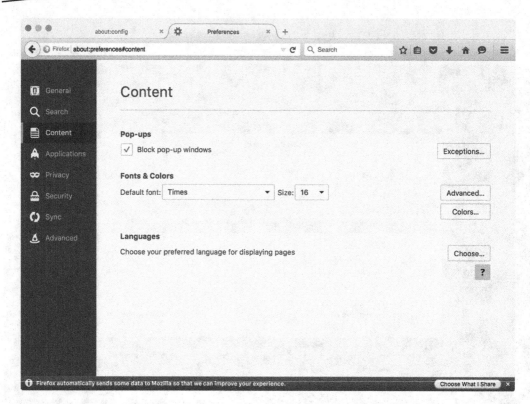

Figure 7-10. Firefox Content tab

There are a number of other settings that can also be configured in Firefox by visiting the about:config page (simply type about:config in the address window of Firefox). Here, you will see a granular run-down of every setting available. This provides a wealth of further customization that can be done, which goes beyond the scope of this chapter. The settings that are configured in the about:config page and in the preferences that we have covered throughout this section are then stored in a Firefox-centric profile. However, if you choose to customize these settings, you should document what you have changed because altering the settings can cause unintended consequences.

Firefox does not conform to a number of Mac OS X standards in terms of how it is developed. This can cause annoyances in a few places. First, Mac OS X is, by design, a multiuser operating system, and so the concept of having multiple profiles within a single user account, while a nice feature, can be difficult to manage. Next, the preferences for Firefox are not stored in standard Apple preferences files (called *property lists*). This can cause a number of headaches when attempting to interact with those preferences from a programming perspective, or when you are looking to perform a mass deployment. (To see how this is done, check out our tech article at www.318.com/techjournal/mass-deployments/mass-deploying-firefox-preferences-for-mac-os-x/) Therefore, you will need to edit a prefs.js file rather than a property list or, depending on the setting, perhaps even an sqlite database, all of which can be found within that profile. Finally, the profile itself isn't consistently named. Profiles are stored in ~/Library/Application Support/Firefox/Profiles; however, they are created with generic names and tracked in the profiles.ini file in that same directory. Any scripting that must be done around Firefox therefore needs to take that into account.

When working with Firefox, you can build changes into your actual application, rather than into profiles. These changes made on the application level can break during the next Firefox update, and will surely break the Application Layer Firewall's ability to interact with Firefox because the signature for the application bundle will have changed (you will need to allow Firefox to access a socket again) We discuss the Application Layer Firewall (ALF) in more depth in Chapter 11.

Securely Configuring Mail

While browsers are important, they are not the only target on your system. You also need to consider practicing good mail security. Different mail protocols have different levels of security. The default settings for most web hosts now include more secure protocols than the traditional POP and SMTP protocols. Mail.app has also been set up to allow for more protection of passwords in transit and more secure encryption protocols.

Using SSL

As we mentioned before, protecting passwords and confidential information while in transit is accomplished through the use of SSL. SSL should be used in the transport of e-mail as well.

> **Note** Web sites typically use port 443 for SSL. However, when you are using SSL with e-mail protocols such as IMAP, the port can be different. Figure 7-11 illustrates how IMAP might use a different port when secured using SSL.

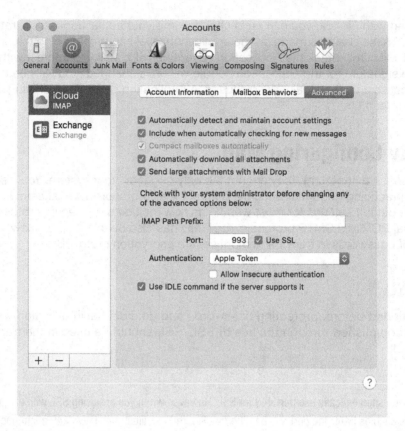

Figure 7-11. Apple Mail's port settings for SSL

Sometimes with SSL you'll be asked to verify the authenticity of a server every time you open your e-mail client. This often has to do with the SSL certificate of your mail host being self-signed. Self-signed SSL certificates typically need to manually be "trusted" (which means you have to click on the Trust sign when the certificate pops up) when you are visiting a site. If you choose not to trust a certificate, then SSL will not allow you to communicate over the secure channel to that host.

> **Tip**   If you are required to accept the certificate every time you visit a site, you can add the site as a secure certificate in Safari by opening the Keychain Access utility and dragging the certificate onto the Keychain Access icon in the dock. You can manage the certificate within Keychain Access.

Now that your communications have been protected using SSL, let's look at how your password is actually sent over the wire. POP is a protocol used for downloading mail from a mail server. IMAP is a protocol used to synchronize mail between a mail client and a mail server.

POP and IMAP are merely protocols for accessing data; they do not instruct a client on how to actually authenticate into the remote host. For this, there are a variety of protocols including MD5, NTLM, KPOP, APOP, GSSAPI, Kerberos, and Password (PlainText). In the realm of layered security, the most important thing to know here is that you need to contact your mail provider and find out exactly what protocols are supported. If it does not support a protocol, you will not be able to use it.

> **Note**   Often the only way to get your Internet service provider (ISP) to introduce support for a new protocol is to request it. When enough people request it, an ISP will find a way to support the protocol.

Some of the mail authentication options are configurable in the SMTP settings, as shown in Figure 7-12. Keep in mind that if your username and password for SMTP are the same as your information for POP and you use SSL for SMTP but not for POP, then you are still potentially exposing your passwords.

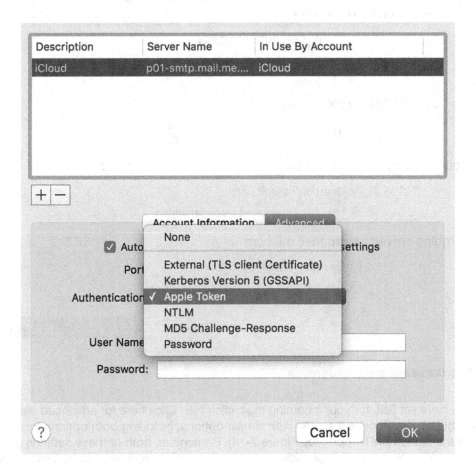

Figure 7-12. Apple Mail's authentication settings

Securing Outlook

You can configure Microsoft Outlook to use SSL in much the same way as Mail. Open your accounts (listed under the Tools menu in Outlook), and choose the account you want to use SSL to secure. On the Account Settings screen, click the "Click here for advanced receiving options" button, and then select the "This IMAP service requires a secure connection (SSL) box."

If your service provider runs IMAP or POP on customized ports, then select the "Override default IMAP" option (or POP, if you are using POP). You can always opt to use the "Always use secure password," which will force encryption on the password when you are checking e-mail (see Figure 7-13).

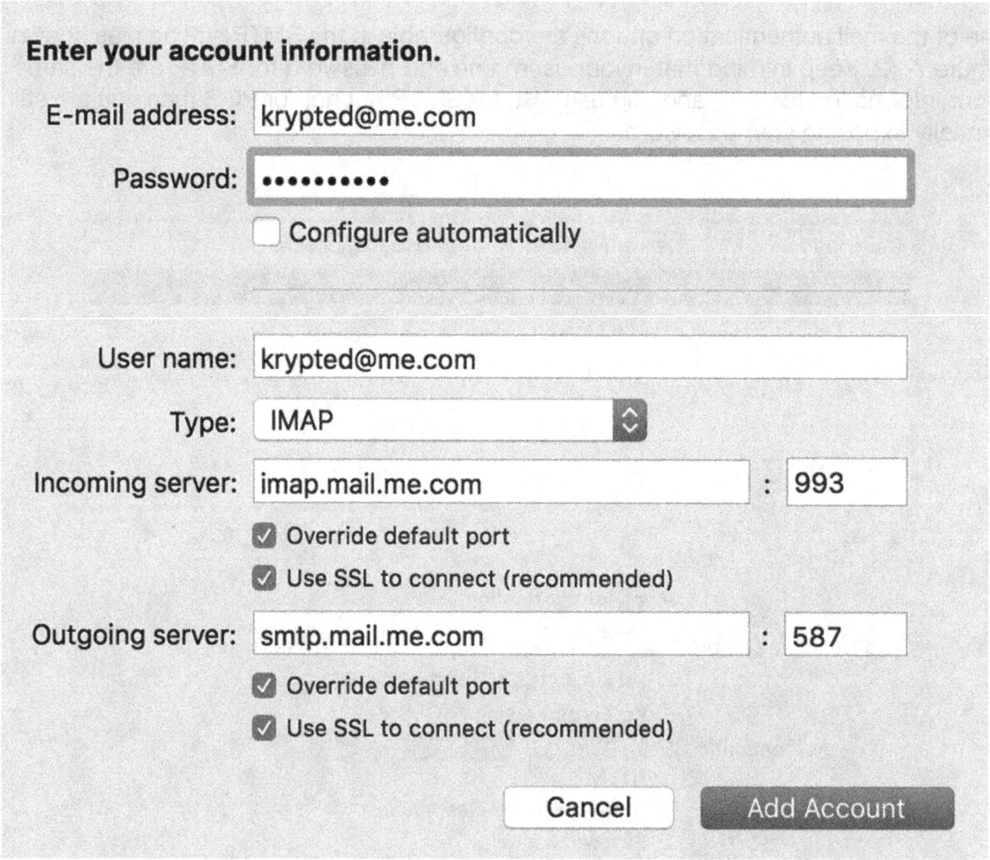

Enter your account information.

E-mail address:	krypted@me.com
Password:	••••••••••
	☐ Configure automatically

User name:	krypted@me.com
Type:	IMAP
Incoming server:	imap.mail.me.com : 993
	☑ Override default port
	☑ Use SSL to connect (recommended)
Outgoing server:	smtp.mail.me.com : 587
	☑ Override default port
	☑ Use SSL to connect (recommended)

Cancel   Add Account

Figure 7-13. Outlook advanced receiving options

Once you have set SSL for your incoming mail, click the "Click here for advanced sending options" button. This opens a screen with similar options, including both options for using SSL and the default SMTP port (see Figure 7-14). Remember, both of these settings are specific to your Internet service provider's mail server settings and need to be verified with them before they can be applied.

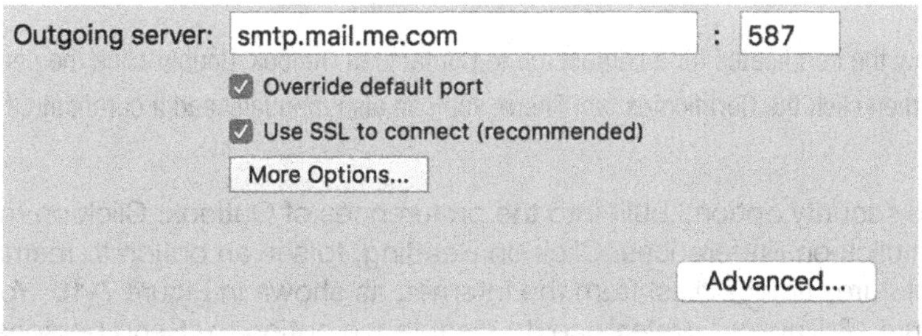

Outgoing server: smtp.mail.me.com   : 587
☑ Override default port
☑ Use SSL to connect (recommended)
More Options...

Advanced...

Figure 7-14. Outlook advanced sending options

Many ISPs are now blocking access to mail being sent over port 25, the default port for SMTP without SSL. One unintended benefit to using SSL is that, once you have set your computer to send mail over SMTP using SSL, you will often no longer run into issues with getting your e-mail blocked when trying to send mail. One unintended annoyance is that you now may have to manage certificates for your mail by accepting, denying, or importing certificates.

To add a different user's certificate to your cached certificates in Outlook, open an e-mail that has been digitally signed, click the Info Bar, and click the View Details button. This opens a screen for viewing a user's certificate data, shown in Figure 7-15.

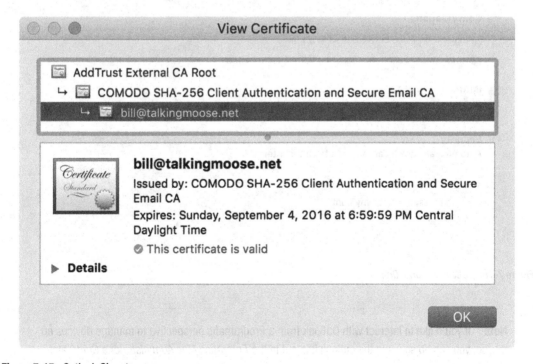

Figure 7-15. Outlook Signatures

> **Tip**   To view the certificates for a contact, go to Contacts in Outlook, double-click the person's name, and then click the Certificates tab. There, you can also manually add a certificate if needed.

You have some security options built into the preferences of Outlook. Click on the Outlook menu and then click on Preferences. Click on Reading, to see an option to restrict downloading pictures (image files) from the Internet, as shown in Figure 7-16. You can also open the "Security & Privacy" preference, to disable the option to "Send personal information to Microsoft to make improvements to Office." While I'm a fan of improving products, the fact that it indicates personal information rather than anonymous information is concerning.

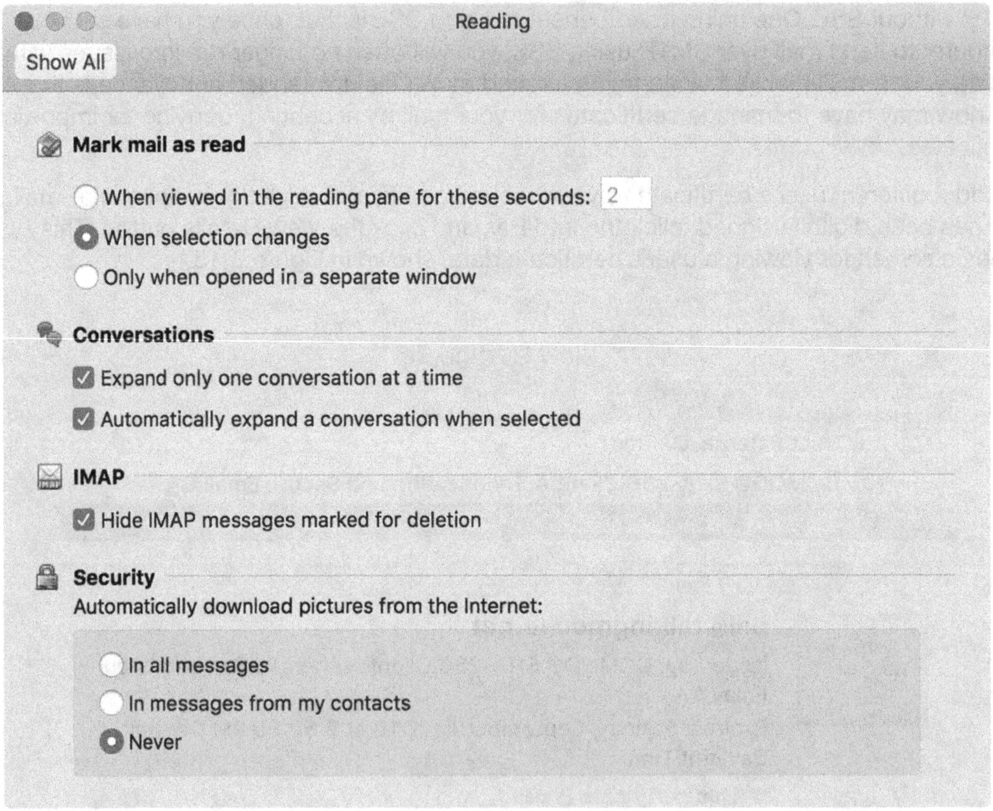

Figure 7-16. Outlook Security Options

> **Note**   If you'd like to interact with Outlook from a Programatic perspective to manage devices en masse, you can do so using the options laid out in the *Enterprise Mac Administrator's Guide*, also from Apress.

Fighting Spam

Our good friends at Wikipedia said it best, "Spamming is the abuse of electronic messaging systems to indiscriminately send unsolicited bulk messages." Spam often involves sending identical or nearly identical messages to hundreds, thousands, and even millions of recipients. Addresses of recipients are often harvested from chain e-mail letters or web pages, obtained from databases, or guessed by using common names and domains. Spam is not just an irritation; it costs corporations, educational institutions, and governmental agencies in the United States alone tens of millions of dollars in lost operations and productivity each year.

An entire industry of software has risen up to help fight spam (much as an entire industry lurks to send spam). On the Mac, the products are limited, and for desktop users we will primarily focus on the built-in spam prevention of Microsoft Outlook and Apple Mail.

The Anatomy of Spam

Before we move on, a bit about the structure of an e-mail as it pertains to spam: An e-mail message has a collection of headers within the e-mail. These include Sender, CC (Carbon Copy), To, Date, and X-Spam-Status. Outside servers that perform spam filtration will assign X-Spam headers. This is meant to make it easier for mail clients to scan messages for spam quickly. The X-Spam-Status contains, among other information, a numerical score (from 0 to 10) that indicates the likelihood that a message is spam. E-mail programs that support the use of the X-Spam headers will compare this score against the score that has been determined as an acceptable risk. When configuring this setting on a mail server, it's important to set the threshold value somewhere in the middle, as it is possible for legitimate messages to get filtered out, causing what is known as a *false positive*.

The headers can be accessed using the rule sets of Entourage and Mail.app. Now let's discuss how to configure our mail clients to deal effectively with spam.

Filtering Apple Mail for Spam

To enable the built-in spam filter in Apple Mail, enter the Mail's Preferences and click the Enable Junk Mail Filtering checkbox. From here, you can instruct Mail on what it should do with the spam using the When Junk Mail Arrives options (see Figure 7-17). Then, select which types of messages will not be filtered. This is where you would configure the client to flag as safe, e-mail coming from entries in your address book, mail coming from people on the previous recipients list, or mail that was addressed using your full name.

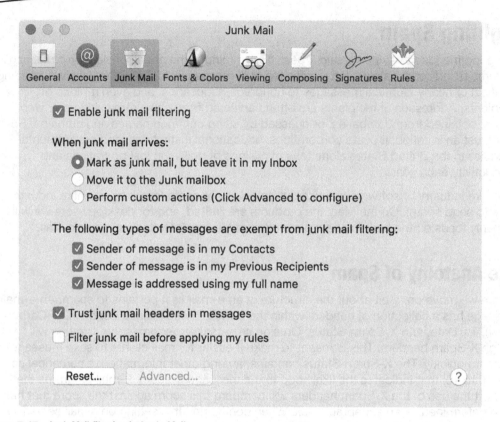

Figure 7-17. Junk Mail filtering in Apple Mail

Within Apple Mail, you also have the ability to select whether to trust junk mail headers. Use the Reset button of the Junk Mail preference panel of Mail preferences to reset the junk mail filter. This will undo any other settings you've made to the filter (such as marking certain e-mails as junk mail).

To make custom rules for your Junk Mail, click on the "Perform custom actions" button and then click on the Advanced button at the bottom to build custom rules (see Figure 7-18). You can also merge criteria to build very specific rule sets.

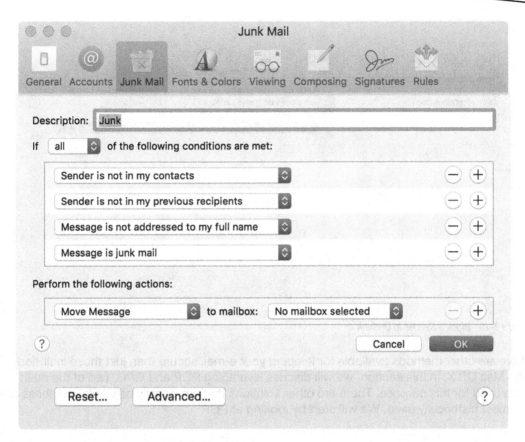

Figure 7-18. Junk mail advanced settings in Apple Mail

> **Note** On the server side of things, the mail server will apply junk mail headers if the mail server is configured to scan mail for spam. More on configuring server spam filters later.

Filtering with Outlook

Outlook, like all modern email programs, also has a built-in spam filter. However, most of the spam management for Outlook will be done within Exchange or Office 365, and any work on the client computer is typically to whitelist or blacklist users. To block a user using the spam filter in Outlook, follow these steps (see Figure 7-19):

1. Click on the account you'd like to block a user for.

2. Select Tools, and click Junk E-Mail Protection.

3. At the Junk screen, click on the Blocked Senders tab.

4. Click on the plus sign (+) in the lower left corner of the screen.

5. Enter the email address of the sender you wish to block.

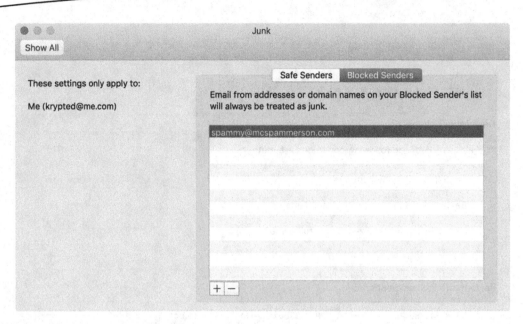

Figure 7-19. Block a Sender in Outlook

There are other methods available for keeping your e-mail secure than just those included with Mac OS X. In this section, we will discuss leveraging PGP and GPG, two of the main tools used for this purpose. There are other solutions that are equally as viable, but these are the most historically used. We will start by looking at PGP.

Desktop Solutions for Securing E-mail

There are other methods available for keeping your e-mail secure than just those included with Mac OS X. In this section, we will discuss leveraging PGP and GPG, two of the main tools used for this purpose. There are other solutions that are equally as viable, but these are the most historically used. We will start by looking at PGP.

Using PGP to Encrypt Mail Messages

PGP Desktop, developed by Phil Zimmerman originally and now available through Symmantec, is an encryption suite (see Chapter 9 for more information on encryption and more specifically at using PGP for full disk encryption) that will encrypt e-mail messages, files, and folders before they are sent. It can be downloaded and purchased at www.pgp.com. PGP Desktop can also be used to encrypt instant messaging traffic in Messages, beyond what is available using the default security options in Messages, and can also encrypt full disks and sign messages so a recipient can verify the authenticity of people sending them email.

GPG Tools

GPG (or GnuPG, downloadable from `www.gnupg.org`) is much like PGP; it allows users to encrypt files and e-mail. It is different in that GPG, and the suite of tools built around it, is open source. GPG is not as feature rich as PGP but does have some compelling features in that it works well with `Mail.app` and, of course, it's free.

To get started with GPG, you will first need to download GnuPG and install it. Once you've installed GnuPG, download and install GPGMail. The most recent releases of both are available at `https://gpgtools.org`. Once you install them, you will see new fields in your `Mail.app` client when you are ready to send mail.

Summary

The Internet has become crucial to our lives as a means of communicating with our friends, family and colleagues. As we've shown, securing our web browsers and e-mail from possible attackers by encrypting our communications is critical for maintaining our identities and financial information in this digital age. In the next chapter, we'll discuss the controversial topic of malware as it relates to Macs and how to combat this threat to Mac OS X.

8

Malware Security: Combating Viruses, Worms, and Root Kits

To many, the very mention of protecting a Mac against malware is actually a pretty inappropriate conversation. But it's an obsession to many at Apple. And because they do a pretty darn good job of protecting users, there's not a lot of concern that needs to be had. However, some caution goes a long way in case things get through Apple's vaunted defense system. That build-in defense system includes technologies like Xprotect, which is like a built-in signature-based anti-virus solution, LSQuarantine, which marks anything downloaded as protected, SIP, which protects Apple's protected space and drivers from infection by third party software, and a robust signing requirement, which makes it difficult for a user to get malware on their system. But it can happen, so we'll look at what you need to do when it does.

In this chapter, we will discuss protecting your Mac from malware. The best way to do so is to run software update frequently. This protects against all of the modern, known threats, including Shellshock, Heartbleed, Poodle, Thunderstrike, Freak SSL, Logjam, and more. Because of Xprotect, when Apple sees a security threat, they can mitigate that threat. And if they need to upgrade a component to mitigate the threat (e.g. Shellshock), only a software update can do that. There are a lot of other techniques to combatting malware, though.

Before we get into combatting malware, what do we mean by malware? *Malware* is a term used by security professionals to reference any software that is designed to infiltrate or damage computer systems without the owner's informed consent. "Informed" is the key word here. A user might consent by clicking an Accept dialog box to allow a software package to install, but might not be fully informed of the vulnerabilities that can potentially be exploited by that software package. Beta versions of new software can sometimes have potentially damaging effects on an operating system, but would not be considered malware because they generally don't intend to harm the operating system (*intend* the operative word here). What we will explore in this chapter are the ill effects that can arise from unintentionally installed software on a Mac, and how to safeguard your machine from them.

Classifying Threats

When discussing how to combat malware threats, it's important to distinguish between the different kinds of threats that can exist on a Mac. To most users, a virus is something that threatens productivity on a machine, and the term is frequently used to classify all malware. But it is important to make the distinction between the two. *Malware* is the overarching term used by security professionals to reference certain kinds of hindrances to the operating system, while a *virus* is just one form of malware. What distinguishes a virus from other forms of malware is the ability to replicate and spread to other files on a computer, thereby infecting them. However, a virus will infect files only on a single computer; it will not automatically copy its code and spread itself to other computers on a network. It can, however, be spread to other computers by infecting files on a network or files on a removable hard drive. This is what distinguishes a virus from a worm.

Worms are not classified as viruses. Worms spread themselves through network connections by automatically copying themselves onto other computers using the security flaws of the target computers. There is a commonly held misconception that Macs cannot be harmed by malware. However, there are indeed worms and other forms of malware that can and do affect Macs. In February 2006, OSX.Leap.A, a Mac worm, spread across the Internet over iChat and infected client computers. The distribution of OSX.Leap.A across the Internet, like many malware threats for OS X, was relatively low. But for those who were infected, the cleanup was a disaster because many applications on the infected systems were hopelessly corrupted, along with their user-specific preferences files.

> **Note**   Most worm threats have a *payload*, the malicious code or program carried out by the worm. If this payload is written in a language that a Mac cannot speak, then the payload will not be able to run, and the worm will not infect the computer. Some threats have a payload that will lie dormant until something triggers its release.

A *Trojan horse* is malicious code embedded within a self-contained application that becomes destructive only when an infected application is opened. Trojans closely resemble viruses because both can cause damage when a file is infected. However, a virus is added to an application after the application is written, whereas a Trojan horse is written, created, and distributed as a single application for the sole purpose of getting you to open it to then allow it to do whatever it wants to with your files. Trojan horses can be used to erase files, get passwords, and send e-mail to other users. The threat to Macs here is real. iWorkServices and Jahlav are two examples of Trojans developed specifically for the Mac. Mac systems can also be carriers of Trojans designed for PC, and can very easily pass them along to PCs through filesharing and the like.

A *logic bomb* is a threat resembling a Trojan horse, but it's architected to initiate when a specific event occurs. Logic bombs are brought into the operating system on the coattails of a virus or a worm, containing the payload that will be launched when the trigger event occurs. It is a ticking time bomb ready to go off on a scheduled date or after being resident in the operating system for a certain period of time. In some cases, programmers have been known (and have been indicted) for deploying logic bombs into their own code in order to make more work for their clients and to change the stock prices for their companies.

A *Backdoor* is an exploitable opening within an application's code. Backdoors are usually designed for the purpose of program debugging by programmers. They're similar to Trojan horses; however, they're meant to troubleshoot bugs in programming code rather than intentionally inflict harm on a machine. Typically, they are merely forgotten entryways accidentally included with the software's final release. Firewalls can sometimes stop a Backdoor from entering the system, but usually the best way to combat these vulnerabilities is to continually update the software with any updates available from the software manufacturer.

A *zombie* is a system that has been remotely triggered to perform a task. Often the tasks zombies perform allow an attacker to originate their attacks from another system undetected. An attacker can also build a virtual army of zombies to attack a target. Zombies, also referred to as *drones*, are often used to perpetrate Denial of Service (DoS) attacks and Distributed Denial of Service (DDoS) attacks. Trinoo and Tribe Flood Network are examples of DDoS attacks created for Unix variants and Windows computers. Another task you see on zombie systems these days is to mine for bitcoins (which might be the only way to get rich with bitcoins).

A *retrovirus* is designed to attack a machine's backup topology. It will wait until all your backup media is infected with the virus before it performs any actions that can cause damage. This makes it impossible to restore the system to an uninfected state once the computer has been infected. Retroviruses are designed to avoid detection by antivirus software. Many of the malware types described in this chapter are available for the Mac, but we have yet to see a retrovirus for Retrospect, PressSTORE, CrashPlan, BakBone, or any other application used to back up a Mac. However, a few specific attacks against Retrospect have been reported, usually exploiting weak passwords.

> **Note**   Retroviruses are not named after Retrospect, the popular backup application from EMC. They're actually named after their biological counterparts which masquerade as a component of one's DNA.

A *macro virus* is a virus attack designed to exploit applications that have the ability to create mini-programs, called *macros*, within documents. Microsoft Word and Microsoft Excel are examples of software that can create these dangerous documents. Thus, most of the known macro viruses in existence are designed for Microsoft Office (even though there are macro viruses such as BadBunny designed for OpenOffice). And these macro viruses are cross-platform, found on both Macs and PCs and can have damaging effects on both Windows and Mac machines.

Table 8-1 summarizes the types of threats discussed in this section.

Table 8-1. *Threat Breakdown*

Threat	Description	Vulnerability for a Mac
Virus	Program that can copy itself and infect a computer without the permission or knowledge of the end user	Rare
Worm	Self-replicating computer program, often used to distribute malicious content, spreading through a computer network	Common
Trojan horse (Trojan)	Code inserted into an application that causes a program to perform actions not intended by the user	Common
Logic bomb	Malicious code triggered by a specific event such as a specific date and time	Rare
Backdoor	Forgotten debugging routines that can be exploited	Rare
Zombie	Remotely triggered applications running in the background of a system used to remotely execute code	Rare
Retrovirus	Attacks against backup systems	None yet
Macro virus	A virus written using the macro feature of macro-enabled software such as Microsoft Office and OpenOffice and then deployed using office documents	Common
Rootkits	A software program written to control an operating system while remaining hidden	Common

The Real Threat of Malware on the Mac

A program called Elk Cloner is credited with being the first computer virus to spread to other computers outside of the lab in which it was created. Since then, viruses and other malware have become increasingly rampant on the Internet, in both commercial and home networks, and have caused billions of dollars in lost productivity. The MyDoom worm alone was estimated by mi2g, a global risk specialist, to have cost $43.9 billion in damages worldwide. This is equivalent to the total revenue earned by GM in the first quarter of 2007.

In March 1999, an e-mail worm named Melissa wreaked havoc across the Internet, so much so that companies unplugged their mail servers from their networks for days because of the flood of e-mail messages Melissa generated. In 2001, two more worms—Code Red and Nimda—generated so much traffic that administrators completely shut down their networks' connections to the Internet. In January 2003, a worm called, very simply, *worm*, imposed so much network traffic that it even sent ATM machines offline. Even Apple had a rather embarrassing incident where it shipped a batch of iPods that had been infected by RavMonE.exe, a backdoor that came from a Windows computer located within Apple's manufacturing line.

Malware are very real threats. And contrary to popular belief, the Mac is not immune to them. Don't believe the community hype. Get antivirus software for your Mac. Yes, it is far more likely that you will suffer from file corruption from a malware attack while working on a Windows machine, but the Mac is still prone to infection. But be realistic about how bad an impact that threats can actually have on a Mac.

Macs typically are "silent" carriers of malware. Most of the time, these come in the form of macro viruses. Many Mac users won't discover that they have a macro virus until a PC user (or more likely, a network administrator) informs them that they were sent one. These viruses are typically written to exploit security holes in Microsoft application software and operating systems. Because Macs at their core are fundamentally different from Windows machines, these viruses won't have the same effect on the Mac and may go unnoticed for a while. But they will attach themselves to outgoing e-mails sent by the e-mail program and infect files sent to friends, colleagues, clients, and family. For example, many viruses are written to specifically attack Microsoft Office for Windows. When an infected file is moved from a Mac to Windows, because of the lack of some security features of Office in the Mac environment, the Mac user may "carry" the virus within the infected file and not even know it until it is passed to a Windows machine. Most commonly, the virus may infect Microsoft Word's normal.dot file, on which all new Word documents are based. This will cause all new Word files created by the infected computer to be infected with the macro virus. The virus may not affect the computer in any other way. This is the case with the most common virus seen on the Mac for almost a decade, the W97M virus, which is a strain of the original Melissa virus from 1997.

> **Tip** If your machine detects the W97M virus, immediately delete the normal.dot file to keep future new documents from becoming infected when created.

There are ways to prevent infecting your Mac with a macro virus. For example, if you open a Word document with macros enabled, you will usually receive an alert letting you know the file has macros. If you receive a macro alert, take a minute to check that document out a little more thoroughly. In fact, check it for viruses (you do have antivirus software running on your Mac, right?) Word will even allow you to examine the macro to see what it does before opening the document. This will help you keep macros that can damage Word and Excel on your computer at bay and keep your office installation at an optimal performance level.

But the real threat of malware on the Mac isn't any of this stuff, it's all of it. And the best protection lies in user education. A user has to accept running any malicious code. If no one ever accepts malicious code, then the system is typically safe.

Script Malware Attacks

For now, Automator is probably the most underutilized and underappreciated gem of the OS X operating system. It is OS X's personal robot, designed to eliminate some of the repetitive tasks that we all must perform while working on our Macs by essentially "automating" them. It is a major time-saver. It can also be a huge malware headache. Automator relies heavily on workflows that are built with *scripts*, which are automatic functions that tell your computer what to do. You can probably deduce that viruses work the same way: they are scripts that tell your computer what to do. For this reason, Automator workflows are huge security risks and should be treated with caution. E-mailing workflows as attachments should be attempted only with extreme caution, simply because the potential for disastrous results from a user accidentally breaking the operating system by opening a poorly made Automator script is way too high. It is important to be conscious of what Automator workflows can do. Before running a workflow, understand exactly what it will do to the system. Only open Automator workflows built by people you trust.

The same is true for AppleScript and shell scripts (which can actually be even more dangerous, although they'd take a little more skill to perfect). Like Visual Basic in Microsoft Office, these two methods of scripting offer powerful functions that can be used to perform a variety of actions such as erasing drives, deleting files, and corrupting operating systems—dangerous operations that malware is famous for performing. With just one dangerous line of code, shell scripts can erase your hard drive while the operating system is running. Or an AppleScript might run a complicated find operation across the entire hard drive, deleting all files of a certain type. There is no undo command in the Terminal (which is where shell scripts originate), and because Terminal commands don't put files in the trash, when they're deleted, they're gone, headed for disk recovery.

Socially Engineered Malware

Gullibility and the good intentions of less-than-savvy users are the chief enablers of socially engineered viruses. These threats are completely based in social interaction. In other words, they do not spread without direct action from a user. E-mail hoaxes are prime examples of socially engineered malware. Typically, an e-mail hoax will contain a message instructing the user to perform an action on their computer, such as deleting certain key system files, which can seriously damage an operating system installation under the guise of making the computer run better. Also, users are often instructed to forward the message to others, allowing the malware to spread to other computers and to negatively impact the bandwidth demand on a network.

Here is an example of an e-mail hoax:

> TO: krypted@me.com
>
> Subject: !!!
>
> Merry Christmas everyone! Be careful out there. There is a new virus on America Online being sent by E-Mail. If you get anything called "Good Times", DON'T read it or download it. It is a virus that will erase your entire hard drive. In fact, you can search for Good Times on your computer and delete anything that looks bad. Forward this to all your friends. It may help them a lot.

Combating e-mail hoaxes is not a no-win situation. There are excellent web sites such as About.com, the McAfee Virus Hoax page, Snopes.com, or the Symantec Latest Threats page that will generally dispel the usefulness of the e-mail right away. Also, Googling the Internet with the exact words from the e-mail in quotes should be all that is required to determine whether a specific e-mail is a hoax. Some anti-spyware software will also combat some of these e-mail hoaxes.

Using Antivirus Software

Antivirus software has one primary function: to examine a system or a network for malware and either attempt to fix the files infected or remove the infected file from the system or network. Most antivirus packages include an auto-update feature that enables them to update their definitions for new threats as soon as they are discovered. But not all anti-virus software deals with malware in the same way. A wide variety of software packages are available for scanning, repairing, and thwarting malware threats on the Mac. In the following sections, we will talk about the general state of antivirus packages for the Mac, touch on a few of the antivirus packages out there, and discuss the pros and cons of how they deal with malware threats.

Built Into Mac OS X

There's a handy security feature built into OS X to help safeguard against some malware threats. In Leopard, Apple added a new quarantine function to the Launch Services API (which is still available), that intercepts new files coming in from supported applications (namely Safari) and scan them for potentially dangerous signatures (or patterns). When opened, a file that has been downloaded from the Internet will issue a warning. For example, if you download Firefox you will receive the error message shown in Figure 8-1.

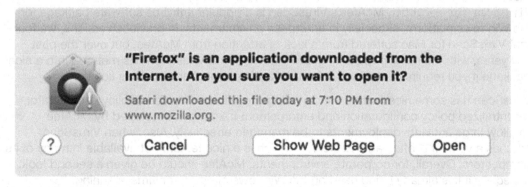

"Firefox" is an application downloaded from the Internet. Are you sure you want to open it?

Safari downloaded this file today at 7:10 PM from www.mozilla.org.

(?)   Cancel   Show Web Page   Open

Figure 8-1. Verify that you want to open a downloaded application

Clicking on the Open button would just allow you to open the application. But in OS X, if the signature matches the signature of a known piece of malware that is defined in the malware signatures, you receive a different error, telling you that the file will damage your computer and that you should move it to the Trash.

The signatures that are installed by default can be found in the /System/Library/ CoreServices/CoreTypes.bundle/Contents/Resources/Xprotect.plist property list, which includes a wonderful list of malware items that Apple has automatically decided you should not run on your computer. This allows other developers to extend signatures by adding more items into the XProtect.plist in Security Updates, or Apple may choose to deploy more items in subsequent software updates.

Antivirus Software Woes

Because malware on Macs are not as chronic as they are in the Windows environment, fewer antivirus products are available for the Mac than for the PC. In addition, those that do exist for the Mac are not as comprehensive, which is, to say the least, disconcerting. In fact, most of the antivirus applications for the Mac will not even clean a file infected (often infected files have valuable data in them removed by the malware); they will instead just quarantine the file with no other choice left but to delete it once quarantined. That is definitely not desirable when the file infected is valuable. Some programs will not even scan e-mail on a Mac, even though Mac users, like everyone else, can carry malware in their e-mail.

Virus definitions are files that tell the antivirus software what a virus will look like, how to clean the infected file when it's found (if the application allows for cleaning of the file), and how to remove the virus from the machine. An antivirus software package often cannot clean a virus unless it knows the signature of the virus within its definition. Only viruses that have been found by the vendor of the application can be cleaned. Therefore, you should regularly check for updates to your Mac antivirus packages.

McAfee VirusScan

VirusScan, from McAfee is one of the best overall centrally managed solutions for the Mac. Found at www.mcafee.com/us/enterprise/products/system_security/clients/ virusscan_for_mac.html, McAfee's VirusScan is a popular antivirus software package for the Windows platform, especially in enterprise environments. In previous versions, we found that VirusScan for Mac suffered from a lack of attention from McAfee, but over the past few years, with the rising popularity of the Mac platform, VirusScan has matured into a nice package if you require centralized command and control of an anti-virus solution.

VirusScan has some nice features. It can integrate with the McAfee ePolicy Orchestrator, a centralized policy configuration and enforcement framework developed by McAfee to allow large antivirus deployments to be managed effectively. Also, when VirusScan catches a virus, it is often able to clean it, which is a nice feature not available in many of its competitors. Overall, for corporate environments, McAfee should be given a second look, especially if it is already being used on the Windows platform for virus scanning.

Norton AntiVirus

Symantec has been cleaning up viruses for a long time. The company leads the way in virus research and mitigation. When new viruses rear their heads, the first place most savvy network engineers consult, no matter the platform, is the Symantec Latest Threats web site.

Symantec's Norton AntiVirus, available through most computer retailers for less than $50, will scan e-mail, automatically update virus definitions, scan files as they are accessed, scan files on demand, and clean up infected files. This makes Norton AntiVirus the most feature-rich product for virus scanning available on the Mac platform today. Symantec's Norton AntiVirus for the Mac also has the most frequently updated virus definition files for the Mac. For example, OSX.Leap.A, a zero-day exploit, was discovered on February 16, 2006, and added to the Norton AntiVirus definitions that same day.

Note   *Zero-day exploits* are released before, or on the same day as, the vulnerability—and, sometimes, the vendor patch—is released to the public. The term derives from the number of days between the public advisory and the release of the exploit.

Norton for Mac is available at `http://www.norton.com/mac`. Norton Antivirus, due to its popularity in the Windows community, is a well-known and well-documented antivirus application. Let's explore a couple lesser-known antiviral suites that pack some powerful features.

ClamXav

ClamXav is an antivirus application that is amongst the easiest to use. It is available at www.clamxav.com in a variety of languages. Although ClamXav lacks many of the features available in some of the commercial packages that are centrally manageable, it is a great and accessible tool that can be used as a first-line-of-defense warning system against malware. The underlying code is actually developed and distributed by the open source community as part of the ClamAV project. The GUI tools that ClamXav brings to the table can then be distributed to large numbers of users to help administrators discover virus outbreaks and perform quarantine measures on infected files.

ClamXav will not clean files; it only scans and quarantines them, which can be helpful on a machine with limited infection. However, on a system where a virus or worm has been self-propagating itself for days, weeks, and even years, this could mean that every single file that the user has ends up getting quarantined. This can cause hours of lost time in rebuilding a file structure to its original hierarchy. ClamXav also does not provide scanning for incoming e-mail, which, as previously discussed, is the primary method for distributing viruses on any computer platform.

Note   ClamXav should not be run on Mac OS X Server.

ClamXav is built on open source technology. At its core, it is a command-line utility, with a GUI built on top of it, allowing administrators to control it easily. You can also configure ClamAV, the back-end package of ClamXav, from the command line.

Installing ClamXav on OS X is fairly straightforward:

1. Download the installer at `www.clamxav.com`.

2. When the download is complete, double-click to open the disk image. Drag the icon from this window to the Applications folder. (See Figure 8-2.)

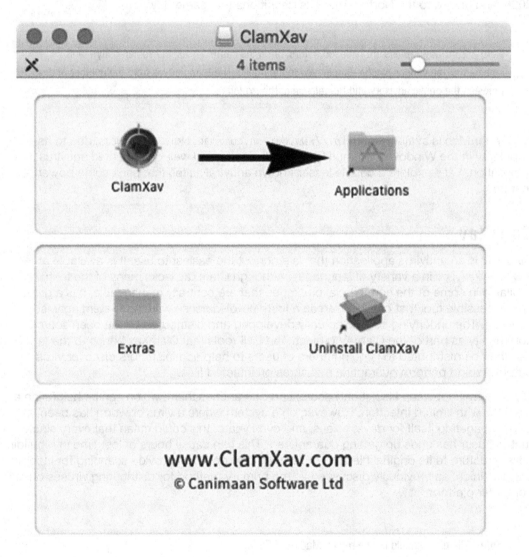

Figure 8-2. ClamXav install

3. Double-clicking the ClamXav icon in your Applications folder will open the license agreement screen, where you will need to click Agree.

4. At the Purchase screen, click Enter Registration if you have a license; otherwise click Free Trial for testing (See Figure 8-3).

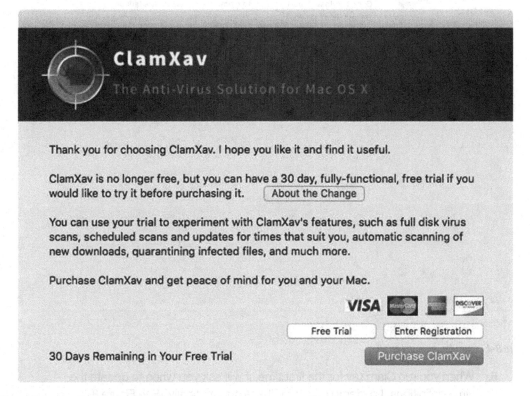

Figure 8-3. ClamXav License Screen

5. The next dialog box, shown in Figure 8-4, will ask you to install the ClamAV engine. Once the installer is finished, ClamXav is ready to run.

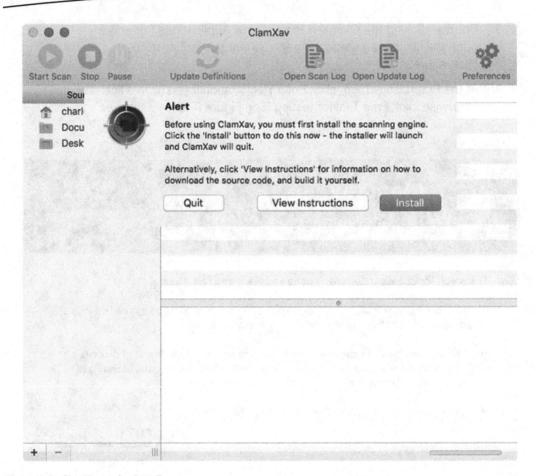

Figure 8-4. ClamXav engine install

6.   When you run ClamXav for the first time, it will ask you when to update the
     virus definitions. I prefer to check for these automatically. (See Figure 8-5.)

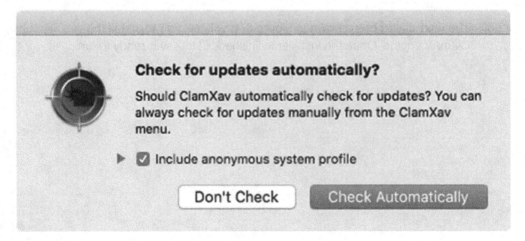

Figure 8-5. ClamXav virus definition update

Click Update Now to go ahead and run your first update.

The main ClamXav screen (shown in Figure 8-6) allows you to select items to scan, to start and stop scans, to review logs, and to set preferences for ClamXav.

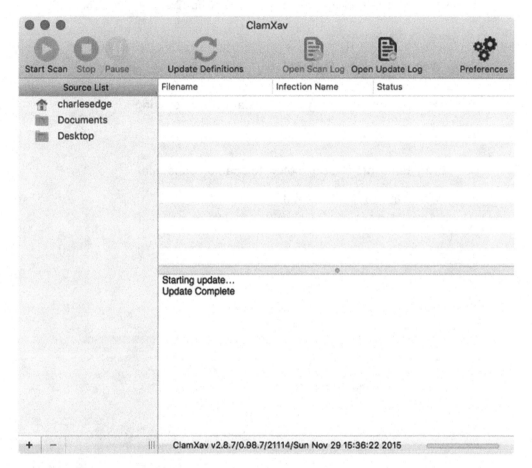

Figure 8-6. ClamXav virus scanner

You can click on the Start Scan button to run a 1-time scan at this point. To automate virus scanning, follow these steps (you can also automate virus definition updates here as well):

1. Click the Preferences button, and then click the Schedule tab of the Preferences screen.

2. Under the Scan pane (shown in Figure 8-7), you can either drag folder items into the pane or add items by clicking on the plus sign at the bottom to add items.

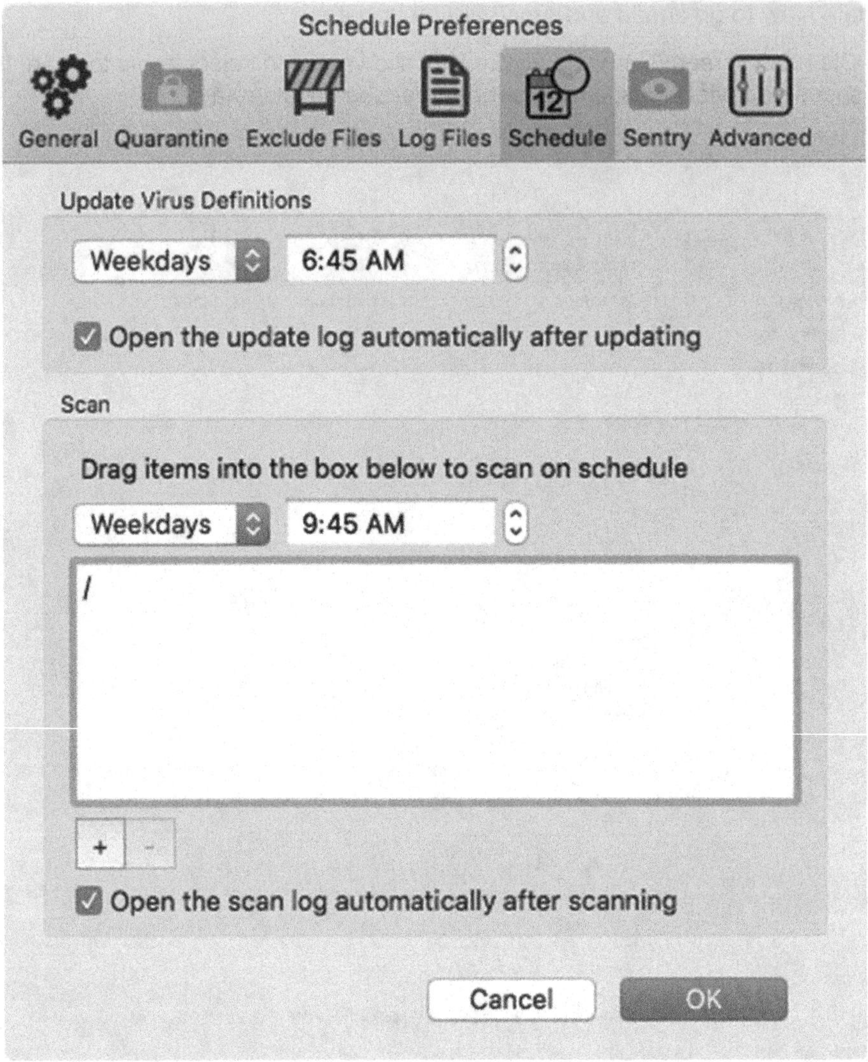

Figure 8-7. ClamXav schedule scan preferences

3. To schedule scans, click on the drop-down window to choose how often you'd like to scan. You can also change the time you'd like to scan. If you would like to get a report of any infected files at the end of the scan, you can check the Open the scan log automatically after scanning box.

4. Clicking OK will commit these changes the next time a scan or update is run.

The Folder Sentry is a nice feature that allows administrators to specify certain watch folders that, when changed, will automatically be scanned. This is good protection for those high-profile crucial document folders that must remain virus-free. The Folder Sentry application runs in the background and activates only when one of the watch folders has been edited. To add a watch folder, either drag the folder from a Finder window into the Folders Being Watched field or add it from the plus (+) sign below (see Figure 8-8). The "Scan inserted disks" option will scan all disks that are attached or mounted on the system. The "Launch ClamXav Sentry when you log in to this computer" option will add ClamXav Sentry to your users' Login Items, launched when the user logs in. The "Delete infected files" option will delete files that are infected automatically when they are detected. Use this option with caution because it is fairly dangerous to automatically delete files without knowing which files are being deleted. Most often, this option is best left unchecked. It's better to review your logs regularly, manually fixing files if they become infected.

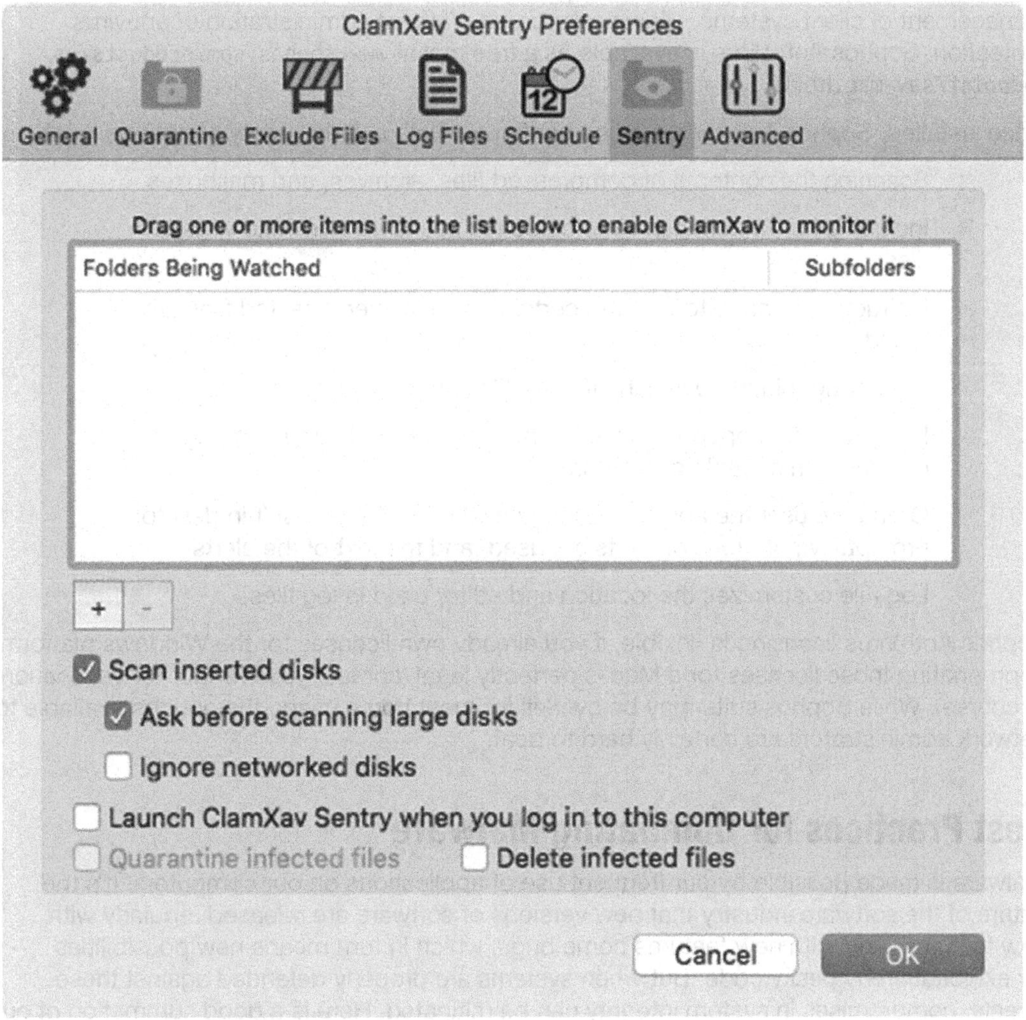

Figure 8-8. ClamXav Sentry Preferences

If you like the software, then we greatly encourage that you purchase it, as you can do much more automation through the command line, making it an excellent pairing with Casper, Munki, or another patch management tool, with or without a centralized management console.

Sophos Anti-Virus

For businesses, Sophos Anti-Virus for OS X is a popular and well-designed antivirus suite that can be purchased for the Mac as well as the PC. Sophos is a well-known leader in the enterprise security field, and its products, while a bit pricey, are some of the best in the industry. We like it because its virus definitions are very up-to-date, it quarantines infected files, and it has an automatic updater for virus definitions as well as disinfection capabilities, standard features for business-class antivirus programs. But what gives Sophos Anti-Virus for the Mac an edge is its unique ability to scale. It uses plug-in architecture integrated into the Sophos Enterprise Console (which requires a Windows computer) for the centralized management of client systems, allowing for cross-platform administration of antivirus protection. Sophos Anti-Virus is available as a free trial at `www.sophos.com/products/es/endpoint/sav-mac.html`.

Once installed, Sophos Anti-Virus can be configured with a wide variety of options, such as:

- Scanning the contents of compressed files, archives, and mailboxes.
- Including non-Macintosh virus detection scans for non-Mac viruses in files.
- Instructing Sophos to perform certain actions when infected files are found.
- Specifying folders to which infected files are moved or copied.
- Many reporting options, including naming of reports and merging of reports from multiple computers.
- Giving the user the ability to configure whether alerts result in desktop prompts, what types of alerts are used, and the text of the alerts.
- Log File customizes the location and editor used in log files.

Sophos Anti-Virus licensing is flexible, if you already own licenses for the Windows platform, appropriating those licenses for a Mac is perfectly legal (contact your vendor for verification, of course). While Sophos suite may be overkill for most home users, the options available for network administrators are certainly hard to beat.

Best Practices for Combating Malware

Malware is made possible by our frequent use of applications on our computers. It's the nature of the software industry that new versions of software are released regularly with new features. And with new features come bugs, which in turn means new possibilities for exploitation by pesky code. But when systems are properly defended against these threats, compromises in system integrity can be mitigated. Here is a good summation of our suggestions for best practices in combating malware.

Every Mac should have antivirus software installed on it, and you should run virus scans regularly to mitigate the damage that can be inflicted from an infection. Scheduled scans are also important to maintain the integrity of an antivirus solution. They often take a while, and it's sometimes very tempting to stop a scan while it's running, but without a regularly scheduled full system scan, you can never be 100 percent sure that a system is completely malware-free. Scanning for viruses and malware regularly, keeping the virus definitions up-to-date, and implementing the security updates regularly are all critical tasks for minimizing the likelihood of an infection.

You should also be wary of opening attachments such as Word documents, Excel spreadsheets, and even compiled applications without scanning them with antivirus software. Resist opening e-mail attachments from people you do not know. If a file requests that you enter an administrative password to your computer, it is a good idea not to open the attachment. Macs are very good about limiting the damage that can be done by malware, but once software is allowed through the administrative password gateway, practically anything can happen to the computer.

It is also easy to fall into the "false sense of security" trap that every administrator falls into after running virus scans: coming up virus-free and assuming the system is in the clear. Virus software is software like any other. As such, it can be compromised or corrupted, and it's entirely possible that the virus scanner is not catching everything. Therefore, you should test your e-mail scanner on a regular basis. There are test virus files that have no ill effects on your computer that can be downloaded and run on the machine. Web sites such as Eicar.org have good tests for anti-virus software integrity (www.eicar.org/anti_virus_ test_file.htm), but they shouldn't be relied on to detect all malware threats.

A complete antivirus solution should not only include a scan and quarantine process, but should also contain a cleaning/repairing component. For example, using ClamXav might yield 30 files in the quarantine, but you'll need another application to actually repair the files. At a minimum, using any of the malware utilities is a good idea because they offer an early warning system for malware infection.

Other Forms of Malware

Malware does not end with viruses. Adware and spyware are other forms of malware that can range from mere annoyances to rather dangerous identity infiltration.

Adware

The term *adware* refers to any software that displays advertisements, whether or not it does so with the user's consent. Adware applications may display advertisements as an alternative to taking payment. These classify as adware in the sense of advertising-supported software, but not as spyware. For software to be classified as adware, it must not operate covertly or mislead the user, and it should provide the user with a specific product or service.

There is nothing unethical about adware. It is a common and valid business practice for companies to advertise via adware. However, when adware attempts to operate stealthily in the background, it becomes spyware. For a good Adware product for the Mac, check out Malware Bytes at https://www.malwarebytes.org/antimalware/mac/.

Spyware

Spyware is classified as any software that covertly gathers information through an Internet connection without the user's knowledge, usually for advertising and marketing purposes. Once installed, spyware monitors Internet activity and transmits that information in the background to another party. It is usually covertly installed, allowing an attacker to gain access to your personal data or track your Internet usage and is often responsible for identity theft, password exposure, fraud, slow Internet activity, and sluggish computer performance. It is often bundled as a hidden component of free or shareware programs downloaded from the Internet.

It is a common misconception that spyware incidents on the Mac are not possible. Although it is true that they are less common and do not install themselves automatically simply by browsing certain web sites, as they do on Windows machines, spyware is a very real threat on any platform. Spyware merely needs to be installed to begin its information gathering and installation can take place using a variety of methods, most notably using files downloaded from web sites.

Because spyware attackers are rather skilled at what they do, as a community, operating system developers have been unable to completely eliminate spyware from ravaging systems. Practicing good browser security can help keep your system safe and secure. (We cover web browser security in more detail in Chapter 7.)

The most common application used to combat spyware on the Mac is MacScan. There are others, but they're not as widely distributed.

MacScan

MacScan by SecureMac is one example of a commercial program that can remove spyware and the data that spyware most commonly harvests on a Mac. MacScan checks for spyware in administrative applications running on a system and in web browser caches (see Figure 8-9), allowing the user to clean this data from the computer. MacScan is available at `http://macscan.securemac.com`.

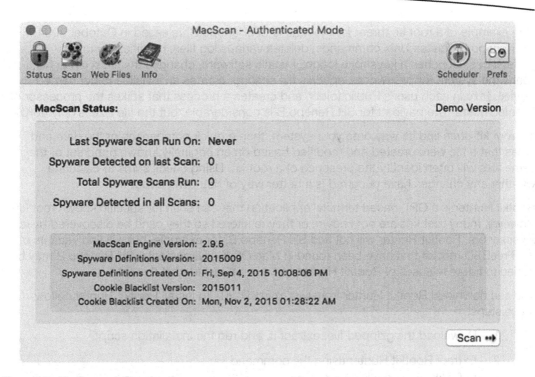

Figure 8-9. MacScan web files cleaner

It is important to point out that MacScan is a basic application, as are many of the spyware-oriented products for the Mac. The products available for the Windows platform such as Spybot Search & Destroy, Ad-Aware, and Spy Sweeper are far more advanced and feature-rich. This is primarily because of the widespread nature of spyware in the Windows environment and the rarity of spyware within the OS X community.

Spyware attacks on the Mac is rare, but they do happen, and staying proactive against this threat takes very little work to be effective. Regularly running an antispyware program such as MacScan can help keep spyware off your computer and provide due diligence for maintaining a spyware-free Mac.

Root Kits

Root kits act like spyware, but are typically much more dangerous. The difference between Rootkits and Spyware lies in the intent. Root kits are specifically designed to allow an attacker to gain hidden unauthorized access to a computer to compromise the integrity of the system. A root kit can be installed on a computer in a variety of ways and will provide those with access unlimited access to the machine as a result. The primary objective of many root kits is to evade detection by the operating system. As such, they often masquerade as other applications in order to hide themselves.

One example of a root kit threat for the Mac is SH.Renepo.B, released in October 2004. SH.Renepo.B deletes Unix commands, deletes various log files, modifies security preferences, launches a keystroke logger, installs software, changes the `hostconfig` file, scans the system for passwords, enables file sharing, creates an invisible folder named `canned.info` in each user's Public folder, and creates a process that spikes the processor of infected hosts. The payload for SH.Renepo.B is considerable, but the file size is only 46KB.

If a root kit does find its way onto your system, then a quick comparison of the date and times that a file were created and modified based on an originally known good set of the same files will often identify the presence of a root kit. Using check sums to calculate whether any changes have occurred is a better way of detecting a root kit.

Rootkit Hunter is a GPL-based terminal application that can scan for specific known root kits. However, many root kits are not known, or they're altered so they can't be discovered by root kit scanners. Rootkit Hunter will not find SH.Renepo.B, for example, but will find variants of the FreeBSD root kit that have been found in Mac OS X environments. SH.Renepo.B may be added to future releases of Rootkit Hunter, but it is not included at this time.

You can download Rootkit Hunter from `www.rootkit.nl`. To install Rootkit Hunter, follow these steps:

1. Download the gzipped file, extract it, and run the installation script.

2. Extract Rootkit Hunter using the command `tar zxf rkhunter-<version>.tar.gz`.

3. Run `./installer.sh` from inside the `rkhunter` directory.

4. Change directory (`cd`) into the `rkhunter` folder, and run the command `sudo ./rkhunter -checkall` to perform all the tests on the system.

Once you have Rootkit Hunter installed, you can invoke it using the following additional parameters:

> `--configfile <filename>`: Uses a custom configuration file.

> `--createlogfile`: Creates a log at `/var/log/rkhunter.log`.

> `--cronjob`: Runs as cronjob.

> `--help`: Shows the Rootkit Hunter manual page.

> `--nocolors`: Doesn't use any colors in the output.

> `--report-mode`: Limits the contents of a report.

> `--skip-keypress`: Doesn't wait after every test (makes it noninteractive).

> `--quick`: Performs quick scan.

> `--version`: Shows the version.

Now we will create an example of a shell script (rkexport.sh) that will run rkhunter and append the output to a new .txt file that could be viewed from the Web, provided that the /admin directory of your site is password-protected. Once you've run rkhunter, you can build on the previous section and run a ClamAV scan of the system and dump the results into the same file:

```
Date >> /opt/apache2/htdocs/admin
Whoami >> /opt/apache2/htdocs/admin
Rkhunter -version >> /opt/apache2/htdocs/admin
Rkhunter -checkall -skip-keypress -report-mode  >> /opt/apache2/htdocs/admin
Clamscan -V >> /opt/apache2/htdocs/admin
Clamscan / -r -i -move=/Quarantine >> /opt/apache2/htdocs/admin
```

This should provide you with output similar to the following:

```
Sun May  7 18:49:04 PDT 2006
Cedge
Rootkit Hunter 1.2.8
* MD5 scan
MD5 compared          : 0
Incorrect MD5 checksums : 0

* File scan
Scanned files: 342
Possible infected files: 0

* Rootkits
Possible rootkits:

Scanning took 110 seconds

*important*
Scan your system sometimes manually with full output enabled!
Some errors have been found while checking. Please perform a manual
check on this machine called Charles.local:

----------- SCAN SUMMARY -----------
Known viruses: 52427
Engine version: 0.88
Scanned directories: 1342
Scanned files: 60046
Infected files: 0
Data scanned: 14.93 GB
Time: 19.096 sec (0 m 9 s)
```

Not all root kits need to be command line or difficult to use. One, available for a few years now, called HellRaiser (most recently called OSX/HellRTS.D) can be configured and sent to targets in only a few minutes, without the need to ever open Terminal. In order to get infected you would have to run a server daemon, and would need to install it, but it can easily be disguised as something like an iChat Smiley or a fake iLife download.

HellRaiser is a RealBasic-based trojan horse that gives control of a Mac OS X system to an attacker. The payload ends up being a root kit accessible through a graphical interface. This can give an attacker the ability to search through your file system and then transfer files, view the clipboard, send audio, send chats, view your screen, show pictures, view spotlight indexes, control mail, reboot and even send shell commands to your computer.

Most major anti-virus applications (eg - Symantec, McAfee, etc) will detect the OSX/HellRTS.D. trojan horse when using the latest definition updates, but you would need to be running one of them in order for it to root out HellRaiser.

HellRaiser is not widely distributed and so most users have a pretty low risk of being infected. If you find yourself infected. If you want to know who it is that is attempting to establish a connection to your computer then you can enable ipfw and then ipfw logging (see Chapter 11 for more on ipfw) for the port that it's attempting to connect over (by default it's 24745).

Summary

Contrary to popular belief, the Mac is not impervious to malware. Viruses, worms and rootkits are very real threats to the integrity of the Mac operating system and as such should be safeguarded against. By understanding what these threats are, how to protect yourself against them, and engaging in ways to combat them, you're that much closer to a more secure and stable computing experience. Now, let's move on to discussing how to secure your Mac's operating system through data encryption.

## Chapter 9

Encrypting Files and Volumes

A common theme that you may be noticing in this book revolves around the concept of confidentiality. In a computer security context, confidentiality is the notion that sensitive data is accessible by only those users who have been approved or authorized for access to that data. For many organizations, and indeed for many malfeasants, data confidentiality is the most significant aspect of security. Certainly sabotage is a significant threat to many organizations, and often a source of incentive for many hackers, but more often than not the end-goal is to gain access to information. Whether it's personal information that facilitates identity theft, or highly valuable corporate secrets, information is highly valuable, both to you and those that would do you harm. In many corporate environments, the policy to encrypt data may be simply due to legal necessity, as there is liability involved with leaking certain data, such as personally identifiable information and payment records. Recent research indicates that loss of corporate secrets can result in an even more dangerous financial windfall for a company. Thus, protecting that data should always serve as job number one for end user's and system administrators alike.

Thankfully, OS X ships with a number of different technologies to facilitate the protection of data, as we have discussed throughout this book. In this chapter though, we will be focusing on one specific aspect of data confidentiality: encryption. Hopefully, if you're reading this book, you already have some prerequisite knowledge as to what exactly encryption is: in short, the obfuscation of data. More precisely, encryption serves as a means to obfuscate and protect data that is stored on a computer system such that it cannot be accessed without the possession of a "secret." In the broad context of data encryption, this secret can exist in many, many different forms from a simple password to a pre-shared cryptographic key, or even biometric data, such as a fingerprint or retinal scan. Certainly this isn't an exhaustive list, and technologies exist in many shapes and sizes to perform this task. Put simply, the primary role of a secret in the terms of encryption is to limit the visibility of the obfuscated data stored on a computer system. Without possession of the secret, the encrypted data is simply a mash of bits and bytes that at first glance may contain no sensible data. However, at the root of all that junk actually lies a very sophisticated mathematical algorithm that serves as a pathway to understanding that which is incomprehensible. The take away is that, without the secret, encrypted data is useless, or at least *should* be useless, assuming you are using a strong cryptographic system. The good news is that, by modern day standards, the best metric that we can hope to achieve, OS X utilizes some pretty rock-solid encryption technologies, ranging from the Keychain, to FileVault, OS X's encryption facilities that are both easy to use and transparent, but are also based upon well regarded mathematical algorithms.

In this chapter we will discuss the ins-and-outs of these technologies, endowing upon you, dear reader, the knowledge and power needed to harness them to their fullest. Without doubt each of these technologies has its own respective strengths and weakness, and it is also without question necessary to fully understand both of these aspects to ensure a truly protected environment. This chapter takes on that heavy burden so that you can confidently employ them for your own means.

Using the Keychain to Secure Sensitive Data

The keychain is an oft-misunderstood feature in OS X. This is rather unfortunate, because it is a very powerful tool for managing passwords and sensitive information, and the keychain entries in the iCloud keychain synchronize between computers using the same Apple ID. There is always a trade-off between security and accessibility, and the keychain provides a very good balance of both, providing an interface that both securely stores data and does so in an interface that is mostly seamless to the end user. We say "mostly seamless" here because there are certainly occasions where the system breaks down, and the result is end user confusion.

The keychain gets off to a bad start simply due to the fact that "password" is a four-letter word for many users; many can't even reliably remember a single password. If at any time any kind of confusion or uncertainty is thrown into the mix, for some reason these users tend to panic, and thus a help-desk ticket is launched, perhaps even followed up by a frantic call. Your job, as an administrator, is to possess a fundamental understanding of how the keychain operates so you can readily and easily dispatch keychain problems, while at the same time educating your users on its proper operation. We seek to facilitate both of these goals in this section.

Keychains

Every user in OS X has a default keychain, called the login keychain. This keychain is provisioned to a user when they first log in to a workstation, and it is assigned a password identical to the password that the user provided at login. From then on, whenever a user logs into a workstation, the login password will be passed to the keychain, and the login keychain will be unlocked. As long as the keychain is unlocked, any applications that have been provisioned access to the keychain will be able to access their respective keychain password entries without user interaction. As you can see in Figure 9-1, there is an unlock icon next to the login keychain entry.

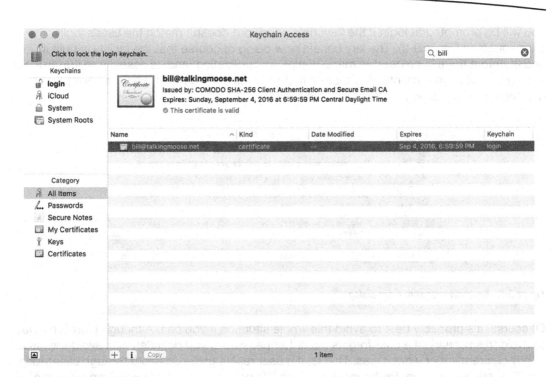

Figure 9-1. Keychain Access

One very key thing to know about the whole system is that each keychain utilizes a self-contained password. This keychain is stored in the user's home directory and its secret, or password, does not directly integrate with Directory Services such as Open Directory or Active Directory. The primary ramification here is that, if a system administrator resets a user's password through the directory system, typically due to the user forgetting their original password, the respective user's keychain is not updated to reflect the new password. Thus, the next time a user logs into an OS X workstation, the new login password that they used will be passed to the login keychain. According to the login keychain, which still contains the old password, the new password will be rejected. Now, whenever the user opens an application that utilizes the keychain, they will be presented with a dialog to unlock the keychain. They'll likely enter their new password again, and it will again get rejected. To the user this is very frustrating: what's the deal, did the password get reset or didn't it? Historically, OS X hasn't really had a facility to help user's recover from this: once the keychain password is out of sync, the only way around it is for the user to go to the Keychain Access utility found in the /Applications/Utilities folder. Once this application is open, the user can reset their login keychain password by selecting the "Change Password for Keychain 'login'" option found under the Edit menu. Once they manually update the keychain password to the same as their account password, the login keychain will be automatically unlocked when they login. This whole reset process is non-intuitive and the keychain password reset utility is buried inside the Keychain Access app, which most end users would never discover on their own.

You will be prompted at login if the keychain password doesn't match the user's login password (see Figure 9-2). The key benefit now being of course that the facility is built in, and therefore there is no need to mass-deploy an application (and its associated fire-at-login settings) to all of your clients. Any feature that reduces management overhead is a plus in our book, so this one in particular is a very welcome.

Figure 9-2. Keychain password reset dialog

Of course, it's probably best to avoid this whole situation if you can. Although there's no way to avoid this scenario if a user forgets his or her password, you definitely can avoid the issue if they can remember what it was. That is, if a user resets their password through client-local facilities, such as System Preferences or Login Window, then the login keychain password will be subsequently updated. The problem is that these password-reset methods require the user to know their old password, so it's not always applicable.

By default, once unlocked (typically occurring at login), the login keychain remains unlocked for the life of the user's session. This means that they will never be prompted to provide keychain access to pre-approved applications. This potentially includes Mail (Mail.app and Entourage), remote servers, Safari and Camino websites (Firefox does not utilize the Keychain), and other application passwords. For instance, if a user has his online banking credentials saved in his keychain, he will be able to go directly to his bank website and get in without ever needing to enter in a password; his banking login information will be auto filled by Safari. This can potentially lend to a security issue, because if he walks away from his computer without locking it, a malicious person could potentially sneak over to his computer and access his bank account. Likewise, if your computer is set to automatically login, then a malicious user can gain access to your accounts simply by rebooting your machine. This obviously presents a problem. Luckily, the Keychain utility has some facilities to address this very issue, which we'll discuss over the next two sections.

> **Note**   By default OS X also has a global keychain, the System keychain. This keychain operates behind the scenes, and is used to store low-level secure data, such as globally trusted certificates, system private keys, auto-login credentials, and trusted wireless network credentials.

Creating Secure Notes and Passwords

The keychain is used by the system to store a variety of confidential information. This includes certificates, certificate trusts, private and public keys, passwords, and secure notes. From an end user perspective, the two most prevalent objects are passwords and secure notes. Conceptually, a stored password is pretty self-explanatory: it's simply a secure object that holds authentication information consisting of the following fields:

- Name: This is an arbitrary name given to the password.

- Kind: This specifies the type of password item, which helps to identify the type of password item. For example, "Web form password," "Application Password."

- Account: This is typically the username.

- Where: This will typically contain a URI (Universal Resource Indicator) such as 'www.mycoolbank.com/login,' although the field does not always conform to URI standard.

- Comments: Miscellaneous information.

- Show Password: The encrypted password data.

Whenever an application needs to access to an encrypted password, it will search your keychain list for items based on its own defined criteria. This criteria will typically match using the fields: Kind, Account, Where, and Password. See Figure 9-3.

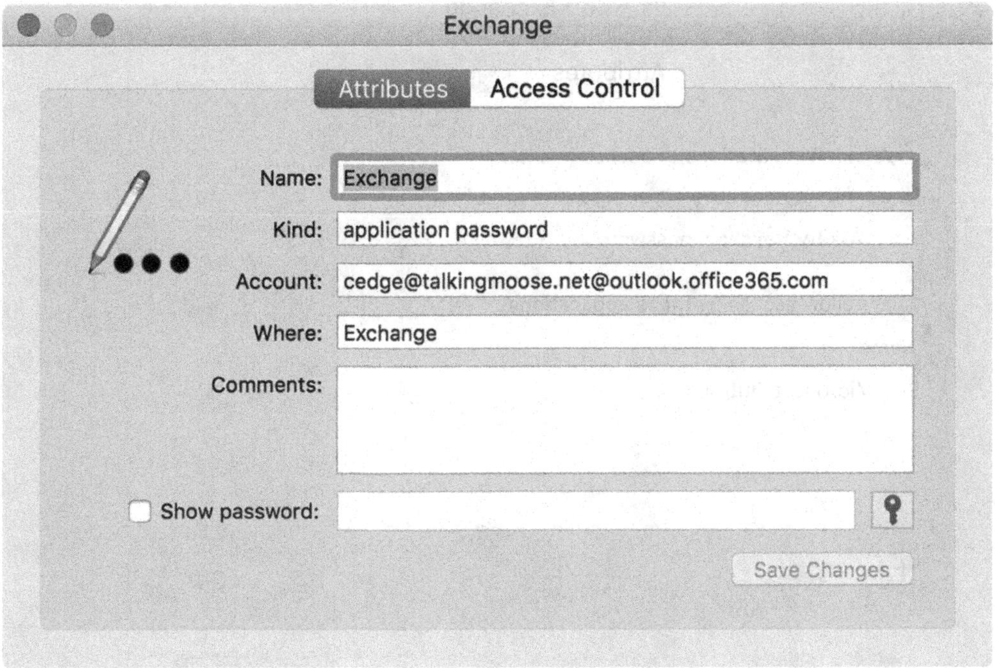

Figure 9-3. Keychain Access password

> **Note**   Of the above fields, only the password field is encrypted; everything else can be viewed
> without entering a password. Because of this, an attacker can potentially use this data for a
> "traffic analysis" attack; by analyzing the clear text data available in the keychain item, they
> may glean information that assists with gaining access to the account. For instance, an attacker
> can view a keychain item to gain access to your username for a website. Having access to
> the username may potentially open the door for them to manipulate a remote password-reset
> procedure. For highly sensitive sites, consider encrypting all data, including username and
> password, in the form a secure note, which we'll discuss more in a bit.

Figure 9-3 illustrates a secure password item for the Exhange account we installed in
Chapter 7, and when accessed, will log in with the account jdoe. The password, as seen,
is masked. By clicking on the check box "Show password," you will be prompted for the
keychain password before it will present the password, even if the keychain is unlocked!
This means that even if you walk away from your computer with the keychain unlocked, your
nosey coworker won't be able to pop open Keychain Access and peruse your password;
they'll need your keychain password for that. However, as stated earlier, they can just go to
Outlook, and the application will auto fill the information. So, they'll be able to login, but they
won't know what your password is. So why is Outlook granted full access to the password,
but Keychain Access isn't? Well, this facility is made possible through the Access Control
tab, shown in Figure 9-4.

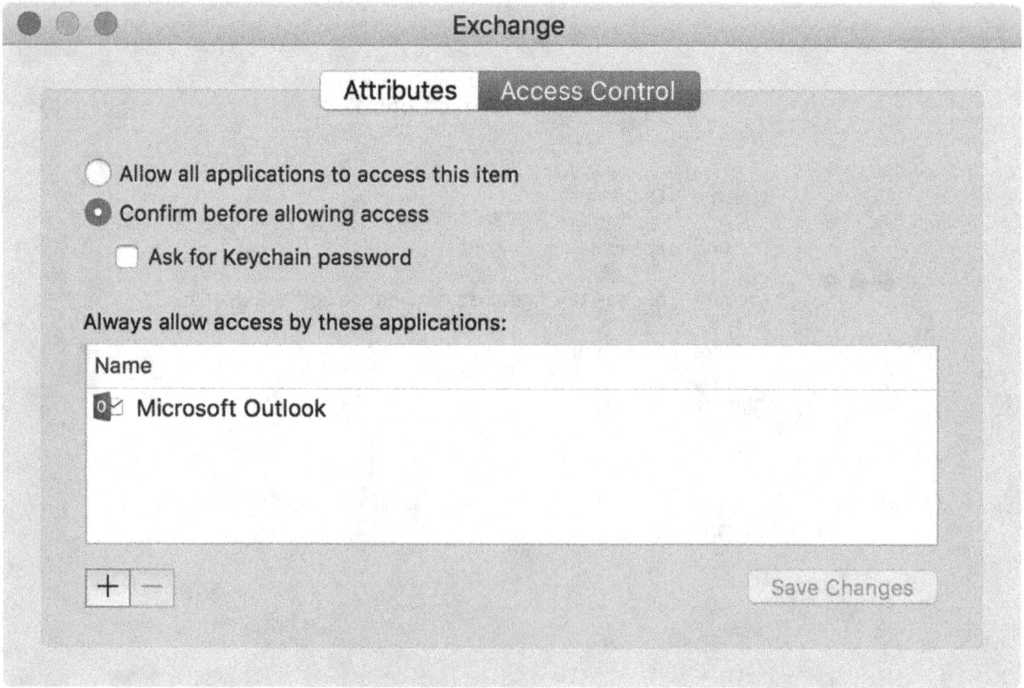

Figure 9-4. Keychain password object access controls

The Access Control tab allows you to specify applications that can freely access the password when the keychain is unlocked. In this case, only Safari is provisioned access, as Safari automatically provisions its own access when it creates the password item. If Keychain Access were added to this list, then you would be able to view the objects password without authentication whenever the keychain is in an unlocked state (so that naturally is a bad idea).

> **Note** Regardless of Access Control settings, no application or facility will be able to freely access a password from a keychain when it is in a locked state.

The second user visible feature of the keychain system that we mentioned earlier is secure notes. Secure notes are similar to password items, but they are meant to store larger sets of data, as seen in Figure 9-5.

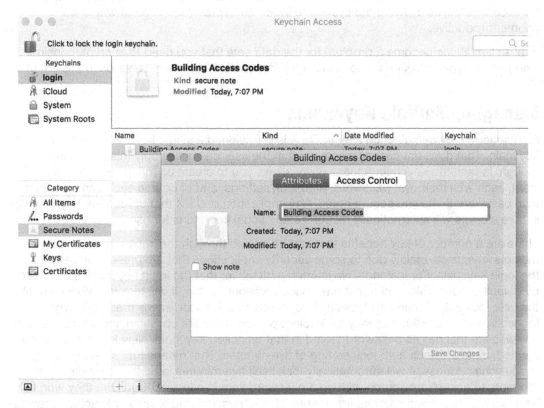

Figure 9-5. Keychain Access secure note

As Figure 9-5 shows, the interface for secure notes is much more apt to storing larger blocks of information than a standard password item. In this example, the user is using a secure note to save building access codes. Placing this information inside of an encrypted secure note is a great idea, especially if this is on a laptop or mobile machine: the chance of such a machine getting stolen is significantly higher, but the impact is greatly reduced if data is encrypted. In such an event, you might be able to sleep a little better knowing that your front door access code isn't sitting in a text file just waiting to be found. As long as your keychain password is relatively secure, your data is also secure.

Unfortunately, there are limits to what you can do with secure notes. While it's a great place to store odds and ends — building access codes, credit card information, personal information such as social security number, and so on — the text box provided supports only basic text, rich formatting is not supported. Because of this, if you have a large amount of data to encrypt, the lack of good formatting might sour your taste a bit, as it could be difficult to visually parse the information that it contains. On top of this, there isn't really a great system for organizing secure notes: there is no hierarchical system for organization; the primary method for organization is search. Unsurprisingly, there's no Spotlight support for secure notes, as allowing the system to index-encrypted note content would be counter-productive.

If these limitations become a problem for the data sets that you need to encrypt, consider using an encrypted disk image to encrypt the information, discussed later on in this chapter.

Managing Multiple Keychains

As mentioned, by default each user in OS X is provisioned a single keychain, the login keychain. That does not necessarily mean that the user can utilize only this keychain, though. In fact, the Keychain Access utility allows you to create as many keychains as you want, each with their own password, auto lock settings, and of course each can contain its own password items and secure notes. Any application in OS X that utilizes the Keychain for secure storage will automatically recognize additional keychains for use.

There are a number of key benefits that can be gained through the implementation of multiple keychains, mainly due to some security implications that are present by default in the login keychain. For instance, we learned a bit earlier that the login keychain is unlocked by default at user login, and that it has no lock timeout; that is, it will remain unlocked until the user logs out, or manually locks it. This means that if a user leaves their node while logged in and unlocked, a sneaky malevolent person could fire up Safari and gain access to any website that has its password stored in that unlocked keychain. New keychains, when created, have a default auto lock setting of five minutes. That means that a user unlocks this keychain for use, it will automatically lock itself five minutes later. If a malevolent user attempts to access a resource utilizing a password item in a locked keychain, they won't have access: the keychain must first be unlocked. Thus, utilizing a second keychain provides a bit more security in that regard.

While it is certainly possible to configure the login keychain to auto lock, or even change its password to a value different then the login password, doing so can sometimes result in an annoyance to end users, as they may complain about having to constantly enter their password. Thus, maintaining multiple passwords can help to achieve security without negatively affecting usability. In such a configuration, the login keychain can be utilized for oft-used and less sensitive information, such as casual websites or commonly used applications that utilize the keychain framework. The second keychain then could be used for data of higher sensitivity such as passwords to financial websites, secure notes containing personal information, or passwords to confidential servers.

For example, this author utilizes three different keychains on his own machine. The login keychain is fairly sparse, and contains only minimal credentials such as passwords to commonly used wireless networks, S/MIME Certificates (utilized by Mail.app to validate e-mail messages we receive from colleagues), and access to various innocuous social websites and web forums. This keychain also contains a few application passwords. For instance, we utilize MobileMe for syncing our data, so we have our MobileMe passwords stored in this keychain to avoid being prompted for a password every time it wants to synchronize. The next keychain is used solely for financial and personal data and credentials. This keychain has extremely aggressive auto-lock settings, and utilizes a password that is over 12 characters long to ensure that it is not a password that can easily be broken through a brute-force attack. The last keychain we maintain contains all credentials that we utilize professionally. This keychain also has extremely aggressive auto-lock settings, and is protected by an extremely secure and unique password. To provide additional security to all of our keychains, we have configured every keychain in our systems, including the login keychain, to lock whenever the machine sleeps. To configure this and keychain auto locking settings, select the menu option "Change Settings for Keychain <keychain name>..." found under the Edit menu in the Keychain Access application (select the appropriate keychain first). This dialog is seen in Figure 9-6.

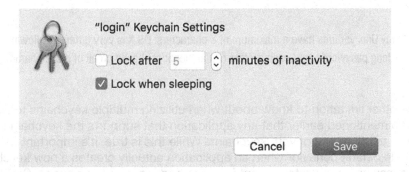

Figure 9-6. Keychain Access keychain settings

Maintaining multiple keychains like this allows us to organize data and assign different credentials and security policies to each keychain. This provides a very secure environment. However, there are still a few considerations that will be missed by most users. First and foremost, it's important to ensure that each keychain (outside of your login keychain) has a globally unique password: if the keychain password itself is the same as a password utilized elsewhere, it is possible that it will be compromised, especially if that password is saved in a keychain somewhere; if a password item in Keychain A has the same credentials as those used by Keychain B itself, Keychain B will be compromised if Keychain A is first compromised. If Keychain A in this example is the login keychain, then this is exceptionally bad. Because the login keychain utilizes the same password as the user's password by default, its credentials are more exposed.

Consider this: a user's login password is stored in the form of a hash on the local hard drive. On an OS X client machine by default a user's password is stored solely in the form of a SHA-1 hash inside the folder /var/db/shadow/hash. Thankfully, this file is protected with root-only access, so to access this file, a malicious user will need to either compromise your machine remotely, or gain physical access. Additionally, SHA-1 has proven to be a tough nut to crack, and is generally considered in the security industry to be a very secure algorithm. So the presence of this hash isn't a huge problem in and of itself. The problem is that SHA-1 is not necessarily the only hash format that is stored in this file. For instance, if you enable Windows file sharing for a user, an NTLM hash is then added to the user's hash file. Not all hashes are created equal, and NTLM has proven to be very susceptible to attack. In fact, a six-digit password stored in the NTLM hash can typically be cracked in a matter of minutes. Like a series of dominoes, once the login password is obtained, the login keychain is felled. If the login keychain has a single saved password containing the same password as one of your other keychains, then those keychains are also compromised, along with all of the items that they might contain. Suddenly this one small weakness has resulted in all encryption being negated.

To avoid such a chain reaction, common security practices can save the day. First and foremost, make sure that your login password is secure: at least eight characters, containing at least one alphabetic character, one capital character, one number, and one special character. The longer the password, the more secure it is from cracking. Additionally, avoid enabling Windows file services on an OS X client machine, particularly a mobile one. Lastly, as we cannot re-iterate enough, each keychain should be protected by secure, unique passwords. This is where you want to utilize those strong, harder-to remember passwords.

> **Note**   Many Unix variants have a maximum of 8 characters. OS X is very different, allowing you to make very long passwords, and each system can authenticate based on all of those characters.

There is one other limitation to know about when utilizing multiple keychains to secure your data. We mentioned earlier that any application that supports the keychain framework would be able to utilize any of your keychains. While this is true, it's important to understand the default behavior when an application actually creates a new keychain item. For instance, say you browse to www.nytimes.com and log in to the website. Say it's the first time you've done so, and so the system prompts you if you would like to save your password, and you click yes. When this happens, the application saves the new password item into your default keychain: there is no way to say specifically which keychain to create the item in. So, after first creating that password item, if you wish to place it into a different keychain, you can do so by using drag-and-drop in the Keychain Access application. The good news is that the login keychain doesn't necessarily have to be the default keychain, though it is by default. To change the default keychain, highlight the desired keychain in Keychain Access, and select the menu option "Make Keychain <keychain name> Default," found under the File menu. From then on, this keychain will be utilized whenever an application creates a new entry.

The keychain, if utilized properly, can provide a way to organize and secure passwords and secure notes on multiple levels. With such a baseline system in place, it allows a user to further leverage security best practices. Users can now create many differing passwords, each unique to their own entity: they can use a different password for Facebook, Google, Twitter, a different password for U.S. Bank or Wells Fargo, for Mint.com. By utilizing a different password for each service, the user ensures that they are reducing the impact of security vulnerabilities to any of these services. If Facebook gets hacked and the user's credentials exposed, the user can maintain piece of mind knowing that that password, unique to Facebook, cannot be utilized to gain access to his other services. This is not something that most users can boast. In fact, we think it likely that most users have one password, and they use it everywhere. Someday, that user might be scratching their head to find there bank accounts emptied and their credit cards maxed, all because they trusted their credentials to a foreign entity, which could not competently protect it.

OS X's keychain empowers the end user to avoid this scenario; a user can create hundreds of different passwords, one for each site, and those passwords can now all be stored safely and securely behind the scenes. The only password they'll need to remember is that used for the keychain itself: whenever a password to a particular site is needed, the user only need ensure that the keychain is unlocked and it will be utilized by the system. This is a very powerful system: learn it and love it; it will be your friend.

Using Disk Images as Encrypted Data Stores

Although the keychain serves as a great tool for securely storing passwords and small blocks of information, it is not great for storing any type of data that requires formatting, and it has absolutely no facilities for storing files. For this type of data encryption need, we instead turn to disk images. A disk image is essentially a virtual volume that can be mounted on a computer and then used to store files. When a disk image is mounted, it appears just like any hard drive or CD would, and is accessed in the same manner as a hard drive: you simply create folders and save files to it. Disk images have been around the Mac OS for a long time, and are most commonly used today for the digital delivery of software and their subsequent updates. For instance, you navigate to http://support.apple.com and download a software package; it will be downloaded in the form of a diskimage file, as denoted by its .dmg extension. This file, when opened, will result in the mounting of a volume on the computer, typically named in a similar fashion of the disk image file itself, though that is not always the case; a disk image's volume name is independent of its file name. Figure 9-6 shows an example disk image file, in this case the Office 2016 Installer, named Microsoft_Office_2016_installer.zip. When the .dmg file is opened, a volume named 'Microsoft_Office_2016_installer' is mounted, and a window is opened displaying the root of its filesystem.

In Figure 9-7, as in all scenarios where disk images are used to distribute software, the disk image presents a read-only volume. Disk images capable of modification are certainly possible, and in keeping with the tradition of this chapter, are fully capable of being fully encrypted. That is, a disk image when created can utilizes AES (Advanced Encryption Standard) encryption such that whenever a folder or file is written to its mounted volume, that data is first encrypted before being written back to the disk image's file on the disk. This allows a disk image to function as a virtual bin of folders and files that can be transported securely. In order to mount the disk image's volume (and thereby access its data), you must first enter in a password, which is then used to decrypt the data. If that password is unknown, the data will be inaccessible (though as we'll find out later in this section, there are some back-door options that can be utilized).

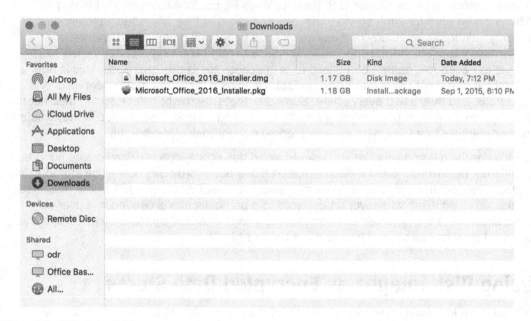

Figure 9-7. Mounting a disk image

Throughout this section we will discuss the use of disk images to aid users in maintaining the confidentiality of their data by keeping it from unwanted interlopers. From creation to maintenance and also potential caveats, we will demonstrate effective methods to utilize encrypted disk images to achieve this end.

Creating Encrypted Disk Images

Creation of a disk image is accomplished through the Disk Utility application found in the folder /Applications/Utilities. Once open, a new image can be created by clicking on the New Image icon in the tool bar, or by selecting the menu option "**New ➤ Blank Disk Image...**" found under the file menu.

Note   If you have a disk selected when you click the New Image button in the tool bar, Disk Utility will create a disk image based upon the contents of the selected disk, rather than a blank image.

As can be seen in Figure 9-8, there are a number of options presented when creating a new disk image. The first and most important option for creating an encrypted disk image is of course the encryption option, where we can choose between 128 and 256 bit AES encryption. AES is generally well respected, and has been officially endorsed by the U.S. government for use with classified data. The difference between the two options presented here lies solely in the length of the key used to encrypt the data. In this case, even though the key is only twice the size of 128 bit AES, the increased level of security that it provides is an order of magnitude larger. Even though 128 bit AES is generally thought to be extremely secure, attacks on data encrypted with 128-bit AES are becoming more and more plausible. Still, even today the NSA has approved 128-bit AES for the transmission of classified data, though TOP SECRET classified data requires at least 192-bit AES. Considering this, for the vast majority of environments, 128-bit AES will provide adequate data confidentiality. Functionally, the type of encryption used operates behind the scenes, with the only user perceptible difference being in the form of computer speed. Due to the increased complexity of performing mathematics with the larger key, computer performance will be degraded when writing the data. For most day-to-day operations, the difference in speed will be imperceptible to the end user; however, when performing I/O heavy duties, the performance impact will become more prevalent in the form of high CPU utilization.

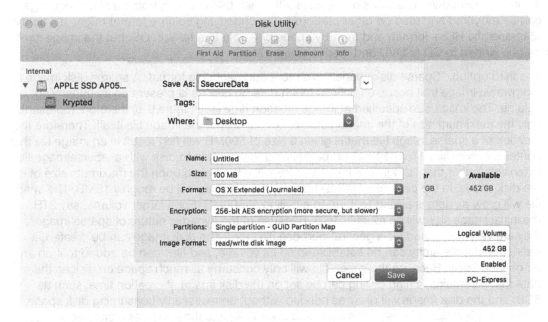

Figure 9-8. Creating a disk image using Disk Utility

The next option to consider when creating a new disk image is the image format. This option is actually one of the more pertinent options when it comes to the long-term use and maintenance of the disk image itself. Here, we have a number of options. First, we have the option "Read/Write disk image," which is the most traditional type of disk image used by the Mac OS through the years. A read/write image is a fixed size image: the size of the image is specified at creation time, and the disk image file is allocated to disk. The disk image file, regardless of how much data its volume contains, will always occupy the specified size. Thus, a 500MB read/write disk image will immediately occupy 500MB of space on disk, and it will continue to occupy 500MB of space throughout its life. Because of the fixed-size nature of this format, it is not particularly well suited for most use-cases involving data encryption requirements. If you are only looking to encrypt data for transport, then a fixed size encrypted read/write disk image will certainly fit the bill. However, for a day-to-day encryption store that may grow indeterminably, you'll likely find this format to be limiting.

> **Note**   An interesting side-effect of using a read/write encrypted disk image is that someone observing the image can't tell how much encrypted data it contains.

The next option, DVD/CD Master, is very similar in function to the "Read/Write disk image" option. The primary difference is in the lower level format of the disk image file. A DVD/CD Master formatted disk image is actually written to disk as an ISO compatible format. That is, you can change the .dmg file extension that is used on these disk images can be changed to .iso, and the image file can be processed by cross-platform disk utilities, such as those used in Linux or Windows. This does not necessarily mean that the data from such a disk image can be mounted and read on other platforms, the underlying volume format might still be the Mac-specific HFS+ format, and thereby undecipherable to a foreign OS, but the image itself can be written to CD or DVD and then read on a Mac.

The third option, "Sparse disk image," is a more approachable format. A sparse disk image is a growable image that occupies only as much data on disk as is present on its underlying volume. The image size specified at image creation time (see Figure 9-8) therefore represents only the maximum size of the image volume, not the size of the image file itself. Therefore the creation of a sparse image file that is given a size of 500MB will first result in an image file that contains only minimal formatting and partitioning data written to disk with a .sparseimage file extension (rather than .dmg). The initial file size will differ based upon the maximum size of the disk image. In the case of a 500MB volume, the initial file will be roughly 10MB. The image file will grow as data is added to it, up to a ceiling of 500MB. For a larger volume, say 2TB, the initial image size will be roughly 1GB. Because of the dynamic nature of sparse images, they are very well suited for a general-purpose file store. The disk image can be created, a defined folder hierarchy can be established on its volume, and files can be added to it on an as-needed basis. Because the image file will only consume as much space on disk as the data that it contains, a high ceiling can be set on the disk image at creation time, such as 8GB, and the disk image will grow as needed without unnecessarily consuming disk space. There are a few side effects to this aspect, but we'll dig into those details a bit later on (see section "Limitations of Sparse Images and Reclaiming Space," later on in this chapter). Because of their dynamic nature for most purposes, a sparse image file will be the go-to option.

> **Note**   Volumes residing on a sparse disk image cannot be resized; therefore, it is a good idea to be somewhat liberal when setting the size of the volume. It also is not a great idea to specify a size that is overly large, as it will result in lost space due to partitioning and formatting overhead on the image file.

The last option, "Sparse bundle disk image," is a different take on a sparse disk image. Like a sparse image, a sparse bundle will grow as needed based upon the content of its volume (up to the size specified at image creation). The difference between the two lies in the way that a sparse bundle is written to disk. Instead of creating a single monolithic file to represent all contents of its virtual volume as a sparse image does, a sparse bundle actually writes its data to disk in the form of directory that contains multiple files. Each of these files, referred to as a band, only contains a small subset of data within the disk image volume. As new data is written to the sparse image, new bands will be created as needed. When existing data is altered on the volume, only the bands that hold the contents of that file will change on disk. This has a couple of benefits: first, it is more resistant to data corruption: in the event of disk corruption, the chance of a catastrophic failure of the disk image's volume is reduced. With individual bands, only the files whose data is written to that corrupted band will be lost. Contrast this with the single monolithic model of a .sparseimage file, which can be susceptible to complete data loss should that single file become corrupted. Sparse bundle disk images have another very valuable property. One significant issue found with monolithic image files is that whenever there is a change, no matter how minute, the underlying disk image file is changed.

Keep in mind that a volume isn't changed solely by your actions; there are many underlying facilities that can result in small changes in data. For instance, the Finder will commonly modify .DS_Store files in any directory that it navigates. Spotlight, if enabled, can cause changes to the volume. Quicklook can cause the generation of proxies, which can also modify the volume. Realistically this means that any time the image is mounted, the file will change.

This has an important ramification for system administrators who are backing up your system, or perhaps on you, the user, if you utilize home directory syncing or back up your own machine. Such utilities, when run, detect file changes, and in such an event will copy/backup the file, typically over a network connection. All of these utilities operate at the file level, not the block level. This means that to back up or synchronize a file, the entire file has to be backed up, not just the changes. Basically what this means is that your backup system has to work overtime to ensure these backups are performed. If you have a sparse image with only a few documents on it, this isn't likely a big deal. However, if your image contains a lot of data, then that can cause significant problems.

Consider an image with 50GB of data on it. If the image file is mounted, the effectively the underlying file will be changed. If you make a habit in opening that file, that's 50GB that needs to be backed up each time, which is a lot of data. If your backup or synchronize window isn't long enough, this could effectively act as a denial of service of your backup or synchronization process: other files might not be addressed by the system due to constant delays introduced by your huge file. This denial of service effectively acts as a breach of security in the area of redundancy. Encryption should not come at the expense of your backups, and as such, a sparse image can be detrimental at this scale. Whenever you have both encrypted files and backups, you have to make the decision of whether to back the files up in their encrypted or plain form. Backing up the plain form makes recovery easier (especially if the only person who knows the password leaves the company), but means it's easier for confidential data to leak from your backups than from the original location.

If your backups are in a secure site and your main system is a laptop or iPad, then having plain backups actually isn't so bad. Unfortunately, with a sparse image structure, backing up data in its encrypted form isn't a very plausible reality.

This is where sparse bundles really shine, and is no doubt the primary rational behind the creation of the image format. With a sparse bundle, only the bands that are actually modified will be backed up or synchronized. Thus, with the same 50GB image, if a Word document is updated on the disk, only the bands that contain that file will be affected, and only those bands will need to be copied by the backup or sync. By default, sparse bundle bands are 8MB each, so such a small change will result in a backup of only that band, as well as band containing the file system table. It's possible for a file to span multiple bands, but either way the end result is a backup of a couple dozen megabytes, which is significantly more manageable then a backup of 50GB. This isn't quite as efficient as a backup of the data in its unencrypted form (in which case, the backup delta would be the size of the Word document itself), but the use of bands helps to utilize an approachable file size to facilitate incremental backups.

In order to ensure that all bands of sparse bundle saved to disk maintain coherence and cohesiveness, they are all saved into the sparse bundle directory. This directory is given an extension of ".sparsebundle," which is interpreted by OS X so that is actually presented through the interface as a single file; similar in behavior to the way that the OS handles on .app or .pkg bundles, which are also commonly directories (.pkg packages can now actually be saved to disk as a single flat file, but historically they have actually been directories). Thus, when viewed from the Finder, a sparse bundle image looks at acts like a single file; the user will be completely oblivious to its actual make-up. Figure 9-9 shows both a sparse image and a sparse bundle as presented in the Finder. As can be seen from the rear image, they are both presented as files. However, if you were to view the contents of the sparse bundle by right-clicking on it and selecting "Show package contents," you will clearly see the underlying contents, including some configuration files and the separate bands.

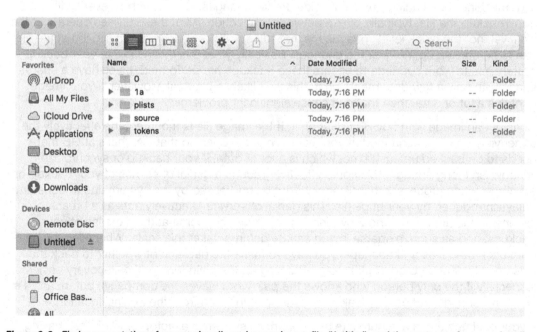

Figure 9-9. Finder presentation of a sparsebundle and sparseimage file (Untitled), and the contents of a sparsebundle image (the directories)

Just as a sparseimage adds flexibility over standard static disk images due to their reduced spaced consumption, sparse bundles introduce additional flexibility over sparse image files in regards to disk efficiency with larger data sets. Because of this, they are a good choice over sparse image files as image capacity grows. The downside to sparse bundles comes at the expense of their structure. Because they are in fact directories at a low level, there is possibility that files can be misplaced or removed. This is particularly problematic when the file will be presented on alternate platforms, as these platforms will not present the bundle as a single file, users viewing the file from such a platform will see a directory, which contains a large number of files, as seen in the front-most image of Figure 9-9. In such a case, if a user modifies or moves one of these files, then the integrity of the sparse bundle image will be compromised. Thus, in cross-platform environments, there can occasionally be problems caused due to this. Regardless, sparse bundles do offer tangible benefits over sparse images, so if you feel that your disk image will contain a large amount of data, then sparse bundles are worth a look.

Once you have chosen the appropriate image format, there remain a couple of options before creating this image. Specifically, we'll want to define the partition type used for the image. By default, this will be the Apple Partition Map, which is an older partitioning format dating back to OS 9. This will work fine, though it may be desirable to utilize the GUID partition map, which is a newer partition map with broader cross-platform support. Effectively on a single Mac-only volume, Apple Partition Map will fit the bill without much fuss. If this disk image is to contain data that will be utilized on multiple platforms, it might be desirable to utilize a Master Boot Record (MBR) partition map, which is utilized by Windows (Later versions of Windows add limited support for GUID partition tables). Alternatively, the option "CD/DVD with ISO data" will utilize a partition map that can be read by Macs, Windows, and Linux machines.

With the appropriate partition format specified, the last step is to specify the file system. For the majority of environments the desirable format is "Mac OS Extended (Journaled)," which is the standard Mac OS filesystem. For cross platform support, the best option is "MS-DOS (FAT)."

With volume name, size and format, encryption settings, partition format, and image format selected, you are now ready to create your disk image. Once created, the disk image can be mounted as needed, and sensitive data can be saved directly to the volume. If the disk image was created with encryption enabled, all data on that volume will be encrypted on the disk. If the disk image file (or sparse bundle directory) is exposed, they will be reasonably secure as long as the password used to encrypt the data is also secure.

> **Tip**   When mounting disk images in the Finder, permissions on the disk image are ignored; all files on the image volume are assigned ownership to the mounting user. This means that any POSIX permissions assigned to the disk image will be bypassed. However, ACL's applied to "Everyone" will be honored, as they are global across all users and will not be subjected to ownership masking.

There is one small caveat to the disk image system utilized by OS X. In order to access the encrypted data on a disk image, its volume must be mounted. Once that volume is mounted, it is presented on the local file system as another disk. The problem with this is that if the systems runtime is compromised, then referencing the filesystem path at which the image is mounted can access the unencrypted data. This means that if the user is subjected to malware such that a foreign program is executed in his environment, then that malicious program will be able to be accessed by that program. Thus, if an encrypted disk image is opened on a compromised system, it can be assumed that the data on the mounted volume will be detected and read; confidentiality of the encrypted data will be breached. Considering this aspect of utilizing disk images for encryption, it is a good practice to get in the habit of only having secure volumes mounted explicitly when needed: mounting an encrypted disk image opens a window to the data, keeping that window closed as much as possible is key to keeping the data safe; keeping an encrypted disk image mounted at all times may expose data unnecessarily.

Interfacing with Disk Images from the Command Line

Thus far, we have demonstrated the process for creating encrypted disk images using the Disk Utility GUI application. In some cases, it may be desirable to automate the process. For instance, as an administrator, you may wish to create an encrypted disk image for the purposes of backup. Or, you may be looking to mass-deploy encrypted disk images to a multitude of users. In cases such as this, using Disk Utility to interactively create a disk image might not be the most efficient use of time. Interactive creation of disk images will severely hamper your ability to automate backups that would utilize them. Economies of scale apply to large user environments inhibiting the practicality of manually creating an encrypted disk image for each of your users. Luckily, Mac OS X offers a very capable command line suite for creating and manipulating disk images.

The primary utility for dealing with disk images from the command line is the `hdiutil` command. This command can be used to create, mount (attach), and unmount (detach) image files, among other things. Mounting and un-mounting disk images is rather trivial to accomplish with this tool. To do so, we just call `hdiutil` with the `attach` verb, and then pass in the path to our disk image file. The command and subsequent output are shown here:

```
$ hdiutil attach ~/Desktop/mySecureData.sparseimage
Enter password to access "mySecureData.sparseimage":
/dev/disk3              Apple_partition_scheme
/dev/disk3s1           Apple_partition_map
/dev/disk3s2           Apple_HFS                    /Volumes/mySecureData
```

As can be seen by the output, the user is prompted for a password, the image file "mySecureData.sparseimage" is assigned device of /dev/disk3, and is mounted at path /Volumes/mySecureData.

> **Note** If you want to automate the mounting of an encrypted disk image for backups, you will need to automate the supply of the password, too, which means that the password is going to be sitting somewhere in cleartext for your script to grab. In the case of an ObjectiveC application, it is possible to utilize the keychain framework to store this value, but even then, the keychain must be unlocked at the time of use.

Once mounted, the encrypted disk image behaves just like another physical drive in the system. There are a few things to note about this. First and foremost, as stated, when an image file is attached, any POSIX permissions laid down on the volume will be effectively bypassed, due to the fact that ownership of all items on the disk image's volume is masked to the running user. On top of this, the volume is mounted to the typical OS X directory in /Volumes. This can create a security issue on nodes that have more than a single logged in user: if you mount your disk image on a computer with another active user session, they will not only be able to see that the disk was attached, but they will also be able to navigate to the volume and likely read data off of that volume. Remember from Chapter 4 that a user's default umask setting in OS X is set such that any newly created files have global read access. As such, concurrent user sessions will likely have access to the unencrypted data, which isn't good. To avoid this issue, there are a couple of options. The first is to simply ensure that the top level of the disk image volume has adequate protections. While ownership is not respected by default with disk images, the mode is. This means that, if a directory only has read and execute permissions granted at the ownership level, other users will not be able to view any data on the volume. To accomplish this, a user can simply remove all access from other users by using the Permissions tab of a Finder Get Info window. Or, you can use the chmod command as shown here:

```
$ chmod 700 /Volumes/mySecureData
```

After running this command, only the mounting user will have access to the data. While for the most part this will work out, it is possible to further secure the data on a mounted volume by passing custom mount parameters to hdiutil when mounting an image. Through the use of -owners option, it is possible to force a disk image to mount in a manner that enforces permissions as laid down on the image volume. On top of this, you can specify a custom mountpoint, other than /Volumes, for the mounting of your volume. Lastly, we can use the -nobrowse option to prevent the volume from being recognized as such by the Finder: instead it will treated just like any other folder on the system, and will prevent the volume from showing up in other user's devices list. To mount an image with such options, utilize the following syntax:

```
$mkdir ~/SecureData
$ hdiutil attach -owners on -nobrowse -mountpoint ~/SecureData↵
 ~/Desktop/mySecureData.sparseimage
```

After executing this command, the volume found in the mySecureData sparse image will be mounted to a folder named "SecureData" at the root of the user's home directory. You'll notice here that we are using the mkdir command to first create the directory prior to running the hdiutil command: if the designated mountpoint does not exist, then the mount operation will fail. Because we are passing the –owners flag with a value of "on,| we are ensuring that any ownership on the volume is preserved, which allows you to utilize normal file system permissions to secure data on mounted volumes. For more information on utilizing file system permissions, refer to Chapter 4.

To unmount or detach the image, we simply use the detach verb and pass it the volume path:

```
$ hdiutil detach /Volumes/mySecureData
"disk3" unmounted.
"disk3" ejected.
```

Alternatively we can provide the disk path:

```
$ hdiutil detach /dev/disk3
"disk3" unmounted.
"disk3" ejected.
```

As can be seen, with either syntax the device disk3 is ejected from the system.

Creation of disk images requires a bit more lengthy syntax, and is achieved by using the create verb. The process allows for the specification of all parameters that we were presented from the GUI and more:

```
$ hdiutil create -size 100M -fs "Journaled HFS+" -volname "myImage"↵
 ~/Desktop/myImage.dmg
created: /Users/cedge/myImage.dmg
```

In this case, a 100MB image file named myImage.dmg is created on the desktop. The volume name of the image is specified by the -volname parameter, in this case "testImage." By default, the format of the image file is "Read/Write," a GUID partition scheme is used, and no encryption is used on the disk image.

To create a sparse image with encryption we can use the following syntax:

```
$ hdiutil create -size 8G -fs "Journaled HFS+" -volname "myImage" -type SPARSE↵
 -encryption AES-128 ~/Desktop/mySecureImage.sparseimage
Enter a new password to secure "mySecureImage.sparseimage":
Re-enter new password:
created: /Users/cedge/mySecureImage.sparseimage
```

Here, we were prompted for a password to use for encryption. We can also use the –stdinpass if we want to specify the password programmatically:

```
$ echo -n 'myPassword1$' | hdiutil create -size 8G -fs "Journaled HFS+" -volname↵
 "myImage" -type SPARSE -encryption AES-128 -stdinpass↵
 ~/Desktop/mySecureImage.sparseimage
created: /Users/cedge/mySecureImage.sparseimage
```

In both of these cases, we're encrypting the image with AES-128 bit encryption. In the first example we had to interactively enter our password; in the second example, we're passing a password of 'myPassword1$' via the echo command (the -n prevents echo from sending a trailing newline after the password), which is then read in as the password to use to encrypt the image. This is very handy in cases where you have to programmatically generate images for end users, and have a default password template or routine that should be used on new images. This password can then be changed on the image by using the Disk Utility GUI application or from the command line. To change an encrypted image's password from the GUI, you can drag the image file into the source list for disk utility, highlight it, and then from the Images menu, select "Change Password...". Or, with no image selected in the Disk Utility source pane, select "Change Password..." and you will be prompted to navigate to a disk image in the file system. To change a password from a command line using the chpass verb:

```
$ hdiutil chpass ~/Desktop/mySecureImage.sparsimage
Enter password to access "mySecureImage.sparseimage":
Enter a new password to secure "mySecureImage.sparseimage":
Re-enter new password:
```

Whether changing the password from the command line or graphical interface, the original password must be known in order to successfully complete the operation. So that begs the question: if an end user can change a password on a disk image, and that password must be known to access data on the image, what's to prevent the user from locking out you, the administrator, from accessing the data's contents? Well, nothing, and that is likely a problem in an environment that seeks to use encrypted disk images to secure company data. A loss in accessibility to company data represents a security failure, and therefore is likely unacceptable, depending on the company's attitude to risk and the impact of such unavailability. Well, luckily there are some steps that you can take to protect your organization against this scenario. Apple's disk image implementation has full support for certificate authentication based upon PKE (Public Key Encryption), which we've discussed elsewhere in this book (see Chapter 6). When creating a new disk image, it is possible to specify a certificate that can be used to authenticate an image, rather than (or in addition to) a password. When an image is created in such a fashion, as long as a user has access to the certificate's secret, its private key, then the user will have access to the data on the encrypted image. This means that as an administrator, you can generate a disk image for each of your users, and these users can access the disk image via a standard text-based password. By passing a certificate for secondary authentication, you can ensure that you retain access to the data even after the user has changed the default password. As an administrator, you are no longer a subject to the loss of data: as long as your retain the private key that corresponds to the certificate that set upon the image at creation time, then you will be able to decrypt the data and mount the disk image.

To accomplish such a task, it is first necessary to create our identity, that is, our certificate and private key. This is a standard private key + certificate combination that is used in the majority of SSL-related tasks. In the case of creating an identity for securing disk images, it is recommend to use a key/cert pair that is dedicated to this task. That is, don't re-use the same certificate that you use to secure your website or your mail system for instance. That being said, you can use these same identities if you absolutely must. The identity that you utilize for disk image authentication does not necessarily need to be signed by a trusted root Certificate Authority (CA), though if you maintain your own CA, you can sign to provide validation, we can specify that an image respect both a password as well as a certificate; if a certificate is not present in a user's keychain, then a password fallback can be used. This is perfect for our needs; we can use the certificate when creating all of our images, which will grant us global access to them all, regardless of each image's individual password. End users will continue to utilize their own password for the disk image, even changing them, and will never need access to our private key. If the end user leaves or forgets the password, we can simply recover it using our own closely guarded private key.

> **Caution** By granting a single identity access to all disk images, it becomes absolutely imperative that the certificate's private key be closely guarded at all times. If this key is compromised, so too are all images created with its certificate.

To create a disk image that utilizes both a password and a certificate for authentication, we simply add an additional option, -agentpass, to our previous command. When the -agentpass flag is specified, hdiutil will prompt for an interactive password:

```
$ hdiutil create -size 8G -fs "Journaled HFS+" -volname "myImage" -type SPARSE↵
 -encryption AES-256 -certificate ~/Desktop/MyCo\ Disk\ Encryption\ Identity.cer↵
 -agentpass ~/Desktop/mySecureImage.sparseimage
Enter a new password to secure "mySecureImage.sparseimage":
Re-enter new password:
created: /Users/cedge/Desktop/mySecureImage.sparseimage
```

If the image is being made programmatically, then the -stdinpass flag can be used to read data in from standard input:

```
$ echo -n 'myPassword1$' | hdiutil create -size 8G -fs "Journaled HFS+" -volname↵
 "myImage" -type SPARSE -encryption AES-256 -certificate ~/Desktop/MyCo\ Disk\↵
 Encryption\ Identity.cer -stdinpass ~/Desktop/mySecureImage.sparseimage
created: /Users/cedge/Desktop/mySecureImage.sparseimage
```

From here on, whenever the image is mounted, disk utility will first search through all of a user's keychains for the corresponding private key; if it is not found, the user will be prompted to enter a password. If you need to mount the image from a machine that doesn't have an active console, you can specify the path to the keychain using hdiutil:

```
$ hdiutil attach -recover /Library/Keychains/MyCo\ Disk\ Encryption.keychain↵
 ~/Desktop/mySecureImage.sparseimage
```

```
/dev/disk1              GUID_partition_scheme
/dev/disk1s1            EFI
/dev/disk1s2            Apple_HFS                   /Volumes/myImage
```

In this example, we utilize the -recover option and specify the path to a keychain file that contains the appropriate identity. In this case, we are referencing a keychain that was made specifically for this purpose, "MyCo Disk Encryption.keychain" stored in the global library. This keychain contains solely the certificate/key pair that makes up the MyCo Disk Encryption Identity that we previously made. By creating a unique keychain for this, we can specify a very strong passphrase for this keychain and store it in a secure place. In the event that data recover is needed due to a lost password, the keychain can be imported on the administrators machine and facilitate access to the data.

> **Tip**   Or, the identity can be stored in a standard password-protected PKCS#12 container, which can be directly exported from Keychain Access, and then re-imported when needed.

Thus far, we've demonstrated how to create sparse images using hdiutil create and passing the –format option a value of SPARSE. However, there are a number of other formats that are worth knowing about, and each requires a specific identifier to be passed to the –format flag. Table 9-1 illustrates the available formats.

Table 9-1. New Image Formats Used with 'diskutil create'

Format	Comment
UDIF	This is a standard read/write fixed-size disk image.
UDTO	This is format is the equivalent of "DVD/CD Master" in the Disk Utility GUI.
SPARSE (UDSP)	A sparse disk image.
SPARSEBUNDLE	A sparse bundle disk image.

These options may be very familiar, and for good reason: the list is identical to the options presented in the Disk Utility GUI. However, there are a few additional properties that can be specified from the command line when dealing with sparse bundle images that are worth noting. As mentioned, a sparsebundle image is actually comprised of numerous separate files, or bands, which comprise the entire volume. By default, each band in a sparse bundle image is 8MB. Apple likely chose this default size because it is a good compromise between small and large file access. The truth of the matter is that one size doesn't necessarily fit all, and for some data sets, a small band size can adversely affect performance. This is especially true in large data sets. Consider a 500GB sparse bundle image; in such a scenario, the sparse bundle would actually contain over 60,000 bands! For instance, a backup system could process and protect 15,000 32MB bands much faster than it could process 60,000 8MB bands. Another situation where a smaller band size can adversely performance is if you plan to store larger files on your image volume. If you plan to routinely store files that are in excess of 8MB, then can be adversely affected due to the extra overhead needed for the additional I/O operations. Even though you are only accessing a single file on the image volume, the underlying file system will have to open up the individual bands that store that segment of the file. For instance, a 128MB video, just a few minutes of

HD, will actually require 16 file requests. That's a fair amount of overhead, so the user may benefit from a larger band size. To create a sparse bundle with a custom band size, you use the -imagekey flag, which accepts key value pairs. For instance, to create a sparsebundle image that utilizes 32MB bands, we can use the following syntax:

```
$ hdiutil create -size 8g -type SPARSEBUNDLE -imagekey sparse-band-size=65536 -fs↵
 "JHFS+" -volname "myImage" ~/Desktop/myImage.sparsebundle
```

With this command, we are creating a sparse bundle image with a maximum size of 8GB, a "Journaled HFS" + file system (for which JHFS+ is a shortcut), and we have specified a band size via the sparse-band-size key. With this key, we specify the number of 512 byte blocks that exist on a given band. In this case, we have specified 65,536 blocks. At 512 bytes per block, we have a total band size of 32MB (512 x 65,536 = 33,554,432). You might be thinking that 33,554,432 bytes is more that 32MB, keep in mind we're operating at a low level here, and thus are operating at base2. So if we were to be completely accurate, we would say that we're specifying a band size of 32 mebibytes (MiB). With such an image, we are helping to improve the efficiency of data as laid out on the sparse bundle. The negative side to this is that we have now effectively raised our minimum backup size as well. With an 8MiB band, a small file change will only result in a backup of 8MiB. On a disk image with 32MiB bands, even a small change will require the entire band to be backed up, so that the same backup procedure would be at least 32MiB. Because of this, choosing a band size that is overly large can result in inefficiencies as well. Really, the exact value will depend on the environment, and values can range from 2048 (1MiB bands) to 262144 (128MiB bands). If in doubt, just use the default values, they work out pretty well, and they are the officially supported size. If you are an administrator and feel like an 8MiB band is not optimal for your environment, then you have the power to fine-tune the size to best fit your use-case.

And that, in a (rather large) nutshell, is the landscape for utilizing disk images for data encryption. Hopefully we have laid out a good blueprint for you to follow, and have established a good fundamental understanding of their strengths and weaknesses. Likewise, we hope we have imparted upon you the knowledge required to utilize disk-image encryption to ensure confidentiality of your data, and as well as providing fail-safes in the form of certificates so that encrypted data can be retrieved in a worse-case scenario.

Encrypting User Data Using FileVault

FileVault is a technology in OS X that allows users to seamlessly safeguard their personal data vis-à-vis encryption. FileVault is configured on a boot volume, and once enabled, accounts are allowed to unlock that volume; all encryption and decryption of the volume is handled behind the scenes. In the event that a computer is physically compromised, any accounts on the system that have FileVault enabled will maintain a rather high probability of avoiding compromise of confidentiality, subject to the strength of the password used to encrypt the data, and whether the machine was logged in and running at the time of theft. In the case of FileVault, this password is equivalent to the user's login password. Without access to the password, provided that it is of relatively secure strength (8+ characters with a number, capital letter and at least one special character), the data stands a good chance of remaining secure.

Although you may be unfamiliar with FileVault itself, you actually already possess a good deal of knowledge as to the inner workings of the technology, provided of course that you have been paying attention. In case you haven't guessed, FileVault technology is at its heart based upon the use of disk image encryption. If you skipped the previous section. Using Disk Images as Encrypted Data Stores, this would probably be a good time to stop and flip a few (dozen) pages back.

When FileVault is enabled for a user, the entire contents of the user's home directory are relocated from the standard location of /Users, and is instead transferred onto a disk image in the form of an encrypted sparse bundle and stored in at /Users/username/username. sparsebundle. When a FileVaulted user logs into an OS X workstation, the system will attempt to mount the encrypted sparse bundle image stored at this location with the password provided by the user at login, and the respective image is then mounted at the traditional home directory path: /Users/username. This technique provides for a completely user-transparent system; from their perspective, their home directory is found at the usual location of /Users/username. However, unbeknownst to them (or beknownst), any changes to files or subdirectories in there home are instead written to the sparse bundle image in an encrypted form. When the user logs out, the home directory is unmounted, at which point the data only resides on the disk in a secure encrypted form.

Caution   When a user is logged in, whether FileVault is enabled or not, the user's data is accessible in an unencrypted form at their home directory path, and as such is susceptible to malware or other runtime exploitation: access to the data is controlled solely by POSIX or ACL filesystem access controls.

The assumption to all of this working, of course, is that the user's login password is identical to that used to encrypt the contents of the FileVault image. By default this is the case, but it is certainly not an unconditional certainty. In this respect, the situation is not unlike that which we previously discussed for the login keychain. In both situations, the ability for the OS to seamlessly access the protected data, whether contents of the login keychain, or contents of the FileVault image, is correlated to the condition that the login password be identical to that used for encryption. The scenarios for these two passwords (login + login.keychain or login + FileVault) to become out of sync are identical. Like the login keychain, if a user changes his password locally on the machine, whether through a forced password change at the login window, or through a voluntary action of utilizing the Accounts System Preference pane to manually change a password, the corresponding login keychain and FileVault disk image will be subsequently updated behind the scenes.

To enable FileVault, first open the Security & Privacy System Preference pane and then click on the FileVault tab. Here, click on Turn On FileVault... as seen in Figure 9-10.

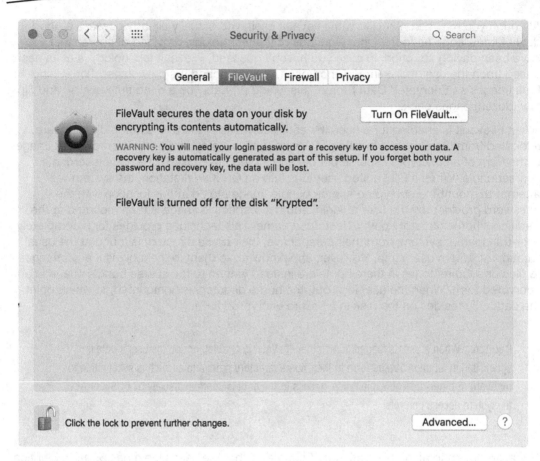

Figure 9-10. Enable FileVault

Next, you'll be prompted whether you want the active iCloud account to be allowed to unlock the disk and reset the disk password if it's forgotten. If you like iCloud, then you'll likely want to use this. If you consider iCloud a security risk then you'll likely want to create a recovery key that does not leverage the iCloud account. Once you've decided whether you'd like a copy of your recovery key saved in iCloud, click Continue.

Figure 9-11. The password reset dialog presented in the Accounts system preference pane

When prompted, click Restart to reboot the computer and begin the encryption process.

Once FileVault Is Enabled

Enabling FileVault for a user is a pretty easy endeavor, and is accomplished on a small scale through the Security System Preference pane. As seen in Figure 9-12, the interface presented is fairly minimalistic, and provides for only one button, used to disable FileVault for the current logged-in user.

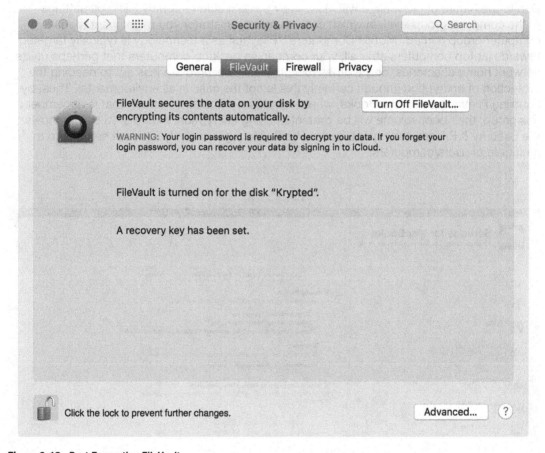

Figure 9-12. Post Encryption FileVault

We'll discuss the master password in just a bit; that indicator function is fairly obvious though there are a few specifics that are good to know. When you click the button to Turn On FileVault, the system will convert the volume into an encrypted volume. Upon doing so, the system will inform the user that the system needs to reboot to convert the volume.

In a larger scale managed environment, it may be desirable to enable FileVault across a large spread of users, or computers. To facilitate this, FileVault fully supports MCX and profile management. If you are unfamiliar with MCX, or Managed Client OS X, it can best be summed up as a technology supported by Mac OS X Clients and managed by OS X servers through the implementation of Open Directory. As its name implies, MCX is a system that allows for the management of various preferences and permissions applied to a user base, and can be applied to individual users, groups of users, individual computers, or groups of computers. Profiles are a means of implementing managed preferences. MCX and profiles are discussed in more detail in Chapter 16.

Due to the nature of FileVault, it will most likely be desirable to deploy FileVault settings at the computer group level, in which case as an administrator you might want to make a computer group named "Mobile Computers". FileVault as a technology is typically targeted towards laptop computers after all, your companies desktop computers that perhaps utilize network home directories, or are otherwise physically secured are less apt to needing the protection of encryption (though certainly this is not the case in all environments). Thus, by enabling FileVault for all MacBooks, whenever a user enrolls a computer that is a member of this group, their boot volume will be protected using encryption. Figure 9-13 below shows the Security & Privacy settings utilized in Profile Manager to apply FileVault settings to a multitude of users/computers.

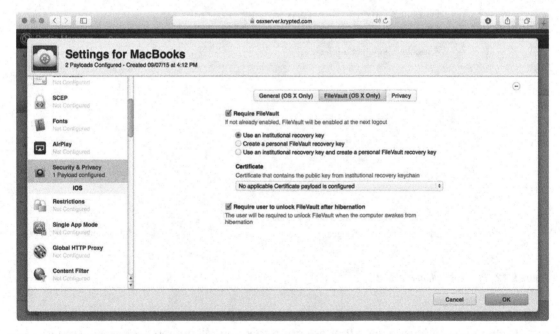

Figure 9-13. Deploying FileVault MCX settings Using Profile Manager

The FileVault Master Password

As we discussed in the previous section, there is a potential liability factor that a company assumes when deploying encryption of user data, as it means that there is a higher potential for the loss of sensitive company data, simply due to the potential loss of encryption keys. However, as we learned previously, companies can mitigate this liability by using a secondary access provision through the use of certificates. Fortunately, by default, FileVault uses such a certificate to provide a backdoor to this data. In the FileVault context, the terminology that Apple applies to this is a master password, and in fact, a master password must be set before a user can enable FileVault. This master password is in fact a FileVault-specific keychain whose contents consist solely of a certificate and private key identity that is used specifically for FileVault certificate-based authentication. The master password is simply the password that is used to secure the FileVault keychain itself. With this setup, the master password can be rotated without concern that existing encrypted volumes need to have the new password applied to it. As we all know (hopefully?), it's a good idea in security sensitive environments to routinely rotate sensitive passwords, and certainly the backdoor password to decrypt company data qualifies as sensitive.

Deploying the centralized identity isn't a terribly difficult task. As you saw in Figure 9-13, you can set a FileVault Master Password using a profile and via MDM. To accomplish this, all an administrator needs to do is to set a master password on the system used for deployment and then select it.

FileVault command Line

In some cases, the technologies we've mentioned will not meet the burden of criteria of a corporation's security policies. While FileVault on a technology level provides very strong encryption, it is not without its own limitations. Thus there is a plethora of third party solutions that provide more options than FileVault alone. Most of these are based on FileVault, the APIs Apple provides for FileVault, and the command line options around fdesetup.

FileVault 2 has a command line configuration utility called fdesetup. To use fdesetup to encrypt a boot volume, first check FileVault's status to make sure that the disk isn't currently encrypted. Do so by entering the fdesetup command along with the –status option (wait, no — required any more!):

```
sudo fdesetup status
```

Read the help page before starting to use fdesetup, as options change now and then. To do so, use the help verb:

```
fdesetup help
```

Once you have confirmed that FileVault is not currently in use, enable FileVault with the enable option, as follows:

```
sudo fdesetup enable
```

Unless additional parameters are specified, you will be greeted with an interactive prompt. Here, provide the primary user's short name and password. Once you have enabled FileVault, a Recovery key is returned. The Recovery key should stored somewhere safe, a task you can use a script to perform to a write-only share used for key escrowing. If you need more complicated logic, check out one of the 3rd party solutions provided later in this chapter or the open source Cauliflower Vest, at code.google.com. If you run fdesetup and you've deployed a master keychain, you will need to point the -keychain command at the actual keychain. For example:

```
sudo fdesetup enable -keychain /Library//Keychains/FileVaultMaster.keychain
```

To define a certificate, you will use the enable verb and then indicate the certificate path:

```
sudo fdesetup enable -certificate ~/filename.cer
```

Adding additional users other than the one who enabled fdesetup is a bit different than the first:

```
sudo fdesetup add -usertoadd julia
```

To remove users, just remove them with a remove verb followed by the -user option and the username:

```
sudo fdesetup remove -user julia
```

The remove and add options also offer using the -uuid rather than the username. Let's look at Juia's uid :

```
dscl . read /Users/julia GeneratedUID | cut -c 15-50
```

From the above command, take that GUID and plug it in as the uuid using the -uuid option. For example, to do so with the remove verb:

```
sudo fdesetup remove -uuid 31E609D5-39CF-4A42-9F24-CFA2B36F5532
```

All of these commands can be run interactively or using the various fdesetup options to define variables you would otherwise provide during the interactive prompt. One other option we'll look at here though is -defer. The –defer option allows you to run the fdesetup tool at the next login, rather than attempting to do so at runtime. Here, we will write the key to a plist and use it with a script at a later time:

```
sudo fdesetup enable -defer /temp/fdesetupescrow.plist
```

Or define users concurrently (continuing to use the julia test user):

```
sudo fdesetup enable -user julia -defer /temp/fdesetupescrow.plist
```

FileVault can also use accounts from a Directory Services. These will synchronize with the Directory Service routinely, as their data is cached. To manually run a synchronization, use the sync verb:

```
sudo fdesetup sync
```

This is really just scratching the surface of what you can do with fdesetup. There are a number of third party solutions that provide far more extensibility, such as WinMagic SecureDoc.

Check Point

Check Point Endpoint Full Disk Encryption is a full disk encryption (FDE) technology for OS X that meets Common Criteria EAL4 FIPS 140-2 standards. Check Point allows you to use a key that is escrowed, as you could script with FileVault.

On its back-end Check Point FDE utilizes AES-256bit encryption, the same government-approved standard available for use with encrypted disk images. Authentication provided by the pre-boot environment supports a number of different facilities. Most commonly, a standard username and password can be utilized to provide access to the data. Alternatively, dynamic tokens, such as RSA or crypto card, are supported, allowing for very secure one-time token authentication. Regardless of the method used, backdoor access can be obtained by administrators or privileged users in order to gain access to the data: therefore the recovery of the data is not solely dependent on the user remembering their password. Likewise, if a user forgets their password in the field, the product has full support for remote recovery even if the laptop does not have an active connection to the Internet. This gives administrators the ability to restore access to a remote user via a standard voice-confirmation phone call. By granting temporary access, the user can regain access to the data and then reset their password. This is a pretty cool feature, and does improve accessibility, another critical component of information security. However, remote recovery systems are not without flaws, and can open up a can of worms, allowing an attacker to socially engineer the help desk or gain permanent backdoor credentials without having to compromise the user's password or token.

In the end, Check Point is a very secure and robust product, and has very manageable features, particularly when working in large environments. For more on Check Point Endpoint Full Disk Encryption, see http://www.checkpoint.com/products/full-disk-encryption/.

Symantec Endpoint Encryption

Symantec is a well-known and trusted encryption technology. Like Check Point, Symantec Endpoint Encryption provides full support for OS X, and can be used to ensure that the volumes attached to your system are fully protected. Full disk protection is provided through a very similar approach to Check Point, where the user is prompted to authenticate prior to the system being able to read the OS X system on an encrypted disk, and therefore boot off of it.

Symantec Endpoint Encryption was once called PGP whole disk encryption (WDE) and has a very robust feature set, and supports numerous encryption algorithms, including the familiar AES-256 algorithm that we have seen throughout this chapter. PGP also supports a very strong hashing algorithm in the form of SHA-2-256, which provides very strong encryption on the stored keys themselves. Upon first configuring whole disk encryption, Symantec Endpoint Encryption creates a public and private key which operate in a similar manner to other PKI systems that we have discussed in this chapter: the public key is, as its name implies, a public file that can be distributed to anyone that might intend to send you encrypted data. The private key is essential to the decryption of any data generated with the public key; and therefore should be guarded with utmost care. The private key itself is protected with your passphrase, and this passphrase is required in order to utilize the private key to decrypt data. Once these keys are created, it is then possible to utilize them to begin to encrypt data stored on your local disks.

While Symantec Endpoint Encryption provides for strong security in and of itself, the strength of the solution is greatly improved through the use of a management suite that includes a Universal Server component. The Universal Server allows administrators to define and enforce various security policies, such as requiring any removable media to utilize encryption.

For more information on Symantec Encryption Desktop, see `https://support.symantec.com/en_US/article.TECH174563.html`.

WinMagic SecureDoc

SecureDoc is a promising player in the Mac encryption game, and has a compelling product. The system operates in much the same way as previously mentioned FDE products, making use of FileVault 2 and for iOS, profiles.

SecureDoc can be deployed to a single node, or to a fleet of nodes. If you're looking to engage in the latter, you'll likely want to deploy a SecureDoc Enterprise Server (SES), which provides a number of management and deployment capabilities that will make your life easier when trying to deploy the FDE system en masse. SES has full support for both Mac and Windows clients, and provides for platform-agnostic centralized management capabilities, which can be used for deployment and configuration of encryption identities/keys, security policies, and for provisioning user access. SES provides for centralized log collection, allowing for global auditing of security events. Lastly, the SES provides for remote password assistance capabilities.

SecureDoc has had Mac support for a few years now, and has gained a decent reputation in this time frame, as the system is generally well regarded. Its support for numerous authentication schemes, such as Active Directory and CAC/PIV, along with its support for booting off of encrypted volumes, rank it among the more capable of Mac-friendly FDE products.

For more information on SecureDoc, check out `http://www.winmagic.com/products/full-disk-encryption-for-mac`.

Summary

In this chapter we discussed in detail methods to provide security to your data in the form of encryption. As we have learned, OS X ships with a number of encryption technologies that can be used to increase the security of a running client: the Keychain for encrypting passwords and secure notes, disk images for encrypting user data, and FileVault can be used to encrypt the entirety of volume. While these technologies do provide a decently strong method for securing data, the protections they offer are not always enough at scale, and additional functionality or protection may be needed. In these cases, multiple third party solutions abound that cover a wide variety of data security needs. Determining the appropriate technology to use in your environment will depend on your needs and policies, but the diversity of the options available will typically ensure that OS X can exist in your environment and adhere to your defined security policy.

For the next chapter, Securing Network Traffic, we will shift focus from protecting data physically residing on a disk to instead ensuring data confidentiality when transmitted over a less secure and more public medium: the network.

## Part III

Securing the Network

## Chapter 10

Securing Network Traffic

Infiltration is a very real problem for network administrators, one that can lead to confidential data being leaked outside of your controlled environment. Every day, new attacks are developed that try to breach a network's security perimeter. Building a secure network requires that a number of key software and hardware components are implemented and configured correctly. But securing a network is not just about acquiring the right network hardware to block unwanted traffic. What is more important is understanding how a network works, how Internet traffic is managed, how information flows within that network, and what services need to be secured that control the traffic. One cannot fully secure what one does not understand.

Once these crucial elements have been explored, the methods of ensuring data packet protection we'll go on to discuss will make sense. In this chapter, we will explore the essential concepts of network structures. Within those concepts, we will then discuss the steps you can take to make your network stronger against security breaches and unwanted network traffic.

Understanding TCP/IP

The Internet runs on a suite of communication protocols commonly known as *TCP/IP*. This stands for Transmission Control Protocol/Internet Protocol, which were the first two protocols to be defined. Over the years, the suite has expanded to include other protocols, such as User Datagram Protocol (UDP), a stateless Internet Protocol used for streaming media, and Domain Name Service (DNS), the protocol used to connect names with IP addresses and the most popular protocol used on the Internet. In order to understand network traffic, it's important to understand what TCP/IP is and how it works. It is the suite of protocols upon which the majority of modern networks, including the Internet, are based. It is also one of the most common vectors exploited by network-based attacks.

This family of protocols is commonly interpreted as a set of *layers*, each comprising a different portion of the complicated task of moving data between systems. Each layer presents its own security problems, and effective security must address each layer independently.

> **Note** There are several *layer models* used to explain IP traffic. For the purposes of this condensed discussion of IP traffic, we will stick to the four-layer model laid out in RFC1122.

The path that data takes over the TCP/IP stack begins and ends at the user-level *application layer*. Here, "applications" doesn't refer to a user-level program, such as Mail.app, but refers instead to the higher-level protocols that make the network useful: HTTP for serving web pages, POP and IMAP for receiving mail, and SMTP for sending mail. Securing the application layer can consist of limiting the applications that a user has access to, as discussed in Chapter 3. It can also entail using application-level encryption—everything from manually encrypting sensitive data using PGP (explained in further detail in Chapter 9) to automatically encrypting data using a secure protocol, such as SSH, which is discussed further in Chapter 15.

Application data is then presented to the *transport layer,* where a protocol, typically TCP, establishes a connection between the source and destination computers, providing reliable delivery of a stream of data from one computer to the other. In order to achieve this, TCP encapsulates the data into *packets*, manageable chunks of data with a source address and a destination address. In order to make sure the packets get to the correct application at the other end, TCP uses the concept of a *port*. This is a virtual construct that acts as an endpoint for the communication between the two computers. TCP ports are identified by numbers, and different protocols will usually "listen" in on the ports assigned to them.

> **Note** This isn't strictly true, as a server will start a listener on any port you configure it to, provided there isn't a listener for an application running on that port already. Some people recommend running services such as SSH on nonstandard ports as an added security precaution. You can see what port each service uses in the `/etc/services` file.

One of the most important steps in securing any network is limiting the number of incoming ports to only those that are necessary. For example, if a machine is not serving web pages, it should not accept traffic on port 80, which is the default port for HTTP. Unwanted software can bind itself to commonly used ports, giving malicious activity an air of legitimacy, and so even if you are not explicitly using a port you should still block traffic to it if that traffic is not required.

Moving packets from one address to another happens at the *network layer*, and is generally handled by IP. Packets move from machine to machine via a series of intermediate steps, commonly referred to as *hops*. If we use the analogy of commercial shipping, this resembles packing up items into boxes and attaching shipping labels to each box. The labels have a shipping address that includes a street address (IP address) and a name (port number). There's also a return address with the same information. Once the shipping company (the network layer) delivers the packages to the appropriate building, it's the responsibility of the shipping and receiving department (the transport layer) to ensure that all packages have arrived and are accounted for, and are delivered to the appropriate resident. That resident (the application layer) can finally assemble the contents of the packages.

> **Note**   Packets are explained in further detail later in this chapter.

An example of security at the network layer is Network Address Translation (NAT), which presents a single IP address to the outside world, while maintaining a separate internal addressing scheme for the local network. Although it doesn't necessarily secure your network from outside attacks, the less information an outside attacker knows about your internal network, the better. This concept of "security through obscurity" increases the difficulty of exploiting vulnerabilities. Having a single incoming access point rather than a large number of systems connected directly to the Internet can make it easier to deal with certain risks, such as Denial of Service (DoS) attacks. However, this would not help protect your systems from other hosts on your internal network.

The *link* or *physical layer* comprises the physical implementation of the network. For example, a wired Ethernet network consists of a Network Interface Card (NIC) in each host connected to the network, and the cabling and switches that connect them. Another example is a wireless AirPort network, accessed with AirPort cards in laptops and hosted by AirPort base stations. There are also fiber-optic ports, satellite signals, and DSL modems of the various Internet service providers, all parts of the physical layer.

The bigger your network is, the more vulnerable the physical layer. For a home user, physical security is as simple as using WPA2 encryption and a strong password on an AirPort network, as discussed in Chapter 12. For a large office, a larger number of switches and routers need to be secured. It is also important to look out for and stop unauthorized access points, spoofed MAC addresses, and Denial of Service attacks that may be launched, even unwittingly, by users.

Each layer has its own part to play and is generally ignorant of the implementation details of the other layers, which allows the TCP/IP stack to be rather scalable. The post office doesn't tape up the package, and it isn't concerned with what is done with the contents of the package once the recipient receives it. All it cares about is moving the package from one address to another. Similarly, when you pack your boxes, you neither know nor care whether they will be put in the back of a truck and driven across the country or packed with other items into a large container and flown across the country on a cargo jet. All you are concerned with is that they get there.

However, as a security expert, you can't afford the luxury of this ignorance. You should be aware of that which you can control, and you should mitigate that which you can't control.

Now that we've run through a quick synopsis of what network traffic is, we'll discuss some of the various network topologies, management techniques for that traffic, and ways to safeguard network traffic from possible attacks.

Types of Networks

To some degree, there are about as many types of networks as there are network administrators. But they are all built using varying themes on one of two network architecture types: peer-to-peer networks and client-server networks.

Peer-to-Peer

A peer-to-peer (P2P) computer network is one that relies primarily on the computing power and bandwidth of the participants in the network to facilitate the interactivity on the network, rather than concentrating it in a centralized set of network servers and routers. (See Figure 10-1 for a graphical representation of a P2P network.) P2P networks are typically used for connecting nodes via ad-hoc connections. Such networks are useful for many purposes: assembling marketing materials, conducting research, and acquiring digital media assets (probably the most common use).

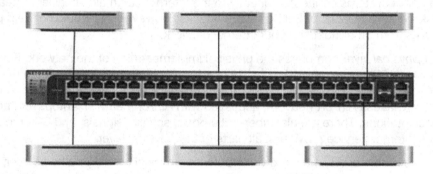

Figure 10-1. Peer-to-peer networks

A wide variety of peer-to-peer applications are available for use, and each has its own specific feature set that makes it popular. BitTorrent sites and other peer-to-peer networks allow you to publish music, documents, and other media to the Internet and to access media published by others. However, peer-to-peer networking applications can use a considerable amount of bandwidth when they are not configured properly. Multiple computers running peer-to-peer applications can flood any network, from DSL to cable modems and even fiber. You will also need to configure them correctly to make sure you are not sharing private information, such as your address book or financial data.

Considerations When Configuring Peer-to-Peer Networks

When configuring a peer-to-peer networking application, you will usually want to share files on your computer as well as download files from other computers. If you do not share files to the P2P network, then your download bandwidth can be automatically limited by the application, and some computers will not even allow you to download files from them. Sharing is an essential part of peer-to-peer networking, so you'll probably devote some bandwidth to others downloading your material. However, you should limit the bandwidth these applications are using as it can seriously affect other processes on your computer that perform their duties on the Internet.

Each application comes with the ability to limit incoming access in some way. One way to limit the bandwidth is by limiting the number of incoming connections that are allowed to access your data. Each program does it a bit differently. Look through the settings for those that allow you to configure the number of concurrent incoming and outgoing connections.

Another way to limit incoming connections is throttling bandwidth. Consider that someone accessing your computer may be running a cable modem or fiber-optic network, and might have available bandwidth of 10Mbps or more to access your files. If you are running only a DSL connection and they have FiOS, let's say, their machine could cause your connection to be saturated while your computer is trying to keep up the pace. This could also cause your Internet speed to slow to a crawl. You can limit incoming connections to make sure you always have plenty of speed available for browsing the Internet. When configuring the settings of a P2P application, look for a section that allows you to limit maximum upload and download speeds. By limiting concurrent connections, you help ensure that your network does not become flooded with P2P traffic (which can result in a Denial of Service attack on your entire network if you're not careful).

Another concern with peer-to-peer applications is limiting access to certain files. On P2P networks, users often share their entire Documents folder, exposing private data, such as their mail database and financial information, to the world. When installing a peer-to-peer application, make sure you know which folder is being shared and that the contents of that folder are limited to data you want accessible from outside your environment. For example, when using a file-sharing utility like LimeWire, you will be asked to choose a folder for shared data. Create a new folder in your home directory to share data from, and only allow LimeWire to share from that folder. You will also be asked to select which file types you would like to share with LimeWire. You should allow it to share only those types that you actually need to share.

One administrative concern with peer-to-peer file sharing is its potential to be used for illegal sharing of copyrighted material. Although preventing this type of traffic by blocking network ports is possible, it can sometimes be a moving target because some of these P2P protocols use random ports dynamically. The Mac OS X firewall (covered in greater detail in Chapter 11) can block P2P traffic by preventing traffic generated by specific applications. Blocking P2P traffic using the firewall requires diligence. There are a number of Gnutella clients for Mac OS X, and if you block all but one, you've left a window open. Some Internet appliances and filtering packages can be configured to tag traffic that appears to be P2P, tracking the session based on these tags, and thus overcoming any reliance on blocking traffic on any specific port.

Client-Server Networks

Over the years, as P2P networks grew, they became unwieldy, making it more difficult to keep tabs on the computers that were linked together. This led to the development of client-server networks. Client-server networks are not ad hoc. Services on client-server networks are statically provisioned and centrally managed. In this model, much of the management of the network—assigning IP addresses, warehousing data, and managing bandwidth—happens at the server level, and not on the individual workstations. Because of this, client-server networks quickly became the primary weapon in combating unwieldy networks (see Figure 10-2 for a graphical representation of a client-server network).

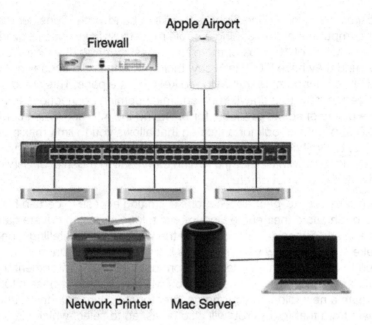

Figure 10-2. An example of a client-server network

Understanding Routing

As data moves between networks, you need to tell it where to go. Moving data through networks is called *routing*. The following sections show how to route data packets and how to secure the routing techniques used to move that data along. First, we will explore what packets are and then examine the various types of devices that packets encounter as they traverse the Internet. This includes gateways, routers, and firewalls.

Packets

To understand how routing data works, we first need to explore what a packet is. A *packet* is a general term for a bundle of data, organized in a predetermined way for transmission over computer networks. IP packets consist of two parts, the *header* and the *data*. The *header* marks the beginning of the packet and contains information, such as the size of the payload and the source and destination address. The *data* is the information being carried by this particular packet.

> **Note**   Packets are sometimes referred to as *datagrams*. The terms are not interchangeable, however. A datagram is a type of packet, but not all packets are datagrams.

Different protocols use different conventions for distinguishing between different sections of a packet, and for formatting the data. The Ethernet protocol establishes the start of the header and the other data elements by their relative location to the start of the packet. For the purposes of understanding other technologies discussed throughout this chapter, just keep in mind that there are different ways to form a packet based on the protocol that is being used.

A good analogy when thinking about packets is to treat data transmission like moving into a new house. When moving our things, we tend to be efficient. Instead of loading one piece of furniture on to the truck, driving to the new house, unloading it, and then driving back for another piece, we move multiple pieces at a time. We also don't cram everything into one giant box. We load our stuff from one room and put it in a box (or boxes) and label it before moving on to the next room. The header is the container (or box) for data (our stuff). The application packing up the data writes the name of the data in the header, much as we would write where the stuff in the box would go on a label on the box. This allows the network router (or movers) to know which room each box is destined for and typically which room the stuff came from. The router (or moving truck) will create a list of what was transmitted (moved). Most transfers of data will move more than one packet (box), breaking files into data packets (boxes) to move them more efficiently.

Gateways

A *gateway* is a device that connects two physical or logical networks. Some gateways mediate between networks that use different base protocols, and some relay traffic between two networks using the same protocol. All gateways should have a minimum of two addresses, one on each network to which they're connected.

Routers

A gateway that forwards IP traffic between two networks is referred to as a *router*. Routers forward packets from one network to another. They use routing tables to help guide those packets to their destination. A *route* is the path that is taken by data traveling from one system or network to another. Routers maintain a table in which they will cache the paths the packets take to get to their destination, which makes communication between devices much quicker than it would be otherwise. The address of each device that the data touches on the path to its destination is a *hop*. Each entry in a routing table specifies the next hop (or several hops), resulting in reduced lookups and improved performance. Each hop maintains its own routing table unless it is the device that initiated or terminated the connection. These routing tables need to be consistent, or routing loops can develop, which can cause a number of problems. If the path from your system to another forms a loop, your system will be unable to contact the other system. Your system might also cause an inadvertent denial-of-service attack on other systems by resending packets along the looped route, taking bandwidth away from legitimate traffic.

One way to view hops is by using the `traceroute` command in Mac OS X, which will show each hop between your computer and a remote device. The `traceroute` command is followed by the remote hostname. For example, a `traceroute` for `www.apple.com` recently resulted in the following output:

```
traceroute to www.apple.com.akadns.net (17.251.200.32), 64 hops max, 52 byte packets
 1  192.168.1.1 (192.168.1.1)  3.501 ms  2.816 ms  2.659 ms
 2  10.67.152.1 (10.67.152.1)  4.271 ms  6.450 ms  6.128 ms
 3  10.1.176.1 (10.1.176.1)  4.670 ms  5.834 ms  5.067 ms
 4  147.225.49.89 (147.225.49.89)  4.686 ms  5.809 ms  5.337 ms

 5  152.161.241.70 (152.161.241.70)  10.346 ms  17.047 ms  10.958 ms
 6  72-254-0-1.client.stsn.net (72.254.0.1)  11.563 ms  12.283 ms  15.622 ms
 7  206.112.96.178 (206.112.96.178)  11.334 ms  10.764 ms  13.055 ms
 8  63.66.208.221 (63.66.208.221)  12.194 ms  14.915 ms  15.028 ms
 9  sc0.ar1.sjc5.web.uu.net (63.66.208.21)  32.809 ms  12.049 ms  10.935 ms
10  0.so-3-0-0.xl2.sjc5.alter.net (152.63.49.58)  10.811 ms  10.897 ms  10.336 ms
11  150.ATM4-0.XR1.SJC2.ALTER.NET (152.63.48.2)  18.823 ms  13.592 ms  14.346 ms
12  0.so-7-0-0.br1.sjc7.alter.net (152.63.48.253)  17.073 ms  16.109 ms  21.148 ms
13  oc192-7-1-0.edge6.sanjose1.level3.net (4.68.63.141)  12.819 ms  13.318 ms  16.430 ms
14  vlan79.csw2.sanjose1.level3.net (4.68.18.126)  15.149 ms
    vlan69.csw1.sanjose1.level3.net (4.68.18.62)  15.668 ms
15  ae-81-81.ebr1. level3.net (4.69.134.201)  15.655 ms ae-61-61 13.229 ms
16  ae-4-4.car2.level3.net (4.69.132.157)  210.512 ms  182.308 ms  41.987 ms
17  ae-11-11.car1.level3.net (4.69.132.149)  15.889 ms  31.446 ms  16.157 ms
18  apple-compu.car1.level3.net (64.158.148.6)  18.413 ms !X *  21.754 ms !X
```

Firewalls

A *firewall* is a device or software that is designed to inspect traffic and permit, deny, or proxy it. A firewall can be a dedicated appliance or software running on a host operating system. Firewalls function in a networked environment to prevent specified types of communication, filtering the traffic you want to be able to receive from the traffic you do not want to receive. Mac OS X has a built-in software firewall that you can use to limit incoming traffic. This will allow you to control traffic in a way that keeps attacks at a minimum. In Chapter 11 we discuss the software firewall in more depth.

Many firewalls will help reduce the likelihood of Denial of Service attacks against one of your computers. However, some firewalls are susceptible to these attacks themselves, opening your environment to the threat of not being able to do business. To help with this, most firewalls support the ability to have a fail-over firewall, which can automatically become the active firewall in situations where the main firewall goes down.

Port Management

Since the introduction of malware and spyware, it is becoming more common to restrict incoming and outgoing access on commonly used (and abused) ports, such as port 25. For example, if you don't need mail services in your environment (perhaps because e-mail is hosted elsewhere), then it is likely that you will want to eliminate outgoing SMTP traffic from passing through your router. If you're not hosting mail internally, you will also want to make sure that all inbound mail-related traffic (SMTP, as well as POP and IMAP) is being denied as well.

As discussed in previous chapters, most savvy network administrators will also restrict incoming access to their networks to all but a select number of ports, and for good reason. Many older protocols, such as FTP, are inherently insecure, or there are weak implementations of these protocols that should not be accessible from the outside. Restricting access is the primary job of most firewalls and is often called *access control*. When looking into configuring the access controls on your firewall, keep in mind that every open port is a security risk, and each one needs to be treated as such. Allow incoming access only for services that are required.

Properly securing your backbone and perimeter will greatly reduce the likelihood of a successful attack. For example, many root kits will attempt to establish an outgoing connection over a certain port to an attacker's computer. If this connection cannot be established, the root kit is less likely to cause harm in your environment. Therefore, it is important to restrict outgoing as well as incoming access.

> **Note** We discuss root kits in more detail in Chapter 8.

> **Tip** Keep in mind that port management is a common task, and an administrator's network management time should be allocated to this vital aspect of network security. Users on a network will frequently ask for certain ports to be opened that are not standard for many environments. Understand that this type of request is common across many networks, and each request should be considered very carefully.

DMZs and Subnets

A *demilitarized zone* (DMZ) is a perimeter network, or a network area that sits outside an organization's internal network. A DMZ is used to hold public-facing servers that need to be accessible to the Internet and are therefore more likely to face attacks. The purpose of this design is to mitigate the damage should one of these hosts be compromised. Important or sensitive information should never be kept in a DMZ. On consumer-grade routers, a DMZ typically refers to an address to which all suspect traffic is forwarded. In home environments, the DMZ is often configured incorrectly. We often find that it is used to forward all traffic to a specific address, rather than researching which ports need to be accessible for each service and only forwarding that traffic to the DMZ. This becomes a big security threat to the computer or network device that has all the traffic forwarded to it.

Whether you choose to use a DMZ depends not on the size of your company but on whether you are using protocols that you think might easily be compromised. For example, FTP is not a secure protocol. Relegating the use of FTP in your environment to a system that lives outside your local network would prevent standard FTP attacks from affecting the entire network infrastructure.

Some administrators might choose to use a second subnet instead of a DMZ to keep certain types of traffic separate from the primary network. Subnetting an IP network allows a single large network to be broken down into what appears (logically) to be several smaller ones. Devices on the same subnet have the same *subnet mask*, a number that determines which part of an address signifies the network range and which signifies the hosts in that range.

Rather than allowing your users to see one another, you could put them on separate subnets and not allow UDP traffic to pass across the various subnets implemented in your environment. It is even possible to split a network into multiple subnets. Keep in mind, however, that the more complex the subnetting gets, the more difficult it becomes to troubleshoot problems on the network. For example, when a wireless network is introduced into an environment, and a separate wireless subnet is created, wireless users may have difficulty automatically finding printers on the main network. The printers will need to be manually installed using their IP address.

Spoofing

When access controls are configured based on IP addresses instead of network security policies, access attacks can occur. *Spoofing*, or the act of masquerading on a network with a valid IP address that was not legitimately given, is one of those access attacks and is a common way for attackers to establish access. To spoof an IP or MAC address, an attacker need only discover the MAC address or IP address of someone they know can access a network and then change their own MAC address to the one that the network is familiar with.

Let's take a command-line look at how to change your MAC address. First run an ifconfig command to get your current MAC address. Then use the lladdr option of ifconfig to change your MAC address slightly:

```
cedge:/Users/cedge root# ifconfig en0
en0: flags=8863<UP,BROADCAST,SMART,RUNNING,SIMPLEX,MULTICAST> mtu 1500
        ether 00:17:f2:2a:66:12
cedge:/Users/cedge root# sudo ifconfig en0 lladdr 00:17:f2:2a:66:21
cedge:/Users/cedge root# ifconfig en0
en0: flags=8863<UP,BROADCAST,SMART,RUNNING,SIMPLEX,MULTICAST> mtu 1500
        ether 00:17:f2:2a:66:21
```

If any application was blocking traffic from your machine based on its MAC address, the traffic will now be allowed. Once a machine on a network changes its MAC address, other machines will see this change and issue a line similar to the following:

```
kernel: arp: 192.168.55.108 moved from 00:17:f2:2a:66:12 to 00:17:f2:2a:66:21

    on eth0
```

Armed with this information, you can now set up a scanner in your logs to be notified when this line appears and then investigate all changes of MAC addresses. One way to get around this type of attack is by redirecting the access to other sentry machines that are set up to monitor these kinds of spoofing attacks. This is a deceptive active response to fool attackers into thinking attacks are succeeding, allowing an administrator to monitor what the attacker is trying to do. If you are running Snort (discussed further in Chapter 17), then your system should notice the MAC spoof and disable communications from that host automatically, thus defending you against an attack from a spoofed IP address.

Stateful Packet Inspection

Using stateful packet inspection (SPI), a firewall appliance holds the significant attributes of each connection in memory. These attributes, collectively known as the *state* of the connection, include such details as the IP addresses and ports involved in the connection and the sequence of packets traversing it. The most CPU-intensive checking is performed when the connection starts. All packets after that (for that session) are processed rapidly because it is simple and fast to determine whether they belong to an existing, prescreened session. Once the session has ended, its entry in the state table is discarded.

Most modern firewalls, including those in some Linksys and Netgear routers found at your local consumer electronics store, have basic SPI features, as does the Mac OS X Snow Leopard software firewall. Consumer-grade appliances have a limited amount of memory and cannot inspect as many packets as rapidly or as closely as a more advanced device, such as some CheckPoints, SonicWalls, or Ciscos. Typically, SPI on these firewalls will check only the source of the packet against the source defined in the header.

Deep packet inspection (DPI) is a subclass of SPI that examines the data portion of a packet and searches for protocol noncompliance, or some predefined pattern, in order to decide whether the packet is allowed to pass. This is in contrast to the simple packet inspection found in stateless firewalls, in which only the header portion of a packet is checked. DPI classifies traffic based on a signature database (as does SPI) and will allow you to redirect, mark, block, rate-limit, and of course report based on the classification.

Many DPI devices, rather than simply relying on signature-based detection, can also identify patterns of potentially malicious traffic in the flow of traffic. This allows devices to detect newer attacks rather than react to predefined attacks, providing for a more secure network. If your environment has the budget to acquire a firewall that performs deep packet inspection, you should strongly consider adding one to your network. For the security it provides, it is well worth the investment.

Data Packet Encryption

When two computers on different networks are communicating, they are often sending packets across multiple routers, allowing traffic to be susceptible to a variety of security holes at each stop along the way. Even with good inspection on a firewall, an attacker can still perpetrate a *man-in-the-middle attack*, an attack in which someone spoofs a trusted host while sitting between your server and a user accessing your server. A man-in-the-middle attack is designed to intercept all the traffic between two points, either to eavesdrop or to insert malicious traffic. To keep prying eyes off your data, it is important to implement encryption techniques on your communications, rendering the data unreadable to the interceptor. If your data are passing from your home to your office, for example, you would implement a VPN. If you are taking customer data over web sites, then you might consider using SSL. We discuss using VPN and SSL further in Chapter 15.

Understanding Switches and Hubs

Hubs are dummy devices that connect multiple computers, making them act as a single segment on a network. With a hub, only one device can successfully transmit data at a time. When two computers submit data at the same time, a collision occurs, and a jam signal is sent to all the ports when collisions are detected. This makes one computer able to cause collisions and force an entire network to slow down while packets that were jammed are re-sent by all the computers that attempted to communicate during the jam. Hubs will also allow any computer to see the packets sent by all other computers on the hub.

Switches are more advanced than hubs and provide expandability, allowing more switches, ports, and computers to exist on a network. Switches perform collision detection and isolate traffic between the source of a packet and its destination. Because each computer is not automatically able to see all the traffic from other computers, this is a more secure communications environment. Switches are less likely to become flooded with collisions and offer faster throughput and lower latency.

We advise against the use of hubs as a general rule, unless you have a very explicit reason to use them, because they can act as potential collision centers and cause security breaches. However, hubs do still have limited usefulness in networks. Switches respond to loops, but hubs do not. When a cable is plugged into a switch twice, it can cause unwanted network traffic. In areas where many users are plugging in their laptops, a cable can get plugged back into a switch by accident, and some network administrators will use a hub to keep this from occurring. Additionally, protocol analyzers connected to switches do not always receive all the desired packets, because the switch separates the ports into different segments. Connecting a protocol analyzer to a hub will allow it to see all the traffic on the network segment. Finally, some cluster environments require each computer to receive all the traffic going to the cluster. In these situations, hubs will most likely be more appropriate than switches.

> **Note**   Many managed switches can be configured to act as though they are hubs, so you can get the capabilities you require while maintaining flexibility for more advanced features. However, this can be a security risk; and so when it's convenient you should disable remote configuration on switches.

Stacked switches are switches designed to accommodate multiple switches in a network. When a switch is stackable, it will have dedicated ports for adding more switches that allow speeds of 10 Gb or faster between the switches, using special stacking cables. These are often converted into fiber connections so that latency is optimized over long distances.

Managed Switches

As networks and features of networks have grown, managed switches have become more popular. *Managed switches* can control internal network traffic and are used to split a network into logical segments, giving more granular control over network traffic and providing more advanced error detection. Managed switches also offer more advanced logging features to help network administrators isolate problem areas. Some managed switches are also stacked, although not all of them are capable of stacking.

A standard feature to look for on a managed switch is VLAN support. VLAN, short for *virtual LAN*, describes a network of computers that behave as if they are connected to the same wire, even though they may actually be physically located on different segments of a LAN. They are configured through software rather than hardware, which makes them extremely flexible. One of the biggest advantages of VLANs is their portability. Computers are able to stay on the same VLAN without any hardware reconfiguration when physically moved to another location. This also works the other way; one physical LAN can be split into multiple logical networks by the VLAN software running on switches. This can be useful when implementing a DMZ, as you can isolate your DMZ traffic without actually creating an isolated physical network. Nearly all managed switches have a VLAN feature set.

Newer and more advanced switches also have the capability to perform rogue access point detection, or detection of unwanted access points and routers on a network. Since Apple joined the ranks of operating system vendors that have introduced Internet Sharing as a built-in feature, many networks have been brought to a grinding halt by rogue routers providing IP addresses to networks. Problems with rogue access points have been especially common in networks with large numbers of freelancers who bring their laptops into the office and connect to the wireless network without turning off the Internet Sharing that they were using at home. This establishes an ad-hoc Denial of Service to the rest of the network, because they receive bad DHCP leases with bad TCP/IP settings. This situation can require administrators to comb through every machine on a network to isolate which user has enabled the Internet Sharing features on their computers. Rogue access point detection is also helpful for making sure that random users on networks do not plug in wireless access points or routers they may think are switches. Rogue access points are discussed in further detail in Chapter 12.

Most managed switches also provide some form of MAC address filtering. A *MAC address* is a unique identifier attached to most forms of networking equipment (you can find your Mac's MAC address in the Network pane of System Preferences by clicking the Advanced button). With MAC filtering, a network administrator can define a destination address so that packets can be received only from a specific port and allow only those same packets to be forwarded to another port. Using MAC address filtering, only users who are connected to port A can access the server connected to port B; packets from other ports, even packets whose destination address is the server on port B, will be dropped. MAC filtering is also referred to as *network access control*, although this could refer to port filtration rather than MAC filtration.

Here are some other features of managed switches:

> **PoE**: Power over Ethernet allows power to be supplied to network devices over an Ethernet cable, rather than over a power adapter.

Spanning tree: This closes loops on networks. If more than one open path between any two ports were to be active at once (a loop), then a *broadcast storm*, or large amount of network traffic, could cause the network to become unstable.

Priority tagging: This specifies ports that are of a higher priority, allowing mission-critical traffic to be differentiated from traffic that's not.

Link aggregation: This uses multiple network ports in parallel to increase the link speed beyond the limits of any one single cable or port. Link aggregation, also known as *teaming*, is based on the IEEE 802.3ad link aggregation standard.

Flow control: This manages traffic rates between two computers on a switched network. It is not always possible for two computers to communicate at the same speed. Flow control throttles speeds for faster systems by pausing traffic when it is running too fast.

Using managed switches historically meant that large portions of an IT budget would need to be spent on acquiring them. However, with the increased number of manufacturers now involved in developing managed switches, that is no longer the case. Managed Netgear and D-Link switches (such as the one featured in Figure 10-3) provide many of the advanced features found in Cisco and other top-of-the-line switches for a fraction of the cost. This has made them increasingly popular. Features offered on D-Link and Netgear switches include link aggregation, flow control, network access control, spanning tree, and priority tags.

Figure 10-3. D-Link 48 port managed switch

Many administrators of Mac environments are not comfortable deploying managed switches in their environments, because they are typically command-line-only configurations, and some of the protocols they use can be incompatible with other devices on the network. To address this concern, Apple has recently begun to align with industry network standards, enabling Mac network administrators to become more comfortable using managed switches to support extended features of Mac hardware products. One example of this is the use of link aggregation (using two network interfaces as one) on Mac servers, a feature that requires a managed switch in order to be configured properly.

Restricting Network Services

Network services are the building blocks of many network environments. Connecting to the Internet, DNS, DHCP, and other protocols is the main reason for having a network in the first place. One of the best ways to ensure security for file sharing, web services, and mail services is to limit the access that computers have to them. Some computers may need access to these resources; denying them can be detrimental to the workflow. Others may not need access, and giving them access could be potentially damaging. For example, you might allow users local to your network to access your file server but will probably never want to allow access to the file server for users outside your network.

When architecting a network, you need to handle each service separately. Analyze which services go in and out of every system in an environment. If protocols will be accessed only from inside the network, such as file sharing and directory service protocols, then they should not be routable. Restricting access to protocols to users outside your network can be handled using the firewall, as mentioned earlier in this chapter. For larger environments, restricting access to services from other computers within your network is often handled using the switches in your environment. Draft a document, such as the one in Figure 10-4, that lists the servers in your environment, the services they will be providing, and which ports they run on. This can help tremendously when trying to secure all the services needed in a networked environment while maintaining their usability.

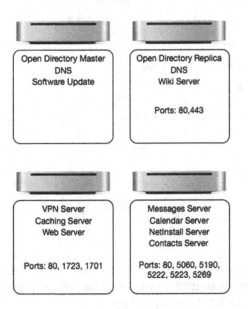

Figure 10-4. Servers, services, and ports

For smaller environments, restricting access between computers is usually handled on a per-service basis by using a local firewall running on the computer providing the service. For more information on configuring the software firewall in Mac OS X, see Chapter 11. For firewall configuration for Mac OS X Server, see Chapter 16.

Security Through 802.1x

802.1x is a protocol that is fully supported in OS X. The 802.1x standard can greatly increase the security of a network environment by requiring users to authenticate before they can access the local network for Ethernet or wireless networks. The 802.1x standard can use a third-party authentication authority, such as Open Directory or Active Directory, or you can use preshared keys. Authentication to the network rather than just the computer is a fairly new concept for most Mac environments. This level of advanced networking is fairly complex and must be given an appropriate level of planning.

Enabling 802.1x is accomplished by deploying a profile. These profiles can easily be created in Apple Configurator (Figure 10-5) or Profile Manager. You can then view 802.1x settings by opening System Preferences, clicking the Network pane, choosing the appropriate interface, and then clicking the Advanced button. At this point, you can click the 802.1x tab (Figure 10-5) and select the network to join.

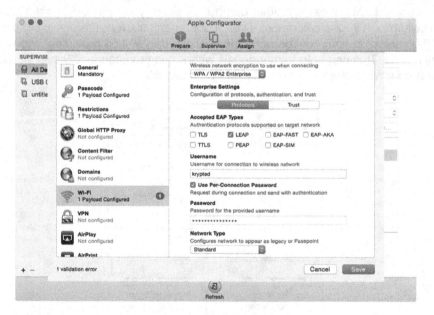

Figure 10-5. Setting up 802.1x

Once you have chosen your network, click the authentication protocol you want to use in the Authentication section, and then click Configure. This will allow you to configure settings for the specific protocol to match the settings of your server.

There are some serious vulnerabilities in the 802.1x protocol. Most significantly, it authenticates only at the beginning of the connection. For example, after authentication is successful and the connection is established, it's possible for an attacker to hijack the authenticated port by getting in between the authenticated computer and the port. As discussed earlier, this is called a man-in-the-middle attack.

Proxy Servers

One way of filtering traffic on your network is through the use of a *proxy server*. A proxy server allows services to establish network connectivity using one server as a sort of traffic cop. The proxy server is situated between computers and the Internet, and processes requests for external resources on behalf of the users of the network (see Figure 10-6). Using proxy servers, administrators can prevent users from viewing predetermined web sites. In addition to increasing security, proxy servers can improve network performance by allowing multiple users to access data that is saved in the proxy's cache. On the first access of this data, there will be a slight performance loss. Any subsequent attempts to visit the site or access the data will see a performance gain, since the content can be served from the proxy. Therefore, proxy servers accelerate access only to content that is accessed repeatedly.

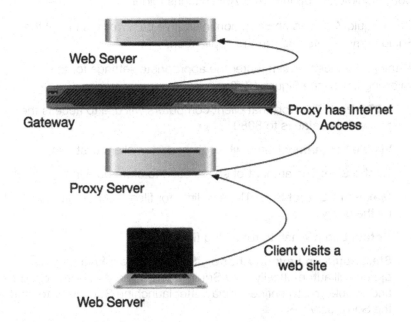

Figure 10-6. Proxy server network configuration

Proxies themselves can be exploited as a means to forward malicious HTTP traffic, such as web-based spam e-mail referrals. When setting up a proxy, it is important to take into account security concerns, such as which clients on the network will have access to the proxy. Often proxy servers have a whitelist (a list of allowed addresses) that can be used to allow access to IP addresses individually or by subnet. This should be configured to allow only those machines on the local area network to access the proxy services.

If external access is required, consider running the proxy on a nonstandard port and requiring authentication, perhaps utilizing an existing directory service, such as Active Directory or Open Directory. This, combined with strong password policies, should help protect against unauthorized access to the proxy.

Squid

Squid is an open source product that allows network administrators to configure proxy services easily. It has a robust set of access control options that can be configured to allow or deny access based on user or group access as well as other criteria such as scheduling proxy servers to be enabled at certain periods of time. SquidMan is a utility developed by Tony Gray to provide Mac users with a GUI to assist with installing and configuring a precompiled version of Squid.

To install SquidMan, follow these steps:

1. Download the installer from `http://web.me.com/adg/squidman/ index.html`, and extract the SquidMan `.dmg` file.

2. Copy SquidMan.app into your Applications folder.

3. Open SquidMan, and enter an administrative password to install the Squid components and run the application.

4. At the preferences screen, enter the appropriate settings for the following fields (see Figure 10-7):

   - **HTTP Port:** The port that client computers will use to access the proxy. This defaults to 8080.

   - **Visible hostname:** Name when viewed from client systems

   - **Cache Size:** The amount of space used to store data in the cache.

   - **Maximum Object Size:** The size limit for files that are to be cached by the proxy.

   - **Rotate Logs:** When to rotate log files.

   - **Start Squid on Launch After a _ Second Delay:** Enabling this option will automatically start Squid when SquidMan is launched and enable you to define a delay after launching SquidMan to start the Squid services.

   - **Quit Squid on Logout:** This allows you to determine if you'd like to keep Squid running when the active user logs out of your proxy server.

   - **Show Errors Produced by Squid:** This prompts users with pop-up windows when errors occur. This is helpful if someone is sitting at the desktop of the proxy server when it's running. However, if the desktop of the system is never looked at, then you will probably refer to logs to discover errors.

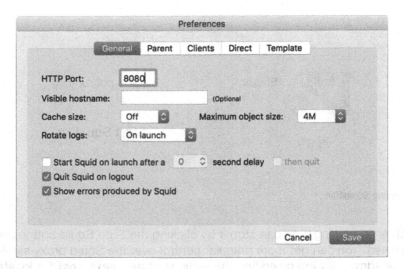

Figure 10-7. SquidMan preferences: changing ports and hostnames

5. Click the Parent tab, and use this location to choose whether you will have your Squid server use another Squid server as its proxy server. This can make troubleshooting difficult in proxy environments. Keep the defaults here unless you have multiple Squid servers.

6. Click the Clients tab and enter the appropriate IP addresses in the Provide Proxy Services For field. When entering IP address ranges, you will need to also enter the subnet for the IP range.

7. Use the Direct tab to configure any exclusions to the list of domains that will be proxied by the server. This will be helpful when troubleshooting a parent proxy environment.

8. Click the Template tab, and use this location to edit the Squid configuration file manually. Here, the maximum object size and cache directories can be increased beyond the variables available in the GUI.

9. Once the settings have been configured for SquidMan, use the Start Squid button of the main SquidMan screen to start Squid (see Figure 10-8).

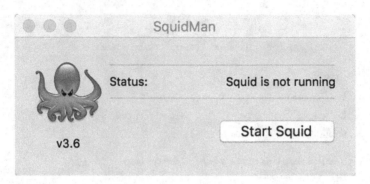

Figure 10-8. *Starting SquidMan*

Once SquidMan is running, you can stop it by clicking the Stop Squid button on the main SquidMan screen. You can get more granular control over the Squid proxy services via command-line administration by editing the settings of the `squid.conf` file located in `/User/<username>/Library/Preferences/squid.conf` once SquidMan is launched for the first time.

> **Note** The help files for SquidMan are very thorough in their explanations of these settings.

Summary

Layers of security breed resilient networks. When securing networks, layer your approach. Start from the center, the computer itself, and move outward, looking at which services should be accessible by which computers. Then, layer the security levels by grouping the computers and building policies to limit access on each of those groups. Determine your firewall policies, both internally and externally. Consider your network's physical layer as you implement security policies based on location within the network. This kind of layered approach gives strength to your network's security blueprint.

Chapter **11**

Managing the Firewall

Put simply, a firewall is a network traffic moderator. It uses a set of rules to determine what kind of traffic is allowed in and out of your computer or network. The term is a bit ambiguous, because there are many types of firewalls. In Chapter 10, we discussed the importance of using a firewall to act as a gateway into your network, denying and allowing network traffic on a network-wide basis between your computers and the outside world. This is what we refer to as a *hardware appliance firewall*.

For the purposes of this chapter, we will discuss the intricacies of the built-in firewall of OS X, the software in your operating system that determines which traffic your computer will accept. This is referred to as a *software firewall*. The differences between a software firewall and a hardware firewall can be rather significant. For example, a software firewall primarily limits how services from other computers on the same network talk to services on your computer, something hardware appliances typically do not do. A software firewall can also act as a barrier to network traffic of any type that might slip past your firewall appliance. In this respect, a software firewall can act as a powerful second line of defense against malicious attacks.

It is important to note that the firewall built into OS X should only act as the last (and most inner) layer of defense. Inexpensive routers from companies such as Linksys, Netgear, D-Link, Xsense, and hundreds of others offer firewalls that cost less than $100 and have many features that are not configurable in the OS X firewall. In many smaller environments, such as homes and offices with fewer than ten users, these firewall appliances used in conjunction with the Mac firewall are more than adequate to protect computers accessing the Internet, because they hide IP addresses from the Internet and expose only the IP address of the router.

Explaining how your software firewall works and how it can be configured requires us to dive into the specific services that your software firewall can blocked and how to teach your computer to allow or deny them. These services are often known as *network services*.

Introducing Network Services

The primary purpose behind most network traffic is for computers to communicate with one another. There are a wide variety of communication paths, or *routes*, that computers take to do this. And there are different purposes, or *roles*, for these varied communication paths. One communication path might have the intent of sending printing commands to a printer, while another might need to send an Internet request to an Internet gateway, or *router*. A network service then communicates with other devices using a structured mechanism for conversing, known as a *protocol*. For firewalls to manage these various protocols, they use rules. A *rule* is a set of parameters that enables the firewall to allow or deny access to a protocol on a computer.

In networking, there are a variety of protocols. Each comes with a default port assigned to it. *Ports* are what computers use to sift through the variety of protocol traffic in order to understand what network service the traffic is destined for. Port numbers fall anywhere between 0 and 65,535, and each protocol is assigned a number so that each type of traffic can be handled differently. When communications between computers occur, applications understand how to connect to each other based on the port number and protocol they use. Rules for applications and network services are then built using port numbers or sets of port numbers. Even though it's possible for thousands of different port numbers to be actively in use at one time, most applications use only a few common ports.

Fortunately, we usually don't have to keep track of port numbers, because the programs we use to access ports (such as Safari for web browsing or Entourage for reading e-mail) usually standardize the use of port numbers. IANA standardizes the port numbers, but they can be customized. For example, if you access a website, you are probably using HTTP, which uses port 80 as its network port. If you send a friend an e-mail, the Mail app is likely using port 25, because it is the default port for outgoing mail traffic. However, if you were to build a web server that runs over port 8080, such as the one built into many inexpensive routing or firewall devices, you would need to specify that web traffic moves through that port.

> **Note**   When working with firewalls, you will often need to know about port numbers in order to allow or block certain types of traffic. If you want to allow incoming access for the Web, for example, which would turn your computer into a web server, you would open port 80 on your computer. It's good practice to frequently reference port number tables in order to remember which ports typically work with various protocols. OS X also has a file, /etc/services, that lists the port numbers and the protocols that use them.

To demonstrate the way the network process structure works, let's look at an essential service of the Mac OS, the Apple Filing Protocol (AFP). AFP is a network communications service that allows the sharing of files between computers. It allows one machine to talk to other machines running AppleFileServer in order for files to move back and forth. AppleFileServer runs on the computer, sharing files as a process. That process listens on port 548. Another computer requests traffic over port 548, and when the host computer is listening, it responds, and a communication link between the two computers is established. And this all happens in a matter of milliseconds.

Many processes are easy to identify. Processes that listen for traffic can also be running as hidden processes or as a different user. mDNS (called Bonjour or Rendezvous in Mac OS X 10.3 and later and Rendezvous in 10.2 and earlier) is the protocol that allows other computers to discover information about your machine. mDNS (the process is known as the *mDNS responder*) runs over port 5353 as the root user, a user hidden by default. This means that if you were to log in as any registered user on a machine besides the root user and open the My Processes section of Activity Monitor, you would not find any processes running the mDNS protocol, because root processes are hidden. If you were to change the filter from My Processes to All Processes, you would find the mDNS responder, which is the actual process that is typically referred to as Bonjour.

Now that we've discussed what a network service is and how it talks to your computer, we'll move on to looking one of two components of the software firewall in OS X. The *Application Layer Firewall* (or ALF) component of the software firewall will allow or deny an application from establishing communication over the network, not based on its ports but based on the application itself. Rather than open and close ports on your computer, an ALF grants access based on whether the application itself has access, not through the configuration of ports.

The second component of the software firewall is the command line pf tool (described in detail later in this chapter), which opens and closes ports. The combination of the two provides a maximum of security if you so choose to use them (and is a serious annoyance if they are configured incorrectly).

Controlling Services

To get started controlling the application layer firewall, you will first need to define the services on your computer that need filtration. For ease of use, Apple has included the most common in the Sharing System Preferences pane. To get there, open System Preferences, and go to the Sharing pane (see Figure 11-1). If the padlock icon in the bottom left-hand corner of the screen is in the locked position, click it to be able to configure settings for the Sharing preferences. To enable a service, select the box that corresponds to each service; after you've checked the box, wait for it to start. This is the quickest and easiest way to enable a service.

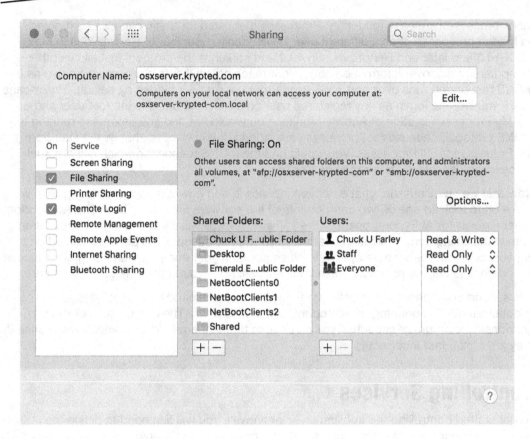

Figure 11-1. Sharing system preferences

> **Note**   If you enable services for the strict purpose of testing, we recommend that you then disable them when you are finished with your testing.

To disable a service, open Sharing in System Preferences, highlight the service you want to disable on the Sharing pane, and click the Stop button. You can actually watch services appear and disappear in Activity Monitor as you start and stop them and review the resources (in terms of memory and processor utilization) that the services are using. This allows you to learn more about services as you go.

Services are accessible from any computer once they are started (we'll discuss fixing that later in this chapter). Because the firewall works based on applications, Apple lists commonly used services by name rather than by port number. For example, you will see File Sharing on the Services pane versus port 548. By adding File Sharing and some of the other more common Apple-centric ports by default, Apple has made basic service management tasks simple to perform. This allows you to quickly enable or disable outgoing and incoming traffic for the ports you will most commonly need to access.

For another computer to connect to yours, you'll need to know your IP address or the computer name that corresponds to your IP address, and the user will need to know which address to use. To find the IP address of your machine, look at the bottom portion of the Sharing pane (Figure 11-1) where the computer name is also displayed. Usually when you connect to resources on another computer, you can browse to them using various programs, such as the Finder or Bonjour Browser, and you will see the computer referenced by name. This makes things easier for users wanting to connect to your computer from your local network. However, you might need the IP address when connecting over the Internet or when the name does not appear on its own.

Table 11-1. When to Enable a Service

Services	When to Enable	Dangers
File Sharing (AFP port 548)	Enable when you want other Mac users to have access to files on your computer.	If you have weak passwords (or no password), then others could gain access into your file system. There have also been a few exploits specifically targeting AFP that have been released.
File Sharing (SMB)	Enable when you want Windows users to have access to files hosted by your computer.	If you have weak passwords (or no password), then others could gain access into your file system. Additionally there are a number of vulnerabilities in the CVE database for Samba.
Remote Login (SSH port 22)	Enable when you want a command-line or Secure Shell (SSH) interface into your system.	Systems with SSH exposed to the Internet are prone to brute-force attacks, where an attacker attempts repeatedly to guess your password. This will show up in your logs, waste your bandwidth, and, if you have weak passwords, give an attacker full control over your computer. Additionally, while strong passwords do mitigate the chance of success they do not obviate it.
Bluetooth Sharing	Enable to exchange files with devices over Bluetooth.	Allows sharing files through Bluetooth.
Remote Management (VNC port 5900)	Enable when you want to allow remote control over the desktop of your computer.	Weak passwords and poor configuration could give an attacker access to everything on your computer.
Remote Apple Events (SNMP ports 161–162)	Enable when you want to turn on SNMP monitoring so other systems can review vital statistics about your system.	Others could gain too much information about your system if SNMP is not configured appropriately.
Printer Sharing (port 1179)	Enable when you want other users to access your printers.	There are very few access controls for printing services, but CUPS does allow for extremely granular control over the printer sharing aspect of Mac OS X.

Anytime you are configuring the firewall on a Mac, you must first determine which services to enable and which to disable. Remember to run only those services that are required to receive *necessary* communications from other computers. Unless a service is absolutely required, do not enable it. Because they have direct access to your machine, each service running on your computer represents another possible vulnerability whereby an attacker, bot, bug, or other malware might crawl into your system and wreak havoc. Table 11-1 indicates when the default services included with OS X should be run and the potential pitfalls enabling them could bring.

Configuring the Firewall

Once you have enough information to understand what services you are trying to control by configuring the firewall, you're ready to move on to the nuts and bolts of working with those services and/or the firewall itself. First things first: let's turn the Application Layer Firewall on.

Working with the Firewall in OS X

Out of the box, the OS X firewall is disabled. Mac OS X clients can be enabled using the Firewall tab of the Security system preferences (see Figure 11-2). Make sure the padlock icon at the bottom of the screen is unlocked in order for you to make changes to the System Preference pane. To enable the firewall, click on the Start button.

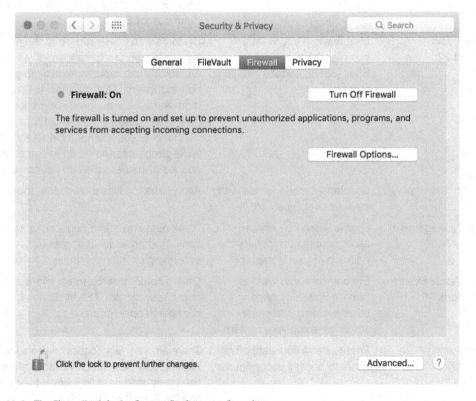

Figure 11-2. The Firewall tab in the System Preferences Security pane

Enabling the firewall allows incoming connections only to certain Apple services by default, such as Personal File Sharing or Web Services. If you are using the firewall in OS X, then you cannot disable these from the Firewall System Preference and must configure them from the Sharing System Preference pane instead (unless you use the command line tool ipfw, as we discuss later in the chapter). You can see this in Figure 11-3, which shows the default settings that were enabled by enabling the firewall. As you can see in the figure, SSH is allowed, because it is a sharing service that is enabled. You cannot remove any sharing services that show up here. But if you disable them in the Sharing System Preferences, they will no longer appear in the firewall.

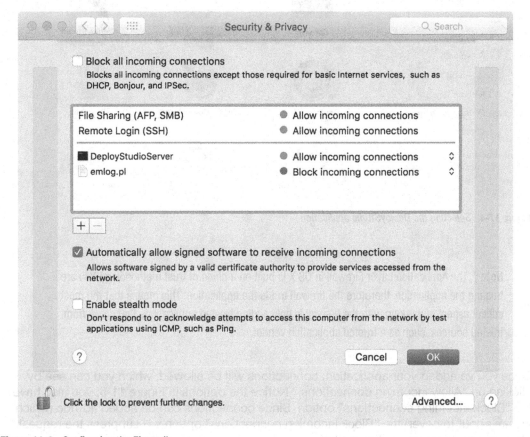

Figure 11-3. Configuring the Firewall

> **Note**   The Firewall and Internet tabs are not located in the same place in OS X Server. These options are configured using Server Admin on Mac OS X Server, as we discuss later in Chapter 16.

To enable third-party services or applications to accept or make communications requests, you must add them based on the application rather than the port. This gives each you access to open its required ports on the firewall.

To enable other services, click on the plus (+) sign and then browse to the application. For example, in Figure 11-4 we will choose DeployStudio, a popular server for imaging OS X systems. Once you click on the application, click on the Add button to add it to the list.

Figure 11-4. *Selecting the DeployStudio application*

> **Note**   The Application Layer Firewall in OS X is built on a chain of trust methodology. You are trusting the application, therefore the firewall trusts the application. This means that the most critical aspect of working with the firewall is only adding trusted applications that come from trusted sources, such as a trusted application vendor.

Once you've added your application, connections will be allowed, which you can see by clicking on "Allow incoming connections." Notice the options in Figure 11-5; you also have the "Block incoming connections" option. Since connections can be added ad-hoc (which we are about to cover) the "Block incoming connections" option will suppress the request to allow you to add a connection ad-hoc.

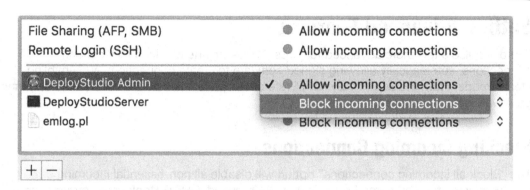

Figure 11-5. Configuring the Firewall to allow incoming connections

To add an application ad-hoc, simply attempt to establish a connection to your computer from that application. For example, open Cyberduck (assuming it is not in your list already) and you will see a dialog box asking if you want to Allow or Deny access for the application, as can be seen in Figure 11-6. Clicking Allow will add it with the Allow incoming network connections settings or clicking on the Deny button will Deny incoming network connections.

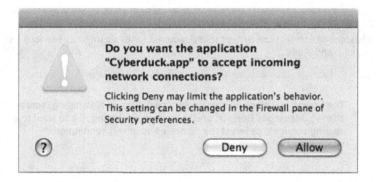

Figure 11-6. Accepting an application ad-hoc

Once you have configured which applications can and cannot communicate with computers outside of your system, it's time to configure the Advanced settings on the Security pane's Firewall button.

Note   If you encounter services that cannot function once you have enabled the firewall, you can quickly determine whether the firewall is the problem. Try disabling the firewall to see whether it is blocking those services (click the Stop button on the Firewall tab of the Sharing pane). If the problem persists, then the firewall is not the culprit. If this resolves the issue, then the firewall is most likely the problem.

Setting Advanced Features

There are also a few more advanced features. These include blocking all incoming connections, automatically allowing signed software to create connections and enabling stealth mode. From the Security System Preferences pane, click on the Firewall tab and then on Advanced… to access these options.

Blocking Incoming Connections

The "Block all incoming connections" option will disable all non-essential incoming connections on the computer. Because they are required, DHCP, Bonjour registration, and other services that will lead to instability will be left enabled. However, all sharing services will be disabled, as will any third-party applications that have been allowed. To disable incoming connections, check the "Block all incoming connections" box in the Advanced options in the Firewall System Preference pane.

Notice in Figure 11-7 that once this feature has been enabled, you cannot configure any other features of the firewall in OS X. Once enabled, sharing services will be disabled, and you'll be unable to configure any of the other options as well.

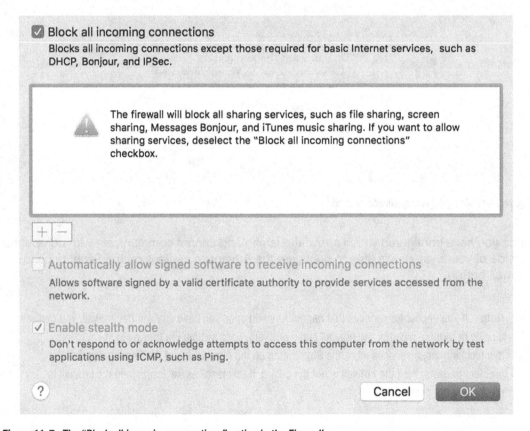

Figure 11-7. The "Block all incoming connections" option in the Firewall

Allowing Signed Software to Receive Incoming Connections

Perhaps one of the most dangerous options in the Firewall is to allow all signed applications access to receive incoming connections. This option, shown in Figure 11-7, will rely on application signatures, which is good, but will allow all signed applications to communicate, which is bad. An application is considered signed if the application bundle has a signature, a designated requirement, and if the signature matches the requirement. The signature is then used when the application is opened to verify that it has not been altered since it was signed and to detect that it is the same application if it is a new version of the same application.

To determine if an application has a signature, browse to the application in question and then Ctrl-click (or right-click if you have a multi-button mouse) on it and then click on Show Contents. From here, open the CodeSignature folder and check that there is a CodeResources file (see Figure 11-8). If so, then there is a signature. But who signed the app? And when was it signed? In some cases, this method of verifying the signature will not work as intended and so the codesign command, covered in more detail in Chapter 6, can be used as well.

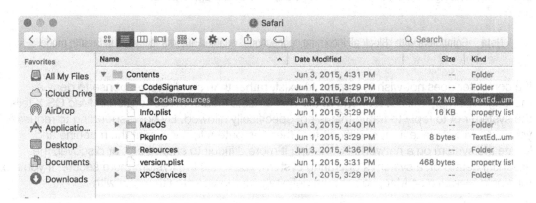

Figure 11-8. Looking inside the Safari bundle

> **Note**   All applications built for the iPhone must be signed, and someday we hope to see this replicated in Mac OS X as well!

To check the signature of the application and obtain more granular information about it, Apple has provided the codesign application. While this tool is covered more granularly in Chapter 6, a good example of its use would be to obtain very verbose output of the Safari application with the following command:

```
codesign -vvv Safari.app
```

The output would simply indicate that the Safari.app checks clean against the tests performed:

```
/Applications/Safari.app: valid on disk
/Applications/Safari.app: satisfies its Designated Requirement
```

Going Stealthy

When Computer A sends a request to Computer B, Computer B determines how to respond. Responses contain either the data requested or a rejection to the request, which is sent back to the requesting computer. If a process is running and traffic is allowed, then Computer A will get a message from Computer B allowing it to connect. If a process is not running or a firewall rule is active that prohibits Computer A from connecting to a given port on Computer B, then Computer A will get a deny message from Computer B. This process occurs before a web page is loaded or before a password is requested.

This seemingly innocuous process is the basis for much of the process by which computers communicate, and can also be used to expose rather important details about your system. By analyzing the patterns in delivery times and the actual content of responses to requests for traffic, it is possible to determine the operating system you are running, the patches you have installed on your operating system, and in many cases the type of hardware that is in your system. Armed with this information, a hacker can easily attack a system. So, how does one safeguard against this? One employs the use of Stealth mode.

> **Note**   Computers with "Block all incoming connections" enabled automatically run in Stealth mode.

If a computer does not wish to appear to exist, rather than sending a response to deny a message, it simply will not respond at all. The "Enable stealth mode" option in Mac OS X tells the system not to reply to traffic that is not specifically allowed. By not responding to requests, your system will make it more difficult for other computers to fingerprint the machine and locate the system on a network. By making it more difficult to *enumerate*, or discover, the essential details of, a system's operating system, you make the system more secure. If you are running a firewall on a Mac, you should definitely be running stealth mode with it.

Stealth mode causes the system to not reply to response requests, or *echo requests*. However, this doesn't make it completely impossible to locate a system on a network. It is still possible to get the system time information or *ARP requests* (which show details about the network settings on your computer) on a machine that is running stealth mode. One reason for this is that stealth mode simply tells the computer not to respond to network requests that aren't running. However, because Apple built zero-configuration networking into the operating system, there are a large number of services that are running and easily discoverable, making it easy to enumerate the Mac OS. One way to help mitigate this discovery is to use custom ipfw rules, which we discuss in further detail later in the chapter.

Testing the Firewall

Once you have closed the ports and configured your firewall to your liking, you will want to test impact of your security change and verify that the services you have denied are no longer accessible. Performing a port scan is the best way to test the configuration. A port scan will check whether a service is available to other systems. Apple has included a port scanner in Network Utility, which is located at /System/Library/CoreServices/Applications (see Figure 11-9). Port scanning is explored in more depth in Chapter 10.

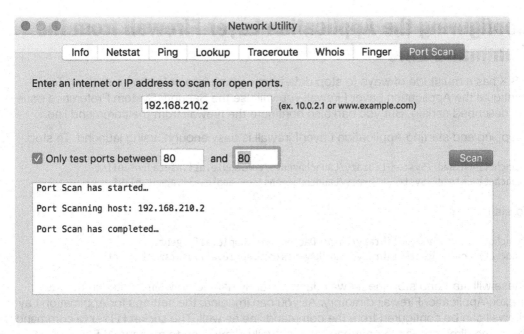

Figure 11-9. Port scanning with Network Utility

Note The ability to run a port scan on versions of OS X older than Tiger is disabled unless the BSD subsystem is installed. The BSD subsystem is installed by default; if it is explicitly not installed, and the system is then upgraded to newer versions of OS X, in most cases the BSD subsystem will not be installed.

Network Utility, although robust, can tend to run rather slowly. For a quicker, dirtier port scan, there is a hidden command-line scanning utility, called stroke, that will allow you to use the port scanner included with Mac OS X much more quickly to scan ranges of ports. The stroke command is just the command-line version of the port scanner in Network Utility, separate from the GUI, causing it to run much faster. It is located in the /System/Library/ CoreServices/Applications/Network Utility.app/Contents/Resources folder. To invoke the stroke command, you will need to use the Terminal application to access it. For example, if you wanted to scan ports 25 (SMTP) to 80 (HTTP) of a mail server to see what services are listening on what port, using the stroke command, you would type the following:

```
/System/Library/CoreServices/Applications/Network\ Utility.app/Contents/Resources/stroke
mail.mydomain.com 25 80
```

This command would result in something much similar to what Network Utility would display, only it's quicker because it's coming from the command line:

```
Port Scanning host: 208.57.132.195
        Open TCP Port:      25
        Open TCP Port:      53
        Open TCP Port:      80
```

Configuring the Application Layer Firewall from the Command Line

OS X has a multitude of ways to stop data from coming into or leaving a system. To configure the Application Layer Firewall you will use the Security System Preference pane (as described earlier). But you can also configure the firewall from the command line.

Stopping and starting Application Layer Firewall is easy enough, using launchd. To stop:

```
launchctl unload /System/Library/LaunchAgents/com.apple.alf.useragent.plist
launchctl unload /System/Library/LaunchDaemons/com.apple.alf.agent.plist
```

To start:

```
launchctl load /System/Library/LaunchDaemons/com.apple.alf.agent.plist
launchctl load /System/Library/LaunchAgents/com.apple.alf.useragent.plist
```

These will start and stop the firewall daemon (aptly named firewall) located in the /usr/libexec/ApplicationFirewall directory. As you can imagine, the settings for Application Layer Firewall can be configured from the command line as well. The socketfilterfw command, in this same directory, is the command that actually allows you to manage ALF.

When an application is allowed to open or accept a network socket, it's known as a trusted application, and ALF keeps a list of all of the trusted applications. You can view the status of applications using socketfilterfw with the --listapps option, as follows (assuming /usr/libexec/ApplicationFirewall is the current working directory):

```
./socketfilterfw --listapps
```

You can also use the command line to add a trusted application using the --add option followed by the path of the application to be trusted. For example, to add FileMaker to the list of trusted apps, you'd want to use something similar to the following, pointing to the binary, not the app bundle:

```
./socketfilterfw --add
"/Applications/FileMaker Pro 14/FileMaker Pro.app/Contents/MacOS/FileMaker Pro"
```

> **Note**   You can also use the codesign command to sign applications, verify signatures and enable debugging, using the -s, -v options and -d options respectively.

Finally, there are a number of global preferences for the firewall that can be configured using the /usr/libexec/ApplicationFirewall/com.apple.alf.plist preferences file. The com.apple.alf.plist file there is a bit temperamental. Changes there simply don't seem to have the desired response. Therefore, stick with the one in the /Library/Preferences directory. Some keys in this file that might be of interest include globalstate (0 disables the firewall, 1 configures for specific services and 2 is for essential services like the GUI), stealthenabled, and loggingenabled.

Using Mac OS X to Protect Other Computers

OS X provides users with the ability to share an Internet or network connection with other computers. Internet Sharing is a handy utility that Apple included in its operating system that allows you to use your computer as a router in much the same way that a firewall appliance is used, as discussed in Chapter 10. Sharing an Internet connection can be extremely useful in a pinch, however, it should be disabled when not in use.

Enabling Internet Sharing

The controls for enabling Internet Sharing are located on the Internet tab of the Sharing pane (see Figure 11-10). This pane allows you to choose the port connection to share from, which is similar to how you would configure your WAN, or outside Internet connection on a firewall appliance. You can also choose which network adapter you'd like to use to share the connection. This option is similar to the LAN, or internal network accessing clients, option on firewall appliances.

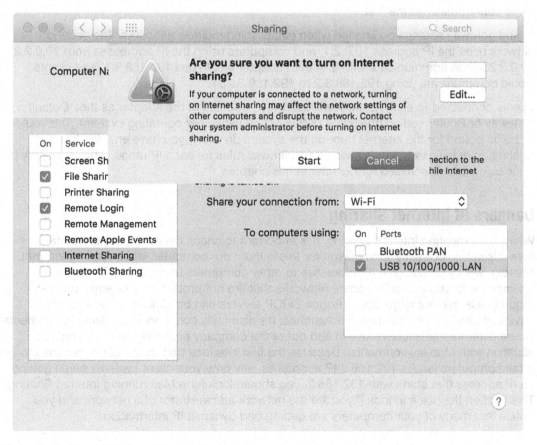

Figure 11-10. Internet Sharing settings

Once you have set your sharing settings and started the Internet Sharing service, you'll need to assign IP address information for client computers in order for them to access the Internet. If they are set to use Dynamic Host Control Protocol (DHCP), a protocol used specifically for handing out IP addresses, the Internet router (which could be your computer or an AirPort using Internet Sharing) will provide dynamic IP addresses to them. Or you can assign static IP addresses to them. To use a static IP address, you'll need to know the network settings on your computer or router and configure the other computers in the same way. At this point, any system that can connect to your computer's IP address can access the Internet, provided it has the correct information and is patched or wirelessly connected to your computer.

Configuring Clients

The first network you'll establish using Internet Sharing on your system will use the IP address of 192.168.2.1. This will allow all client systems that are connected to the network to connect to the Internet. To connect to the Internet, client computers will need an IP address that falls between 192.168.2.2 and 192.168.2.254. The subnet mask that would be used in this setup is 255.255.255.0. All subsequent subnets and networks would use the same subnet mask as the first.

IP and gateway settings do change when establishing multiple networks. The second network uses the IP address 10.0.2.1, and computers using the IP addresses from 10.0.2.2 10.0.2.254 can communicate with it. A third adapter would use 192.168.3.1, and clients would communicate using 192.168.3.2 to 192.168.3.254.

Clients connected to each network will use the IP address of the adapter as their Default Gateway or Router setting (the name of this option varies per operating system). This routes all traffic bound for the Internet through the system on which you have enabled Internet Sharing. In many cases, you'll need to add firewall rules for each IP range, which can only be done using ipfw, discussed further later in this chapter.

Dangers of Internet Sharing

When implementing Internet Sharing, it is important to check the configuration to make sure it is set up correctly. One reason for this is that your computer, when running Internet Sharing, will by default give IP addresses to other computers using DHCP. If you set it up improperly, you can cause entire networks that are not protected sufficiently against rogue DHCP servers to go down. Rogue DHCP servers can be difficult to track down in environments that use inexpensive switches. It's also fairly common in creative environments where different freelancers move in and out of the company on a daily basis (a common situation with Mac environments). Because the first interface that provides connections to other computers issues 192.168.2 IP addresses, any time your client systems begin getting an IP address that starts with 192.168.2, you should look for a Mac running Internet Sharing. This is often the place to look if you are the network administrator of a network and you notice that many of your computers are getting bad dynamic IP information.

Also, connecting to a network and sharing a connection using the same adapter for both your Internet connection and your client computers can cause serious network problems. In a cable modem or DSL environment, you'll more than likely cause your service to be turned off. If your service does not get cut off, congratulations, you've successfully bridged your network to the network of your Internet service provider. This can cause any computer on their network, of which there are likely tens or hundreds of thousands, to have the ability to access any computer on your network. This is only a risk if you have two Ethernet cards, patch the cables incorrectly *and* if you are sharing an Ethernet connection.

If we wanted to share a network connection and had only one network interface, such as an Ethernet card, our best way to accomplish this would be to install a second Ethernet card into the system to share the connection. Sharing a network connection over an AirPort card is risky, and you'll need to address some security concerns. The most important concern is the fact that the security of the network is based on wireless protocols which, by their very nature, are seldom properly secured. Traffic sent over a wireless network is easily interceptable, potentially exposing passwords and other private information. We will discuss this further in Chapter 12.

Working from the Command Line

Although it is possible to adequately configure the firewall through the OS X Sharing System Preference or through third-party applications, sometimes you'll want to get even more granular. For example, you might want to perform a more advanced security lockdown such as denying outgoing traffic for certain ports while continuing to allow incoming traffic on those same ports. Or you might want to disable communications to and from certain IP addresses rather than across the board. These and other specific tasks, such as bandwidth throttling, can be accomplished only by using the command line. They cannot be accomplished with the GUI. Before we delve into the specific commands, we need to discuss some of the ways to get more granular with controlling your firewall and why it is important to maintain this control.

Getting More Granular Firewall Control

A *network adapter* is a physical connection that your computer makes to a network. Network adapters include your Ethernet interface), your Wi-Fi interface (whether it is built into your computer or a card that you have added), modems, and any other item that allows your computer to access other computers.

Because of the nature of complex networking, sometimes you'll want to assign differing rule sets to different interfaces or different IP addresses within different interfaces. For example, you might want to put multiple e-mail domains on separate IP addresses within the same network interface. There are definite benefits to this. The configuration of multiple IP addresses can bring a more fault-tolerant network connection to the server, it can provide other features with the mail server, and it could be used to run various services over the same port on the same system. However, these configurations can be difficult to set up using the graphical tools built into the OS, because each instance of a network interface must be configured separately. By default, all firewall rules created on the Sharing pane are applied to all network interfaces. To make these configuration changes possible, you will need to use the command line to configure the firewall.

Configuring multiple IP addresses on a Mac is a fairly straightforward process. Each network interface is not limited to using one IP address. Adding an IP address to a network interface is fairly simple. You can do this by opening the Network system preferences pane, clicking the + icon, choosing the appropriate adapter, and clicking the Add button. This creates a second listing for the duplicated network interface and allows you to give it an IP address. If you have multiple IP addresses, you will notice that although network requests can be sent to multiple interfaces on the system, they will always reply from the one that is the primary interface. An example of a system using multiple IP addresses for the same interface, in Figure 11-11, shows that the instance of the Wi-Fi occurs twice: once under the heading of Wi-Fi 2 and once under the heading of Wi-Fi.

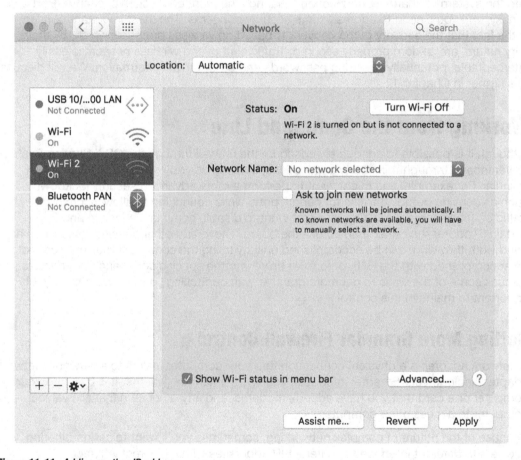

Figure 11-11. Adding another IP address

As mentioned previously, a really important security measure to take with your network is to lock down certain types of outgoing traffic on specific ports. For example, in an educational environment, a system administrator may want to lock down most types of outgoing Internet traffic. Remote control applications, instant messaging applications, and file-sharing peer-to-peer software all tend to be unnecessary on client computers in a classroom environment. Because these programs make requests for outgoing traffic, they will need their ports locked down for them to be properly secured. In the workplace, you might want to block streaming Internet music stations to help conserve precious bandwidth, or you might want to restrict staff from using a file-sharing protocol to keep them from taking creative assets out of your environment. All of this must be configured using the command line.

Some outgoing network traffic blocking can be configured using a firewall device at the edge of your network, but not all. Even if it is possible at the firewall-device level, it's wise to impose a rule at both the software level and the hardware level to circumvent a breach at one of your layers of defense. This layered, or tiered, approach to security helps keep your network as secure as possible. Another layer is pf, a firewall that allows you to configure your system to block outgoing traffic for certain ports, a feature not available otherwise.

Note   Later in this chapter we will discuss blocking outgoing traffic, but it is important to point out that you can block outgoing traffic only by using either the command line or a third-party application. You can block incoming traffic by using the built-in firewall in System Preferences.

Using pf with IceFloor

The default port-based firewall used in OS X is pf. This firewall can be used by editing the pf.conf, pf.os, and pf.anchors files. You can also use the pfctl command to manage the firewall. But there's an easier way in a little tool called IceFloor. IceFloor provides a graphical interface to managing pf. To get started with pf through IceFloor, install IceFloor from `http://www.hanynet.com/icefloor/index.html` and complete the setup wizard. Once complete, open IceFloor.

Configure Basic Firewall Options

The first tab in IceFloor is Firewall. This is where you configure basic pf rules and start pf. The left column is an address group, or a collection of addresses. The right column is a list of services. For example, you can use the plus sign in the left column to add your LAN IP addresses and then click on those and define which services that are available to IP addresses coming from your LAN IPs. Then, as you can see in Figure 11-12, you can start the pf service by clicking on the Start PF button.

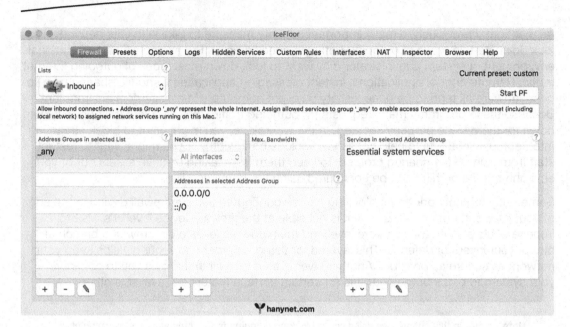

Figure 11-12. Use IceFloor to fonfigure basic firewall options

Under the Lists section, by default, you'll see that you're configuring how pf handles Inbound connections. You can also manage Outbound connections, as well as inbound and outbound connections that are filtered through NAT, if you're using your server as a routing device for other computers.

The Presets tab is used to enable a collection of known services for a given purpose, kind of like a Blueprint in Apple Configurator. Since we'll be managing aspects of the firewall a bit more specifically, click on the Options tab to see some global options for the firewall. As seen in Figure 11-13, these include the following:

- Preserve Apple PF anchor: pf uses anchors (similar to includes in Apache) to include other rules from other files. Apple has a set of anchors and it's recommended to leave them in tact.

- Allow Multicast DNS: When disabled, disables all zero configuration networking (mDNS). I would recommend being very careful with this option.

- Enable Emerging Threats protection: Enables the ET ruleset. For more on that, check out http://rules.emergingthreats.net. I'd enable this option.

- Enable <sshguard> and <spam> PF tables and block rules: Updates the pf tables to include options for www.sshguard.net/docs/setup/firewall/pf/, which protects against brute force attacks, adding an additional layer of security to the pf firewall.

- Stealth Mode (block policy drop): Disables responding to requests for ports that aren't open

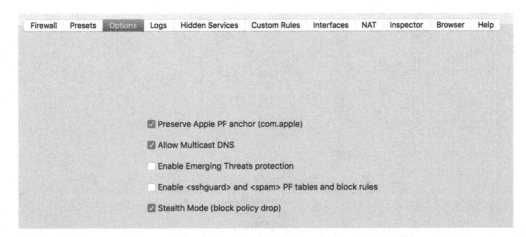

Figure 11-13. Configure global pf options

Click on the Logs tab. Here, you have a number of options for dealing with the logs for pf as well as how pf logs data. These options include the following:

- Open PF Logs in Console: Opens the pf logs in the Console app.

- Real Time Logs in terminal: Runs a tail of the logs in the Terminal.

- Export PF Log File...: Brings up a Save dialog box to save a copy of your pf log file so you can view it in other applications easily, or move it to another system (e.g. for forensic analysis).

- Show IceFloor Activity Log: Opens the icefloor.log file in the Console app

- Logging Exceptions: Allows you to enter a port, range of ports, address, or range of addresses to disable logging for.

- Logs Analysis: Opens a screen that allows you to filter and sort logs for various common administrative tasks (like looking for the computers that have port scanned your system).

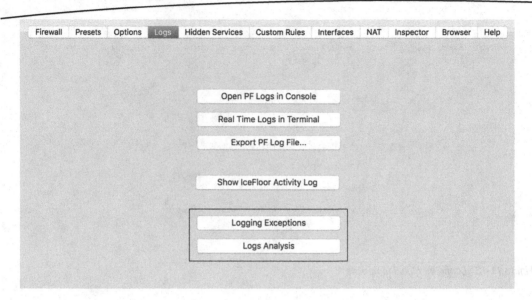

Figure 11-14. Configure pf Logging

There are a number of tabs that we're not going to spend much time on in this chapter. These include:

- The Hidden Services tab allows you to configure port knocking. Port knocking is outside the scope of what we're covering in this book, but it's pretty cool and you should read up more on what you can do with this increasingly common security through obscurity technique.

- The Custom Rules tab allows you to create custom rules that are helpful for further learning to use the command line interface of pfctl and the anchor files. You can get very granular here, and even lock yourself out of remote systems, so be careful with what you choose to configure.

- The Interfaces tab allows you to view information about each active interface installed on the system.

- The NAT tab allows you to configure Internet sharing more granularly than you can with the Sharing System Preferences. For example, you can choose whether to route traffic over shared VPN connections. *Note*: Uses pfnat instead of natd.

- The Inspector tab shows live information about the system.

- The Browser tab provides access to other the active rules, the icefloor. conf file, active tables, active addresses, etc.

- The Help tab is probably the most important tab in IceFloor, as it makes accessing the User Guide for the product quick and easy, as you can see in Figure 11-15.

Figure 11-15. Access the User Manual

The purpose of IceFloor isn't exactly to mass deploy computers running it. Instead, it provides a quick and easy way to make somewhat complicated rulesets without fully learning how to use the pf commands and configuration files. If you'll be deploying pf, you will eventually need to learn these commands. But, graphical tools such as IceFloor can provide long-term guidance as well as the short-term bridge to get you going with complex technologies.

Summary

ALF can be used to limit access that specific applications have in accessing network resources. In this chapter we spent a good amount of time looking at ALF. We first looked at configuring ALF from the System Preferences and then from the command line. We then switched into looking at a different firewall, which controls network access at a port level, meaning that all configurations per port are made for all applications. Given that there are no built-in graphical controls for pf, we only looked at configuring pf from IceFloor; however, there are a number of other options that will allow you to configure pf in great detail from the command line.

All of these changes are made on wireless and wired clients alike. Next, in Chapter 12, we will focus on those changes that you can make to your wireless configuration and wireless environment.

## Chapter 12

Securing a Wireless Network

At the Black Hat conference in August 2006, David Maynor and Jon "Johnny Cache" Ellch shocked the Mac community by demonstrating to the world something that hackers had known for a long time: the Mac could be hacked, easily. Maynor and Ellch, two security professionals with long-time careers in the security industry, were able to release what is known as a *proof-of-concept attack* by exploiting the wireless Atheros drivers built into the Mac operating system. Using a script called setup.sh, which turned a Mac computer (with its wireless card turned on) into an access point, an attacker could gain control of an unsuspecting Mac user's laptop. Another hacker script, called bad_seed, could then be run from the host computer to exploit the vulnerability in the target computer's wireless driver; this would give an attacker access to a Terminal session on the target computer running root (which is a "superuser" that is allowed full control of the computer). The exploit was not released, but it did provide proof that the Mac community was a long way away from an operating system immune to wireless attacks. While the Mac may be more resistant to attack, no system has every been truly immune.

I don't believe in spreading Fear, Uncertainty and Doubt (or FUD) to sell security products. Instead, I've tried to be a pragmatist through this book, looking at easy and safe ways to secure your Mac without degrading the user experience. The concept used in the wireless exploit was not specific to Apple computers, but pointed instead to general flaws in wireless networking protocols as a whole.

In this chapter, we'll cover securing Apple AirPort-based wireless networks. We'll begin with an introduction to wireless networking in general and then move into securing an Apple AirPort base station. Later in the chapter, to help show the importance of wireless security, we will showcase some common wireless hacking tools. We'll illustrate just how easy it is to listen in on wireless traffic, emphasizing why security measures are so important.

Wireless Network Essentials

From a basic security perspective, wireless networks can be rather challenging. Many amateur wireless setups are left unsecured and transmitting information in clear text, thereby exposing user credentials, e-mails, and other data submitted over the network to anybody in the vicinity, and causing unnecessary security risks to sensitive information. It is all too easy to plug in an open wireless device on a wired network, causing a breach in the network that can then be exploited by someone listening in from an outside location such as a parking lot or nearby coffee shop. These and other potential security threats make it important to practice good security when configuring wireless networks.

To properly secure a wireless network, it is key to first have a fundamental understanding of what a wireless network is. A wireless network is different from an Ethernet network or another type of local area network (LAN), although the topologies often follow many of the same standards covered in Chapter 10. In fact, a wireless network is often referred to as a wireless LAN (wLAN).

Logging in to a wireless network is like connecting to a hub with all the other users of that network. But rather than traveling across copper wires to interconnect devices like LAN networks, wireless networks use channelized, low-powered radio waves running on the same frequencies as microwave ovens and cordless telephones. The 2.4GHz and 5GHz bands are pretty crowded these days, with Bluetooth technology (2.4GHz to 2.485GHz) only complicating matters. This can often place a large amount of conflicting signal traffic on these channels, causing data to get lost or fragmented in transit.

The speed and reliability of a wireless network depends on the hardware and proximity of the devices. Ranges between wireless devices are typically limited to a few hundred feet, depending on signal strength and the efficiency of the equipment. The greater the signal strength the longer the distance the signal can be detected, which increases the chance that packets can be intercepted.

> **Note**   A key element to focus on when studying wireless security is what happens with data that is not properly delivered between wireless devices.

Wireless networks that encompass a large area will be composed of multiple wireless devices, because of the short-range capacity of wireless connectivity and the tendency to saturate a single device with multiple users. Wireless access points (WAPs) are the devices used to distribute the wireless signal across this network. They accomplish this using a *radio*, the device within the WAP that talks to the client computer's wireless card, creating a wireless signal. WAPs will often connect directly into a wired network, exchanging data with the wired network via an Ethernet connection. This connection is known as a *backhaul*.

Wireless networks use the IEEE 802.11 protocol, which differs from other wireless protocols in how it processes the wireless signal and the frequency used for connectivity.

There are a number of flavors of 802.11 used in wireless networking as it applies to Macs. While the formal definition for each protocol is by frequency (or wavelength) and signal design, they are commonly referred to as having different speeds, referred to in megabits per second. The most common flavors are 802.11b running at 11 megabits per second, 802.11g running at 54 megabits per second, 802.11n running at 108 megabits per second, and 802.11a, which uses the 5GHz band for internodal communications. Lastly, 802.11ac runs at various speeds up to 1.3 gigabits per second.

> **Note**   802.1x is a highly secure wireless protocol typically found in larger network infrastructures. If your network can leverage this technology, check out our section on integrating 802.1x into your environment in Chapter 10.

Introducing the Apple AirPort

Over the years, Apple has released a variety of products in its family of WAPs, typically referred to as Apple AirPorts. Today, we're back to two devices, the Apple AirPort Extreme and the Apple AirPort Express, described in detail at http://www.apple.com/airport-extreme/http://www.apple.com/shop/product/ME918LL/A/airport-extreme?afid=p238|sKLFkj8Sn-dc_mtid_1870765e38482_pcrid_91262096527_%26cid%3Daos-us-kwg-btb and http://www.apple.com/airport-express/http://www.apple.com/shop/product/MC414LL/A/airport-express?fnode=58 respectively.

The AirPort supports a variety of encryption protocols that can be used to secure the wireless network. Encryption protocols that are specific to wireless networking include the following:

> *WPA2*: Also known as 802.11i, WPA2 uses the AES block cipher to make cracking keys difficult. Unless you have a RADIUS server, WPA2 is the best form of encryption to use on an AirPort with Apple clients.

> *WPA2 Enterprise*: Similar to WPA2 in supported encryption standards, WPA2 Enterprise also adds support for usernames, which can be obtained using a RADIUS server, such as FreeRadius and Microsoft Windows Active Directory servers.

> *WEP*: This is the weakest of the security features supported by Apple AirPort. Windows computers need to use the hex equivalent to log into the network. This can be found using the Equivalent Network Password option in the Edit menu of the AirPort Utility. You should not be using WEP unless you have devices so old that this is the only encryption protocol they can support.

The Apple AirPort devices were designed to be easy to use. In many environments, the Apple AirPort will work right out of the box. However convenient this may be, the default settings are widely known, so an AirPort left with the default settings running represents a considerable security risk for any network.

> **Tip**   AirPorts do not always need an Ethernet cable connection to become part of the network. If there are other AirPorts on the network, it is possible to use the wireless network of an existing AirPort network as the network connection that the AirPort will use. This is what is known as a wireless distribution system (WDS) cloud. A WDS network can allow you to extend a wireless network for great distances, and create a wireless network that goes far beyond the 300-foot limitation documented by Apple.

AirPort Utility

The Apple AirPort is configured using an app called AirPort Utility, which is on every Mac in /Applications/Utilities. The AirPort Utility has built-in controls for disk sharing and a user-friendly, wizard-like approach to configuring AirPorts of all types, including older AirPorts.

Configuring the Current AirPorts

When you start the AirPort Utility, you're immediately able to browse all the AirPorts on the network at once in a view that shows how the devices are interconnected with one another (Figure 12-1). This list includes all AirPorts that are visible over the Ethernet interface, as well as AirPorts on the wireless network.

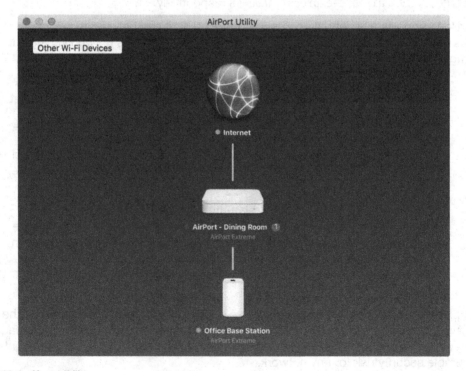

Figure 12-1. Airport Utility

Click on any AirPort to see basic information about that device, including the MAC addresses of connected clients and addresses configured on the device. Click Edit. (Figure 12-2) to log into the device.

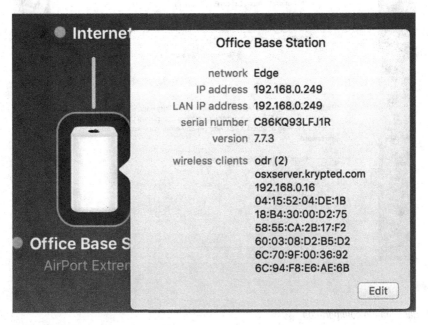

Figure 12-2. Device Basic Settings

When you log into the AirPort, you are initially placed into the Base Station tab. Here you will configure a password to manage the AirPort. This is one of the most important security tasks you have: select a strong password. There are no password lockouts if an incorrect password is entered too many times, or alerts of such a thing happening. Therefore, you should use as strong a password as possible. Additionally, as you can see in Figure 12-3, you configure Back to My Mac options for the AirPort here as well. This allows you to log into the AirPort from any computer that is configured to use Back to My Mac, using the same account that you're using for the AirPort. This type of option can be helpful if you need to configure an AirPort remotely from somewhere else, such as the office while your kids are trying to access NetFlix from home. Otherwise this should not really be used as the account provides a second potential vector for unauthorized users to inappropriately access the device.

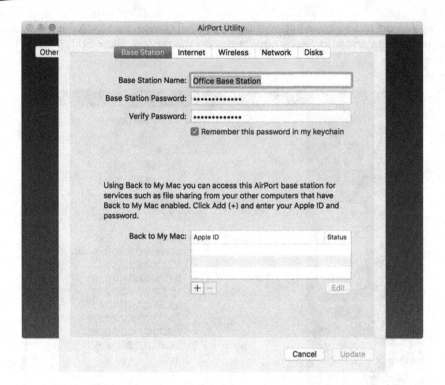

Figure 12-3. Base Station configuration

Click on the Internet tab. Here you'll configure static or dynamic IP addresses if you're also using the AirPort as a router. In this case, we're using the AirPort as a router behind another firewall. This allows us to segment traffic between various networks. For example, when using this network you won't be able to see any of the devices on my home network. There is also a Guest Network option, but I have a number of networks at my house for various tasks, so I use this guest network for writing books (like this one) and provide the Guest Network option for allowing friends to access my network.

The options available here include the following (shown in Figure 12-4):

- Connect Using: Typically, this will be Static (where you manually assign settings) or Dynamic, where the Internet Service Provider assigns settings to you.

- IPv4 Address: The IP address of the router. This can be dynamic, if your Internet Service Provider provides you with one, or Static, if you assign one manually. (Your ISP will usually provide you with the static IP address to use if this is the case.) Because this is looking upstream at another router on this network, I was able to arbitrarily assign it an IP address within the block I use for the upstream network.

- Subnet Mask: Usually supplied by your Internet Service Provider, the Subnet Mask limits the size of the network.

- Router Address: This is the gateway that your router will use to connect to the Internet.

- DNS Servers: The DNS servers the AirPort will use to resolve any hostnames that the AirPort needs to resolve.

- IPv6 DNS Servers: These are used if you are able to use IPv6 for your network. Typically they will deploy onto the device automatically. Therefore, unless your Internet Service Provider tells you otherwise, you won't need to configure IPv6 DNS Servers.

- Domain Name: A default domain name provided to clients that obtain IP addresses dynamically (if there are any) from the AirPort.

- IPv6 WAN Address: This is used if you're able to use IPv6 for your network. Typically the WAN Address will deploy onto the device automatically through your Internet Service Provider. Therefore, unless your Internet Service Provider tells you otherwise, you won't need to configure IPv6 DNS Servers.

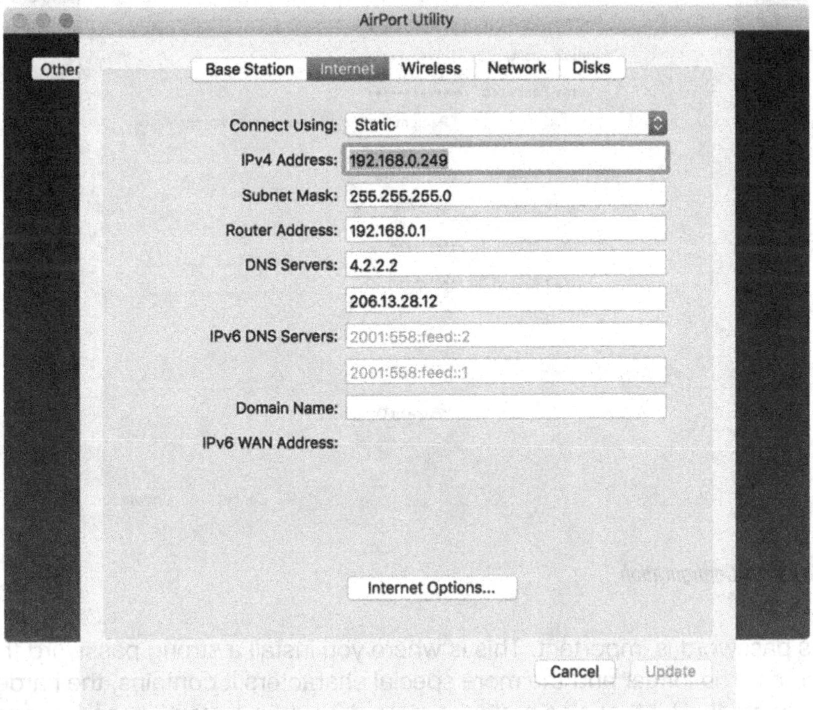

Figure 12-4. Internet Configuration

There is little security in the settings you choose here other than the 192.168.* private addressing scheme. These settings are mostly just to make the device work with the rest of the network infrastructure. We're still not supplying a network to end users, just configuring this device to join our main network. Click on the Internet Options button to configure more IPv6 settings, but we will not cover Ipv6 in this chapter as it has little to do with the security of your AirPort network.

Next, click on the Wireless tab. This is where we configure the protocols referenced earlier in this chapter. Assuming the AirPort is providing a wireless network to other devices on your network, the Network Mode setting is usually set to Create a wireless network, as configured in Figure 12-5. Here, you can also disable the wireless antenna by selecting the Off option, or configure WDS by choosing to Extend a wireless network.

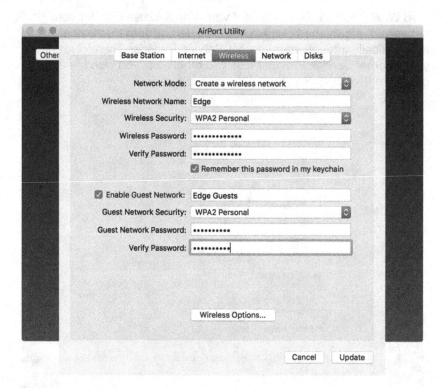

Figure 12-5. Wireless Configuration

The wireless password is important. This is where you install a strong password that is difficult to crack. The longer and the more special characters it contains, the harder a password is to crack. But that also makes it more difficult to remember and means the wireless password might get written down, reducing the security of your environment. Using the "Remember this password in my keychain" option will save the wireless password to the computer where you're configuring the AirPort so you don't need to enter it again, once you save your settings by clicking that handy Update button to save your settings.

The Enable Guest Network option allows you to configure a guest network. Devices in this network will not be able to see the devices in your main network. Here you have similar security options, but when set up properly none of these settings are nearly as important as on the main wireless network, as this is a smaller and more limited network.

Click on Wireless Options. Here, you can enable or disable the 5GHz networking on the AirPort and change the channels used to provide wireless signal. Changing channels is usually done to cut down on interference in your network caused by other WAPs on your own or neighboring networks. However, it's important to keep in mind that the more robust the security of the connection to your access point from other devices, the less of your data that can be intercepted. As you can see in Figure 12-6, you can also choose to hide your network. This means that the network name (SSID) only shows up in computers requesting to join a wireless network if the network name is manually typed in. This is known as SSID suppression on many other brands of devices. I like the option, but it can create support issues in larger environments if you're always having to send someone to enter a network name for users. Also, it does not really hide the network. Several common network utilities will ignore the "hidden" feature in the radio signal and show the network to the utility and its operator.

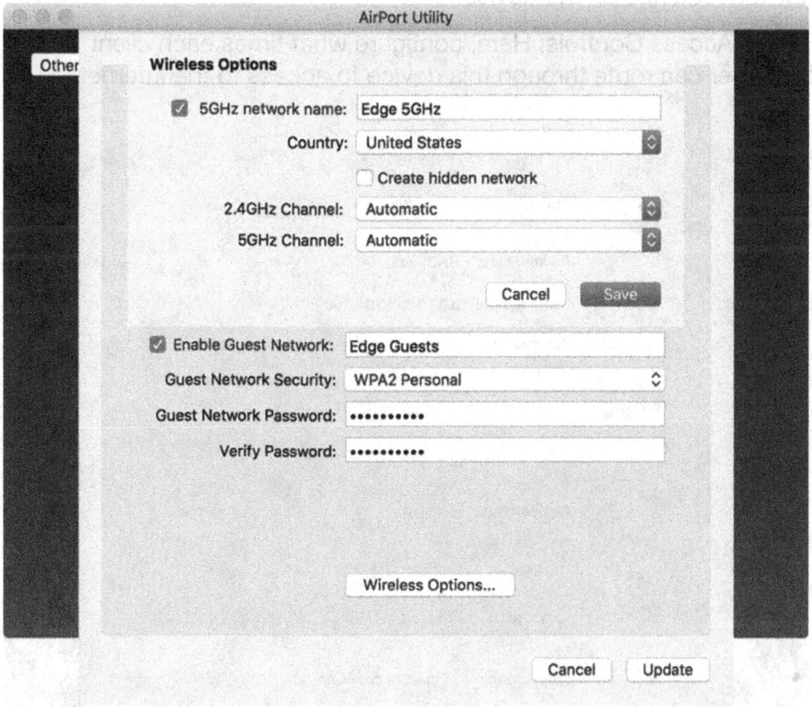

Figure 12-6. Wireless Options

Once you're happy with the settings for your wireless network, click on Save or Update. Keep in mind that if you are making an update to the configuration of a live network then clicking on Update will shut down and restart the network. If you have a critical connection open then you may have to wait for a better time to enable the update. After making the change to this setting, click on the Network tab. In the

Router Mode field, you will choose to use Off (Bridge Mode), which disables the router functionality of the device (so it uses an upstream router to provide clients with IP addresses and a gateway to the Internet), or you will choose to use DHCP and NAT. Assuming you are using DHCP and NAT, you will have a few items to configure (Figure 12-7):

- DHCP Reservations: Every computer on a network has a unique MAC address as well as a unique IP address. Here you can assign a static IP address from your new network to a computer with a given MAC address.

- Port Settings: Also known as port forwarding. This option allows you to configure which TCP ports are forwarded to which LAN IP addresses when they come into the network, using the static or dynamic IP address assigned earlier in this chapter when we configured the Network settings on the device.

- Enable Access Controls: Here, configure what times each client computer can route through this device to access to the Internet.

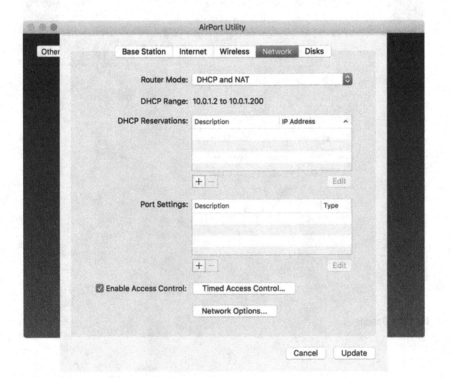

Figure 12-7. Network Options

Limiting the DHCP Scope

If the AirPort is acting as a routing device and there are multiple computers for which the AirPort is directing traffic, then you should use the built-in DHCP feature on the AirPort. The DHCP feature will configure the AirPort to hand out IP addresses to client computers and devices on the network. A good way to secure the network is to limit the number of IP addresses assigned to networked computers. Limiting the number of assignable IP addresses to the exact number of computers on the network is a good way to ensure that only certain computers are able to use the address. Not allowing an unlimited number of computers to join the network limits the threat of unknown systems compromising your environment (although not as much as limiting access based on MAC address would as we will discuss later on).

To configure DHCP, click Network Options from the Network tab in AirPort Utility (see Figure 12-8). Next, click the DHCP Range field, and select the IP address scheme to use. When choosing an IP scheme, make sure there are no other IP schemes already in place on the network that might conflict. Once an IP scheme is selected, enter the first IP address the router should use in the DHCP scope in the DHCP Beginning Address field. Then enter the last IP address in the scope in the DHCP Ending Address field. For example, if five computers need to have IPs distributed to them, then you'd use 10.0.1.2 as the first address and 10.0.1.6 as the last address. Click the Save button to commit the changes to the AirPort (and Update from back on the Network screen).

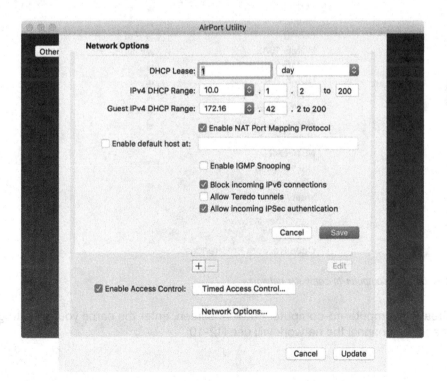

Figure 12-8. DHCP settings

Securing Computer-to-Computer Networks

A *computer-to-computer network* is similar to other wireless networks except it does not have a central base station. In previous versions of OS X, computer-to-computer networks were known as *ad hoc networks*.

The security features available on computer-to-computer networks are limited. WEP is disabled by default, and WPA is not available. When creating a secure computer-to-computer network it is imperative to implement a secure, encrypted connection. To create a secure computer-to-computer network connection, click the wireless icon at the top of your screen (see Figure 12-9), and choose the Create Network option.

Figure 12-9. Creating computer-to-computer networks

At the Create a computer-to-computer network screen, enter the name you'd like to give the network and the channel the network will use (12-10).

Figure 12-10. Enable the computer-to-computer network

Other computers will now be able to connect to your network. This is mostly useful for sharing files back and forth with one another.

Wireless Topologies

A wireless network's placement within a network can greatly impact the security level of the network. Many wireless networks, for ease of use, will want to have NAT disabled, allowing Bonjour connections into devices on the wired network. For larger networks where security is paramount, network administrators should strongly consider putting an Apple AirPort in a demilitarized zone (DMZ). A DMZ sits outside the corporate firewall and can have a completely different set of rules for how network traffic is managed.

The default configuration of an Apple AirPort has NAT enabled. This removes the ability of the wireless clients to communicate over broadcast networks with upstream networks. However, clients can still communicate by IP address with upstream networks. Therefore, this is not actually a DMZ but instead a subnetwork of your main network. Communications are still possible and less controllable.

The preferred location of AirPorts and wireless access points is in a DMZ. It is important to note that placing the wireless access point in a network above rather than below (in terms of the network architecture) will render your NAT wireless clients unable to communicate directly with your corporate network. They will need to establish a VPN tunnel to talk to the network. With this setup, traffic can be most effectively encrypted.

This network topology is often employed in larger companies, and in the future we expect more and more wireless protocols to be developed around it.

Wireless Hacking Tools

Several tools can be used when looking to enumerate or break into wireless networks. Many of these have graphical user interfaces (GUIs) that allow less-savvy users to perform very complicated tasks, such as mapping out WEP keys for physical areas and discovering wireless networks with relative ease, even if they don't have any background in hacking. We'll spend some time covering these tools so you'll know what to look out for when securing your wireless network.

KisMAC

KisMAC is the OS X version of Kismet, a wireless network utility for Linux and FreeBSD. KisMAC development was managed by a developer in Germany, but political considerations in 2007 forced the project to move to Switzerland. The project changed hands again and eventually ended up in the United States at http://kismac-ng.org. It has since been forked to IGRsoft and renamed to KisMac (or KisMac2), and it can be found at http://downloads.igrsoft.com/beta/KisMac2.zip. KisMAC is a free network scanning utility based on Kismet. KisMac is used to detect wireless networks and crack their passwords. Once downloaded, simply open the app and click the Scan button. As you can see in Figure 12-11, KisMac initially lists all of the wireless networks that are visible by KisMAC scanners. KisMAC will show the signal strength and type of encryption for each of the networks, making it very easy to find AirPorts that are close to you as well as isolating networks with weak signal strengths.

KisMac v0.3.4

#	Ch	SSID	BSSID	Enc	Type	Sig...	Avg	M...	Pack...	Data	Last Seen	Ch...
0	1	Mapsi's Network	B8:C7:5D:0A:1A:4B	WPA	managed	0	0	0	0	0B	2015-08-26 03:43:07 +0	
1	9	hennen	00:15:05:35:80:8F	WPA	managed	0	0	0	0	0B	2015-08-26 03:43:21 +0	
2	14?	Edge	88:1F:A1:2F:3C:BF	WPA	managed	0	0	0	0	0B	2015-08-26 03:43:21 +0	
3	2	NETGEAR	A0:21:B7:93:C7:3C	NO	managed	0	0	0	0	0B	2015-08-26 03:43:21 +0	
4	1	HOME-A4BE	E0:88:5D:77:A4:BE	WPA	managed	0	0	0	0	0B	2015-08-26 03:42:45 +0	
5	6	USI Wireless	00:0D:67:0B:86:7C	NO	managed	9	9	11	0	0B	2015-08-26 03:43:21 +0	
6	6	Edge	88:1F:A1:2F:3C:BE	WPA	managed	33	33	43	0	0B	2015-08-26 03:43:21 +0	
7	11	HOME-F417	88:F7:C7:98:F4:17	WPA	managed	0	0	0	0	0B	2015-08-26 03:43:21 +0	
8	6	usiw_secure	00:0D:67:0B:86:7D	WPA	managed	9	9	15	0	0B	2015-08-26 03:43:21 +0	
9	1	HOME-29D5	C4:27:95:CD:29:D5	WPA	managed	0	0	0	0	0B	2015-08-26 03:43:21 +0	
10	9	CenturyLink8039	40:8B:07:C6:15:A5	WPA	managed	0	0	0	0	0B	2015-08-26 03:43:21 +0	
11	11	Bucky	10:C3:7B:C5:84:60	WPA	managed	0	0	0	0	0B	2015-08-26 03:43:21 +0	
12	11	CenturyLink7620	A0:A3:E2:21:38:25	WPA	managed	0	0	0	0	0B	2015-08-26 03:42:02 +0	
13	6	share-guest	20:AA:4B:9F:82:51	NO	managed	0	2	2	0	0B	2015-08-26 03:42:02 +0	
14	1	xfinitywifi	E2:88:5D:77:A4:B0	NO	managed	0	0	0	0	0B	2015-08-26 03:42:34 +0	
15	11	xfinitywifi	8A:F7:C7:98:F4:19	NO	managed	0	0	14	0	0B	2015-08-26 03:43:21 +0	
16	1	xfinitywifi	C6:27:95:CD:29:D7	NO	managed	0	0	0	0	0B	2015-08-26 03:43:21 +0	
17	11	J&P Network	00:25:BC:8D:82:7B	WPA	managed	4	4	4	0	0B	2015-08-26 03:43:21 +0	
18	6	City of Minneapoli	00:0D:67:0B:86:7F	NO	managed	6	6	6	0	0B	2015-08-26 03:43:21 +0	
19	4	Flapjack	94:10:3E:83:CC:58	WPA	managed	0	0	0	0	0B	2015-08-26 03:43:21 +0	
20	4	Flapjack-guest	96:10:3E:80:CC:58	NO	managed	0	0	0	0	0B	2015-08-26 03:43:21 +0	

Figure 12-11. KisMAC base stations

When scanning, KisMAC can show details about a given network. Simply click on one of the networks and click on Details to see everything KisMAC has been able to ascertain thus far, as you can see in Figure 12-12.

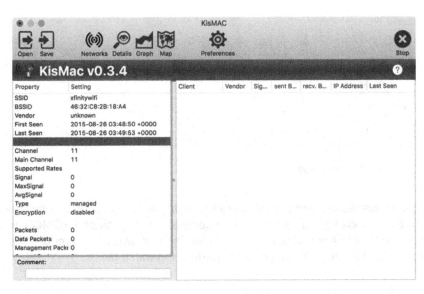

Figure 12-12. KisMAC graphs

Other programs such as Mac Stumbler and iStumbler can give the same information, but the more advanced password cracking and wireless scanning features found in KisMAC make it a more compelling application for the hacker to use.

Cracking wireless networks with KisMAC is possible only if a second wireless network interface is installed on the machine. The second network interface runs in a passive monitoring mode, while the first active network interface sends out probe requests and waits for answers. Be aware that this is no longer the bleeding edge of hacking technology, but it is still very effective in testing out the "hackability" of your network.

Packet reinjection is a WEP cracking technique used to crack wireless networks. With this attack, KisMAC will try to send captured packets of data in order to cause another computer to respond. If the computer responds, KisMAC will send these packets repeatedly. If KisMAC detects any answers, then it will go into injection mode. Injection mode generates a lot of traffic, causing more easily captured pieces of data to be generated. Wireless networks with WEP can be broken within an hour, and sometimes only ten minutes or less.

Many wireless access points offer a key generation process using an easy-to-remember passphrase. Unfortunately, many wireless manufacturers implemented a very dangerous algorithm, called the Newsham 21-bit attack, for the generation of 40-bit WEP keys. This algorithm generates keys with an effective strength of only 21 bits. KisMAC is able to *brute-force*, or attempt all possible combinations until the correct password combination is found (see Figure 12-13), finding these keys quickly. Wireless access points from Linksys, D-Link, Belkin, and Netgear are confirmed to be vulnerable to the Newsham 21-bit attack.

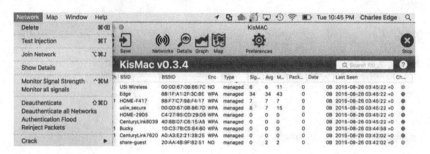

Figure 12-13. *Cracking into base stations*

Most network interfaces that are available are PCMCIA cards, which is an interface that MacBook and MacBook Pro users cannot use because of the lack of a PCMCIA interface on the machines. Still, there are a couple usually listed in the KisMAC preferences that you can acquire if you'd like to use your computer for performing these tasks.

Detecting Rogue Access Points

If a rogue access point is suspected on the network, it is possible to use KisMAC to quickly locate the WAP. If you have a GPS unit, the Map menu provides users with the ability to set their current position on a map and then follow the wireless signal to the rogue access point's source using signal strength readings.

To set up a map, you will need to import an image and switch to the Map tab. You should now see a map. Click the Set Waypoint 1 entry in the Map menu and click a position in the map for which you know the geographical position. KisMAC will now ask you for this position. If you have a GPS device attached to your computer, your current position is set as the default coordinates.

Now use the Set Waypoint 1 entry to set up a second waypoint. After you have set up these two points, KisMAC can use the image as a map (see Figure 12-14). Networks are automatically displayed. You can also show your current position by clicking the Current Position entry in the Map menu.

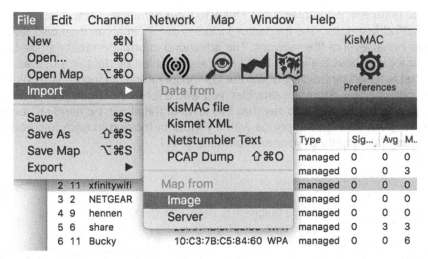

Figure 12-14. Setting up a map for KisMAC

iStumbler and Mac Stumbler

iStumbler is a good discovery tool for OS X that is available under a BSD-style open source license and allows users to find AirPort networks, Bluetooth devices, and Bonjour services. You can download iStumbler from `www.iStumbler.net`. After downloading, open the application and it will automatically scan the wireless networks that are accessible to the computer running it. The default graph (see Figure 12-15) will show the wireless network name, the type of security employed on the wireless network, the signal, the vendor of the WAPs, the wireless channel, and the Mac address of the wireless base stations.

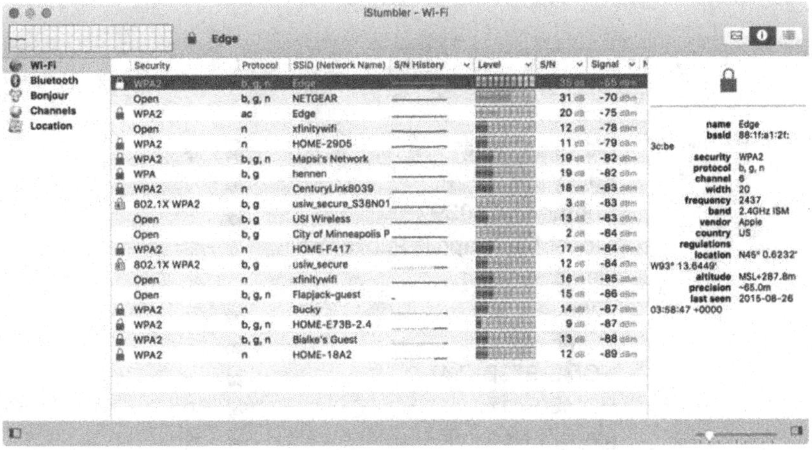

Figure 12-15. iStumbler

It will also compute a graph that displays a history of the wireless network's signal strength. You can view this in a stand-alone window by selecting Monitor from the AirPort menu. The monitors can be used to help in troubleshooting wireless signal issues by finding overlapping SSIDs, finding rogue access points, and helping determine which channel to use in a physical location that is highly saturated with wireless access point channels and signals.

Another nice feature of iStumbler is the ability to view details about wireless networks using the AirPort Inspector. The Inspector includes details such as the noise level and the average signal level of the network. The advanced information that can be obtained using Inspector is accessible in the Edit menu and enabled by default, but it also mirrors much of what is found by holding down the Option key and clicking on your Wi-Fi menu bar item (Figure 12-16). iStumbler provides you with a lot more information than we can cover in this chapter. Suffice it to say that this level of detail can be handy if you are troubleshooting an issue on the phone with a vendor or looking to hack into your wireless network to test the security of your environment.

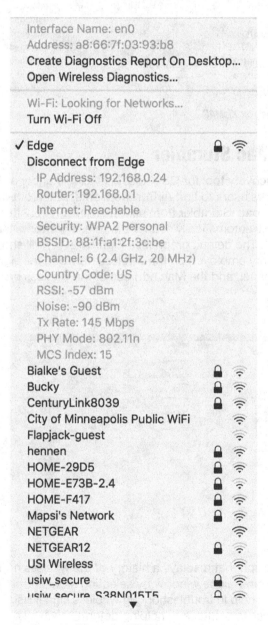

Figure 12-16. Hold down the option key and click on your Wi-Fi menu bar item

Ettercap

Ettercap is a tool used to execute "man-in-the-middle" (MITM) attacks on a LAN. Features include sniffing network traffic, network analysis, and content filtering. It can also be used to intercept packets, to perform ARP spoofing, and to perform character injection. It will perform password collection for a variety of protocols including Telnet, FTP, POP, SSH, ICQ, SMB, MySQL, HTTP, IMAP, and Yahoo Messenger. Ettercap can perform OS fingerprinting, kill network connections, and check for other poisoners. It can also do all of this on wired networks.

You can download Ettercap from https://ettercap.github.io/ettercap/.

Network Utility

Built into OS X is the Network Utility, which still provides some useful information about the Mac it is running on as well as the network that Mac is attached to, whether that be an Ethernet network or a wireless network. This utility has been moved to /System/Library/CoreServices/Applications/

NetSpot Pro

NetSpot Pro (and the non-Pro version for home users) is a WiFi planning, surveying and mapping utility that allows detection of many characteristics of WAPs in an area. The SSIDs and characteristics can be saved in a file, and can be mapped to an area. These maps can be exported to a KML file for storage and later comparison and analysis over time to see how a WiFi environment changes. The app has good tech support and a user forum. It can be found here, http://www.netspotapp.com. Discovery setting in NetSpot Pro displays several useful characteristics when scanning a physical space or area for WiFi signals that are in the space (Figure 12-17).

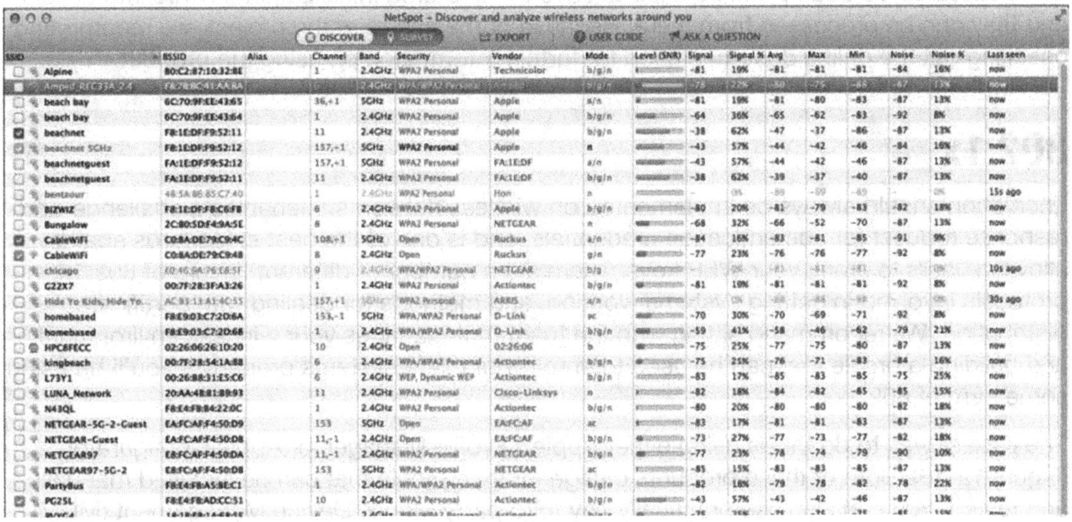

Figure 12-17. Discovery setting in NetSpot

The Survey setting in NetSpot Pro allows adding WAP locations and characteristics to a map or outline of a physical space or area for documentation or later analysis (Figure 12-18).

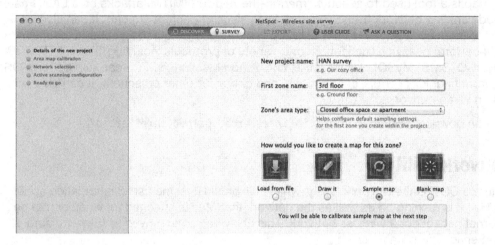

Figure 12-18. Survey setting in NetSpot

Cracking WEP Keys

To drive home why it is so important to practice good security with your wireless environment, let's look at cracking a few types of wireless security protocols. Let's start with a WEP key. There are three steps we will need to go through in order to crack a WEP key. First, we need to locate the AirPort using a tool such as KisMAC.

Second, we need to generate a minimum of 400,000 WEP initialization vectors (random bits of data used to decrypt wireless traffic). We will capture the traffic using Aireplay to generate the required initialization vectors. Aireplay is available at http://www.aircrack-ng.org. Once captured, Airodump will be used to save the captured initialization vectors into a file and they can be processed from there. Because of the nature of the project, we recommend checking out the online documentation for further information on using the product.

802.1x

Encryption should always be implemented on wireless networks. It enables a challenge-and-response request for authentication credentials, and is one of the best safeguards against allowing users to crack your WEP keys. There are a number of different flavors of 802.1x, protocols involved in getting systems working, and methods for dealing with certificate distribution. We recommend sitting with the team that manages your wireless environment and building a profile that can be used to enroll your client systems properly if you'll be using some form of 802.1x.

The easiest way to do this is using either Apple's Profile Manager, or Apple Configurator (Figure 12-19). Both of these products can generate a profile that can be installed manually and tested. You can also use practically any third party Mobile Device Management (MDM) solution to deploy a profile.

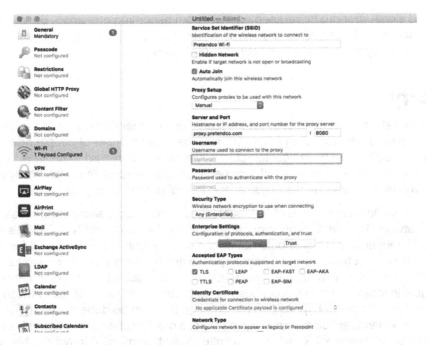

Figure 12-19. Manually build profiles for 802.1x configurations

Once a profile is installed, use the 802.1x tab of the Wi-Fi interface you're configuring for connectivity in order to manually connect and test your configuration. 802.1x can be either very easy or very frustrating. By working with your network administrators, you can have them review logs and help you get each setting configured appropriately.

General Safeguards Against Cracking Wireless Networks

Encryption should always be implemented on wireless networks. It is one of the best safeguards against allowing users to crack your WEP keys.

Determining the strength of encryption is always a trade-off between security and speed. The more encrypted, the slower the network will be because of increased time for the mathematics to do encryption and decryption at both ends. But increased levels of encryption also mean increased time to crack passwords, which makes your network a tougher problem for potential password crackers. Most wardrivers will not bother with heavily encrypted networks, moving on to less well-protected environments. Keep in mind that the encryption strength is not only determined by the number of bits that the encryption is using but also by the complexity of the passphrase being used if only because more complex passwords are harder to crack when using a dictionary attack. Corporate environments concerned about wireless security will use WPA2 Enterprise and 802.1x, which goes beyond simple WEP keys by employing a RADIUS server on the network. (RADIUS is Remote Authentication and Dial In User Service. It has been around for a long time but is still widely used and is very useful for network security.) This allows the administrator to use a server that can lock accounts if someone is attempting to break into them using password policies and other account management security measures described in Chapter 16.

Having good signal strength helps keep packets from becoming orphaned. Because orphaned packets make cracking wireless networks easier, maintaining good signal strength is another good way to keep wireless networks protected.

Summary

Securing your network is a must in today's security environment. Because of the damage or loss that can happen on a local area network and the sheer number of people now able to effect such damage, it is now critical to act locally as well with regard to network security. This starts with the wireless network, if only because of the exposure to potentially nefarious operators who may be outside the physical and logical perimeter of your space.

In this chapter we looked at some of the techniques used to both secure and break into a wireless network. Password protection, MAC address filtration, and NAT firewalls are good security techniques. They should not be the only security measures used for securing wireless networks, but they are good first steps toward securing wireless networks. While breaking into any networks should be reserved to labs and securing your own networks, our main goal in looking at these practices was to portray how easily some of these security mechanisms are to bypass and the damage that can be done once they have been circumvented. When practicing your skills in wireless cracking be sure to act only on your own network or on a network for which you have explicit permission to act on. Many regions have laws that forbid password cracking or attempts to penetrate WiFi networks, with real penalties for doing so.

Now that we are finished looking at wireless networks, in Chapter 13 we will look at one of the most critical of services on the inside of your network, file sharing.

Part **IV**

Securely Sharing Resources

File Services

Configuring file-sharing security can be one of the more challenging aspects of working with shared computer data in a networked environment. The challenge is twofold—how do you keep files accessible to those who need them while simultaneously keeping them inaccessible to those who don't? Sharing files over a network is also an inherently dangerous activity. Other computers' users can access files on your system without physically gaining access to your computer; thus, if it is configured incorrectly, the wrong data can easily get into the wrong hands, which can prove to be catastrophic. However, in most environments, it is crucial that multiple computers have access to data on a single computer. How do we manage this file-sharing conundrum?

In Chapter 3 we discussed how to apply security settings to users and groups. In this chapter, we will discuss these security settings as they apply to sharing files. We'll explore the security differences in file sharing between Macs on a peer-to-peer network and a central file-sharing networked system, and we'll look at how to strengthen these file-sharing policies in a networked Mac environment using the native tools within OS X (Apple Filing Protocol when file sharing with other Macs, and Samba to connect a Windows-based machine to a Mac).

The Risks in File Sharing

Giving others access to files on your computer can be risky on many levels. First, you risk someone obtaining access to the system who shouldn't. For example, when a file is remotely deleted from your system, the file does not go to the trash, you do not get alerted about the deletion, and anyone who knows the right password typically can delete files. If the wrong folders on a system are shared, you can also give someone the ability to delete critical files, whether intentionally or not. For all of these reasons, and with the risks of confidential data being accessed over file-sharing protocols, you need to properly lock down the security of any file sharing on your systems.

In Chapter 3, we discussed creating a limited Sharing Only account. This feature was added into Mac OS X Leopard for this very reason, and when creating accounts solely to give access to files, we recommend using this account type over any other.

Peer-to-Peer vs. Client-Server Environments

Before we discuss how to configure file-sharing permissions correctly, it's important to summarize the differences between peer-to-peer and client-server file-sharing environments. See Chapter 4 for an extensive discussion of the two network types.

It is common in a networked Mac environment to have a handful of computers, each with file sharing enabled, with users trading files back and forth between each other without a central repository for the files. This type of environment is known as *peer-to-peer networking* (P2P). Security in a P2P environment is generally straightforward and tends to be rather loose. Anyone with access to the computer usually has access to files on that machine.

Note   Peer-to-peer in this context is not the same as it is when using an application to access files hosted anonymously on the Internet. In this context, peer-to-peer is strictly meant to indicate sharing files over network connections in small environments.

As environments mature and grow larger, the distributed file sharing of P2P will give way to centralized file servers in what is typically described as a *client-server*, or *two-tier*, environment. Client-server environments offer a single and centralized location for users to access files that are needed by multiple users. In a client-server environment, backup and security begin to play a much more critical role, because files are now accessible by multiple users who have access to that repository. File permissions become critical to maintaining security. The permissions and backup strategies are easier to deal with in client-server environments for two reasons: first, because client-server environments have dedicated servers to handle many of the tasks that clients will handle in P2P environments; and second, because in a client-server environment, most data is stored on a server.

There are some inherent challenges to migrating from a P2P to a server-based file-sharing environment. Some users might have a hard time moving away from their old method of sharing files. The proper permission controls are often not set up correctly on the centralized data, if they are set up at all. Client machines might continue to share files after the transition simply because they weren't configured not to share them. This can lead to security issues that can be disastrous if not managed appropriately.

File Security Fundamentals

Before we dive into how to secure file services properly, let's discuss some fundamentals of file security in OS X. This will include the LKDC, POSIX and ACLs (covered more fully in Chapter 4).

LKDC

Because Apple is concerned about protecting peer-to-peer environments just as much as client-server environments, it has equipped every copy of OS X with a Kerberos Local Key Distribution Center (LKDC). The LKDC, based on a Kerberos authentication scheme (Kerberos is discussed in Chapter 16), secures AFP, CIFS (Samba), and VNC services (covered in Chapter 15). The LKDC implementation helps to secure communications, because it requires the nodes communicating with one another to prove their identity prior to communicating. Once a system has initiated communication, keys are used instead of passwords when authenticating users and services. This keeps passwords from being sent over the network, helping to keep them secure.

By forcing the same identity requirements that are common in client-server environments, the LKDC protects against eavesdropping and replaying sessions (where traffic is captured and replayed to get around security mechanisms). And the LKDC is implemented by default in every Mac, meaning there is nothing to do to set it up! The LKDC is dedicated to providing and protecting authentication. But how does the system determine what you are authorized to access? It starts with POSIX.

Using POSIX Permissions

Chapter 4 discussed POSIX permissions in OS X at length; this section summarizes the topic in the context of file permissions. OS X is an SUS-compliant operating system. POSIX is a standardized feature set developed to make operating systems compatible with Unix-based operating systems. POSIX permission levels are divided into three categories: read (users can access the file), write (users can write data to it), and execute (users can run the file, such as an application). When viewing these permissions from the terminal command ls, read is indicated by an r, write is indicated by a w, and execute is indicated by an x.

> **Note** For more information on changing permissions from the command line, see Chapter 4.

When you look at the permission designations for files, you'll see they are displayed in the order of *owner*, *group*, and (if needed) *everyone*. The owner is the user that owns a file, can set permissions on the file, and is listed in the text following the permissions of the file. The group of a file is listed next. The "everyone" designation is given to every user accessing a file who is not listed in either the owner or the group designation and is also known as a guest user of that file.

> **Note** When looking at file permissions, you might find that an admin or wheel group is listed in a file's permissions. These are part of the built-in users and groups that a system defaults to upon installation of the operating system. Chapter 4 discusses admin groups in more depth.

The output of the permissions for a file will use the following syntax:

```
(permissions) (owner) (group) (everyone) (file size) (last modified)
```

The ls command followed by the –al option can show you the permissions, as indicated in the following example:

```
cedge:/Users cedge$ ls -al
total 16
drwxrwxrwx    8 root      admin      272 Aug 24 22:07 .
drwxrwxr-t   35 root      admin     1292 Agu 13 20:27 ..
-rwxrwxrwx    1 cedge     admin     6148 Aug 23 13:55 .DS_Store
-rwxrwxrwx    1 root      wheel        0 Aug  1 2015 .localized
drwxrwxrwx   16 318admin  318admin   544 Aug 26 2015 318admin
drwxrwxrwt   10 root      wheel      340 Aug 23 13:14 Shared
drwxrwxrwx   38 cedge     cedge     1292 Aug 13 15:40 cedge
drwxrwxrwx   12 postgres  postgres   408 Aug 24 22:22 postgres
```

> **Note** The d in front of the permissions in the previous example indicates that the item is a directory rather than a file.

Getting More out of Permissions with Access Control Lists

Traditionally, OS X has been limited to the standard POSIX permission model of read, write, and execute. This system has served Unix-based operating systems well for many years now; however, it is starting to show its age. The main concern is that it isn't very flexible, and several special modes, such as the *sticky bit* (a setting that indicates that only the owner can delete a file from the respective folder), have been added over time.

For more complicated permission structures, access control lists (*ACLs*) provide you with the most granular control available over permissions for files and folders. An ACL is a list of permissions attached to files and folders. These replace POSIX permissions in the traditional sense of OS X security. ACLs give the Mac a set of permissions equal to that found in Microsoft Windows. ACL information is stored in the extended attributes of the Mac OS Extended file system (HFS+).

It's easiest to understand ACLs if we break down how they work and are applied. There are two key system properties that allow ACLs to function:

- The generated unique identifier (GUID) is a value that is used many times in OS X because it can be guaranteed to be unique across computer systems. Your user account has both a traditional Unix-style UID and a new GUID.

- An access control entry (*ACE*) is the individual rule that determines what access is given to any particular user or group.

> **Note**   An ACL is a list of ACEs that can be attached to a directory or file, providing permissions similar to those used in Microsoft Windows.

The following are the possible permissions that can be applied to files and folders with the new ACL model. This is a huge jump from the read-write-execute model we are used to on OS X. Here are the permissions:

- Change Permissions
- Change Owner
- Read Attributes
- Read Extended Attributes
- List Folder Contents
- Traverse Folder
- Read Permissions
- Write Attributes
- Create Files
- Create Folder
- Delete
- Delete Subfolders and Files

> **Note**   When defining ACLs, you should typically do so at a group level. Reserve user-level ACEs for special cases such as deny rules for problematic users. For more on defining the users and groups that make up ACEs, see Chapter 4.

Sharing Protocols: Which One Is for You?

Computers can connect in various ways to talk to one another. The way in which computers communicate is known as a *protocol*. When configuring global settings for a file-sharing environment, you must consider that computers connecting to each other will more than likely use different protocols to communicate. For example, one protocol, Apple Filing Protocol (AFP), will typically be used when connecting two Macs, and an entirely different protocol, Samba (SMB), will be used to connect a Windows-based machine to a Mac. However, one fact remains constant among these protocols: permissions must be set when accessing resources from one computer to another.

Apple Filing Protocol

AFP is a presentation-layer network protocol that is the primary protocol for providing file services for Mac computers. AFP is rarely used outside the Mac platform, so little security attention has been paid to it as a protocol from security researchers. However, you should take certain steps to ensure the security of the files and data that use AFP to communicate.

To configure AFP sharing, you must first enable AFP on the computer. To enable AFP in OS X, open your System Preferences, and click the Sharing preference pane (see Figure 13-1). Select the File Sharing check box. The File Sharing indicator button will turn green.

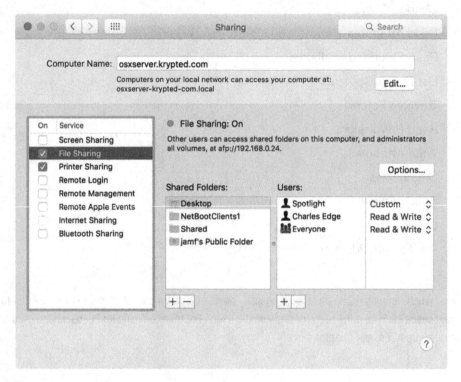

Figure 13-1. Enabling file sharing

> **Note**   Configuring AFP is different and much more feature-rich in OS X Server than in the OS X client. For more information on this portion of the AFP configuration, please see Chapter 16.

Now that you've enabled file sharing, you will want to limit access to files and folders. To do so, review the shared folders in the Shared Folders list. Here you can stop sharing any folders that should not be shared by clicking the minus (–) sign in order to "unshare" them. Once you have verified that everything in the list should be there, you can now create new shared folders. To do so, click the plus (+) sign, which will open a window that allows you to browse your folders (see Figure 13-2). In this window, find the folder you want to share, and click the Add button.

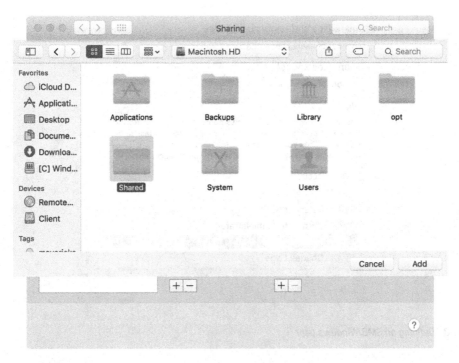

Figure 13-2. Browsing to a folder

Once you have shared a folder, you can move on to setting sharing permissions. To do so, first review the list of users and groups (for more information on configuring users and groups, see Chapter 3) in the Users list. Click any of the users and groups that should not have access to the data in the Shared Folders list, and click the minus (–) sign while those users or groups are highlighted to deny access. After you have removed users who should not have access to the folder, click the plus (+) sign to add users who should have access. At this point, you will see a window with all of your users. Any users who already have access to the directory will be disabled. Find the users you want to grant access to, select them, and click the Select button to add them to the Users list.

Setting Sharing Options

Click Options to select which protocols you will use. On this screen, simply select the check box for each protocol to enable it, as you can see in Figure 13-3. For the purposes of this discussion, we have selected SMB. Here you can also configure which users will have access to the SMB service.

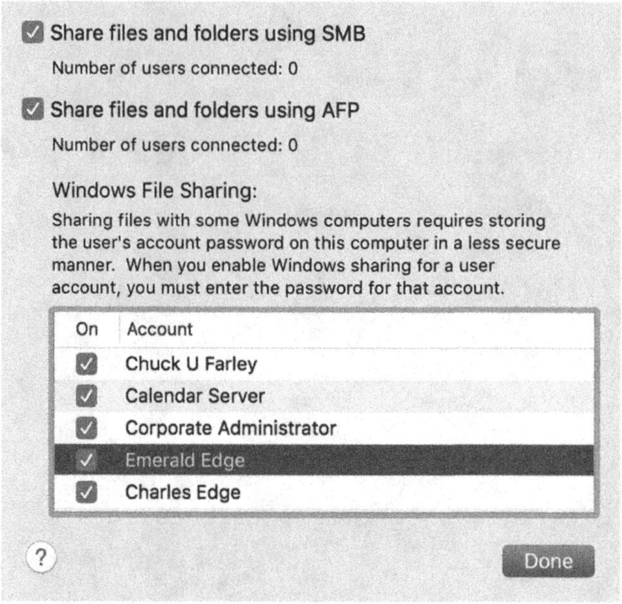

☑ Share files and folders using SMB

Number of users connected: 0

☑ Share files and folders using AFP

Number of users connected: 0

Windows File Sharing:

Sharing files with some Windows computers requires storing the user's account password on this computer in a less secure manner. When you enable Windows sharing for a user account, you must enter the password for that account.

On	Account
☑	Chuck U Farley
☑	Calendar Server
☑	Corporate Administrator
☑	Emerald Edge
☑	Charles Edge

(?)   Done

Figure 13-3. Defining an SMB/Windows user

Samba

You should only enable SMB, or any of the services discussed here, if you actually need them. When adding users to this list, you will be asked to enter a password (see Figure 13-4). The reason for this is that the respective user's password file must be modified to allow for an older style of password, which is used by the Samba Windows file-sharing engine.

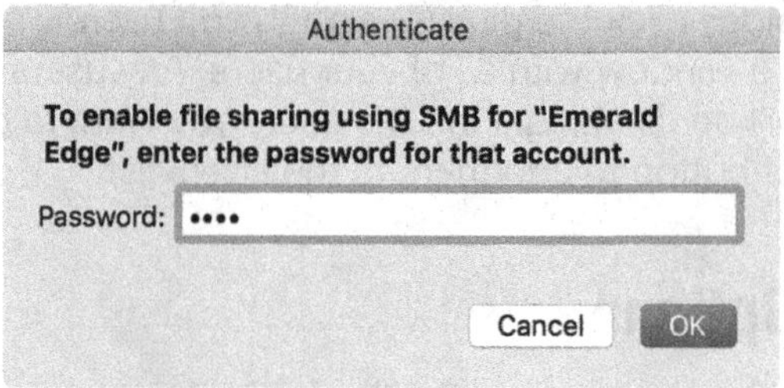

Authenticate

To enable file sharing using SMB for "Emerald Edge", enter the password for that account.

Password: ••••

Cancel   OK

Figure 13-4. Providing the password for a Windows user

It's important to note that you are decreasing the overall security of your system by using the SMB service. Apple does not enable the storage of these weak passwords by default, because dictionary attacking these older LAN Manager (LM MD4) passwords has been fairly simple. Any attacker who has gained root access to your system could view this weak password "hash" in your password file and potentially recover your login password. It might seem counterintuitive to worry about security concerns for someone with root access, but remember that even the root account cannot view a user's encrypted keychain file without knowing that user's password. Therefore, in this instance, if an attacker has gained complete control of the system, they could be able to decrypt files that are based on the user's login password, such as keychains or file-vaulted home folders.

> **Note**   If you use the same password for all services, then compromising this password could lead to compromising the password for all of your services that use it.

Once you are satisfied that your files and folders have an appropriate level of permissions assigned to them, it's time to turn to other protocols that computers will be using to access resources on your Mac. First on the list is the Samba protocol.

Once you have enabled a Windows user, you will be able to connect to the system using SMB. To test this from a Mac, click the Go menu from the Finder, and select the "Connect to a Server" option. In the Connect to Server window (as shown in Figure 13-5), type **smb://** followed by the IP address of the computer to which you are connecting. When you click Connect, you will be asked to enter the password and will be given a list of share points that have access through SMB. Make sure the user you are logged in as has access only to the locations that you want the user to be able to access.

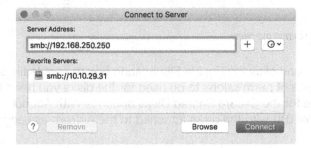

Figure 13-5. Connecting to an SMB share point

Using Apple AirPort to Share Files

The File Sharing feature of OS X provides the most granular approach to a workgroup-oriented file-sharing scenario that you can get without upgrading to OS X Server. There will be instances, however, when users may want to configure the File Sharing feature to run off an AirPort base station. Modern Apple AirPorts have the capacity to share files using a portable hard drive connected over USB to the AirPort device. To share files using the Apple AirPort, plug an external hard drive into the AirPort, open the AirPort Utility in the /Applications/Utilities folder, authenticate, click the AirPort to configure, and then click the Edit button for that device.

Click Disks to see a window similar to that shown in Figure 13-6. This window will list the disks and volumes attached to your AirPort along with their names and capacities. It will also list the users attached to the AirPort if you configured Secure Shared Disks with the "With accounts" option.

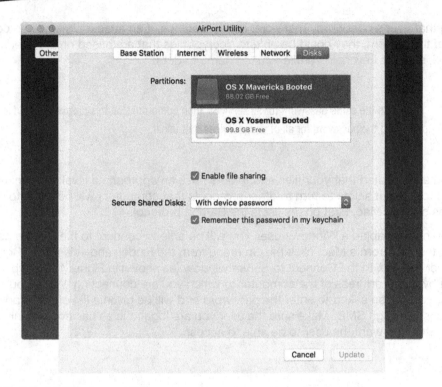

Figure 13-6. AirPort disk sharing overview

Select the Disks tab, and click the Enable File Sharing box to enable file sharing. You can now configure the type of permissions to be used for the disks you need to share. The most secure setting to use for the Secure Shared Disks option is With Accounts, which allows you to create accounts for use with the disks attached to the AirPort, as seen in Figure 13-7.

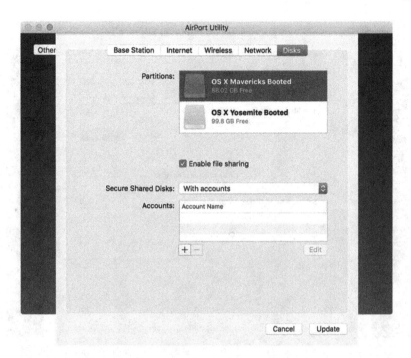

Figure 13-7. Configuring file sharing on the AirPort

> **Note**   It is common to refer to a wireless access point, such as an Apple AirPort's shared disk, or a
> hard drive connected to a network, as *network-attached storage* (NAS).

Once you have set your base station to use accounts for shared storage, create the
accounts that can access the shared volumes. To do so, click the plus sign. At the account
creation screen, provide a username and password to access the shared disk. Then choose
the level of access the account should have. Here, you can choose Read and Write (as
we did in Figure 13-8), which is able to do anything on the disks, Read Only, which can
only view contents, and Not Allowed, which is an account that is able to see the shared
repository of data, but not access any of the volumes. Each account will have the same set
of permissions for all disks.

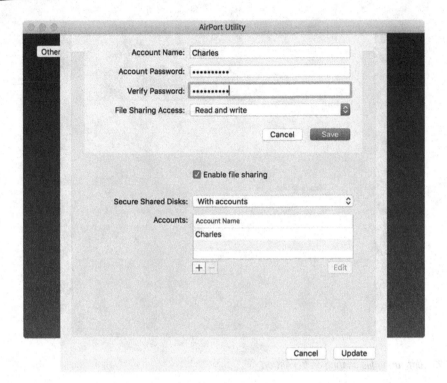

Figure 13-8. Create accounts on the AirPort

Caution   There is little protection for these accounts; the user names and passwords do not benefit from policies, the users and passwords are not shared between various systems, and there is no adaptive firewall as with OS X or OS X Server to protect the device whatsoever.

Third-Party Problem Solver: DAVE

From time to time, file and application incompatibilities will arise that cannot be solved by enabling the Samba protocol. Or you'll need to use SMB signing to communicate with Windows servers. In these and other cases, the default capabilities of Samba in OS X are often not enough. In these situations, we recommend turning to third-party applications to solve this problem. DAVE is one of these problem solvers. DAVE, distributed by Thursby Software (www.thursby.com), enables file and printer sharing compatibility between Windows and Mac operating systems.

Note   Before installing DAVE, disable Samba on the Sharing preference pane in System Preferences. DAVE cannot be installed if Samba is currently enabled.

SMB authentication primarily occurs over LANMAN, NTLMv1, and NTLMv2. LANMAN used a weak (by modern standards) authentication protocol known as LM Hash. NTLMv1 was a great step forward and represented the introduction of a challenge-response protocol. With NTLMv1, the server authenticates the client by sending a random number, known as the *challenge*. The client uses the challenge and a password, or *ticket*, known by both the client and the server. The client identity then is configured using the result of combining the two. The server verifies that the client has calculated the correct result and verifies the identity of the client. NTLMv2 is also a challenge-response protocol, but with more steps involved to enhance the security of the challenge-response process.

Of these, NTLMv2 is by far the most secure; however, it has been replaced in many situations by Kerberos. If Kerberos is available, then the DAVE client will always use it. This level of granularity is more than is found in OS X otherwise. Add in the ability to name and set up workgroups and other traditional Samba options, and you can easily see why Dave has a place in environments that use OS X to provide files to Windows clients.

Permission Models

In larger environments, system administrators have been grappling with various methods to handle file permissions for a good while now. Over the years, the Mac administrative community has developed a few methodologies as standard practices for managing permissions. In this section, we'll touch on these permissions methodologies, or models, to give you a better understanding about the ways that file-sharing permissions policies can be implemented on Mac networks.

Discretionary access control (DAC) allows data owners to administer file permissions themselves. In a DAC model, administrators often spend less time assigning permissions (which often means spending more time restoring accidentally deleted files). Discretionary access control systems permit users to entirely determine the access granted to their resources, which means they can (through accident or malice) give access to unauthorized users. The owner of any resource has access to control the privileges to that resource. There are often no security checks ensuring that malicious code is not distributed or that the owner of a file or folder is well trained enough to be assigning permissions in the first place. This is the default model and, unfortunately, the most common model for controlling permissions. However, in addition to time spent on restoring deleted files, DAC is also limited in that security breaches can be caused when users who do not understand the appropriate access levels for files within their organization assign permissions that cause security breaches.

Mandatory access control (MAC) is a model that can augment or even replace DAC for file permissions. MAC's most important feature involves denying users full control over the access to resources that they create. The system security policy (as set by the administrator) entirely determines the access rights granted, and a user cannot grant less restrictive access to their resources than the administrator specifies.

MAC has the goal of defining an architecture that requires the evaluation of all security-related information and making decisions based on what is done with data and the various data types in use in your organization. MAC is a strict hierarchical model usually associated with governments. All objects are given security labels known as *sensitivity labels*, and are classified accordingly. All users are then given specific security clearances as to what they are allowed to access. A common term when working with MAC is *lattice*, which describes the upper and lower bounds of a user's access permission. In other words, a user's access differs at different levels.

Role-based access control (RBAC) involves limiting access to files based on the responsibilities of a user. When using a role-based security model for access controls, each role in an organization is created for various job functions. The permissions to perform certain operations are assigned to specific roles. Users are then assigned particular roles, and through those role assignments they acquire the permissions to perform particular system functions. Role-based access requires that an organization review the various positions and build access levels for resources based on those roles.

As an organization looks to scale, it should define roles based on potential future hires. As organizations grow, they are more likely to build out new organizational charts that contain current and future positions within the organization. This often represents a good building block for developing roles, which become users or groups in the directory structure. Security groups can then be used within any document management system or enterprise resource planning (ERP) solution that an organization might decide to deploy. This is the most common permissions model being used today because it accommodates growth within an organization while being careful to limit permissions definitively.

Summary

Throughout this chapter we have discussed securing your file shares. While many of the security mechanisms that have been put in place by Apple will help, such as the LKDC and various encryption protocols, they will not be effective if your password is not secure. They can also be easily circumvented if you do not have good password policies, such as requiring a password to be changed at certain intervals (see Chapter 16 for more on password policies). Therefore, the most important aspect of securing your files over file shares is to practice good password security.

In Chapter 14, we will turn our attention to perhaps the most popular way to access data today, web servers.

iCloud Security

iCloud is a cloud service provided by Apple. A basic iCloud account is free and provides a connection to calendars, contacts, and other services that integrate with your Mac. Because iCloud has services that integrate with the Mac, it's more than a traditional cloud solution, though. An iCloud account has options that include tracking the physical location of your Apple devices and potentially escrowing keys used for decrypting hard drives and remotely controlling computers. Because the iCloud account provides access to your computer, securing the account and the connection between the computer and the account is of paramount importance. This security starts with the Apple ID and extends to the settings used when setting up iCloud-based services on your Mac.

The Apple ID

Each iCloud account will have an Apple ID. This Apple ID is the gateway to most of the services described throughout the remainder of this chapter. When doing large-scale deployments, you will not need to deploy an Apple ID or even iCloud accounts for every single user. But it certainly helps if you do so. The Apple ID is a unique identifier provided by Apple, used to access a number of Apple services. This includes the most popular of these services: music purchased through iTunes. But also includes iCloud, Messages, and the iBookstore.

Much of the security concerns regarding Apple IDs arise from the fact that an Apple ID can be used to access a computer or synchronize data to iCloud or iCloud Backup even after an OS X computer or iPhone has been wiped. This is more of a concern on iPhones and iPads, where wiping a device should provide a sense of security that the data on the device has been removed due to the Managed Open-In feature of iOS, which restricts data within apps provided by an MDM solution from leaving the secure enclave of that solution. While you can wipe an OS X device, there are far more ways to synchronize data with third party services on a desktop operating system, and concerns around data security are lessened. A lot of software vendors now provide their software through the Mac App Store. And until all of the Mobile Device Management (MDM) vendors support device-based Volume Purchasing Program (VPP) access, this will be pointed out as a flaw to that program. iOS 9 and OS X 10.11 bring device-based VPP, but at the time of the writing of this book, that feature has yet to be implemented by the main VPP vendors.

So what can you do? MDM solutions do not report what Apple ID is being used to access software. However, you can use the defaults command to obtain information about Apple IDs in use on an OS X computer. You would do so by using defaults to read the global defaults domain. In the following example, we use the grep command to constrain our output to Apple IDs:

```
defaults read | grep AppleID
```

What an Apple ID Provides Access To

Today, most devices are going to need an Apple ID. The Apple ID becomes the gateway to most of the services described throughout the remainder of this chapter. The following is a list of Apple services that need an Apple ID:

- App Store: Buy Apps on the iOS and Mac App Stores and have them automatically download to your devices.

- Apple Developer programs: Access beta copies of software and developer tools.

- Apple Music: Apple's music service that uses a monthly fee rather than purchasing each song individually.

- Apple Music Radio: Stream radio to your devices over the Apple Music Radio service.

- Apple Online Store: Purchase hardware and software through the Apple.com.

- Apple Retail services: Access to Concierge, Joint Venture, and programs, including the Apple Store app.

- Apple Support Communities: Access the Apple support site, ask questions, and answer any support requests you know the answer to.

- Apple TV: Access Content purchased on Apple from an Apple TV and control the TV with the Remote app on an iOS device.

- Back to My Mac: Provides remote access to a computer, even when that computer is using NAT behind a different firewall.

- Device Enrollment Program (DEP): Automatically associate devices owned by an organization with a Mobile Device Management (MDM) solution.

- FaceTime: Video conferencing with friends and family.

- FileVault Key Escrow: Option to keep the FileVault recovery key stored on a server.

- Find My Friends: Shows the physical location of friends you have added using the Find My Friends app, using GPS

- Find My Mac: Shows the physical location of your Apple devices using the iCloud web interface

- Game Center: Access scores in apps that support Game Center integration for friends using the Game Center app.

- iBooks Store: Access books and other multi-media content on the Apple iBooks Store.

- iChat: Legacy chat system from 10.8 and below.

- iCloud Calendars: Sets up the client for the Calendar app to work with an iCloud account.

- iCloud Contacts – sets up the client for the Contacts app to work with an iCloud account.

- iCoud Drive: allows certain apps to write data into storage on iCloud servers.

- iCloud Keychain: Synchronizes passwords and certificates between computers.

- iCloud Mail: Configures the Mail app to work with an iCloud account.

- iCloud Photos: Displays the photo stream and integrates iCloud Photo Library with your Mac and allows for iCloud Photo Sharing.

- iCloud Notes: Synchronizes notes created in the Notes app with an iCloud account.

- iMessage: Instant message with other iMessage users rather than using text messages.

- iTunes Genius: Tracks purchases on iTunes and allows you to find similar content to music in your library and purchase history.

- iTunes Home Sharing: Share data within apps such as iTunes and Photos from within a given Local Area Network (LAN).

- iTunes Match: Access music that was ripped from CDs and other media.

- iTunes Store: Purchase music that can be downloaded and listened to offline.

- iTunes U: Access podcasts posted by education institutions.

- Handoff – Shows the same content on an iPhone or iOS devices as on an OS X device if apps are built with Handoff support.

- My Apple ID (`appleid.apple.com`): Access information about an Apple ID and reset passwords and addresses for the Apple ID.

- Volume Purchase Program: Purchase applications in bulk and deploy those applications using codes, Apple IDs, or devices.

Securing the Apple ID

Given the number of services that an Apple ID provide access to, you will find that you need to secure an Apple ID. The first and most important part of securing the Apple ID is to use a strong password. Because Apple requires their customers maintain a good level of security, they have implemented password policies to keep users secure. These policies mean that Apple ID passwords must follow these rules:

- Have at least one capital letter
- Have at least one number
- Have at least 8 characters
- Not be used in the past year
- Not be the same as the user name
- Not have any consecutive, repeating characters (e.g. aa or bb)
- Not be a common password (e.g. ABCD1234)

While Apple doesn't require it, we strongly recommend using special characters (e.g. !, *, or $ are pretty common) and that there be nothing that can identify you in the password, such as your child's name, dog's birthday, or the day you were married.

Apple also provides users the ability to reset access to an account. Here, you are given three security questions. When selecting these, don't use easily identifiable information. For example, I was using my high school mascot for one, and then I realized my high school was listed on my Wikipedia page and therefore easily ascertained.

You can instead (and this is definitely recommended) add two-factor verification to your iCloud account. Doing so enhances security by requiring you to use a code sent to one of your Apple devices on another Apple device when you go to access certain features on that device, including resetting passwords and changing information on an account. If you haven't done so already, you can enable two-factor authentication at https://appleid.apple.com/.

Changing passwords can be a terrible bore. You may find that when you have a lot of devices that require a new password to be entered or that you end up needing to remember this new password at annoying times. However, there's no accounting for brute force, which is attempting iterations of a password until an attacker guesses the correct password. Therefore, set a routine reminder to change your password. This can be every 30 days or 90 days, but it should be reset routinely.

There are other things to be careful of. For example, anyone with an iCloud account is likely to get at least an occasional phishing scam email. If you get an email that seems like it came from Apple and opens a domain other than apple.com, don't click on anything. These are likely simply directing you to portals that exist for the sole purpose of stealing the credentials to your Apple ID. Don't send your account information to anyone. Don't use an Apple ID on a public computer without clearing the remnants of the ID off the system when you stop using that device. Don't sell or give a device away without first removing your Apple ID from the computer. And don't distribute passwords to IDs over email.

The Apple ID can provide a lot of access to your computer. In addition to securing the Apple ID itself, you should also secure the account on devices that you own, and in some cases, do so on a service-by-service basis.

Suppress the iCloud Options at Startup

The first time a new user logs into a Mac, they should be prompted to provide credentials for an iCloud account. If your organization chooses not to use iCloud, you can disable this option by running the following command:

```
sudo defaults write /System/Library/User Template/Non_localized/Library/Preferences/com.
apple.SetupAssistant DidSeeCloudSetup -bool TRUE
```

Once run, new accounts will no longer prompt users to provide iCloud credentials (and possibly use an iCloud account for their login to the computer). You can undo the option by running the following command:

```
sudo defaults write /System/Library/User Template/Non_localized/Library/Preferences/com.
apple.SetupAssistant DidSeeCloudSetup -bool TRUE
```

Once this option is enabled, users will still be able to access iCloud; however, users will not be prompted to do so at their first login. You can also disable iCloud, which we'll cover in the next section.

Disable Access to iCloud

I hate disabling iCloud. We can debate the validity of killing iCloud access in any environment. However, it's an organization's option to allow or disallow iCloud and so our goal in this chapter is simply to provide the options to limit, restrict, or provide access securely, and to provide a solid understanding of the security ramifications of doing so.

The easiest way to disable iCloud access is going to be through a Mobile Device Management (MDM) solution, such as Profile Manager and the Casper Suite. To disable iCloud Drive and possibly leveraging iCloud for account passwords, open Profile Manager and create a new profile (or edit an existing profile). From there, select the OS X Restrictions payload. Click on the Functionality tab to see options for iCloud. As you can see in Figure 14-1, there, you'll be provided with two options: "Allow iCloud documents & data" and "Allow use of iCloud password for local accounts." These disable all access to iCloud Drive and disable using your iCloud password on your local computer respectively.

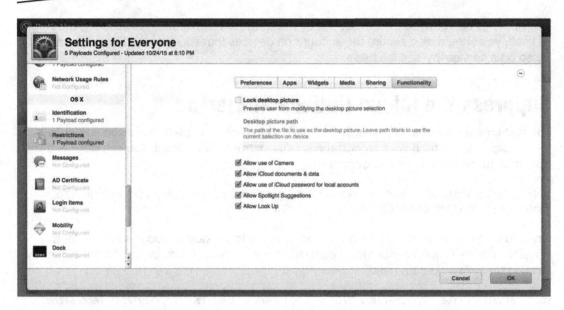

Figure 14-1. Authenticate to iCloud

Once you've configured the appropriate options, you can click on OK and save the profile. You can also use custom profiles to configure the options that we used the defaults commands to set, shown previously in this chapter.

Secure iCloud On Macs

To setup iCloud on a Mac, open System Preferences and click on the iCloud System Preference pane. From here, you will be prompted for a username and password for your iCloud account, as shown in Figure 14-2. Once entered, click on Sign In.

Figure 14-2. Authenticate to iCloud

Once the account is authenticated, you'll be prompted on which features to allow access to. The main thing this screen is for is to give you the option to opt out of Find My Mac. Let's leave these both checked, as in Figure 14-3 for now, and we'll look at all the options later in this chapter. Click Next.

Figure 14-3. Enable iCloud Services

Once an account has been configured, you can see many of the iCloud services available on a Mac in the iCloud System Preference pane, shown in Figure 14-4. This is where an iCloud account is configured on each computer and once configured, where the settings for each service that iCloud provides are enabled. If you won't be using a service, disable it. Most services are enabled by default, when you initially provide your iCloud credentials to access a system. But any service that's enabled and not being used can provide access to resources that maybe shouldn't be provided to.

Figure 14-4. The iCloud System Preference pane

In some cases, allowing access to a given service actually provides you with a more secure environment. For example, if you sync your Notes with a computer not otherwise backed up and the computer gets erased, you will still have access to your notes despite loosing access to the data on that one computer, as the notes are synchronized to iCloud. This is all, of course, provided that you secure access to the Apple ID that can access these notes.

In addition to checking and unchecking each service to configure that service on the computer, you will have an Options button for some services. These services can be granularly configured.

iCloud Drive

The first of these services that we'll look at is iCloud Drive. You can store your files on iCloud Drive and they will synchronize with Apple's cloud. This makes iCloud Drive similar to services such as Box, Dropbox and Google Drive. Click on the Options button for iCloud Drive and you will see each application installed on the computer that can leverage iCloud Drive for file storage. As you can see in Figure 14-5, these are currently mostly Apple-based applications, such as Photos and QuickTime. Uncheck each that you do not want to be able to use files on iCloud Drive or save files to iCloud Drive. Click Done when you've appropriately configured access.

Documents
Look Me Up By Email
Apps that store documents and data in iCloud will appear here.
Automator
Preview
QuickTime Player
Script Editor
TextEdit
Photos Agent
Apple Configurator 2
Done

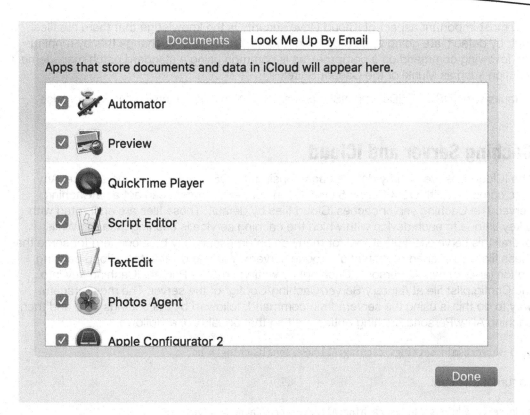

Figure 14-5. *iCloud Disk Options*

Once you have configured iCloud Drive, you'll see it listed (by default) in the sidebar of any Finder window, under the Favorites section (Figure 14-6). Once iCloud Drive has synchronized your files, you'll see the layout of your iCloud drive in that folder and be able to access the files directly, opening them in any application you so choose.

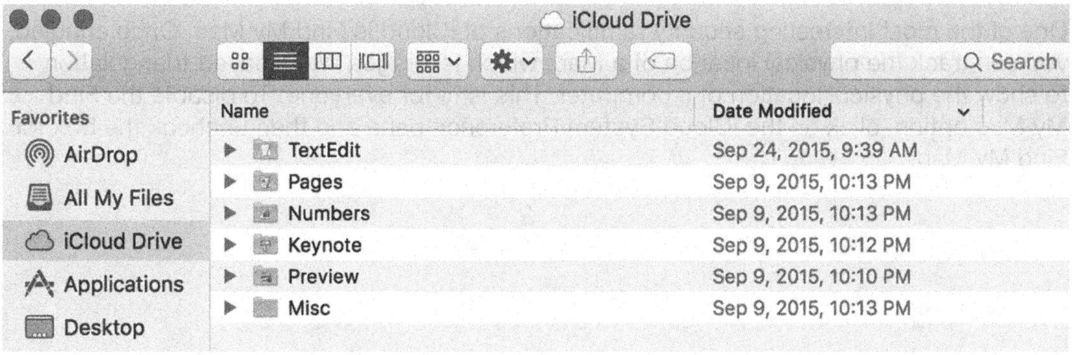

iCloud Drive
Search
Favorites
AirDrop
All My Files
iCloud Drive
Applications
Desktop
Name
Date Modified
TextEdit
Sep 24, 2015, 9:39 AM
Pages
Sep 9, 2015, 10:13 PM
Numbers
Sep 9, 2015, 10:13 PM
Keynote
Sep 9, 2015, 10:12 PM
Preview
Sep 9, 2015, 10:10 PM
Misc
Sep 9, 2015, 10:13 PM

Figure 14-6. *iCloud Drive Folders*

The most important aspect of iCloud Drive security is the knowledge that there are files that, by default, are going to be stored on iCloud. You can easily change this by running the following command on a computer, as is common using a standard patch management solution such as Munki or the Casper Suite:

defaults write NSGlobalDomain NSDocumentSaveNewDocumentsToCloud -bool false

Caching Server and iCloud

The iCloud files are also by default cached using the OS X Server caching service. Any Mac computer with OS X Server 5 installed in your environment can act as a Caching server. The Caching server caches iCloud files by default. These files are encrypted with a key unique to each device with which the caching service is caching data for. While overall this service is a great tool for many an enterprise, it may be a concern for some that these files are cached on potentially rogue servers. You can disable the iCloud caching option (also known as Personal Caching) by writing an AllowPersonalCaching key into the Config.plist file at /Library/Server/Caching/Config/ of the server. The most graceful way to do this is using the serveradmin command, followed by the settings verb and then caching:AllowPersonalCaching option, setting that equals no, as follows:

```
sudo serveradmin settings caching:AllowPersonalCaching = no
```

To turn it back on:

```
sudo serveradmin settings caching:AllowPersonalCaching = yes
```

This can also be done by dropping a Config.plist file into the correct location for new server installations. You can also leverage this file to keep track of what computers that you have enrolled in a patch management system are running this service. If you see the file, the service has been enabled.

Find My Mac

One of the most interesting security ramifications of iCloud is Find My Mac. Once enabled, you can track the physical location of a Mac, which leverages Wi-Fi-based triangulation to show the physical location of a computer. This isn't for everyone. To disable the Find My Mac option, click on the iCloud System Preference pane and then uncheck the box for Find My Mac.

Figure 14-7. Disable Find My Mac

Once the setting saves, you should no longer see the Mac on a map when you log into the iCloud web portal.

Back to My Mac

Back to My Mac allows you to log into your Mac from another computer that has your iCloud account installed. When you use two computers that run Back to My Mac, you will see computers that can be controlled using Back to My Mac by clicking on them in the sidebar of a Finder window. This feature works using NAT-PMP, as you can see in Figure 14-8.

Figure 14-8. Back to My Mac

Provided your iCloud account is secure, this feature is secure; however, if you wish to mitigate the risk associated with someone else gaining access to your iCloud account, uncheck the box for Back to My Mac.

The Mac App Store

The Mac App Store represented a completely new idea in software distribution. All software on the Mac App Store can be accessed through an Apple ID. Some of this software you pay for, some you don't. From a security perspective, it's worth nothing that Apple reviews all software before the apps get posted to the App Store. As you can see in Figure 14-9, even operating systems are distributed through the App Store.

Figure 14-9. The Mac App Store

When possible, use software from the Mac App Store. Any software posted on the Mac App Store is vetted by Apple prior to becoming available on the store. Additionally, software from the iOS App Store that is managed with MDM can have features limited by the MDM to secure content. While these types of options are not currently available for the Mac, it is only a matter of time before they are.

Summary

Apple provides a number of services with an iCloud account. Some of these can introduce risks into an environment. Others can help further secure an environment. I personally use most of the options that we looked at disabling in this chapter. But I don't have official security requirements for my personal systems that many organizations have with their large fleets of computers. Each organization should review each option available and then determine which should be allowed and which should not. Then only disable the features that you don't want to use.

Summary

Chapter 15

Remote Connectivity

As a security expert, consider this all-too-real scenario: a passenger sits in the airport, working on his computer, waiting for the plane to start boarding. While sitting there, surfing on the wireless airport network, he notices that almost every laptop in sight is a Mac. On a hunch, he opens Bonjour Browser to discover that many of these laptops have various remote management tools (the Apple Remote Desktop client or Screen Sharing, based on VNC), SSH or Telnet enabled. He also notices that many of these computers are not password-protected, and are therefore easily controllable by anyone with the gall to tap into the computer. Within 10 minutes, nearly all the laptop lids are closed with their owners suspiciously looking around, attempting to determine which passenger was entertaining them with the "joke of the day" on their display.

On a serious note, this is possibly the best-case scenario for these unsuspecting Mac owners in the airport. With Screen Sharing, Apple Remote Desktop (ARD), SSH, and many of the other remote access options improperly secured on these machines, it would be possible to cause much more damage than simply sending a humorous message to their desktops. Deleting files, capturing passwords, reconfiguring operating system preferences, and issuing damaging commands from a shell are all possible. It would also be very easy to simply submit a program that would run in the background and provide access to anyone attempting to control it, using what is called a *root kit*. (Root kits are explained in further detail in Chapter 8.)

More often than not, communication over public networks is not properly secured. When sitting in an airport, coffee shop, hotel, or any other publicly available network, it is important not only to password-protect the means of communicating, but also to encrypt the traffic you are sending over the network. Sending information in an unprotected manner across a public network can be painfully embarrassing, not to mention expensive. This chapter will focus on securely configuring and using the most common remote management applications (both built-in and third party) in the Mac community.

Remote Management Applications

Apple has created a number of remote management programs that are included with Mac OS X. In this section we will cover the two that are available graphically: Apple Remote Desktop and Screen Sharing. We will also cover Back to My Mac, which uses Screen Sharing to establish connectivity between two systems via the MobileMe service.

Apple Remote Desktop

Apple Remote Desktop (ARD) allows administrators to remotely control and administer OS X systems, either from within your company's network or from outside of it. ARD can be used to send shell commands to workstations, transfer files to client systems, and install software remotely on computers. ARD also allows for very extensive reporting of user history, application usage, and software versions.

Screen Sharing

Mac OS X 10.5 introduced a feature called *Screen Sharing*. Screen Sharing allows you to control a remote system and send and receive clipboard contents, simply by clicking on an icon in the sidebar of a Finder window. Screen Sharing is also built into Messages, allowing for very easy remote management from an Instant Messaging session. Screen Sharing provides only very limited capability compared to ARD, but it can be very useful for remote support or emergency server management.

> **Note**   Although opening the Screen Sharing application is most easily done from the sidebar of a Finder window, you can also open the application from the /System/Library/CoreServices/ Applications folder. This means that you do not have to see a client, but can connect over an IP address; this is handy for connecting to remote locations where the computers will not appear in your sidebar for OS X.

Both Screen Sharing and Remote Desktop use the Virtual Network Computing (VNC) protocol to observe and control remote systems. The VNC system (and Screen Sharing) by itself does not provide for the same level of control as ARD. For example, you cannot send Unix commands over VNC or set up tiered access to VNC. ARD is easy to set up, and its customizable security features make the operating environment much more secure than VNC alone. Apple has expanded beyond the capabilities of VNC in its development of ARD, and has added a lot of new features while maintaining backward compatibility with clients such as Chicken of the VNC, UltraVNC, and RealVNC. If you do not have the ARD client installed, then you can still use VNC to access another computer remotely using Screen Sharing, but although this is equally as secure (it uses Kerberos to protect passwords by default), Screen Sharing has less configurable options than the Remote Desktop component of Apple Remote Desktop.

Because VNC is a multiplatform remote connectivity protocol that allows you to remotely view and control Mac, Windows, or Linux systems, the Mac can be managed by any platform and likewise manage any platform, provided the client has a VNC server running. Other operating systems can connect using a standard VNC client, allowing you to quickly tap into another computer, no matter what kind of machine you're connecting from. This is obviously a dangerous aspect of VNC, as an attacker can compromise your system by remotely accessing it if the VNC client is not secured properly. If you do not want to allow other systems to connect to yours, then we recommend disabling this feature entirely (it is not enabled by default). If you would, however, like to allow other systems to be able to connect to yours, there is a way to set this up securely. Let's walk through setting up screen sharing in a secure manner.

Enabling Screen Sharing

To enable Screen Sharing, open the Sharing preference pane. Then click either the Screen Sharing or Remote Management check box (see Figure 15-1). Checking Screen Sharing will allow for only remote control and observation. We'll discuss remote management shortly. Once you have started the Screen Sharing service you will be able to click on the "Allow access for" section, and set it to "Only these users."

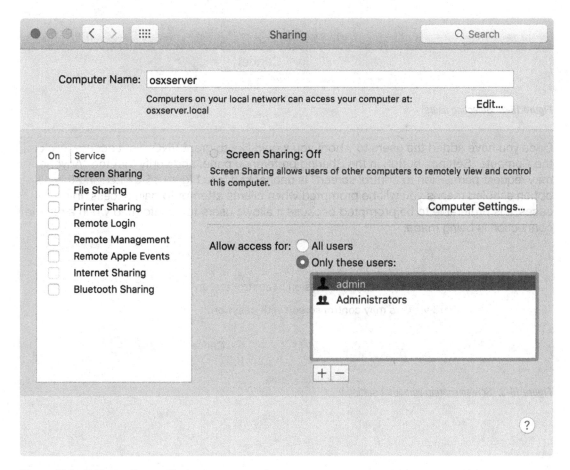

Figure 15-1. Setting up Screen Sharing

One of the most critical aspects of securing Screen Sharing is limiting which users are allowed to connect to your system remotely. The "Allow access for" section is where you would configure which users (from the Accounts pane in System Preferences) have access to share any of these services by clicking the plus (+) button. Select the user from the list in the dialog box (see Figure 15-2) that you would like to grant access to this preference, and then click the Select button.

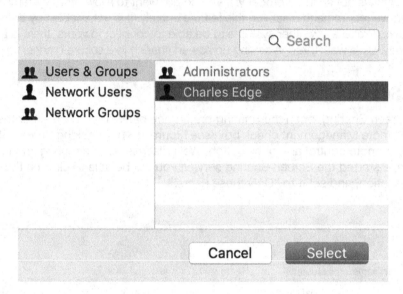

Figure 15-2. Selecting users

Once you have added the users to whom you would like to grant VNC client access, click the Computer Settings button in the Sharing preference pane, and verify that the "Anyone may request permission to control screen" is unchecked (see Figure 15-3). Leaving this option enabled means you will be prompted when clients attempt to gain access. In many cases, it is preferable to be prompted because it allows users to be informed when a remote connection is being made.

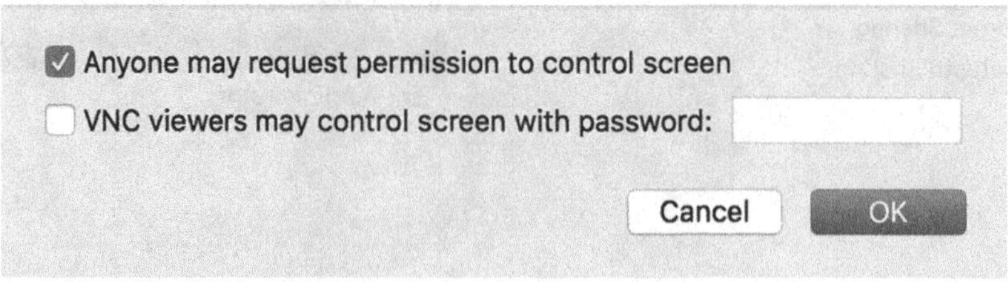

☑ Anyone may request permission to control screen
☐ VNC viewers may control screen with password: [   ]

Cancel   OK

Figure 15-3. Screen sharing computer settings

If you know that users without ARD (such as Windows workstations or those using Chicken of the VNC) will need to control the machine with a different VNC client, click the "VNC viewers may control screen with password" box. Otherwise, leave it unchecked, because allowing any VNC access increases the susceptibility of a system.

To control your computer, VNC clients on the local network can connect to it via IP address or Bonjour. As a Bonjour-enabled service, Screen Sharing is also available via Wide-Area Bonjour, courtesy of .Mac.

Implementing Back to My Mac

If you have a current iCloud account, the Back to My Mac feature of iCloud allows you to connect to any computer that has your .Mac username and password entered in the iCloud pane of System Preferences. This eliminates the need to forward ports on your router, because it accesses the remote system using the iCloud system preference. The OS X built-in Screen Sharing feature is used to allow both Back to My Mac and VNC to connect to your computer. You can stop or start Back to My Mac using the Back to My Mac option in the iCloud preference pane (see Figure 15-4).

Figure 15-4. Back to My Mac in the iCloud preference pane

Configuring Remote Management

Screen Sharing is great for home use, but ARD is far superior for larger environments with more requirements. If you only need remote control, then Screen Sharing will typically suffice. If you have large numbers of systems to manage, or you need the ability to remotely install software or send Unix commands, then Remote Management is likely going to be of more use to you. In the Sharing preference pane, the management features are referred to as Remote Management, and can be controlled granularly on a per-task basis. The Remote Desktop application, used to control Macs using ARD, is licensed separately. If you enable Remote Management, Screen Sharing will automatically be disabled. Remote Management includes the VNC access managed by Screen Sharing.

Enabling Remote Management

To enable Remote Management, click the Remote Management service in the Sharing preference pane (see Figure 15-5). From here, you should set the "Allow access for" option to "Only these users" and add the users who will have access privileges as you did for Screen Sharing in the previous section.

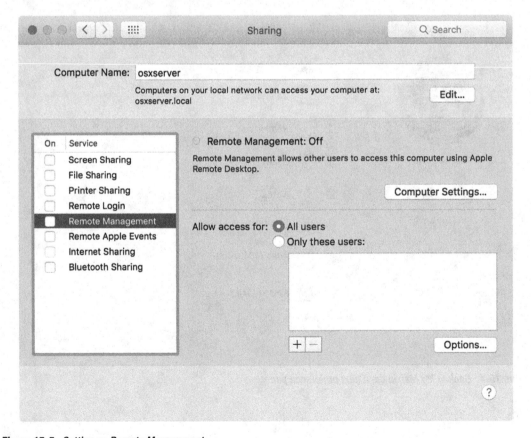

Figure 15-5. Setting up Remote Management

In the Sharing preference pane, you can also select what level of access other users have to your system. The Remote Management panel also lets you select what level of access a user should be given by clicking the Options button. Check the boxes (see Figure 15-6) for the appropriate level of access you want to grant. Remember that for every user, only the minimum required level of access should be given. For example, if you want the ARD to be used to build reports on a machine only, then you would click the Generate reports box and nothing else.

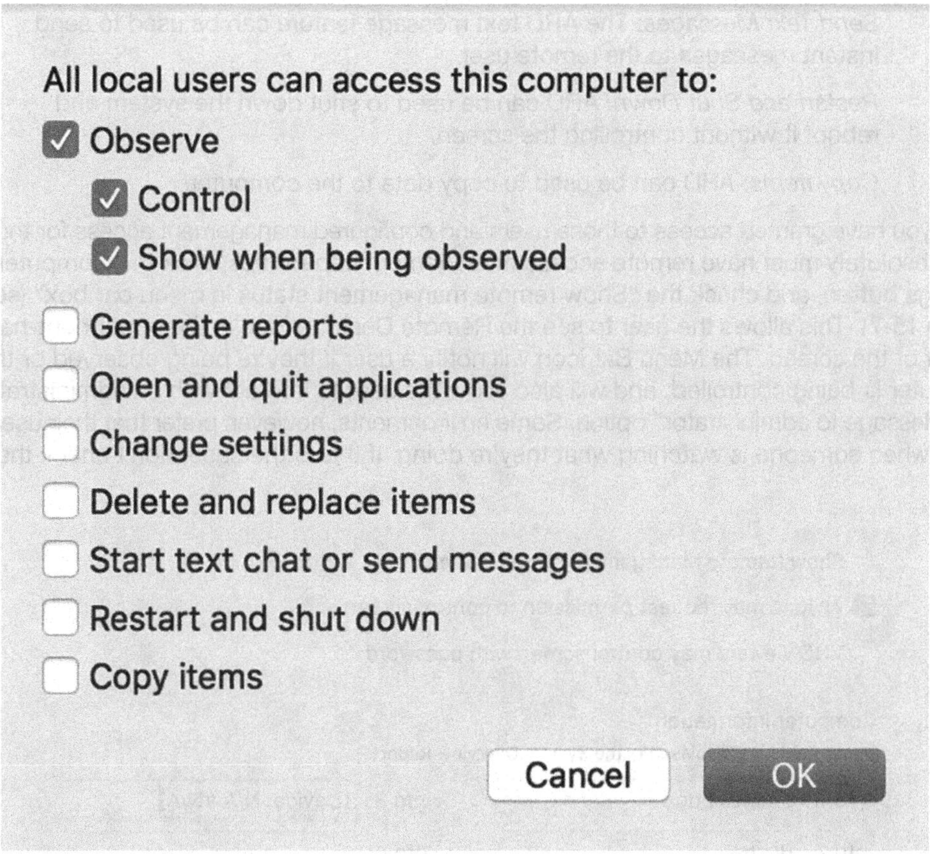

All local users can access this computer to:

- ☑ Observe
  - ☑ Control
  - ☑ Show when being observed
- ☐ Generate reports
- ☐ Open and quit applications
- ☐ Change settings
- ☐ Delete and replace items
- ☐ Start text chat or send messages
- ☐ Restart and shut down
- ☐ Copy items

Cancel   OK

Figure 15-6. Remote Management options

Here are descriptions of the settings that can be enabled:

Observe: Remote users can see the activity on their computer, but cannot take control of a session.

Control: Remote users can see the activity on their computer and can take control of the mouse and keyboard. Keep in mind that, if they can take control of an administrative user, they have the capability to elevate their own privileges.

Show When Being Observed: Users being observed will see an icon in the toolbar indicating that their computer is being controlled.

Generate Reports: Remote users can view software, hardware, and other information about your system.

Open and Quit Applications: ARD can be used to open and quit applications without using the remote control function.

Change Settings: Application and System Preferences Settings can be changed without using menu options from within the Remote Desktop application.

Send Text Messages: The ARD text message feature can be used to send instant messages to the remote user.

Restart and Shut Down: ARD can be used to shut down the system and reboot it without controlling the screen.

Copy items: ARD can be used to copy data to the computer.

Once you have granted access to those users and configured management access for those who absolutely must have remote access management capabilities, click the Computer Settings button, and check the "Show remote management status in menu bar box" (see Figure 15-7). This allows the user to see the Remote Desktop icon in the upper right-hand corner of the screen. The Menu Bar icon will notify a user if they're being observed or their computer is being controlled, and will also allow the user to interact with an administrator via the "Message to administrator" option. Some environments, however, prefer that their users not know when someone is watching what they're doing. If this is the case, don't check the box.

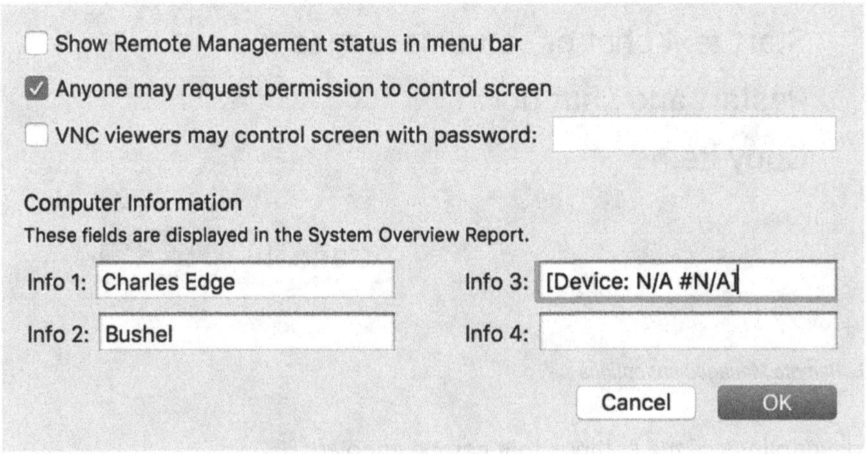

Show Remote Management status in menu bar

☑ Anyone may request permission to control screen

VNC viewers may control screen with password:

Computer Information
These fields are displayed in the System Overview Report.

Info 1: Charles Edge   Info 3: [Device: N/A #N/A]

Info 2: Bushel   Info 4:

Cancel   OK

Figure 15-7. Remote Management computer settings

Note   You can also enable VNC clients to access the system in this screen, but keep in mind that VNC viewers will have a lower encryption protocol than ARD users. Once you are satisfied with your settings, click the OK button to return to the Sharing preference pane.

Using Secure Shell

Telnet was once the primary method for remotely connecting to client systems with command line over remote shells. However, Telnet connections are unencrypted, and therefore insecure forms of transmitting information. As use of the Internet became more widespread, the security implications of having login credentials and user data transmitted in cleartext became unacceptable, and SSH was created. SSH is a better version of this technology, giving an administrator a remote shell (or Terminal access) to send commands to a user computer over a secure connection. These commands can be used to transfer files, connect to other systems, and run any Terminal commands. SSH should be used in those environments where opening a variety of ports to allow remote ARD connectivity is undesirable and where GUI level access is not needed to remotely manage the computer.

Enabling SSH

To enable incoming SSH access to your system, click the Sharing preference pane, and click Remote Login service (see Figure 15-8). From here, click "Only these users," and click the plus (+) button to add users who will be allowed to remotely access the computer using SSH. Checking the box turns the Remote Login indicator light green. You can now use SSH to access the system remotely.

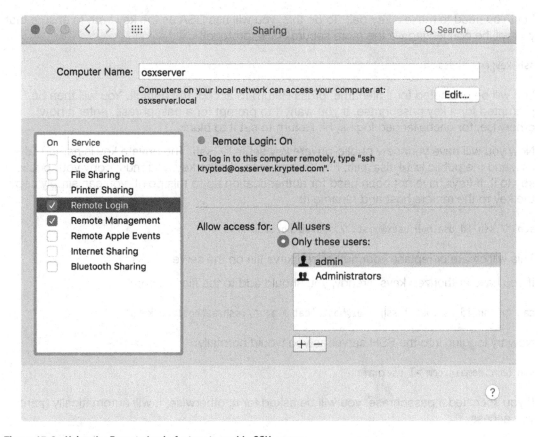

Figure 15-8. Using the Remote Login feature to enable SSH access

Further Securing SSH

SSH is a secure protocol, but you can make SSH even more secure with the command line by using public/private key pairs, which make it unnecessary for your password to go over the wire at all. Your private keys should be secured with a passphrase, to keep your private key safe if your system is compromised. You can store your passphrase in your keychain, but this can prove to be just as dangerous as having no passphrase at all if your system is compromised. Therefore make sure that a passphrase is set and required for every access of your keys.

Connecting to an SSH host will request authentication from the client. If you have a key set, your SSH client will generate a temporary key based on your private key. It will then send this key to the server, and the server will compare it to the public keys that it has. If your public key can unlock the temporary key, you are authenticated and allowed access. If the keys fail, then SSH drops back to password-based authentication and will prompt for a password.

Let's see how this works:

> **Note**   For the purposes of this example, we assume you haven't generated an SSH key yet.

First you need to make a key pair. To do this, you will use DSA as the key type to ensure that you will be connecting via the more secure SSH2 protocol:

```
ssh-keygen -t dsa
```

You will be prompted for a filename; press Return to accept the default. You will then be prompted for a key passphrase. If you want it to prompt for a passphrase, enter it now; otherwise, for unchallenged logins, hit Return to set it to blank.

Now you will have your new public-private key set in ~/.ssh. The private key is named id_dsa, and the public is id_dsa.pub. For the server to use the key, you must copy your public key to it. If keys have not been used for authentication up to this point, you can simply copy the key to the remote host and rename it:

```
scp ~/.ssh/id_dsa.pub user@host:~/.ssh/authorized_keys
```

This will create or replace your authorized keys file on the server.

If you have authorized keys already, you should add to the file like so:

```
cat ~/.ssh/id_dsa.pub | ssh user@host 'cat - >> ~/.ssh/authorized_keys'
```

Now try logging into the SSH server as you would normally:

```
ssh host.domain.com -l username
```

If you specified a passphrase, you will be asked for it; otherwise, it will automatically grant you access.

> **Tip** If you are using single sign-on with a Mac OS X Server, then authentication will be handled by Kerberos instead and won't need to implement key-based login.

When using keypairs without passphrases, it is imperative that the private key not fall into the wrong hands. If a compromised passphrase is suspected, the key should be removed from the authorized_keys file of any computer on which it has been installed, and a new keypair should be generated immediately.

Using a VPN

A virtual private network (VPN) is a private communications tunnel, established within a public network, between two points, one inside a home or corporate network and one outside of it. Safe communication through this tunnel is possible through encrypted network traffic.

Connecting to Your Office VPN

Many organizations have VPN's in place for uses to remotely connect to the office. When you use the VPN to connect to your office, then you are using a public network (in other words, the Internet) to establish a private network (a VPN tunnel). Once you have a private network, then you will more than likely be able to access many of the resources just as you would if you were in the office, albeit a little slower because you are not actually working from the LAN. Let's run through a basic VPN client setup to connect to your office's LAN.

If you are going to set up a VPN client, then you first need to obtain configuration settings from your network administrator. First, you need to know what VPN protocol your network is using. The two main types of VPNs are PPTP and L2TP over IPSec. Once you know the type of VPN you are connecting to, then you will need to know the address of the VPN server. This is often an IP address or a DNS name.

To start, open the Network preference pane, and click the plus sign to open the Select the Interface screen. At the Select the Interface screen, choose VPN as the interface, and then choose appropriate VPN type (PPTP or L2TP) for your environment. Once you have entered this information, click the Create button (see Figure 15-9).

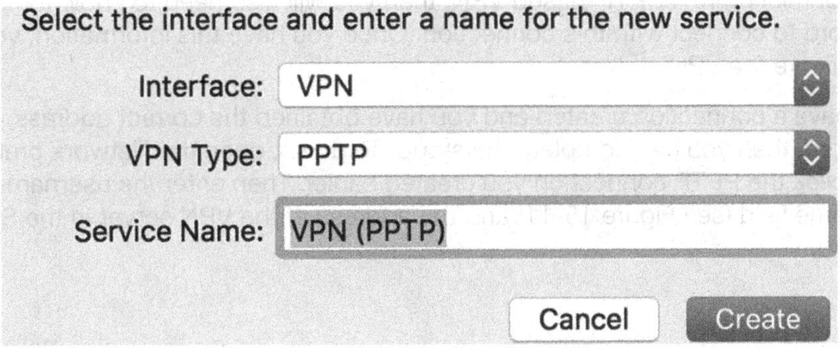

Select the interface and enter a name for the new service.

Interface: VPN

VPN Type: PPTP

Service Name: VPN (PPTP)

Cancel   Create

Figure 15-9. Adding a VPN connection

Setting Up L2TP

If you are given a choice of PPTP or L2TP, then you should use L2TP, because it is more secure. If you will be connecting to an L2TP-based VPN, then you will have a few more configurable options available to you, and you'll need to know more information about the technical nature of network you are connecting to. In addition to some form of user authentication, L2TP also requires machine-based authentication, such as a *shared secret*, a term that can be used to refer to a password. The authentication can also be an SSL certificate (see Figure 15-10), which can be imported or manually added using the Keychain Utility.

Figure 15-10. *L2TP user and machine authentication types*

Setting Up PPTP

If you are connecting to a PPTP-based VPN, then you will also need to know the username and password to connect with this connection. Once you have this information, you will be able to configure the VPN.

Once you have a connection created and you have obtained the correct address, account, and password, then you can complete the setup. To do so, open the Network preference pane, and click the PPTP connection you created earlier. Then enter the username in the Account Name field (see Figure 15-11) and the address of the VPN server in the Server Address field.

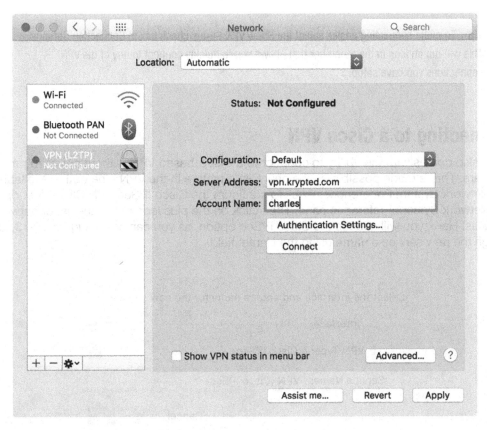

Figure 15-11. Configuring a VPN connection in System Preferences

If you have an authentication method other than the simple password authentication required to establish a connection, click the Advanced button. At the User Authentication screen (see Figure 15-12), select your authentication type and click OK. Once you are finished configuring all the required settings, click Apply in the Network preference pane, and test your connection by clicking the Connect button.

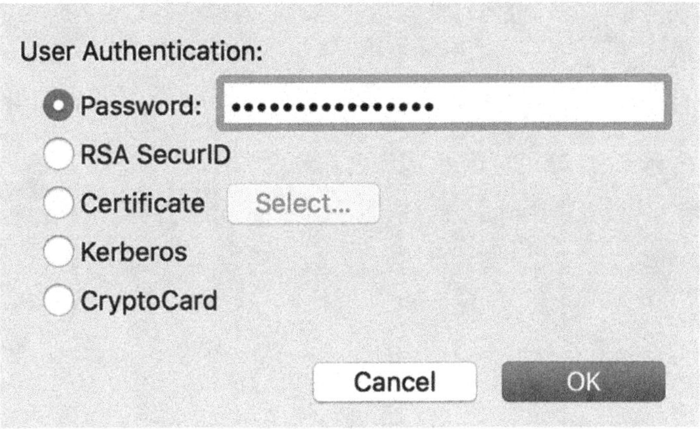

Figure 15-12. PPTP user authentication types

> **Tip**   To make connecting easier, select the Show VPN Status check box in Connection Settings.
> This will put an icon in the menu bar that allows you to quickly connect to any of the VPN
> connections you have setup.

Connecting to a Cisco VPN

OS X also comes with the ability to connect to a Cisco-based VPN without any third party
software. This is made possible by the new Cisco feature in the VPN type option available in
the Network System Preferences pane. To configure the Cisco IPSec VPN Client, first open
the Network System Preference pane. Then click on the plus icon below the list of network
services. Here, you will choose the Cisco IPSec option, as you can see in Figure 15-13, and
assign the new service a name using the Name: field.

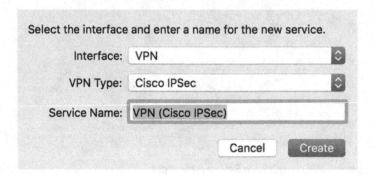

Figure 15-13. Setting up the Cisco VPN client

You will then see a screen with the settings to connect to the IPSec VPN client, as you
shown in Figure 15-14. Here, provide the name or IP address of the server that you will be
connecting to in the Server Address field. You will also need to provide a username and
password to connect to the VPN.

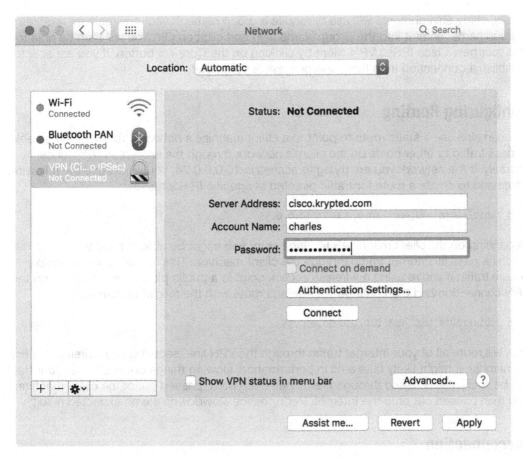

Figure 15-14. Configuring the Cisco VPN client settings

If you need to provide a shared secret then click on the Authentication Settings button and provide it in the Shared Secret field. Or, if your environment uses an SSL certificate, click on the radio button for Certificate and then click on the Select button. You can then select the certificate. See Figure 15-15.

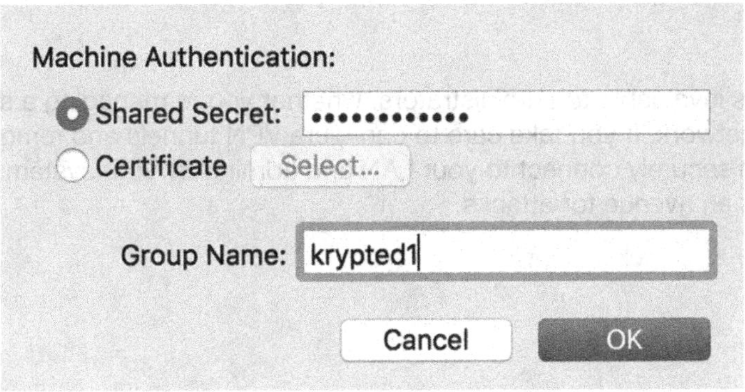

Machine Authentication:

⦿ Shared Secret: ●●●●●●●●●●●

◯ Certificate   Select...

Group Name: krypted1

Cancel   OK

Figure 15-15. Configuring the Cisco VPN Authentication Settings

Finally, many environments will use or require a group name. If your environment requires a group name, enter it into the Group Name field and click on OK. You will then be able to test your new Cisco IPSec VPN client by clicking on the Connect button. If you are able to establish a connection then the setup process is complete!

Configuring Routing

You can also use a static route to point to a client machine's network. You will then be able to pass traffic to other hosts on the client's network through the encrypted PPP tunnel securely. If the network you are trying to access is 10.0.0.0/24, you would use the following command to create a route for traffic directed at specific IP addresses:

```
sudo /sbin/route add -net 10.0.0.0/24 10.0.0.55
```

Depending on the client machine's routing setup, you might be able to have the server machine pass all Internet traffic through the client machine. This is a good way to help secure traffic if you're using a wireless access point in a public place. You can bring up the VPN connection and then change your default route with the following command:

```
sudo /sbin/route add -net 0.0.0.0 10.0.0.55
```

This will route all of your Internet traffic through the VPN link, securing your wireless traffic. Remember, it might likely take a hit in performance, slowing things down a bit, as your traffic will be encrypted, passed through the tunnel, decrypted, passed out of the client machine, and then passed out onto the Internet. Performance slowdowns are an expected result.

Disconnecting

The process to disconnect is fairly simple. On the server, use ps ax | grep pppd to search for the PPP daemon's process ID. Then use the sudo kill <Process ID>command to stop the daemon. The server machine's PPP daemon will bring down the link. This allows the client machine's PPP daemon to quit. Upon quitting, the client machine will log the VPN user out of the connection. At this point, the PPP connection will have stopped, both daemons will have quit, and your SSH connection should be disconnected.

Summary

Remote access is invaluable to administrators, whether you're managing a small office or a large corporate network. If you take care to configure VPN tunnels and remote management properly, you can securely connect to your LAN and administer your systems without making those same tools an avenue for attacks.

## Chapter 16

Server Security

OS X Server is an app that runs on a standard Mac. This app is available on the App store and very straight forward to setup. The Server app contains a faux root of the former OS X Server operating system within the app bundle, which contains a number of binaries that should be secured for those that use an OS X Server. It may look similar, but the Server app brings some very different functionality to an OS X Client,. The differences lie in the fact that Mac OS X Server, like most other servers, should be used exclusively to share data. That data is shared across a variety of protocols, according to the type of data being shared. Therefore, it naturally follows that you will need to take additional precautions to properly secure OS X Server on a per-service basis. In this chapter, we'll primarily focus on the services that are specific to the Server app and how to secure them, paying attention to where the best practices differ from a standard Mac client.

A number of services are included with OS X Server. We will focus on security as it pertains to the most heavily used services: directory services, file sharing, web server services, Internet sharing, user account management, Internet security, and the Messages Server. We'll start with common security themes that persist across each service. Because many of the other services are dependent on directory services, we'll then move on to securing Open Directory, an innovation in OS X Server that distinguishes it from OS X Client. Finally, we'll take a look at each service and the special security precautions that should be taken with each.

Limiting Access to Services

A key aspect of OS X Server is its ability to determine which users can access specific services, as well as its ability to delegate management control over each service to the appropriate users. The granularity of control in OS X Server is much finer than a client not running the Server app. When securing file sharing, for example, you can control which share points each user can access per protocol. And you can create a support user who has the capability of starting and stopping the service while removing their ability to access the data shared by that service. Or, if you'd rather not make a configuration change that restricts a specific user from mounting a share point, you can also set a control that denies access to certain services, or protocols, for specific users.

Service access control lists (SACLs) allow administrators to limit access to services for certain users. To configure SACLs, open the Server app, and click on Users or Groups in the sidebar. Open one of the users and then click on the cog-wheel icon at the bottom of the screen. Click Edit Access to Services… to bring up a list of services. Here, uncheck the box for each service that you do not want to provide access to this specific user or group, as shown in Figure 16-1.

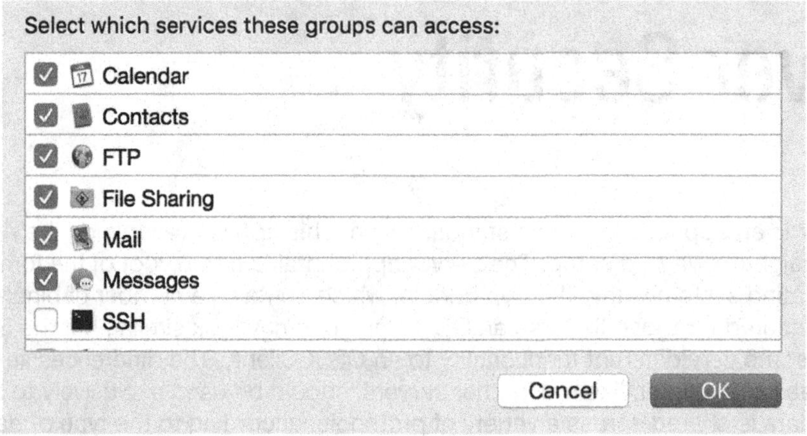

Figure 16-1. Configuring SACLs

You can also use the configuration options for each service to configure access to resources. To do so, click on the service that you would like to restrict access to and then click on the Edit Permissions… button if available. Then, click on on the "only some users" option in the "Allow connections from" field. Click on the plus sign (+) to add a user and provide a name for a user or group in the field, as seen in Figure 16-2. Once added, click on OK to edit each of the groups.

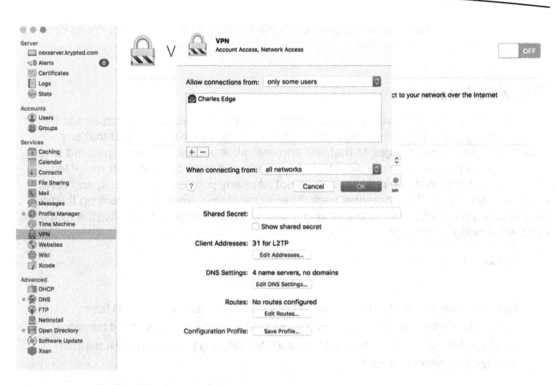

Figure 16-2. Configuring SACLs from the Server app

Each SACL is a group. By editing each SACL, you will edit the group membership for that group. For example, there's a group called _jabber. Members of that group get access to the Messages service. You can also edit SACLs by manually adding users to groups. You can use the dsmemberutil command to do so, or show hidden users in the Server app. To show these accounts, click on the View menu and select Show System Users, as seen in Figure 16-3.

Figure 16-3. Show System Accounts

Once you can see System Accounts, you'll be able to add and remove members as needed, in order to edit access to services.

The Root User

When you setup your first user, the local administrative user's password (such as *admin* or *mycompany admin*) becomes the password of the root user. Keep in mind that any subsequent password changes to that first administrative account are not replicated when you change its password. In practice, this often leads to a stale password for root if left enabled; in other words, the password does not have any policies applied to it, and can provide an entry point for a potential hack. This is one strong argument for leaving the root user disabled on OS X Server and enabling it only when it's needed. To disable the root user, use the following command:

```
dsenableroot -d
```

> **Note**   One caveat to disabling the root user is that you will not be able to promote an Open Directory system to a replica. The root user does not need to be active during standard replication intervals, but will need to be enabled during replica setup. Disabling the root user will result in an error during the setup of the replica.

Foundations of a Directory Service

One of the most substantial aspects of OS X Server and its impact on a OS X-based network is the ability to run directory services. Open Directory, Apple's native directory service technology, is built on open standards such as OpenLDAP and Kerberos. Open Directory gives administrators the ability to centralize usernames and passwords for an environment, which increases security. But a directory service also allows for the ability to deploy policies to workstations over the network in a somewhat automated fashion. Using directory services, it becomes possible to lock down client computers with the security settings you want, to enforce password policies to keep users from having simple passwords, and to limit the frequency that passwords are required on the network, also greatly increasing the overall security of your environment.

While we will focus on Open Directory throughout most of our discussions about directory services, it is worth noting that every OS X computer ships running a local directory service. This includes many of the components found in OS X Server, which allows for optimal security among Mac computers without a server. The local directory service can also be used to deploy profiles, or policies, without the use of a centralized server.

Defining LDAP

A *directory service* organizes information such as users, groups, and computers. The directory service is the interface to the directory and provides access to the data that is contained in that directory. In addition to Open Directory, popular directory services include OpenLDAP, Active Directory, and eDirectory. The one item that nearly all directory service implementations share is the Lightweight Directory Access Protocol (LDAP). LDAP provides access to a centralized data structure commonly used to track information such as usernames, computers, printers, and other items on a network by performing fast queries of the database. LDAP is a popular protocol and allows for a wide variety of uses.

Apple's Open Directory technology runs LDAP on a Berkley Database (bdb), which is made accessible via OpenLDAP for storing user account information. Slapd is the process behind Apple's implementation of the OpenLDAP server. Slapd hosts access to the Berkeley Database where user account information, such as the user ID, is stored. When broken down to their bare components, these accounts are merely sets of *attributes*. Attributes are fields for a given object that constitute the makeup of a standard user, such as a username, a unique ID, a home directory path, and a password slot. Think of it this way: if you were to print out all of your attributes then the data set would resemble a spreadsheet.

> **Note**   When directory services are enabled on the first server of an organization, that server is considered the Open Directory *Master*.

Kerberos

Kerberos is a highly secure computer network authentication protocol developed at MIT that allows individuals, communicating over an insecure network, to prove their identity to one another in a secure manner.

Kerberos helps prevent eavesdropping to discover passwords or replay attacks (resending packets to obtain similar results from the original transmission) and ensures the integrity of the data. It provides mutual authentication much like a client-server model, where both the user and the service verify each other's identity. Let's dive into how Kerberos authenticates its users.

> **Note**   In Greek mythology, Kerberos was the hound guarding Hades—a monstrous three-headed dog with a snake for a tail and innumerable snake heads on his back.

Kerberos Deconstructed

In OS X Server, Apple has modified Kerberos to handle communication with the Apple authd and accountsd services. All of these keep the passwords encrypted internally on the server, but Kerberos allows computers from the outside to communicate securely with the server.

Kerberos is divided into three components: the Kerberos key distribution server, the Kerberized service, and the Kerberos client. This trio communicates with a Kerberos network known as a *realm*. Kerberos guards your passwords and enables single sign-on to configured servers. Kerberos does this by identifying each user and server with a *principal*. A principal is then assigned a time-sensitive *ticket* or (TGT) to submit credentials over the network rather than sending passwords, establishing a session. Kerberos relies on a series of challenges and session keys that then allow a user or server a TGT assigned to the user's principal. The TGT contains the time stamp used by the key distribution server to verify its authenticity.

> **Note**   Apple's implementation of the MIT Kerberos key distribution server (KDC) is krb5kdc.

The TGT is issued as an authentication token to gain access to additional service tickets during the TGT's lifetime. This can be illustrated by logging in at the loginwindow as an Open Directory or Active Directory user, which authenticates you to the directory server and provides a TGT placed in a shared *credentials cache*. Other services such as file sharing will then provide single sign-on based on the TGT.

> **Note**   Clients who are using Open Directory for authentication (known as *binding*) will be automatically configured to use Kerberos using special entries provided and updated by the LDAP server. You can manually initialize the configuration by using the `kerberosautoconfig` command, but this is typically not required.

One of the most critical aspects of Kerberos configuration is time synchronization. If a client or server is more than five minutes apart from its Kerberos KDC server, then authentication will fail. This value is normally best synchronized using the Network Time Protocol (NTP). By default, the network time server is time.apple.com. You can use a custom network time server using the systemsetup command, along with the –setnetworktimeserver option followed by the name of a network time server, as follows

```
sudo systemsetup -setnetworktimeserver time.krypted.com
```

To then enable the network time service, use the systemsetup command along with the –setusingnetworktime option to on, as follows:

```
sudo systemsetup -setusingnetworktime on
```

Another important consideration for Kerberos is DNS. Prior to setting up an Open Directory master or replica, make sure that the server's DNS is accurate in both forward and reverse DNS resolution. To do so, run the changeip command with the -checkhostname option, as follows:

```
changeip -checkhostname
```

Kerberos is frequently called the "keys to the kingdom," on an OS X Server. An improperly configured Open Directory service can give way to those keys. If a Kerberos system is deployed on an OS X Server, it's important to make sure the services on your Open Directory servers are properly patched and securely locked down. Let's discuss the proper ways to do just that.

> **Note**   Typically, a secure Kerberos environment consists of a standalone system that doesn't run any other services and is used as a KDC. However, in OS X Server the Open Directory Master already runs other services, such as passwordserver and LDAP. Therefore, for a fully secure environment we recommend running your Open Directory master on a dedicated host that isn't running any other services other than the Open Directory master service.

Configuring and Managing Open Directory

Because directory services give such a boost to the security of larger environments, we will spend the first part of this section discussing how to set up and bind to Open Directory. Once you have a solid Open Directory environment, we will then show you how to secure Open Directory, more than it is secured in the stock implementation of OS X Server, by disabling anonymous binding and implementing LDAP ACLs. Anonymous binding allows unauthenticated users to be able to enumerate your directory structure, whereas LDAP ACLs control what is visible to unauthenticated users and specified groups for authenticated users of the directory.

To start setting up Open Directory, open the Server app, and click the Open Directory service. Next, click on the ON button, shown in Figure 16-4.

Figure 16-4. Turn on the Open Directory Service

You'll then be prompted for how Network Users and Groups should be configured (see Figure 16-5). This is just another way of defining how Open Directory is setup. Here, you'll have the choice of the following:

- Create a new Open Directory domain: This will setup a new Open Directory master and build a domain. The Open Directory master is automatically the first server setup in a domain and can be transferred to other servers in an emergency. Other Open Directory servers will be replicas to this server.

- Join an Existing Open Directory domain as a replica: Sets up a second, third, fourth, etc Open Directory server. Use this to balance the load between your servers.

- Restore Open Directory domain from an archive: If you have a backup, you can use this option to restore that backup into a new Open Directory master.

For the purposes of this example, we'll go ahead and setup a new Open Directory domain, which is the default option. So click the Next button.

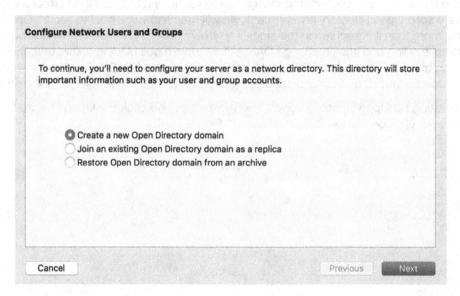

Figure 16-5. Select the Role of the Server

Next, provide credentials for the account that administers the Open Directory service. In Figure 16-6, we provide diradmin as a username and a password. This password should be very secure, as it can manage all of the shared accounts on the directory domain.

Directory Administrator

Enter account information for the new directory administrator account. This user account will have administrative privileges for managing network users and groups.

Name: Directory Administrator

Account Name: diradmin

Password: ••••••••••

Verify: ••••••••••

☑ Remember this password in my keychain

Cancel   Previous   Next

Figure 16-6. Setup Your Directory Administrator Account

You'll then be prompted for the Organization Name and Admin Email Address. These will be used in the SSL certificate for the server (see Figure 16-7).

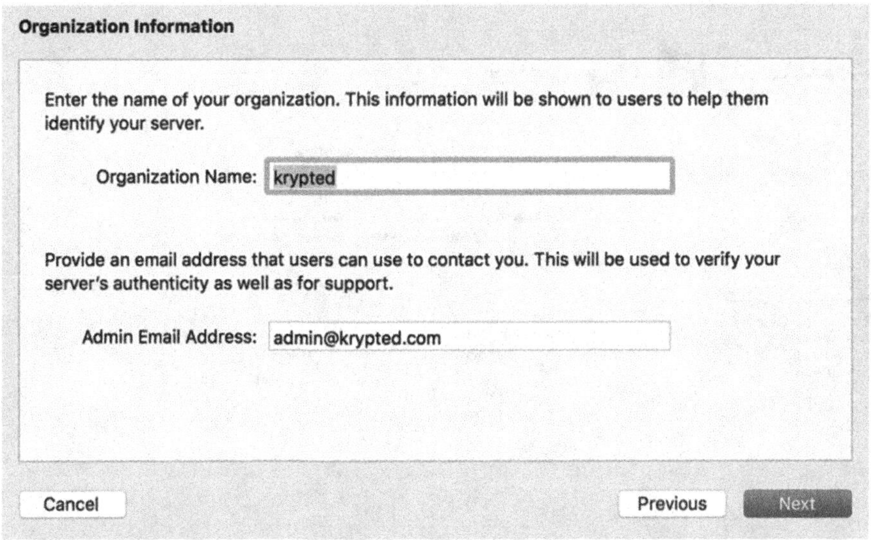

Organization Information

Enter the name of your organization. This information will be shown to users to help them identify your server.

Organization Name: krypted

Provide an email address that users can use to contact you. This will be used to verify your server's authenticity as well as for support.

Admin Email Address: admin@krypted.com

Cancel   Previous   Next

Figure 16-7. Configure the Settings for the Certificate

At the Confirm Settings screen, confirm that the information provided in the previous screens matches the settings to use for setting up the Open Directory service (see Figure 16-8). Provided that the settings are correct, click Set Up.

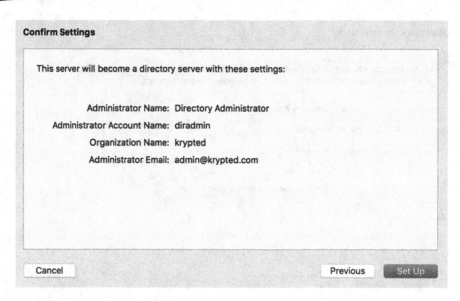

Figure 16-8. *Confirm the Open Directory Settings*

The Open Directory setup is then complete (see Figure 16-9). You will see the name of your server in the Servers: field.

Figure 16-9. *Open Directory Setup Complete*

Once setup, you can create an Open Directory Replica, create accounts in Open Directory and each service created on the master and any replicas will also leverage the shared accounts. And these accounts will use Kerberos to authenticate, if the service is integrated with Kerberos.

Securing Open Directory Accounts by Enabling Password Policies

Password policies include server-side rules that limit the age and strength of passwords that can be used in your environment. Some password policies are available only globally (network-wide, while others are available on a per-user (or per-account) basis. To see global policies, open the Server app, and click on Users. To edit password policies, click on the cog wheel icon and then click on Edit Password Policy... (as seen in Figure 16-10).

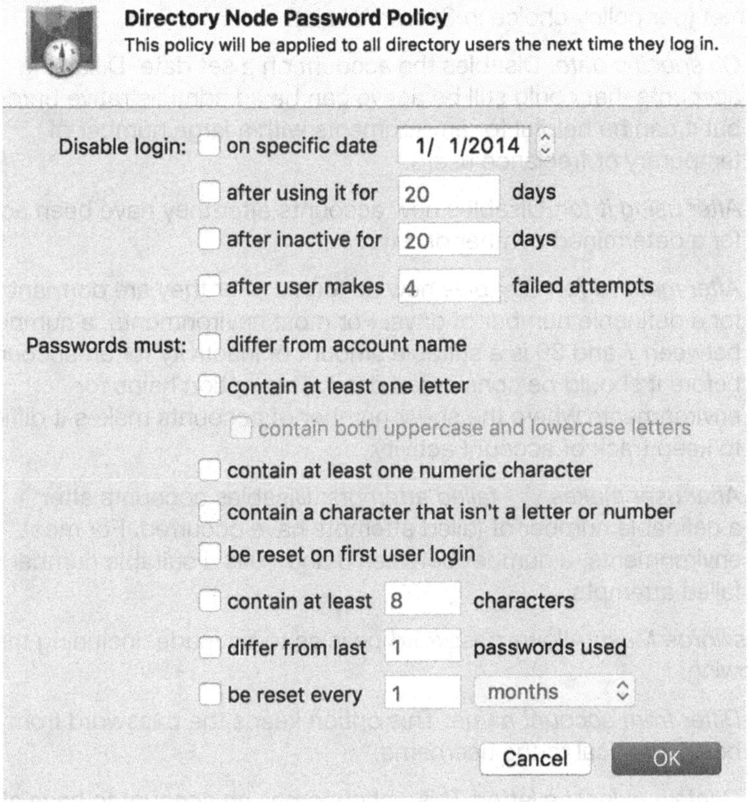

Directory Node Password Policy
This policy will be applied to all directory users the next time they log in.

Disable login: ☐ on specific date   1/ 1/2014 ⌄
                ☐ after using it for   20   days
                ☐ after inactive for   20   days
                ☐ after user makes   4   failed attempts

Passwords must: ☐ differ from account name
                ☐ contain at least one letter
                ☐ contain both uppercase and lowercase letters
                ☐ contain at least one numeric character
                ☐ contain a character that isn't a letter or number
                ☐ be reset on first user login
                ☐ contain at least   8   characters
                ☐ differ from last   1   passwords used
                ☐ be reset every   1   months ⌄

                                        Cancel   OK

Figure 16-10. Configure Global Password Policies

Here,

> **Note**   Global password policies are overridden by user password policies, and do not apply to administrative users.

Two types of global password policies exist: Disable Login controls when accounts are able to log in, and Passwords Must controls various requirements for a password to be allowed. We strongly recommend using as many of these as possible, because they provide a substantial amount of Open Directory security. However, keep in mind that the harder a password is for a user to remember, the more likely they are to write it down, so a certain amount of balance between complexity and ease of remembrance should be practiced here.

Let's briefly discuss each:

- *Disable Login*: Allows logins to be disabled when the following criteria are met (per policy choice in Server Admin):

  - *On specific date*: Disables the account on a set date. Disabling accounts that could still be active can be an administrative burden, but it can be helpful for environments with a large number of temporary or freelance users.

  - *After using it for*: Disables new accounts after they have been active for a determined number of days.

  - *After inactive for*: Disables new accounts after they are dormant for a definable number of days. For most environments, a number between 7 and 30 is a suitable amount of inactivity for an account before it should be considered dead. This option helps for environments where the sheer number of accounts makes it difficult to keep track of account activity.

  - *After user makes ___ failed attempts*: Disables accounts after a definable number of failed attempts have occurred. For most environments, a number between 3 and 10 is a suitable number of failed attempts.

- *Passwords Must*: Allows password policies to be made, including the following:

  - *Differ from account name*: This option keeps the password from being identical to the username.

  - *Contain at least a letter*: This option forces an account to have at least one character from the alphabet (a to z) in the password. This enforces a policy that avoids passwords such as 1234.

  - *Contain both uppercase and lowercase letters*: This option requires at least one letter be uppercase and at least one letter be lowercase. Passwords are case sensitive.

- *Contain at least one numeric character*: This option forces a password to have a number in it. An example of an allowable password would be 1paSsworD1. Passwords should typically have at least one lowercase letter, at least one uppercase letter, and at least one numeric character.

- *Contain a character that isn't a letter or a number*: This option forces a password to have a special character in it, such as a $, *, &, ^, !, or #.

- *Be reset on first login*: This is a good option for new accounts or accounts that have had their passwords reset. This will keep administrators from knowing their users' passwords (a policy that protects the administrator as well as the user). This will provide a certain level of comfort to users that the administrator is not snooping through their personal data. If you need access to an account, then you should be forced to reset a password to obtain it.

- *Contain at least*: This option allows you to define the minimum length of a password in characters. The minimum length of a password is something debatable in any environment. For many, eight is a good number, but this is not as much a technical decision as it is a management decision.

- *Differ from last*: This option allows you to force users to change their passwords to something different every time they change their password for as many times as you specify. Some administrator's think 3 is enough, others say 18 is better. This is a decision that should be made on a management level in many cases.

- *Be reset every*: This option allows you to force your users to change passwords at specific times and to define the number of days, weeks, or months that can transpire before a new password must be set. Passwords should also be changed as often as management will allow.

Securing LDAP by Preventing Anonymous Binding

In the previous section, we discussed the Require Clients to Bind to Directory option, but it is important to note that it affects only automatically configured clients. When this option is enabled, no changes are made to the running LDAP process (slapd). This option enables a preference key in the Open Directory client configuration container cn=config. This preference key will be enforced on Mac OS X clients that read this record (but not on most flavors of Linux or Unix). You can view this client configuration record using dscl:

```
dscl /LDAPv3/127.0.0.1/ -read Config/macosxodpolicy
```

When the setting is enabled, you will see the Binding Required key set to true when you review the output of dscl. However, because only Mac OS X clients read this configuration, they are the only LDAP clients that are actually "required" to bind. In other words, you are not restricting access to your LDAP server; you are in fact requiring binding only for clients that use the Max OS X LDAP plug-in. A standard LDAP browser from a rogue machine can anonymously bind even with this option enabled. If you wish to restrict access to only authenticated users, you must add the bind_anon option to the top of the OpenLDAP configuration file stored at /private/etc/openldap/slapd.conf.

> **Note**   Be aware that configuring slapd to refuse anonymous connections means all clients will be
> required to bind. This includes the Open Directory master, which is automatically configured with
> the local host value 127.0.0.1 upon its promotion to an Open Directory master. You will need to
> update this and all other entries before clients will be able to access the database.

Once connected, test that your binding is working by running the following command:

```
dscl localhost list /LDAPv3/127.0.0.1/Users.
```

The above dscl command should output a list of all users in your Open Directory domain. If it doesn't then return to Directory Access, and make sure your binding username and password are correct. Once you have verified that your server can access your authenticated LDAP server, you can disable anonymous binding. To do so, edit the slapd configuration using your favorite text editor:

```
sudo nano /private/etc/openldap/slapd.conf
```

Add the following disallow bind_anon near the top of the file:

```
#
# See slapd.conf(5) for details on configuration options.
#
# This file should NOT be world readable.
#
disallow bind_anon
```

Next, save the configuration file, and restart the LDAP service by sending it a HUP signal using the following command:

```
sudo killall -HUP slapd
```

> **Note**   Disabling anonymous binding while forcing SSL certificates for binding is the goal here. This will provide a highly secure solution, and the binding process can easily be automated to help alleviate the added administrative burden that distributing SSL certificates and performing an authenticated bind will incur.

Securely Binding Clients to Open Directory

Once you have securely configured Open Directory on your servers, you can then bind the individual client workstations and non-directory services servers to Open Directory. At this point, all of the password policies are enforced, and many of the services' communications will be Kerberized. So, *why bind clients*? If client workstations are not bound, then workstation policies will not be enforced. This includes pushing out Software Update Server settings, mobility and network home folder settings, and any of the managed preferences you may have defined (or will define). Also, usernames and passwords for workstations would not be centralized, which is a key to effectively managing and securing larger numbers of systems as is required in most enterprise environments.

You can distribute managed settings using profiles, Profile Manager, or third party patch management solutions. But being able to use a layered approach to deploying policies is an important aspect of enterprise systems administration.

To bind client workstations, you will need to authenticate as an administrator and use the Users & Groups System Preference pane on the client workstation. This is achieved in different ways on different versions of OS X. In 10.11, the Directory Utility is found in /System/Library/CoreServices/Applications. At the Users & Groups System Preference pane, click on Login Options and then click on Edit… in the Network Account Server field. Here, click the plus sign (+). Enter the name of the Open Directory master that you setup in the Server field, as you can see in Figure 16-11.

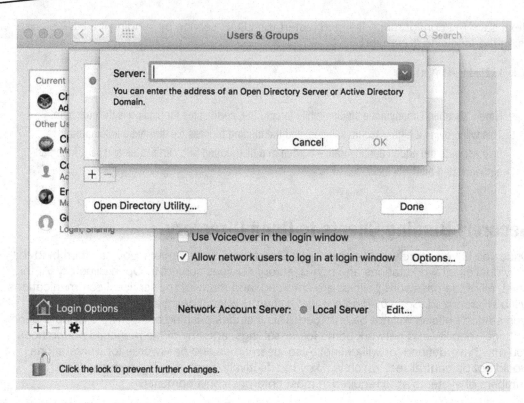

Figure 16-11. Binding to Open Directory

By default, you will then be prompted that "This server does not provide a secure (SSL) connection. Do you want to continue?" This means that the server does not secure communications with an SSL certificate. Click Continue to complete the binding process, as seen in Figure 16-12.

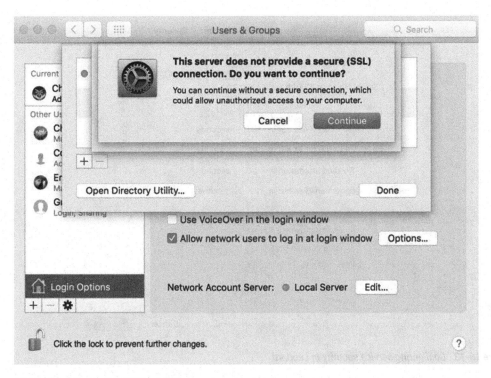

Figure 16-12. Choosing To Bind Without SSL

You can then choose the appropriate items that correspond with the setup of your Open Directory master using the Security Policy section of the Open Directory screen (see Figure 16-13), which is accessed using the Directory Utility and opening the connection to that server. You will want to match these as closely as possible on the client side.

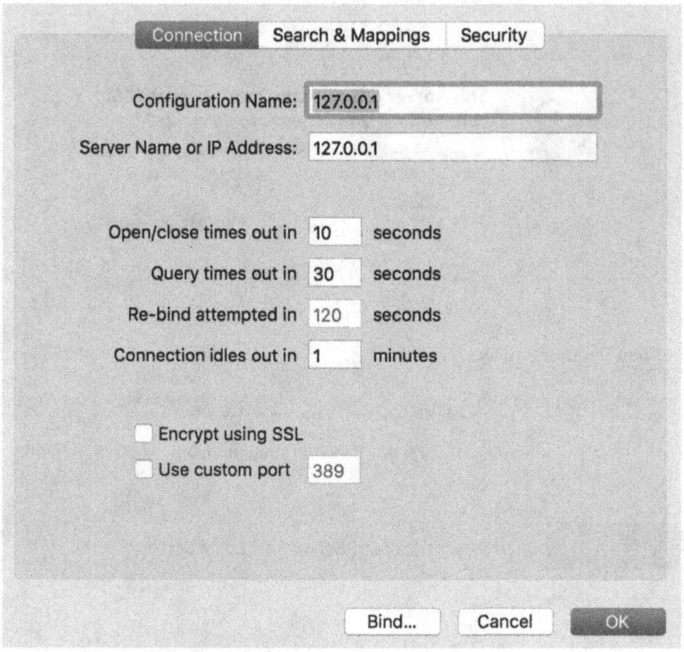

Figure 16-13. Configuring service security in Leopard

Further Securing LDAP: Implementing Custom LDAP ACLs

An access control list for LDAP is a way to manage security for the OpenLDAP database. This is secure, because it enforces who can access and change things in the LDAP database. ACL policies are enforced at the server level. If ACLs are not configured, you can use LDAP data to access information about network layouts, users, and other information without authentication. One example of this methodology is to use the "Force Clients to Bind" option in the Open Directory policy settings in Server Admin. For most of these configurations, however, you will need to jump into the command line to create these ACLs.

> **Note**   You can use ldapsearch from the command line to search LDAP databases without authenticating.

To restrict bound users from viewing attributes of other users, add the following to your /etc/openldap/slapd.conf:

```
Access to dn=".*,dc=your dcname,dc=.com" attr=userPassword
    by self write
    by * auth
Access to dn=".*,dc=your dcname,dc=.com"
    by * read
```

To fully disable anonymous reads, use this series of commands:

```
Access to dn=".*,dc=your dcname,dc=.com"
    by dn"uid=nssldap,ou=people,dc=dcname,dc=com" read
    by * none
```

To restrict access to an LDAP database and allow users to change their own LDAP information in the shared address book, you'll need to add an LDAP ACL to your slapd.conf file. To do this, add the following series of lines (we will go into further detail on LDAP ACLs later in this chapter):

```
access to
attrs=mail,sn,givenName,telephoneNumber,mobile,facsimileTelephoneNumber,street,
    postalAddress,postOfficeBox,postalCode,password by self write
```

> **Tip**   A number of different LDAP ACLs are configured in Mac OS X 10.6 Server out of the box. When you are configuring the access controls, these may conflict with the ACLs already on your network. In short, it can get very confusing very fast. For more assistance with configuring this type of policy see the book *LDAP System Administration* from O'Reilly Press.

Creating Open Directory Users and Groups

Now that you have Open Directory set up securely, you might want to start building out the users and groups for your server. Later you can log into client systems using these accounts, but for now you'll need to set up accounts securely so they can log into the server and access services. You can create users and groups in the LDAP database in OS X Server by using the Server app in the /Applications directory.

To create your first user, open the Server app from the Open Directory master, and click on Users (see Figure 16-14) and then click on the plus sign icon towards the bottom of the screen.

Figure 16-14. Creating a user with the Server app

At the New User screen, provide the name of the user (see Figure 16-15), a password and optionally enter an email address, a quota for how much space on the server the user can access, choose a path for the home folder (network home directories are beyond the scope of this book), keywords to help you find the account in the future and any notes about the account that you choose to include. Then click on Create. The account is then created.

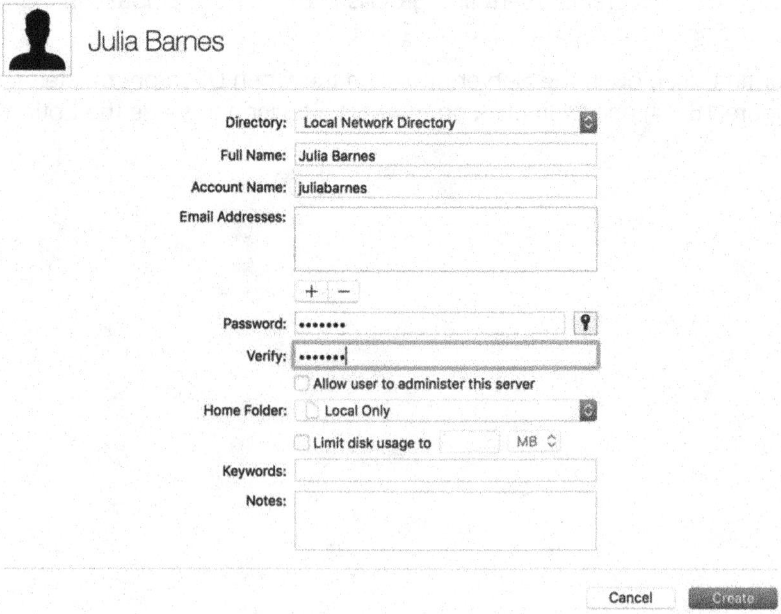

Julia Barnes

Directory:	Local Network Directory
Full Name:	Julia Barnes
Account Name:	juliabarnes
Email Addresses:	

+ −

Password:	••••••
Verify:	••••••

☐ Allow user to administer this server

Home Folder:	Local Only

☐ Limit disk usage to   MB

Keywords:	
Notes:	

Cancel   Create

Figure 16-15. Choosing User Settings

To create a new group, click the Groups option in the Server app and then click the plus sign (+), shown in Figure 16-16.

Figure 16-16. Create A Group

At the New Group screen, provide a name for the group. As you can see in Figure 16-17, you can also optionally provide information for email groups at this point, but that's beyond the scope of this book. Click on Create.

Figure 16-17. Group Settings

Once created, double-click on the group (see Figure 16-18) and click on the plus sign (+) to add members to the group. When you are satisfied with all of the settings for the newly created account, click OK.

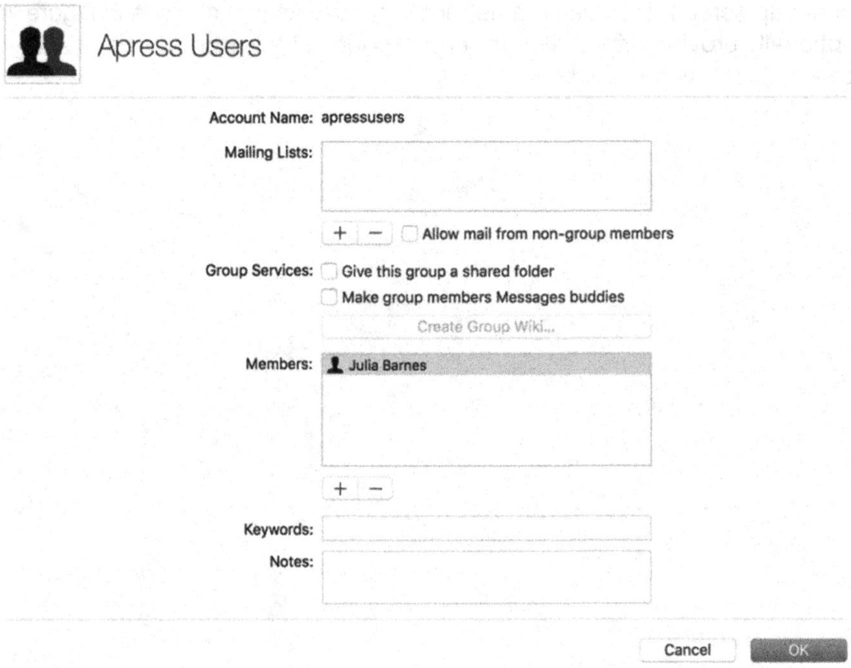

Apress Users

Account Name: apressusers

Mailing Lists:

+ − ☐ Allow mail from non-group members

Group Services: ☐ Give this group a shared folder
☐ Make group members Messages buddies

Create Group Wiki...

Members: 👤 Julia Barnes

+ −

Keywords:

Notes:

Cancel   OK

Figure 16-18. Add Members to Your New Group

Securing Kerberos from the Command Line

Kerberos is a powerful application, and the options you have in the GUI are fairly limited. These settings can be accessed by opening the Ticket Viewer tool from Keychain Assistant. Here you can add and remove Kerberos tickets and view existing tickets. While a GUI tool is provided for Kerberos configuration, the command line gives you far more options to help further secure and test connectivity for it. The command-line tools available to further secure Kerberos include `kinit`, `klist`, `kdestroy`, and many others.

- `kinit` is used to establish and cache Kerberos connections. This is useful when troubleshooting Kerberos errors and looking to initiate Kerberos communications. Options for the `kinit` command include the following:

  - `-F`: Makes tickets nonforwardable

  - `-f`: Makes tickets forwardable

  - `-P`: Makes tickets nonproxyable

  - `-v`: Forces validation

  - `-R`: Renews tickets

- `klist` lists tickets. This is useful when looking to list all of the Kerberos service principals that a user is authorized to access. Options for `klist` include the following:

  - `-4`: Lists only Kerberos 4 tickets

  - `-5`: Lists only Kerberos 5 tickets

  - `-A`: Lists all tickets

  - `-s`: Runs silently

- `kdestroy`: Removes tickets from the cache. This is useful in troubleshooting Kerberos/KDC issues. The following is the option:

  - `-a`: Destroys all tickets

> **Note** As is true with Windows, a RAM-based ticket cache is used instead of a file-based ticket cache, much like most versions of Kerberos for Unix and Linux variants.

Some command-line applications available for the Kerberos server include the following:

- `kdcsetup` creates the first admin account.

Managed Preferences and Profiles

The ability to manage preferences is one of the most powerful aspects of directory services. In previous sections, we showed you how to set up Open Directory to have a centralized repository of usernames and passwords. You can further secure the server itself (and any other servers in our environment) using Kerberos and password policies. We have also shown you how to secure Open Directory accounts by enabling password policies and restricting the types of communications with the server. Now, we'll cover enforcing policies, known as *managed preferences*, on client systems and user accounts. These policies are enforced using a technology known as Profiles. Profiles are property lists, which enforce policies.

Although you can perform these tasks on OS X Server in a distributed management environment using Profile Manager, we'll focus on creating profiles using a tool called Apple Configurator to create the profiles. But keep in mind that while profiles are an excellent way to lock down computers, an actual Mobile Device Management (MDM) platform that supports OS X such as Profile Manager, the Casper Suite, FileWave MDM and others are better suited to the task much of the time, as you can send new profile changes over the air, using Apple's Push Notification service (APNs), which is the same technology that puts a red badge on apps in the dock when they have information waiting for them.

To get started with Apple Configurator, first install the tool from the Mac App Store, by opening the App Store, search for Apple Configurator and then clicking Install or Get (according to whether you have used the tool previously with the Apple ID you're logged in as). Once installed, open Apple Configurator and click on New Profile from the File menu.

At the new profile screen, you will need to provide a name (in this case Passcode Policy) for the profile, as well as a unique identifier (in this case, com.krypted.passcodepolicy) as you can see in Figure 16-19. In the sidebar, you will see a list of options that can be configured. These policies, or manifests, include the following:

> *General*: The name of the policy as well as how the policy can be removed.
>
> *Passcode*: Specifies what passcodes are allowed. For example, whether you are required to use special characters and how long the passcode is.
>
> *Restrictions*: Disables certain features of the operating system, such as the iTunes Store.
>
> *Global HTTP Proxy*: Force devices to use a proxy server for HTTP traffic.
>
> *Content Filter*: Whitelist and blacklist Internet traffic.
>
> *Wi-Fi*: Configure Wi-Fi settings on devices, including 802.1x if you use a secured network.
>
> *VPN*: Setup connections to a VPN server.
>
> *AirPrint*: Install printers automatically.
>
> *Mail*: Automate the setup of IMAP and POP email accounts.
>
> *Exchange ActiveSync*: Automate the setup of Exchange, Kerio, and Google Apps accounts.

Calendar: Automate the configuration of CalDAV calendars from a server.

Contacts: Automate the configuration of CardDAV contacts from a server.

Web Clips: Put links to websites into LaunchPad or as icons on an iOS device.

Fonts: Install font files automatically.

Certificates: Embed certificates in the profile (useful for 802.1x and self-signed certificates to talk to OS X and other types of web servers.

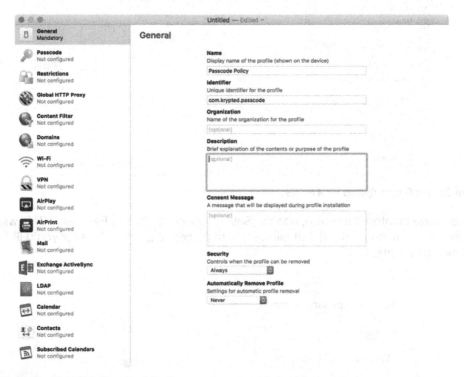

Figure 16-19. The General Options For A Profile

As you can tell from the types of profile settings, you have a lot of options you can automate the configuration of in OS X. Here, we'll look at the Passcode Policy we discussed earlier. The example will configure a passcode of at least 8 characters, with at least one number, one letter, and one special character. The passcode will need to be changed every 30 days and the computer will automatically require the passcode after 5 minutes of inactivity.

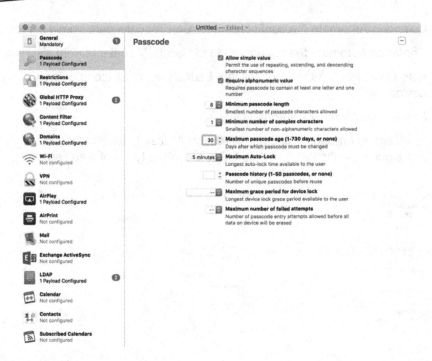

Figure 16-20. *The General Options For A Profile*

Once you have created the profile, use the Save… option under the File menu. This will bring up a dialog (Figure 16-21) that allows you to place the profile wherever you'd like for distribution on clients.

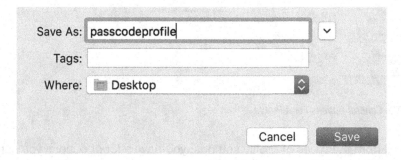

Figure 16-21. *The General Options For A Profile*

Once saved, to install the profile simply open it on a Mac or iOS device and the profile will install. Once installed, you will see a new System Preference pane called Profiles, which you can use to remove the profile if needed.

The features available in a profile (and therefore via MCX) include access to removable hard drives, how the drives appear to users, login items, and Finder settings. However, local administrators of each machine can remove these profiles if they wish. A custom-managed preference can also be pushed to client systems and will enforce custom policies for third-party software or settings that Apple didn't include in the default policies (primarily using property list options available to the `defaults` command).

If you would prefer to use managed preferences without profiles, then Workgroup Manager can be run on a Mac client. Workgroup Manager is how policies were managed up until 10.8 and official support was dropped after 10.9; however, you can still download the Workgroup Manager application from Apple. You cannot install the application on 10.10 or 10.11; however, you can extract the application bundle from the installation package using Pacifist and run the app. As you can see in Figure 16-22, the options are far more limited.

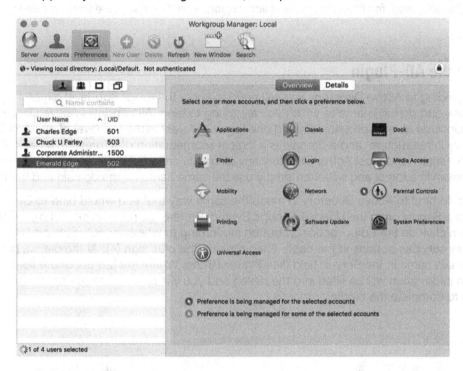

Figure 16-22. Workgroup Manager

although you can manage custom preferences and manifsts, making managed preferences extensible and able to be managed using the directory service without MDM or custom profiles. However, managed preferences are no longer officially supported, so your mileage may vary.

Active Directory Integration

The Apple Active Directory service plug-in (AD-Plug-in) is an extension that Apple added to its DirectoryService API to enable OS X Client or OS X Server to bind to Active Directory, making interconnectivity between Apple's Open Directory and Microsoft's Active Directory easier. The Active Directory plug-in also supports Kerberos autoconfiguration for clients bound into Active Directory using DNS entries known as *service* (SRV) records. The Active Directory plug-in is configured using the Users & Group System Preference pane or by using the dsconfigad command line tool.

When you use the Active Directory plug-in to bind to Active Directory, you can set up Open Directory to connect to an Active Directory domain controller and have items accessible to Open Directory from Active Directory. Because you are connecting to an existing Active

Directory service, you will more than likely have all the policies for binding and passwords in place in your current directory services environment. This architecture is known as a *dual-directory* environment.

Note   You can also use Directory Access to bind to Active Directory, or the third party tool ADmitMac, which has a few options not otherwise provided in the native Active Directory plug-in.

Using the AD-Plugin

When binding to Active Directory, you will need to know the forest (top-level directory structure) and domain name to which you are trying to bind. All Windows Active Directory setups include at least one domain and one forest. A *forest* is the top level of any Active Directory infrastructure, and a *domain* is a logical segmentation of a forest. In a basic Active Directory setup (and most Active Directory environments are a basic setup), you will have only one domain in a forest and will often simply use the same name for the domain and the forest.

You would bind to Active Directory in much the same way that you would bind to Open Directory. Simply open the Users & Groups System Preference pane, click on Login Options and then click on the Edit… or Join… button (according to whether you've already use the directory services options in the past). Then click on the plus sign (+). At the dialog, provide the domain name in the Server: field (see Figure 16-23). When you tab out of the field, the domain information will be filled into the dialog and you will be able to click on the Bind button to complete the binding process.

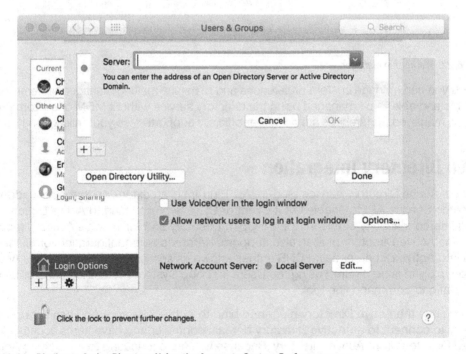

Figure 16-23. Binding to Active Directory Using the Accounts System Preference pane

Provided the system finds the server, click Bind and when prompted, provide credentials with the access to bind to a client in the provided fields. The client is then bound to the Active Directory domain.

> **Note**   If you need to do an advanced setup, the name of the domain needs to match the name of the forest when the domain is a member of a similarly named forest. With a Windows server, when you create the first domain controller and give that domain a name, the forest will also take on that same name. Which is not to say that you cannot have different domains in the same forest; you can, in which case you would leave the forest the same but change the name of the domain. Remember that all domains belong to a forest, and multiple domains can belong to a single forest.

Setting Up Network Homes with Active Directory Clients

A universal naming convention (UNC) is used for mapping drives within the Windows operating system, resulting in drives with lettered mappings (for example, the UNC path of \\server\share can be mapped to the S: drive). These folder mappings can then be used to provide synchronized profiles, known as *roaming profiles*, for Windows clients. The Use UNC Path from Active Directory to Derive Network Home Location option in Directory Utility will allow you to use the Active Directory profile location as a UNC path for network home folders, the OS X equivalent to roaming profiles.

By default, a home directory is not created in this scenario; however, in a Windows environment, many organizations enable this home directory in order to ensure that the users' data is stored on the server for the centralization of sharing, permissions, and auditing, as well as the decentralization of end user, or *edge*, backups. The option offered here will allow you to keep that structure in the Apple environment as well, preserving the Active Directory–planned file and folder structure for profiles to be preserved across platforms.

The "Network protocol to be used" option allows you to then choose one of two protocols from the drop-down menu: SMB or AFP. If you are using Windows servers, then you will likely select SMB, although if you have a solution such as Extreme Z-IP then you may be running AFP off of your Windows servers. This option determines how a home directory is mounted on the desktop. Server Message Block (SMB) is the default protocol used by Windows to communicate with other Windows computers when accessing shared resources (including printers, files, and serial ports). The SMB option here will allow Apple workstations to communicate with the Windows server using the native protocol that Windows uses to communicate with its files and directories. Unix variants can communicate in the same manner using Samba.

Using the AD-Plugin from the Command Line

It may become necessary to bind a Mac to Active Directory using the Active Directory plug-in from the command line. Perhaps you need to force the binding, you want to use a setting not available in the GUI, or you want to use the Active Directory plug-in in a server script. In these circumstances, you will need to turn to the command line. You'll find the command dsconfigad to be very handy in performing these tasks. dsconfigad does not require root privileges to run for all of its options to be enabled and it can be used from the command line to force certain aspects of directory services to work even when the GUI will not bind clients as needed. These include the following:

- -enableSSO enables Kerberos authentication for services, such as AFP, by generating Kerberos principals (commonly used with the magic triangle, described in the next section).

- -ggid maps group ID information.

- -mobile automates the enabling of mobile accounts.

- -preferred enables the use of a preferred server.

- -localhome places the home folder on the local system rather than using a server shared home.

- -f forces the command to run (which is useful when forcing an unbind).

- -packetsign enables packet signing when communicating with domain controllers.

- -namespace enables the use of multiple domains within a forest.

- -packetencrypt enables encryption of data being transmitted between Active Directory and the client system.

- -passinterval configures the number of days between each iteration of the machine password within Active Directory.

These options become very helpful when scripting server bindings, as they allow for easy mass deployment and for the scripting of specific options to be pushed out to clients for binding. A script can also be told to run on the first access of an imaged system. This type of programmatic interfacing between Active Directory and Mac OS X clients and servers is one of the primary focuses of the Enterprise Mac Admin title, also from Apress.

Integrating Open Directory with Active Directory: Dual Directory

Setting up a *dual directory* involves the administrator building an Open Directory infrastructure, binding it to an Active Directory infrastructure and binding managed clients to both Active Directory and Open Directory. It is a common way in the Mac OS X Server community to get Mac management policies and still use centralized Active Directory-based directory services. This seemingly awkward setup results in Active Directory handling password authentication and Open Directory handling policy management, giving administrators a fairly simplistic way to manage their Mac systems, even within the confines of Active Directory. It is also possible to extend the Active Directory schema to include managed client preferences that can be used to provide the managed preferences covered earlier in this chapter on Mac workstations.

> **Note**   You can also use augmented records to provide attributes for clients that are missing in your primary directory service, which requires much of the same infrastructure but has less of a clear integration roadmap. We will continue to focus on the dual directory environment rather than digging deeper into augmented records.

To set up a dual directory, first bind the server into Active Directory, as described in previous sections of this chapter. Then, promote your first server to an Open Directory master (also covered earlier). When you perform the promotion though, provided that you have already bound to Open Directory, you will have an option to leave the Active Directory binding and supplement the promotion with that existing Active Directory binding. Once the Open Directory server is a master and has been bound into Active Directory, it is possible to re-enable single sign-on functionality. To do this, run the following command:

```
dsconfigad -EnableSSO
```

Finally, bind Mac clients into both directory structures (using the same steps for both Open Directory and Active Directory that were mentioned previously). Active Directory will now process user credentials, and Open Directory will now process system policies for the Mac clients.

> **Note**   This is a rather quick explanation on setting up a dual directory environment. You may run into errors or problems along the way with DNS, Active Directory, Open Directory, or server communications. If this is the case, check the extensive documentation on this feature at support.apple.com and around the Internet. Also, see Chapter 3 of *The Enterprise Mac Admin's Guide* from Apress for additional information.

Web Server Security in OS X Server

The default web server in OS X is Apache. Apache is the most commonly used web server for the Unix, Linux, and Apple platforms and so is constantly being improved by security researchers and the open source community. By default, the Apache implementation in OS X is pretty secure. But there are things you can do to further secure the solution.

Using Realms

As discussed in Chapter 14, using htaccess files is the traditional way to password-protect a folder in Apache. However, htaccess can get rather complicated and, if not configured correctly, could cause more security headaches than it solves. Instead, if you have OS X Server, try using realms to limit access to specified directories. In OS X Server, when discussing the web server, a *realm* is a password-protected folder that uses a username and password in OS X to share files. Realms use WebDAV, a protocol designed with this exact purpose in mind, and a protocol which Apple has integrated with Kerberos in OS X Server. With WebDAV you will be using a password from your directory service rather than one stored in an htaccess or passwd.

To use realms, first create a site using a subdirectory you would like to password protect. Create the users and groups who will need to access the directory in the Users and Groups sections of the Server app. Then click on Websites in the sidebar. Here, you'll see a list of all the sites hosted on this server. As seen in Figure 16-24, all servers will by default have two sites installed: Server Website and Server Website (SSL). These contain OS X Server's built-in websites that are used to drive the Wiki and Profile Manager services. These cannot be removed, and are used for all traffic that doesn't have a site otherwise defined.

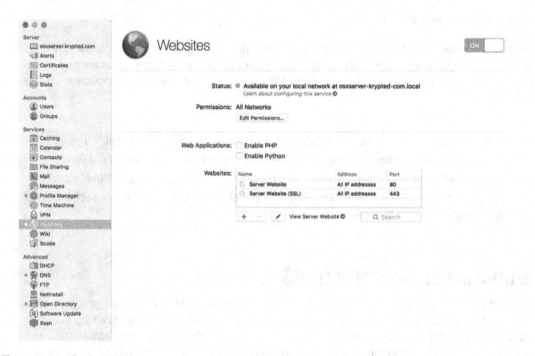

Figure 16-24. Viewing Websites

Double-click on a site to see the site screen (Figure 16-25). Then click on the Who Can Access field to see the options for who can access the site. Here, you can select the following options:

- *Anyone:* Anonymous access is allowed on the site (a traditional web site).

- *A specific group:* Restrict access to this site to a group, which we created earlier in this chapter.

- *Limit access by folder:* Allows you to assign a group that can access each directory of the root directory of a site.

Figure 16-25. Limiting Access To A Site

Click OK to save the settings.

SSL Certs on Web Servers

If you are doing any form of e-commerce, you should be using an SSL certificate (in fact we think that you should be using SSL for every service that has an option to do so). Many would argue that if you are trading any information with a client computer, such as a web form for submitting a support request, you should also be using SSL to encrypt the traffic. To enable HTTPS Access (SSL) on the web server, you will first need to create and install an SSL certificate (we will discuss implementing SSL on OS X Server later in the chapter). Then from the Server app, you will click the Websites service and click the plus (+) sign to add a new site.

Click in the Domain Name field (see Figure 16-26) and enter the appropriate domain name. By default, the port will be 80; enter **443** (the default port for SSL) in the Port field.

Figure 16-26. *Creating a site on port 443*

To assign the appropriate certificate, click on the SSL Security field and select the appropriate SSL certificate, and click Create to complete the setup.

File Sharing Security in OS X Server

File Sharing is more mature in OS X Server than on a standard client system, and thus has a more unified security context across services. For example, to view all the shared folders on a system, first open the Server app, and click the File Sharing button in the Services section of the sidebar. Here, you will see a list of the shares that are provided to other clients through the File Sharing service, along with who is allowed to access those shares, which is shown in Figure 16-27.

Figure 16-27. Viewing shared folders

Double-click on a share (or click the plus sign to create a new share). Here, you will see a number of options displayed in Figure 16-28. These control different behaviors of that share and include the following options:

- iOS: Shares files to iPhone and iPad.

- SMB: Enables file shares over SMB (the native Windows file sharing client).

- *AFP:* Shares files over AFP, the native Mac file sharing client.

- *WebDAV:* Shares files over WebDAV, a typical option found within Apple apps such as Keynote.

- *Guest Users:* Allows guest (or unauthenticated users) to access a share.

- *Only allow encrypted connections:* Forces using SSL to connect.

- *Home Directories over:* Define the protocols to provide home directories over, if you are using Network or Portable Home Directories.

Desktop
/Users/jamf/Desktop

Name: [Desktop]   [Browse...]

Access: ☑ iOS   ☐ Guest users
         ☑ SMB   ☐ Only allow encrypted connections
         ☑ AFP   ☐ Home directories over SMB ↕
         ☐ WebDAV

Permissions: 👥 Everyone   Custom   ↕
              👤 Charles Edge (owner)   Read & Write ↕
              👥 Staff (primary group)   No Access   ↕
              🌐 Everyone Else   Read & Write ↕

              [+] [−]

                                          [Cancel] [OK]

Figure 16-28. Viewing shared folders

Note   From a security perspective, you should enable only the file sharing protocols that are necessary on a per-share basis.

Once you have configured the options for each share point, click in the Permissions section to configure who can access the data shared by the share point. The Users & Groups floating window will appear when you click on the plus (+) sign. ACLs are listed above POSIX permissions, indicating their prioritization; when you drag a user or group into the Server Admin window from the floating users and group window, a blue line will appear indicating that dropping the object into the screen will apply it. Each user and group can then have custom permissions, roughly mirroring custom permissions available on Microsoft Windows servers.

Keeping a server secure also means not allowing users to fill up hard drive space on these shared volumes, which can not only reject other user's ability to save files on the server, but also cause the server to become unstable or even unresponsive. This often means implementing quotas on the volumes. To implement quotas, click on each user and provide the desired quota. Only users with home folders on the volume can be configured for quotas using the Server app. Make sure to issue warnings to your users. They might not be accustomed to the idea of quotas and it may take some time for users to get used to them.

A Word About File Size

One of the challenges of life as a OS X Server administrator is that Mac users (who are often artists and designers) generally work with large files. In the most extreme cases, single files can be in the hundreds of gigabytes. Mac users accustomed to files normally 100MB in size are less likely to notice that they are sending files to each other that are too big for emailing. So, limit files, but make sure to communicate what's appropriate with the users in order to reduce support calls. Explain when to use FTP or file sharing and when not to use it.

AFP

The AFP service in OS X Server is similar to that in on a standard client system. However, OS X Server has a myriad of other features that can be used to further secure the server that increase performance for the AFP service. As we covered AFP in OS X in Chapter 13, we will be picking up where Chapter 13 left off by investigating unique aspects of the AFP service in OS X Server.

Disable Masquerade As Any User

One of the more dangerous options in file sharing is the ability to masquerade your login as any other user. This means that you can log into a standard user account using any administrative password. While this setting was once in the Server Admin app, when that was retired, the setting became a command line only setting. While disabled by default, it's worth checking to verify that it is still disabled. To do so, run the serveradmin command followed by the settings verb and then `afp:` `afp:specialAdminPrivs`:

```
sudo serveradmin settings afp:specialAdminPrivs
```

If the setting is On, then it should be turned off by running the following command:

```
sudo serveradmin settings afp:specialAdminPrivs = Off
```

You will also want to limit the number of users that use AFP to something that is reasonable in order to keep the AFP server from crashing (AFP can only typically handle approximately 350 clients mounting from the volume). To do so, use the serveradmin command again:

```
sudo serveradmin settings afp:maxConnections = 350
```

> **Note**   Guest access is disabled by default for AFP but can be enabled by new administrators. To verify that it is disabled, use the serveradmin command and check afp:guestaccess or just disable with the following command: serveradmin settings afp:guestaccess = no

Kerberized AFP

Kerberos authentication, as mentioned earlier, is a superior authentication method to the standard Diffe-Hellman exchange (DHX) authentication scheme. Kerberos authentication can be required for the AFP server, but it is worth noting a few gotcha's with this configuration:

- When Kerberos authentication is required, only clients with a properly configured edu.mit.Kerberos file can authenticate with the service. This can disable access for any client that is not bound into the Open Directory network.

- Clients must not have a time skew longer than five minutes. This should be configured on the client by using a network timeserver.

- Users within the local authentication database will not be able to authenticate to the AFP server because their passwords are not authenticated using Open Directory. This may prevent the first user created on the system from being able to authenticate because they are created in the local authentication database.

Forcing Kerberos authentication requires AFP clients to use Kerberos to connect to the server, a good way to increase the security of your AFP environment. To force Kerberos authentication, set the authentication type to Kerberos using the serveradmin command. Users that are not in the Open Directory database will not be able to authenticate via Kerberos. This means that those clients with local accounts that do not have proper Kerberos configurations files in /Library/Preferences/edu.mit.kerberos will not be able to authenticate to the AFP server once this setting is enabled. To set the server to only accept Kerberos authentication, we'll use serveradmin again:

```
sudo serveradmin settings afp:authenticationMode = "kerberos"
```

AFP Logging

By default, OS X Server does not log all events. From a security perspective, if there is a compromised server, then you will want as many logs as possible to pull data from, in order to reconstruct the events that transpired on your server.

To maximize logging, use the serveradmin command to configure the AFP service to log more data. Here, we'll do so using the serveradmin

```
sudo serveradmin settings afp:activityLogSize = 100000
```

> **Note**   You will not see the path to files and folders in the logs. Even if logging is maximized, these seemingly important elements will still not appear.

Limiting Access to a Service

FTP is a pretty old protocol at this point. So we're going to use FTP as an example for how to limit access to services running on your server. We would recommend looking for a replacement if you are using FTP. Having said that, if you use FTP, you should take some steps to secure your implementation. One way to do so is using chroots. A chroot command is a technique under *nix whereby a process is permanently restricted to an isolated subset of the filesystem. Because there are insecurities within FTP and therefore in OS X, chroot can be used to further secure FTP. One easy way to obtain this functionality without a lot of command-line configuration is to use Rumpus, a web-enabled FTP application.

Another step to take with FTP, which is fairly consistent across all of the services provided is to limit access to the service by user or by location (via IP address). To do so, open the Server app and click on the FTP service in the sidebar. Then click on the Edit Permissions... button (shown in Figure 16-29) for the FTP service.

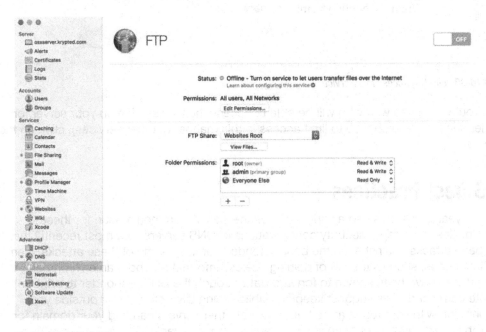

Figure 16-29. The FTP Service

From the Account Access, Network Access screen, click on the "Allow connections from" field and choose "only some users." Here, you can provide the accounts of any users known to the server that can access the FTP service. Ad/or, you can click on the "When connecting from" drop-down list and select "only some network" which allows you to define IP address ranges that can access the server. We did both in Figure 16-30, but you might choose to only do one of these.

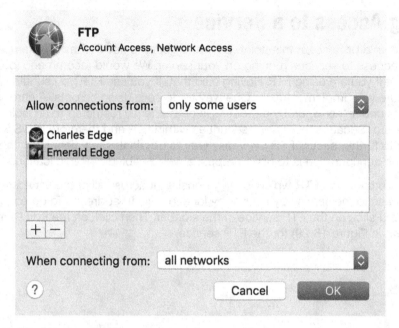

Figure 16-30. Limiting Access to a Service

Once you're satisfied with who will be able to access the FTP service on your server (or another service if you choose to limit access in this manner to other services), click on the OK button.

DNS Best Practices

Over the years, DNS has had a variety of weaknesses. A common reason for these vulnerabilities is improper security configurations of DNS servers. But most recently there have been attacks against even the best-defended servers. Some of these attacks seem fairly innocuous, such as the act of gaining useless information about an environment, while other attacks have been known to forward data through the DNS responder to arbitrarily execute commands. We suggest keeping public-facing DNS on a server outside your environment (with your registrar perhaps) so that other servers can find your domain for mail and web services while not exposing your environment to hacks.

A good number of other services require DNS to function properly, such as Open Directory, Mail Server, and some Apache modules. If the DNS service is overloaded, other services on other servers that use that DNS service will have problems, and also potentially crash. Therefore, we suggest you maintain a separate internal DNS infrastructure that is not accessible from outside your network. It is also strongly suggested that you customize the resources that the DNS service has available to it using sandbox, a means of separating different running services on your server (more on sandbox in Chapter 6).

> **Note**   To ease administration woes, Apple and Microsoft both suggest naming your internal domain something other than what you use for your public presence. Although this may cause more administrative burden, maintaining separate domain names does generally increase the security of your server environment.

> **Tip**   As with all services, you should maximize logging for DNS. To do so, open Server Admin, and click DNS. Then click Settings, and click Logging. Then set your Log Level for the service to Debug.

SSL

Implementing an SSL certificate on your server to encrypt traffic on OS X Server is an essential security precaution to take if you are going to enable most any service (especially for mail, web and collaborative services). If you want to purchase a certificate rather than use a self-signed certificate (including the one installed by default), open the Server app and click on Certificates in the sidebar. Then, click on the plus sign (+) to create a signing request, choosing Get a Trusted Certificate… from the list of options. At the "Get a Trusted Certificate" screen, click on the Next button. At the Get a Trusted Certificate, provide a name for the site in the Host Name field, an email address for the administrator of the server in the Contact Email Address field, and the name of the organization in the "Company or Organization" field, as you can see in Figure 16-31.

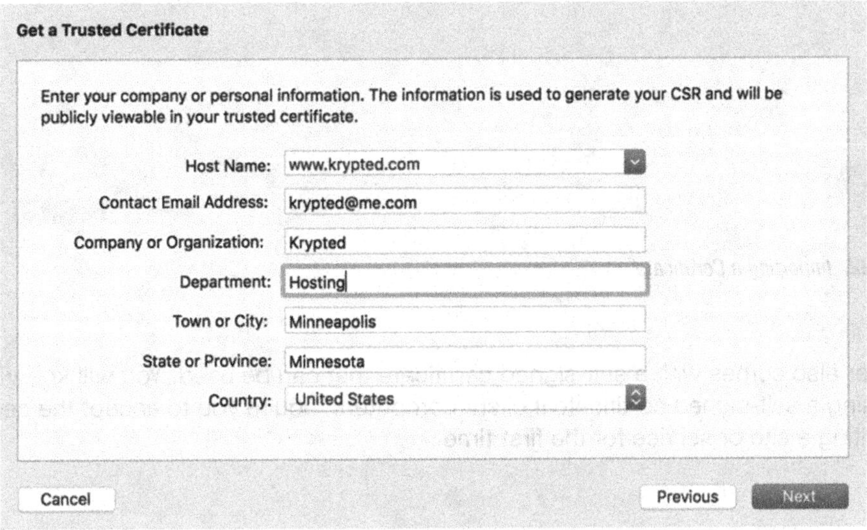

Figure 16-31. Certificate information

You will also need to fill in the Department field, which contains the name of the department the certificate is for (if you are an organization of 1, this won't be a big deal), the City the organization is in, the State the organization is in and the country the organization is in. Click Next when you're satisfied with these settings.

You will then see a bunch of really random looking text. Copy this into your clipboard and then go to a trusted CA, such as Thawte or Godaddy. From there, purchase the certificate and when prompted for a "CSR" provide the next we just copied into the clipboard.

The certificate then shows as pending. Once you receive back a certificate from the CA, use this same screen that shows a list of certificates to click on the certificate you'd like to sign and at the screen shown, drag the certificate from the CA into the Certificate Files section of the screen, shown in Figure 16-32.

Figure 16-32. Importing a Certificate

The server also comes with a self-signed certificate that can be used. You will know that you're using a self-signed certificate if client computers require you to accept the certificate when visiting a site or service for the first time.

Reimporting Certificates

If you need to re-import your certificate, you will need to convert it to a PEM certificate by running the command:

```
openssl x509 -in your.domain.com.cer -inform DER -out
    server.krypted.com.crt -outform PEM
```

Open the resulting .crt file in a text editor and copy the contents. Then, from Server Admin, choose Add Signed or Renewed Certificate from Certificate Authority, and paste the contents in from the previous step. Next your certificate should show that it has been signed by your CA (if you are using serveradmin on the same machine as your certificate server, then the certificate should be trusted as well).

SSH

OS X Server ships with the ssh service automatically enabled. This service, by default, will allow connections on port 22 by any authenticated user known to the server. This has many security implications, such as the ability for standard accounts to run services on ports 1024 and higher. This means that by default any user of your server has the ability to start a proxy or traffic redirector (such as the Internet relay chat client Bouncer) without admin authorization.

Firewall safeguards should prevent remote access to those services, but even in a full firewall lock down, if port 22 is open, there are still many vectors that an attacker with user credentials could use to cause mischief and mayhem, so disable ssh unless you plan to use it. If you use it, make sure to secure it as described in Chapter 15. An example of this type of exploit of ssh would be the ability for users to send large quantities of spam e-mail through the default mail (postfix) system. Spammers controlling compromised systems often use this technique to send large quantities of unsolicited e-mail.

If you are not using ssh to manage servers, disable ssh in the Server app by clicking the server name in the sidebar, then clicking the Settings tab, and finally unchecking the SSH box, as done in Figure 16-33. If you leave ssh enabled, configure service access controls in the Server app by clicking on Access for Users or Groups and then selecting who has access to login through SSH.

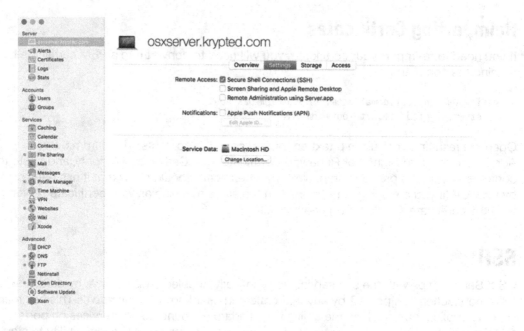

Figure 16-33. Disable SSH

> **Note**   As mentioned in the SACLs section earlier in this chapter, you cannot create an Open
> Directory replica when SSH is disabled. Once the replica is created, then SSH can be disabled, but
> for the replica creation process, it will need to be enabled.

You can also increase security of the SSH daemon by limiting older encryption protocol
versions that have known exploits and by restricting access to certain groups. You can do
this by editing /etc/ssh/ssh_config to include the following lines:

```
Protocol 2
PermitRootLogin no
```

Then type the following:

```
sudo dseditgroup -o edit -a <USERNAME> -t user com.apple.access_ssh sudo
    killall -HUP sshd
```

The serveradmin Command Line Interface

OS X Server is a strange beast. On the surface, it's the greatest gift known to sysadmins, granting admins the ability to perform all kinds of complicated configurations quickly through a nice GUI. It can also dismay many of us who know where Unix-specifics live in the operating system and would prefer to configure things there. So, where are all those settings that override so many of the default Unix configuration files? serveradmin is the command that gives access to much of what you see in the Server app, as well as what you don't see graphically.

To see all the services you can configure and view, use the command serveradmin list. Or use the serveradmin settings vpn command and check the settings applied to the firewall service. serveradmin use starts out with viewing data on a specific service. For example, type sudo serveradmin fullstatus vpn to see a full status on the settings and use of the VPN service. Then use the command serveradmin start vpn, followed by a serveradmin stop vpn. Stopping and starting services on a server using the command line is incredibly helpful as you can actually issue these commands over an SSH session rather than needing to use a remote management utility such as ARD (Apple Remote Desktop) to connect. This can become invaluable when a bad firewall rule locks you, the admin, out of the Server Admin tool. Just issue a serveradmin stop ipfilter command, and you're right back in!

You can also configure settings that aren't available in the GUI. For example, we'll use VPN to customize where we put our logs.

First, type sudo serveradmin settings vpn. Now, look for the following entry:

```
vpn:Servers:com.apple.ppp.pptp:PPP:Logfile = "/var/log/ppp/vpnd.log"
```

To change this setting, type the following:

```
Serveradmin settings vpn:Servers:com.apple.ppp.pptp:PPP:Logfile =
"/var/log/ppp/pptpvpnd.log"
```

Now the PPTP logs will be stored in a separate location than the logs for the rest of the VPN service. This can be done only using the serveradmin command and not with a configuration file. Nifty, huh?

To see all of the useful things that can be done with the serveradmin command, we suggest running a man command on serveradmin.

Messages Server

Instant messaging is one of the cornerstones of modern corporate communication, and it doesn't show any signs of slowing down. With its heavy presence in the modern workplace, it has become very common for business-related communications to be sent over IM. However, because of its humble insecure consumer upbringings, these communications are often not encrypted at all. Many modern packet sniffers have plug-ins or filters specifically designed for tracking session data such as connection passwords and chat transcripts. Because of IM's prevalence and its potential for eavesdropping, securing your IM communication by way of an encrypted chat server should be a top priority.

The OS X Messages Server uses the XMPP protocol with an available option to enable SSL. You can use the default SSL certificate created when your OS X Server was first configured, or you can choose to import your own. If you opt not to purchase a SSL certificate from one of the public CAs, make sure to generate your own certificates for distribution to your clients, as covered in the previous section on SSL.

Customizing the welcome message to new users of your Messages Server is a fairly simple task, and from a security context it allows an administrator to push out an acceptable use policy for their Messages environment. For this, we'll cover the Jabber configuration because Jabber is the open source package on which Messages Server is built.

When you first set up Jabber, the /etc/jabber directory will be created. Inside this folder is a file called jabber.xml. Open the jabber.xml file, and look for the welcome tag. Then, any data between "welcome" and "/welcome" will be the information that is shown in a welcome screen when a new user signs onto the iChat Server.

> **Tip**   Before you edit the /etc/jabber/jabber.xml file, make sure to back it up.

For this example, we will have all new users receive a message that says "Welcome to the Krypted chat Server."

To do this, delete or comment out the information between the existing welcome tags, and add the following information:

```
<welcome> <subject>to our iChat Server</subject> <body> Welcome to the Krypted
    chat Server</body> </welcome>
```

Save the jabber.xml file, and you've now customized the welcome message for your Messages Server.

Securing the Mail Server

The mail server in OS X Server has a few settings designed specifically for security. In Chapter 7 we discussed using the SpamAssassin and ClamAV features to limit mail that SpamAssassin and ClamAV identify as potentially sent from a spammer or system that has been infected with viruses. But what if your server is hijacked and set up as an open relay used to send spam? An *open relay* is a server that allows any user to relay mail through it. To verify your system isn't being used as an open relay, use the following command

```
sudo serveradmin settings mail:postfix:luser_relay_enabled
```

You should receive a "no" as a response to this command.

Limiting the Protocols on Your Server

To reduce the footprint of mail services, you should also limit the number of protocols in use on your server. To do so, you'll need to use the command line. For example, many environments will use only POP or IMAP. If you aren't using one of the two protocols, then disable the other. To disable pop:

```
sudo serveradmin settings mail:imap:enable_pop = yes
```

To disable imap:

```
sudo serveradmin settings mail:imap:enable_imap = yes
```

If you are using a protocol, then make sure that clear text passwords are not allowed. To disable clear text passwords for pop:

```
sudo serveradmin settings mail:imap:pop_auth_clear = yes
```

To disable clear text passwords for imap:

```
sudo serveradmin settings mail:imap:imap_auth_clear = yes
```

Finally, you can also disable hashes that you no longer need (check with each mail client you use to see which is required for your environment). The currently supported options are cram-md5, digest-md5, login and plain. To disable one, remove it from the smtpd_pw_server_security_options:_array_index array. For example, if mail:postfix:smtpd_pw_server_security_options:_array_index:3 = "plain" then you can use the following to remove plain:

```
sudo serveradmin settings mail:postfix:smtpd_pw_server_security_options:_array_index:3 = "plain"
```

After each of these commands, use the ON/OFF button in the service pane of the Server app to restart the mail service.

Summary

In a Mac client-server environment, you're only as secure as a properly configured server. With the knowledge of how to securely configuring file-sharing services, directory services, the root user, Kerberos, realms, mail services and the myriad other capabilities of your OS X Server, you have yet another weapon in your arsenal to defend your networked environment against attacks. Now, let's turn to the next line of defense: network intrusion detection and prevention.

Securing the Workplace

## Chapter 17

Network Scanning, Intrusion Detection, and Intrusion Prevention Tools

Would your network withstand an attack? How easy would it be for someone to break into your network, find anything they want on your Mac, and steal enough information to masquerade as you on the Internet? To answer this question, you'd need to take a good hard look at your network and audit for intrusion vulnerabilities. Imagine having to catalog all the programs, files, and services that run on your Mac, cross-referencing each program and file extension on the Internet, one at a time, against all the known exploits. This auditing process would take a considerable amount of time. Unfortunately, hackers have easy access to a wide variety of auditing tools, and already have a good idea of which exploits to look for. Thankfully, the very same auditing software can help you expedite the process of keeping them out.

This is not to say you shouldn't be mindful of open ports, listening services, and the daily activities of a computer when analyzing security on a machine. You should be. Keep in mind, however, that each item that represents a security risk will need to be handled separately. The more time you can save in the actual audit of a computer, the quicker you will be able to secure the items that are flagged as a security threat. In this chapter, we'll cover the types of scans that hackers and auditors are likely to employ and how to use auditing software to counteract them.

Scanning Techniques

White-box testing is a methodology used when the auditor has full knowledge of the target environment. If you know all the relevant network information about the environment, such as the IP address of each system and what types of computers and network appliances exist, then you do not have to perform any discovery and can move straight into attempting to exploit systems or document threats.

Black-box testing assumes that the person auditing the network knows nothing about the environment. Because security information about an environment can be difficult to obtain, black-box testing should be conducted to assess security threats in the environment. If you're new to the environment, the first step in black-box testing is to understand what kind of information an attacker might be able to obtain. Once you have a full understanding of an environment, the techniques then become similar to those used in white-box testing. For the discovery portion of black-box testing, you can use a variety of techniques, which generally fall into two categories: active or passive scanning.

Active scanning involves targeted probing of a network or a specific host, trying to ferret out vulnerabilities. Many attackers will avoid active scanning, because it will often leave traces in the target system's logs, making their activities easier to trace. Active scanning methods include using a port scanner to find open ports, testing web applications for weak passwords or insecure code, or sending web links to users in the hope that they will visit a web site that will log their IP address and information that might identify potential attack vectors. Active scanning is easily detected as most of these are blatant and high-speed probes. You can then block offending addresses based on the malicious detection.

Passive scanning uses less intrusive means of observation, so as not to leave indications that a scan is taking place. Passive scanning requires much more patience, because the techniques are rather investigative in nature. Searching newspapers and job boards for specific technologies will give indications of what technologies are being used. Requests for assistance on a vendor's support page or a mailing list will tell an attacker not only what technologies are in use, but what problems the users are having, and potentially very detailed information about what solutions are being implemented. You may also be able to gather information about the staff responsible for the network. When looking for information that could be used against an organization, the search must be comprehensive, often including chat rooms, the whois database, newsgroups, web sites, mailing list archives, and the target user or company's web site. A company web site can even give an attacker usernames, e-mail addresses, and the location of CGI scripts on web servers. Sometimes there will even be passwords discovered, or at least hints as to password policies. To help reduce the amount of information about your organization that is on the Web, consider routinely using Google to search for information that is available about your organization. There are a number of advanced Google search operators that make it easier to narrow your search. For example, A search for `site:mysite.com filetype:doc` will return all indexed Word Documents on your site.

Fingerprinting

Fingerprinting is the practice of gathering as much information as possible about your systems or network and using that information to positively identify the hardware and software in use. The goal is to get as much information as possible about a network or host's security, including its remote access capabilities, vulnerable services, and open ports. Successfully attacking a system depends on having this information. Tools that can be used in fingerprinting include general-purpose tools such as host, dig and traceroute, and specialized tools like nmap and Ethereal.

The easiest and safest way to go about finding information about a company is to use publicly available information. This includes researching and collecting phone numbers, addresses, press releases, SEC filings, and other seemingly innocuous information. Company blogs are wonderful mediums for discussing technology, but they can also be a great resource from which to extract information about a company's infrastructure. Many companies post a great deal of information about themselves on their web site, including information about the systems they have deployed, the revisions of services running on these systems, and the security solutions used to protect these services. A lot of this information can be very useful to hackers.

Let's fingerprint the site `apress.com` to find out as much as we can about our publisher. We can hopefully assume that, as a publisher of books on network security, they maintain good security practices.

According to whois, the domain was registered in 1998. The DNS Servers are on Rackspace. We can glean from this that the web servers are also probably hosted on Rackspace. The current registrar for the domain is Network Solutions. Sometimes you can see the name of the person that registered the domain, as well as the technical contact for the domain; however, as you can see in Figure 17-1, this is becoming much more rare than it used to be.

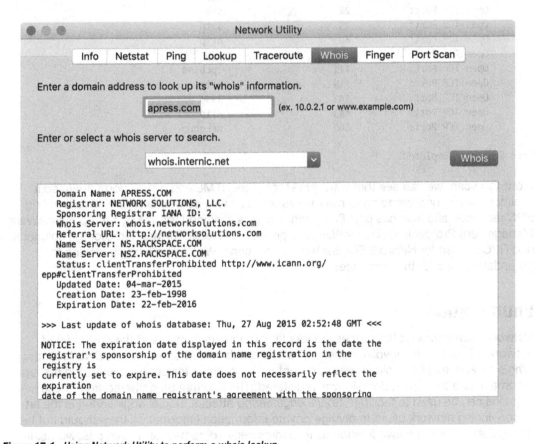

Figure 17-1. Using Network Utility to perform a whois lookup

Next, let's find the IP address of `www.apress.com`. The host command performs both forward and reverse DNS lookups. Running it on `www.apress.com` returns the IP address `207.97.243.208`. Running host on the IP address returns NXDOMAIN, which means there's no reverse DNS mapping for that address. Running whois on the IP address reveals that the address belongs to Rackspace, which confirms that Rackspace is where the site is hosted.

A cornerstone of fingerprinting is port scanning. Apple has provided a built-in port scanner with OS X, under the Port Scan tab of the Network Utility application (located in the `/Applications/Utilities` folder) Later in this chapter we will review nmap, a far more capable port-scanning utility. For now, open Network Utility, and click the Port Scan tab. Then, type `www.apress.com` in the search box, and let's see what services are running on that computer by clicking the Scan button. The most common and important services use the lower-numbered ports, so we'll limit our scan to only ports between 1 and 1000. Our results are as follows:

```
Port Scan has started...

Port Scanning host: 66.211.109.45

        Open TCP Port:          21              ftp
        Open TCP Port:          22              ssh
        Open TCP Port:          25              smtp
        Open TCP Port:          80              http
        Open TCP Port:          110             pop3
        Open TCP Port:          111             rpcbind
        Open TCP Port:          119             nntp
        Open TCP Port:          143             imap
        Open TCP Port:          443             https
        Open TCP Port:          688             unknown

Port Scan has completed...
```

From this scan, we can see that `www.apress.com` has HTML and e-mail ports open, so it is either running or pretending to run mail services as well as web services. It's accepting RPC requests, and also has port 688 open, which is assigned for use by the ApplianceWare Management Protocol. ApplianceWare is a provider of Network Attached Storage solutions, and RPC is used for Network File System connections. We can now begin looking for potential exploits for these services.

Enumeration

Network enumeration is the process of identifying domain names and their associated networks. Enumeration involves querying whois databases and performing DNS lookups. Whois databases often hold names and contact information for people involved in managing a domain, and the date a domain was registered. The information gathered from these inquiries can be used to facilitate *Social engineering* attacks. Social engineering is the art of convincing network users to divulge private information (information they should not be giving out) about the network, such as IP addresses, usernames, and even passwords. In some cases, a lucky (or skillful) attacker only needs to ask a user nicely for their password.

> **Note**   DNS zone transfers are used to pass DNS information between DNS servers. Many environments are mistakenly configured to allow untrusted hosts to perform a DNS zone transfer, which means that any machine masquerading as a DNS server can request a zone transfer in order to obtain DNS information. You can find a wide variety of tools on the Internet that can be used to perform DNS interrogation. For more information on DNS security, see Chapter 16.

Vulnerability and Port Scanning

Scanning can be performed on a single host or a whole network. Scanning with a vulnerability scanner allows you to rapidly review your computer and the computers on your network for known security holes such as outdated software. You can then move on to penetration testing, which typically starts by going a step beyond scanning and into using automated tools that attempt to exploit vulnerabilities.

Be very careful when trying to access any open ports you may find. Brute-forcing an FTP or a web server can land you in a pile of trouble. As a rule of thumb, if attempting to access a service requires a password, you probably shouldn't be there. In fact, in some jurisdictions, accessing a resource without permission is illegal, even when it is configured to allow anonymous access. However, if you access something important and the system doesn't ask you for a password, then this is a problem that should be resolved immediately. Further, you should issue a stern warning that any unauthorized access will be prosecuted.

nmap

Nmap is a network exploration tool that can be installed on OS X from `nmap.org`. It is one of the most valuable tools for a security engineer or penetration tester (someone who attempts to break into a system in order to test its security). It is, as its name suggests, a network mapping tool. With nmap, you can probe an entire network and discover which services are listening on each specific port on every workstation, server, and router accessible. Nmap can also perform operating system fingerprinting. By comparing different fingerprints, nmap gives users an educated guess as to the operating system a target machine is running.

For this section, we'll be using nmap to run scans. The binary can be downloadd and installed from `https://nmap.org/book/inst-macosx.html`.

Nmap is very flexible, and offers a lot of options or flags that let you perform a wide variety of scans. For example, you can perform a TCP `connect()` scan (which initiates a full connection to the host) or a SYN scan (also known as a *half connection*). You can test firewall rules and distinguish whether you are scanning a firewall or a packet filter. You can also throw out decoys to make your real address harder to trace. Table 17-1 describes the nmap options for the actual binary command. The proper usage of nmap includes the following:

```
nmap [Scan Type] [Options] <target(s)>
```

Table 17-1. *Common Scanning Options*

Option	Description
-sO	Scan for supported IP protocols rather than open ports.
-sS	TCP SYN stealth port scan (default if running as root).
-sT	TCP connect() port scan (default for nonroot users).
-sU	UDP port scan.
-sP	Ping scan (find any reachable machines).
-O	Use TCP/IP fingerprinting to guess remote operating system.
-p <range>	Define ports to scan. Example range: 1-80, 8010, 8080, 10000.
-F	Scans only ports listed in nmap-services to speed up scans.
-v	Verbose. Its use is recommended. Use twice for greater effect.
-PN	Don't ping hosts before scanning (needed to scan www.microsoft.com and others).
-D decoy_host1, decoy2[,...]	Hide scan using decoys.
-6	Scans via IPv6 rather than IPv4.
-T <timing>	General timing policy. Settings are Paranoid, Sneaky, Polite, Normal, Aggressive, Insane.
-n/-R	Do not use DNS resolution/always resolve (the default is to sometimes resolve).
-oN/-oX/-oG <logfile>	Output normal/XML/grepable scan logs to <logfile>.
-iL<inputfile>	Get targets from file; use - for stdin.
-S <your_IP>/-e <devicename>	Specify source address or network interface.

Here's an example:

```
nmap -v -sS -O www.krypted.com 10.0.0.0/16 '10.0.*.*'
```

The stealthiest and most widely used nmap-scanning method is SYN scanning, also known as *half open* or *stealth scanning*. There are a couple of downsides to using this method. Unfortunately, most intrusion detection systems (described more later in this chapter) can detect these packets, and some firewalls and packet filtration mechanisms will drop SYN packets, which make it harder to get an accurate list of what ports on the host are open.

With a SYN/stealth scan, you do not actually make a full connection with the host. It will send a SYN packet and request a connection. The host being scanned then responds with a SYN/ACK packet informing you about whether the port is open and responding. As soon as you receive the SYN/ACK packet from the remote host, nmap sends one RST packet terminating the connection. It does not make a full connection or three-way handshake (full connection), which is why SYN/stealth scanning is called a *half open scan*.

Running a SYN/Stealth Scan

Here is what an nmap SYN/stealth scan would typically look like. First, we initialize the scan with the following Terminal command, assuming we are scanning a system with the IP address of 192.168.210.5:

```
nmap -sS 192.168.210.5
```

This command results in the following output:

```
Starting Nmap 5.21 ( http://nmap.org ) at 2015-08-29 20:15 PST
Nmap scan report for 192.168.210.5
Host is up (0.018s latency).
Not shown: 985 closed ports
PORT        STATE     SERVICE
22/tcp      open      ssh
88/tcp      open      kerberos-sec
139/tcp     open      netbios-ssn
445/tcp     open      microsoft-ds
515/tcp     filtered  printer
631/tcp     open      ipp
777/tcp     filtered  unknown
1063/tcp    filtered  unknown
3306/tcp    open      mysql
3689/tcp    open      rendezvous
5100/tcp    filtered  admd
5900/tcp    open      vnc
12000/tcp   filtered  cce4x
60443/tcp   filtered  unknown
MAC Address: 00:0D:93:83:F3:B0 (Apple Computer)

Nmap done: 1 IP address (1 host up) scanned in 5.99 seconds
```

> **Note**   A filtered port, such as the port 515 in the previous scan, usually indicates the machine is running a firewall.

Here is a log of a stealth SYN scan from an intrusion detection system called snort (we will discuss intrusion detection systems, including snort, later in the chapter):

```
[**] [111:13:1] spp_stream4: STEALTH ACTIVITY (SYN FIN scan) detection [**]
09/21-19:18:03 10.0.0.4:80 -> 10.0.0.8:88
TCP TTL:255 TOS:0x0 ID:2304 IpLen:20 DgmLen:42
******SF Seq: 0x90AB763  Ack: 0x0  Win: 0x1000  TcpLen: 20
9-21 19:18:04 10.0.0.4:80 -> 192.168.0.8: 88 SYN ******S*
```

As you can see by the warning message, snort has built a rule set that is able to identify nmap's SYN/stealth scanning sequence.

Other nmap Scans

Nmap scans can be limited to specific criteria. For example, if you wanted to scan only UDP ports 1 through 80 on a server using the IP address 10.0.0.4, you would use the following command:

```
nmap -sU -p 1-80 10.0.0.4
```

If you only wanted to find out what addresses actually have machines responding, you can skip the actual port scan and simply send a ping. This is commonly called a *ping sweep*. For the whole 10.0.0.1-254 network, you would use this command:

```
nmap -sP 10.0.0.0/16
```

Using the -O flag, nmap can also identify many operating systems, based on how the target responds to a large number of tests. The results of a scan are compared against a large database of known OS fingerprints. Nmap can often identify an operating system even when very few services are running.

Scanning a network for vulnerabilities is only one piece of the network intrusion pie. We must now make steps to secure the weaknesses that our scans have uncovered. So that we aren't overlooking anything, we should first look for intrusion instances that may have already been attempted and then implement measures to prevent future attempts.

Intrusion Detection and Prevention

In information security, *intrusion detection* is the practice of detecting attempts (successful as well as unsuccessful) to compromise a network resource. Intrusion detection does not usually involve the prevention of intrusions; however, we will discuss some preventive measures that can work in tandem with intrusion detection. With any intrusion detection solution, it is important that it somehow alerts you to potential intrusions so that you can determine whether your security was actually compromised, allowing you to act swiftly in order to limit the damage. Once you've mitigated the damage, you can examine what the attack vector was, investigate whether it was done maliciously, and then take measures to prevent future intrusions based on this information.

Host-based Intrusion Detection System

The purpose of a host intrusion detection system is to monitor and analyze a system in such a way that an administrator can determine whether a change has occurred on a system. Most host-based intrusion detection systems focus on checking for changes to configuration files or folders containing binary files (applications).

Tripwire

Tripwire is an intrusion detection system that is used to track changes to the files on a computer. Tripwire can scan for files on computers by creating a checksum of the files and folders on a system, and then comparing that against a checksum created at installation time. This enables a fast scan of a variety of files and folders on a computer. Regular Tripwire scans will alert system administrators of changes to the file system that shouldn't be made.

You shouldn't be able to edit some of these locations due to SIP restrictions. However, some folders we recommend scanning regularly still include the following:

```
/dev
/opt
/usr
/usr/sbin
/bin
/mach.kern
/Library/Preferences
/Library/FileSystems
/etc
/System/Library/Extensions
/System/Library/CoreServices
```

Tripwire Installation

The simplest method of installing Tripwire is to first install MacPorts. MacPorts is a package management tools that allows for easy installation of software from a large repository of open source projects. To install Tripwire from MacPorts, you would use the port command.

```
sudo port install tripwire
```

After installation is finished, run the tripwire configuration script. This will create the necessary configuration files and passphrases, and then sign the configuration files with those passphrases.

```
sudo /opt/local/etc/tripwire/twsetup.sh
```

When that's finished, you need to define the baseline state of the computer.

```
sudo tripwire --init
```

To update your Tripwire database after making system changes, run this command:

```
sudo tripwire -m u -r /opt/var/db/tripwire/report/day-month-year-initials.twr
```

To update your Tripwire config, change the /opt/local/etc/twcfg.txt file, and run this command:

```
sudo twadmin -m F -S /opt/local/etc/tripwire /site.key /opt/local/etc/tripwire/twcfg.txt
```

To enforce a new policy, edit the `/opt/local/etc/tripwire/twpol.txt` file, and run this command:

```
sudo twadmin -m p > /opt/local/etc/tripwire/twpol.txt
```

To view Tripwire reports, run this command:

```
sudo twprint -m r -r /opt/local/var/db/tripwire/report/*.twr
```

To scan for changes that have been made to the system, run this command:

> **Note**   A `.twr` file is a Tripwire report file.

```
sudo tripwire -m c
```

To e-mail these changes to the e-mail address listed in the config file, if you have identified an e-mail address, run the following command:

```
sudo tripwire -m c -M
```

Bear in mind that Tripwire will not be able to restore any modified files that it finds. This is another reason that proper backups are important.

Network Intrusion Detection

Host-based intrusion detection scans the system for changes. But it is also possible to use a network intrusion detection system (NIDS), which can scan the network interface of systems to identify traffic patterns based on signatures of known exploits. One example of a popular NIDS application is snort.

Snort from the Command Line

Snort is an open source network intrusion detection and prevention system that is capable of packet logging and real-time traffic analysis. Proprietary solutions that include integrated hardware and support services are sold by Sourcefire, and there are hundreds of additional rule sets and downloads available to extend the snort platform.

Snort can perform protocol analysis along with content matching, and it is often used to help detect attacks and probes. But it's mainly used as a means of finding existing threats to your network infrastructure. Some of the attacks that snort can detect include buffer overflows, stealthy port scans (such as those stemming from nmap), specific CGI attacks, SMB probes, and OS fingerprinting techniques. Snort can also be used for intrusion prevention by dropping attacks as they are taking place or augmenting your firewall to block future attempts from flagged IP addresses. SnortSnarf, sguil, OSSIM, and the Basic Analysis and Security Engine (BASE) help administrators effectively analyze the mountains of data generated by snort.

> **Note**   Snort patches that can be configured to work with antivirus scanning within ClamAV are available from Emerging Threats (www.emergingthreats.net). Any potential threats are isolated into signatures. These signatures are network traffic patterns that are then recorded. When future traffic comes through the network interface that matches these signatures, snort will perform the action that it is configured to perform (more on configuring these later in this section).

The easiest way to install snort is to use MacPorts.

```
sudo port install snort
```

Once it's installed, snort can immediately be run in sniffer mode or packet logger mode, both of which will give you a real-time view of the traffic on your network. Create a folder in your home directory called snortlogs, and then run the following command:

```
sudo snort –dev –l ~/snortlogs
```

This will run snort in logger mode. All the traffic that snort can see will be captured to file in snortlogs for later review.

In order to run snort in NIDS mode, you will need to install rules that snort can match traffic against. To install rules, you need to make a place for snort settings files, rules, and logs:

```
sudo mkdir –p  /var/log/snort
```

Go to the snort rules page at http://www.snort.org, download the latest snort rules package, and unzip it. In order to download rules, you'll need to register as a user with snort.org or use the community rules available at https://snort.org/downloads/#rule-downloads. Once you've unzipped the rules:

```
cd <snort-rules-download-dir>/rules
sudo cp rules/* /opt/local/etc/snort/rules
sudo cp etc/* /opt/local/etc/snort/etc
```

> **Note**   If you are using the community rules, the path the downloaded rules are copied into will be community-rules instead of rules.

Copy the default snort.conf.dist sample file to snort.conf. Keep the original as a failsafe:

```
cd /opt/local/etc/snort
sudo cp snort.conf snort.conf.orig
```

Now it's time to fire up snort and test it. If you have installed snort, then the first thing you will want to do is run the following command to initialize snort:

```
sudo /opt/local/bin/snort –c /opt/local/etc/snort/snort.conf
```

After the initialization information is displayed, you will see live packet capture information on the Terminal screen if you are connected to a network. Now kill the snort foreground process by pressing Ctrl+C to take a look at the summary information. You should be ready to roll if you see packet captures that resemble Figure 17-2.

> **Note**   For official snort training, see `www.sourcefire.com/services/education/`.

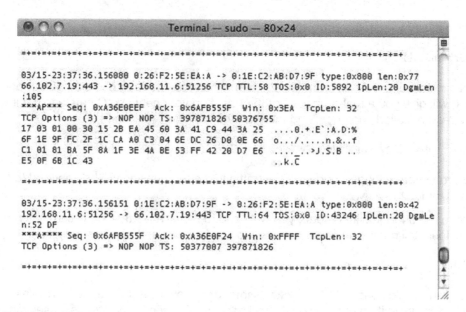

Figure 17-2. Packet capture

> **Note**   snort has no mechanism to update rules automatically. To keep snort updated, you should add a script to your weekly or monthly periodic tasks that will download the current rules.

Honeypots

A *honeypot* is a trap set by a network administrator to detect, deflect, or even attract attempts at unauthorized use of the network. Generally, it consists of a computer, data repository, or network resource that appears to be part of a network, containing information valuable to attackers, but is actually isolated and monitored by the network admins.

Honeypots are valuable surveillance and early-warning tools. Honeypots should have no production value, and should not see any legitimate traffic or activity. They should in no way be connected to actual production networks, and should not be running any production services. Whatever they capture can then be assumed to be malicious or unauthorized. For example, honeypots designed to thwart spam by masquerading as zombie systems can categorize the material they trap 100%accurately: it is all illicit. A honeypot needs no spam-recognition capability and no filter to separate ordinary e-mail from spam. Ordinary e-mail should never come to a honeypot.

Implemented improperly, honeypots can easily be leveraged as Denial and Deception (D&D) hosts. Therefore, be careful when deploying a honeypot in your environment, so there isn't a rogue point that can easily be leveraged as a Denial of Service host. A good strategy is to use a technology like Docker or nightly reimaging to deploy hosts, so they can easily be redeployed when needed. And scan them routinely, bringing them offline when possible. Finally, you can also host them on an external LAN to minimize the impact they can have on a production network.

Web traffic can be reviewed in the same manner. Create a script to put a file in a web directory that tells bots not to search the folder. If a bot then searches the folder, you can update the firewall configuration on that server to block future traffic from the IP address of the originating bot. This is a rudimentary form of a honeypot. MacPorts includes a port of honeyd, a small daemon that creates virtual hosts that appear to be running arbitrary services.

Honeypots can take on other forms, such as files or data records or even unused IP address space (for example, a file that is watched with verbose logging called payroll.xls). A collection of honeypots is known as a *honeynet*.

Security Auditing on the Mac

Several products on the market allow for vulnerability scanning and security auditing on the Mac. Some of them are freeware, and some of them are not. SAINT, Nessus, and Metasploit are our favorites for this critical piece of the security puzzle. Only Nessus and Metasploit are free products. Assume that an attacker will have a copy of each of these and much more advanced tools as well.

Nessus

Nessus is a comprehensive vulnerability scanner and analyzer, which is estimated to be used by more than 75,000 organizations. The core of Nessus is *nessusd*, the Nessus daemon, which performs the actual scanning. nessusd provides a web-based management interface.

Nessus begins by performing a port scan with its own internal port scanner (or it can optionally use nmap) to determine which ports are open on the target and then tries various exploits on the open ports. The vulnerability tests, available as a large body of plug-ins, are written in Nessus Attack Scripting Language (NASL), a scripting language optimized for custom network interaction.

Optionally, the results of the scan can be reported in various formats, such as plain text, XML, HTML, and LaTeX. The results can also be saved in a knowledge base for reference against future vulnerability scans. Scanning can be automated through the use of a command-line client by using the nessus command located in the /Library/Nessus/run/bin folder.

If the user chooses to do so (by disabling the option safe checks), some of Nessus's vulnerability tests may try to cause vulnerable services or operating systems to crash. This lets a user test the resistance of a device before putting it in production.

Nessus provides additional functionality beyond testing for known network vulnerabilities. For instance, it can use Windows credentials to examine patch levels on computers running the Windows operating system and can perform password auditing.

Installing Nessus

To install Nessus, go to the Tenable Network Security web site at `www.nessus.org`, and download the Nessus installer. You'll also need to register for a subscription. All of the audits performed by Nessus are coded as plug-ins. In order to download plug-ins, you'll need to register for either the HomeFeed or the ProfessionalFeed. The HomeFeed is free, but can only be used by home users. If you're planning on using Nessus for professional or government use, you'll need to purchase the ProfessionalFeed. When you register for a feed, an activation code will be emailed to you.

> **Note** An older version of `nessus` that does not require a registration key is available via MacPorts.

During the install, you have the option to choose whether you want the server to start when the system boots or whether you want to start it manually. If the system is a dedicated Nessus server, then you will want the Nessus daemon to launch at boot. Otherwise, it's better to launch manually as needed, especially if Nessus is installed on a laptop (it can be a sizeable resource hog).

After installation, launch the Nessus Server Manager application, enter your activation code and click Register. Once your copy of Nessus is registered, you'll be able to start the Nessus Server (see Figure 17-3).

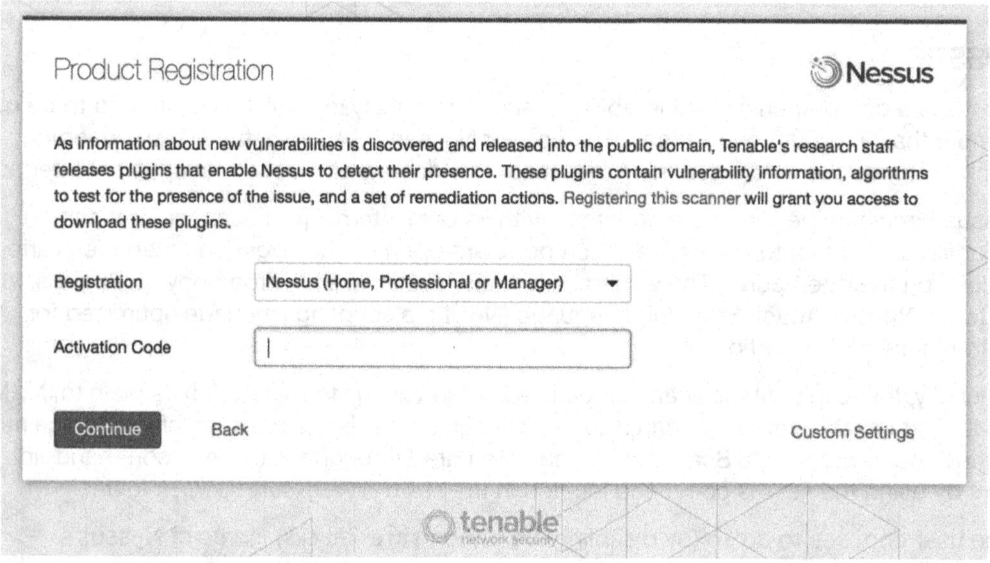

Figure 17-3. Starting the Nessus server

You'll be prompted to authenticate to the system once Nessus starts. Log in and you can then start using Nessus.

In order to scan a target, you'll need to define a *policy*. A scanning policy defines options like types of scan and range of ports to use, and also which plug-ins to use. Each plug-in typically corresponds to a specific vulnerability. Enabling fewer plug-ins will speed up scans, since the scanner will not take the time to perform disabled probes. For example, if you're scanning a Mac OS X Server system, you can probably disable the Cisco plug-in family.

To define a policy, click on Policies, and then click New Policy. At the list of policies, you can choose a template, or perform an Advanced scan. Click Basic Network Scan, as you can see in Figure 17-4.

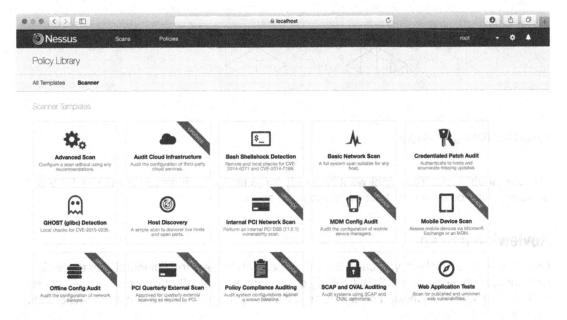

Figure 17-4. Defining a policy

Once you have defined a policy, you can create a scan and select your targets. There are multiple options for defining a target. To define your targets, click on Scans and then click on the New Scan button. At the New Scan screen, choose a scan type (as done in the policies section, click on Basic Network Scan. Then provide a name for the scan and enter a range of IP addresses in the Targets field (see Figure 17-5). Once you've entered the appropriate information, click on the Save button.

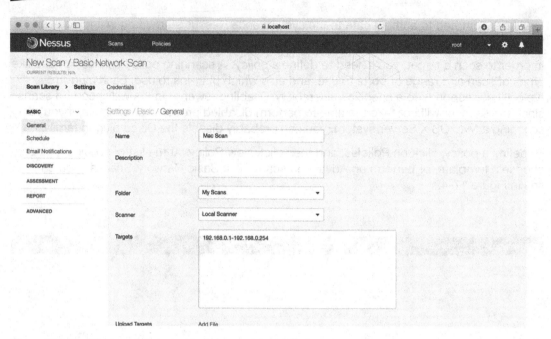

Figure 17-5. Defining your targets

The scan then starts. You might want to give it some time after the scan starts to let the scan complete. Obviously, it may take awhile to run a scan.

Reviewing a Scan

Once the scan is finished, you can click the Report tab to view the vulnerabilities available for your system (see Figure 17-6). Clicking on a scanned host will show you the open ports and running services. Clicking on a service will show you more details about the vulnerability as well as possible exploits.

Figure 17-6. Reviewing the Nessus report

You can export Nessus reports into HTML to make reviewing and saving them easy. There are companies that specialize in running automated scans of servers on behalf of institutions, such as credit card processors and insurance companies. These companies often simply rebrand a Nessus scan by replacing the images in the HTML exports. To export a scan, click the Export button in your report.

Metasploit

Metasploit is a free, open source framework that can be used to launch automated exploits to target known vulnerabilities. The Metasploit framework makes it easy for administrators to use these exploits to discover how vulnerable their network is.

You can download the latest version of Metasploit at `www.metasploit.com`. Download the latest version and you can run a scan on a Mac using Windows or Linux. There are also instructions to run Metasploit on a Mac available at `http://www.darkoperator.com/installing-metasploit-framewor/`.

Summary

If you want to keep your network and your systems secure, you should be mindful of the methods that potential intruders use and be aware of the attack vectors they will try to use. In this chapter, we reviewed some of the more common tools that are used to both enumerate and secure client systems. There are a lot of other tools out there. Take the time to understand the methods that attackers use and apply their techniques to your network, and you'll be better prepared to defend yourself from them.

Additionally, follow Bugtraq and RISKS digest daily and have all CERT advisories for OS X e-mailed to you when the advisories are issued. This will keep you informed on what is happening for the platforms that you support.

Chapter 18

Backup and Fault Tolerance

"Stop hackers dead in their tracks by securing your systems and network." That has been our mantra up to this point. However, there is another piece in the security pie that often goes unexamined. Any conversation about security on a system or network must go beyond discussing the prevention of unauthorized access and into what happens when an incident leaves you hating life. And we start that conversation with backup, because the capacity to recover data minimizes the potential impact of an attack. Securing the data on these systems with a reliable data backup scheme is a crucial element in any security framework.

As digital assets become increasingly valuable, organizations are becoming more and more reliant on their data. Many companies have invested large amounts of labor in building their company data. If they were to suffer a catastrophic loss of data (for some this could mean as little as 30%), due to the number of hours it would take to re-create that data, it would prove impossible to rebuild, and would simply cause them to go out of business. Therefore, backing up data is very important in any security footprint and critical in any organization.

When developing a backup schematic, you should answer some important questions that start with the following (there are more but this is a good start):

- What is the source data to be backed up?
- To what destination device is the data to be backed up?
- How far back in time will the backups need to go?

As we move through this chapter, we will examine how backups are performed for a variety of software packages. We will start by discussing the most simplistic backup topology and work our way up to more complicated backup schemas, including fault-tolerant solutions. This will allow you to see the increasing complexity and weigh it against your needs to eventually choose which is best for you. Once you have a backup solution that you trust, you should continue to refer to this chapter, because as your needs increase, so will the complexity of your backup topology. Backing up a computer is nothing more than a waste of time and equipment, right up until the time when it becomes critical to restore the data. Readers should get into the habit of testing their restoration process (and should document it if it's at all difficult) so that when the time comes, they know they can rely on their backups.

Time Machine

Time Machine is an application in OS X that allows you to back up your computer to a second hard drive (internal, external, over the network, etc) at set regular intervals. Time Machine is a straightforward application that is simple to configure. However, it is fairly limited in granularity and flexibility compared to many 3rd party software packages. The good thing is that Time Machine is installed by default on every new Mac, so you don't need to purchase any additional software. To set up disk-based backups using Time Machine, open the Time Machine Preference pane (see Figure 18-1).

Figure 18-1. Time Machine preference pane

Next, select the target device for your backups. This is where the data that is backed up on your computers is stored. To do so, click on the Select Backup Disk... button and then select the device you want to backup to. Also, if you'd like to encrypt the target disk, check the box for Encrypt backups. Once you are satisfied with your selection click the Choose Backup Disk button (see Figure 18-2).

Figure 18-2. Choosing the backup device

Once you have selected the target disk, the screen will change to reflect the critical statistics of your backup operations (see Figure 18-3). Here you will see the volume you are backing up to, how much available free space is on that volume, the date and time of both the oldest and most recent backups, and when the next backup is scheduled. For many smaller backup environments, this information is the most crucial to track.

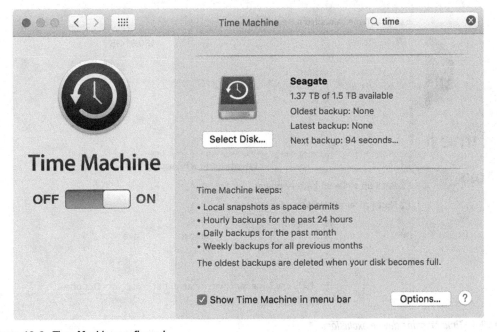

Figure 18-3. Time Machine configured

> **Note**   Knowing which volume you are backing up to means that you know where additional copies of your data are. Sure this increases availability, but the backed up file now needs the same protection from theft and tampering that you applied to the "master" version. This is an important (and to many people, surprising) point: adding security countermeasures doesn't make a system more secure, it makes it differently secure. You have to consider risks affecting those countermeasures, which wasn't the case before they were deployed.

On this screen, you can also click the Select Disk button at any time to change the destination of your backups. This will allow you to fill up a disk and then move to the next disk in your backup scheme. Multiple disks can give you a deep historical backup set of your data, which is crucial if collecting multiple versions of files is important to your backup strategy.

> **Note**   Unfortunately the Time Machine workflow doesn't really support recovery from multiple disks, so different versions of files will end up strewn across the disks with no central catalogue to tie them together.

You can also set what data on your computer will not be backed up. By default, Time Machine will back up all the data on your computer's hard drive. To limit what is backed up, click the Options button, and you will be presented with the "Exclude these items from backup" window (Figure 18-4). Here you can specify which items are to be excluded from the backup sets.

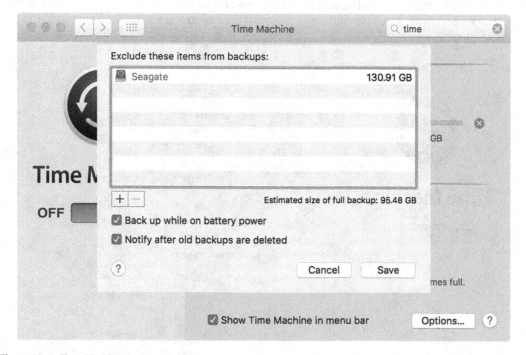

Figure 18-4. Time Machine device exclusions

Next, if you click the plus (+) button, you will be able to browse to folders that are not worth the space to back up. For example, most users do not need to back up the following directories unless they plan to do a "bare-metal" restore (a restore from a hard drive crash without reinstalling the operating system):

- /Applications
- /Library
- /System

Invisible items (which are accessible by unchecking the Show Invisible Items check box) include the following:

- /.Spotlight-V100
- /.Trashes
- /bin
- /opt
- /private
- /sbin
- /var
- /Network

> **Note**   To view the files that are not backed up by default, check the information listed in the file /System/Library/CoreServices/backupd.bundle/Contents/Resources/ StdExclusions.plist.

Which data are backed up is really dictated by your personal backup strategy. Some feel comfortable backing up the whole machine. For others, just backing up the /Users folder is sufficient because that is where the bulk of the irreplaceable data is stored.

> **Note**   If you have been following along with the other chapters, you will now have a heavily modified OS configuration. Having a strategy to replace your chosen configuration and application set is a fundamental aspect of reactive security, and backing the whole lot up with Time Machine is one way to achieve that.

Once you have selected all the items you are going to exclude, click the Exclude button (Figure 18-5), and the initial setup of your backup system will be complete. Time Machine will then run an incremental backup (backups of any files that have changed since the last backup) once an hour, every hour. According to how much data you have, the data can fill up your backup drive rather quickly, because every change to a file, big or small, will cause it to be copied to the Time Machine destination again. For this reason, we suggest Entourage databases not be backed up in Windows Exchange or IMAP environments where a database is backed up elsewhere, as is the case with many corporate environments. We also suggest reviewing the larger files on your systems and deciding whether you need to back them up. If they are changed often, then you will more than likely want to back them up, but educating yourself about the files that you are backing up can often be an eye-opener for you. Virtual machines are a good example. Choose whether to back up the virtual disk file (which is many gigabytes big and frequently changes), or run an incremental backup of the VM's filesystem from within the VM. Also, you should strongly consider investing in a rather large hard drive, 500GB at the minimum, but we often see 2TB drives as a good size for backups if you want historical backups of your data. If malware infected your system three hours ago and your only recovery option is a backup from one hour ago, then you can only recover to an infected configuration.

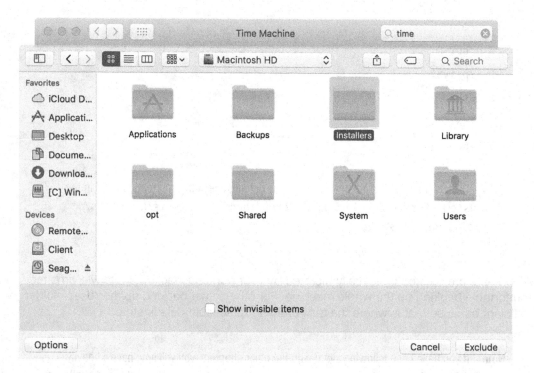

Figure 18-5. Excluding Directories with Time Machine

You can also disable Time Machine backups altogether. To do so, click the Time Machine preference pane, and use the slider to move the backup status to the Off position (see Figure 18-6).

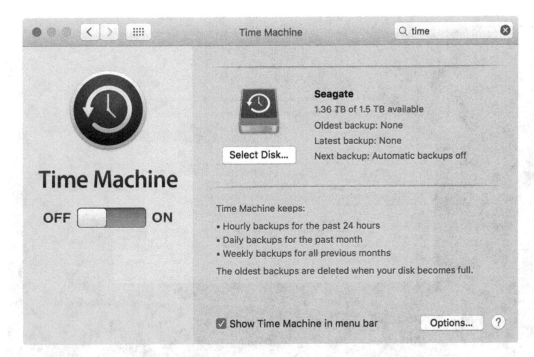

Figure 18-6. Turning Time Machine on or off

Restoring Files from Time Machine

To restore files from Time Machine backups, open Time Machine from the /Applications folder. When the Time Machine restoration utility opens, use the timeline on the right side of the screen to select the restore point you are going to restore to (see Figure 18-7). Next, browse to the file or folder you want to restore, and click the Restore button.

Figure 18-7. Time Machine Restore screen

You can also see the files that were backed up and restore files by browsing to the Backups. backupdb directory located on your target drive. Inside this directory, you will see a folder containing your computer's name. If you are backing up multiple computers to a single device, you will see multiple computer names in this directory. If you open these folders, you will see the date on which a backup was run and the files that were backed up at the time.

> **Note**   Backing up multiple systems to the same drive is putting all of your eggs in the same basket. Hard drives are cheap, but your data probably isn't.

Using a Network Volume for Time Machine

Time Machine is capable of performing backups over the network. These backups can be saved to a disk attached to an AirPort device using AirPort disk sharing, an AFP volume hosted by an OS X Server, a Time Machine server, or any other volumes to which your computer has access. To allow backups over a network volume, make sure the network volume is mounted, and simply select the network volume from the Change Disk menu option in the Time Machine configuration page, as mentioned earlier.

Apple officially supports using Time Capsule and Mac OS X Server share points with the Time Machine checkbox enabled for network backups only. However, if you want to use an unsupported network disk type for your Time Machine archives, such as a different type of server or a NAS appliance, running the following command on workstations will allow you to do so:

```
defaults write com.apple.systempreferences TMShowUnsupportedNetworkVolumes 1
```

SuperDuper

One of the easiest-to-use and most versatile third-party backup programs available for the Mac platform is SuperDuper, an application developed by David Nanian and available from www.shirt-pocket.com/SuperDuper. SuperDuper is more flexible than Time Machine and has more features. If you're willing to plunk down $30 for the software, you'll be given the extra ability to write custom backup scripts, schedule backups, and use sandboxing (a highly useful utility that backs the system up to a separate volume that can be used to boot the machine if it crashes).

After you've downloaded and installed SuperDuper, a configuration window opens that allows you to configure what data should be backed up and where it should be backed up to (see Figure 18-8).

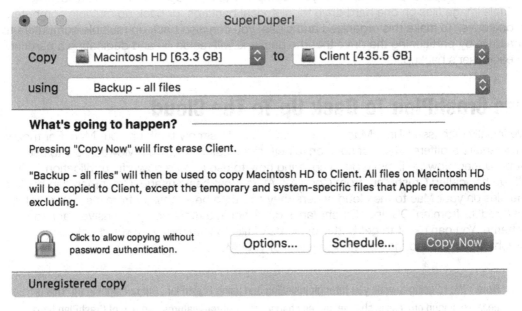

Figure 18-8. The SuperDuper configuration window

Using the default options will back up the entire hard drive. However, you may choose to back up only the /Users folder if you're not concerned with having to rebuild the operating system if the machine crashes, or if you don't fear an attack that might threaten the integrity of the operating system (see Figure 18-9).

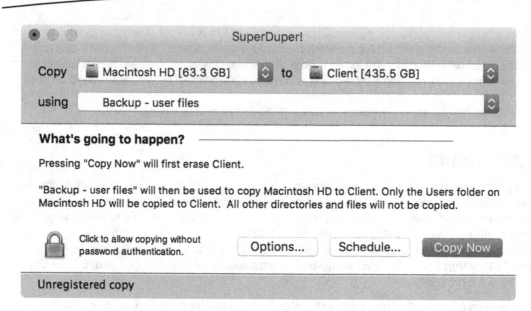

Figure 18-9. Backing up all files with SuperDuper

You can use SuperDuper to back up your computer to an image file. You can also store multiple image files on one hard drive for historical backups, or back up multiple computers to one drive. To make this organized and clean, you can also back up multiple computers to one drive by partitioning the drive that the backups will reside on and dedicating a partition to each user's backup.

Use CrashPlan To Back Up To The Cloud

We initially discussed Time Machine to explain how to simply back up your Mac. For those who require a different type of solution (albeit slightly different), we reviewed how to use SuperDuper. Now we'll move on to covering how to use a more powerful application altogether, called CrashPlan, from Code 42. At its most basic usage, CrashPlan can backup the files on your Mac to the cloud, where they can then be accessed from a system that is restored, or from an iOS app. CrashPlan is one layer in a more comprehensive backup scheme. You can use it to get better backups of files offsite, but you would not use CrashPlan to backup the operating system of your Mac.

> **Note** We're going to walk you through installing and using CrashPlan. But not signing up. This is because signup processes change, prices change, etc. But the features and use of CrashPlan have been pretty static for the past few years, so we feel comfortable showing how to do some standard tasks. Using other tools can be similar; our goal with this section is more to show what you can do with a tool like CrashPlan. Provided that a different tool does everything you want, the concepts should remain the same.

The first step to getting a functional CrashPlan deployment is to purchase and install the application, or use a trial. To do so, first sign up for an account at for CrashPlan from the Code 42 website at www.crashplan.com. Once you've signed up, download the latest version of CrashPlan using the Download Free button on the main screen, shown in Figure 18-10.

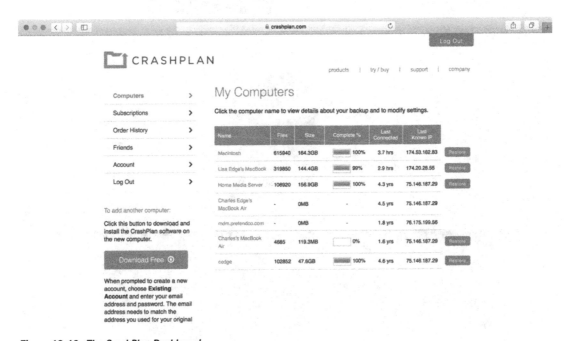

Figure 18-10. The CrashPlan Dashboard

While we're on this screen, before we start the download, notice that you have a very quick and easy view of the computers that I've backed up using my account. Here, you can see how much data I have on CrashPlan's servers, when the last time I did a backup of each, and start a restore of any data that is missing.

Once the CrashPlan download is complete, double-click on the installer, from the extracted disk image, as seen in Figure 18-11.

Figure 18-11. *Performing a standard installation*

At the Welcome to CrashPlan Installer screen, click Continue. Then, when prompted with the license agreement, click Continue (Figure 18-12) to agree to the license agreement or click on Go Back if you'd rather not agree to the license agreement. You can also save a copy of the agreement or print the agreement, for filing away in the future.

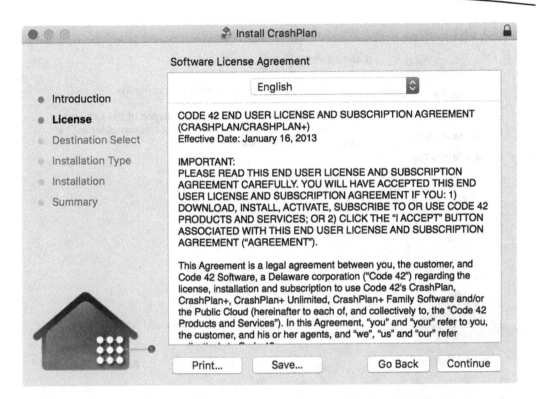

Figure 18-12. Accept the License Agreement

When prompted to verify that you accept the agreement, click Agree. Then, at the Installation Type screen, choose whether you would like to do a Standard Install (which installs the software in /Applications, as seen in Figure 18-13) or a Custom Install, which allows you to choose a custom location to install CrashPlan by choosing the Change Install Location button.

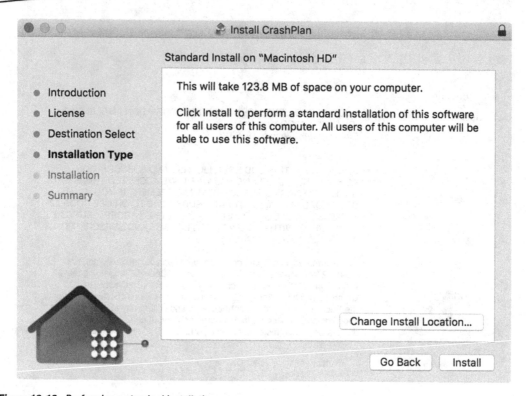

Figure 18-13. Performing a standard installation

If you wish to complete the installation (and for the purposes of this walkthrough you do), click on the Install button. You'll then be prompted to enter an administrative username and password, as seen in Figure 18-14. Here, provide the appropriate credentials and click on Install Software.

Figure 18-14. Provide your credentials

Once the installation is complete, you'll be prompted to provide information to create an account (figure 18-15, or to sign in using an existing account). If you already have an account, use the later option.

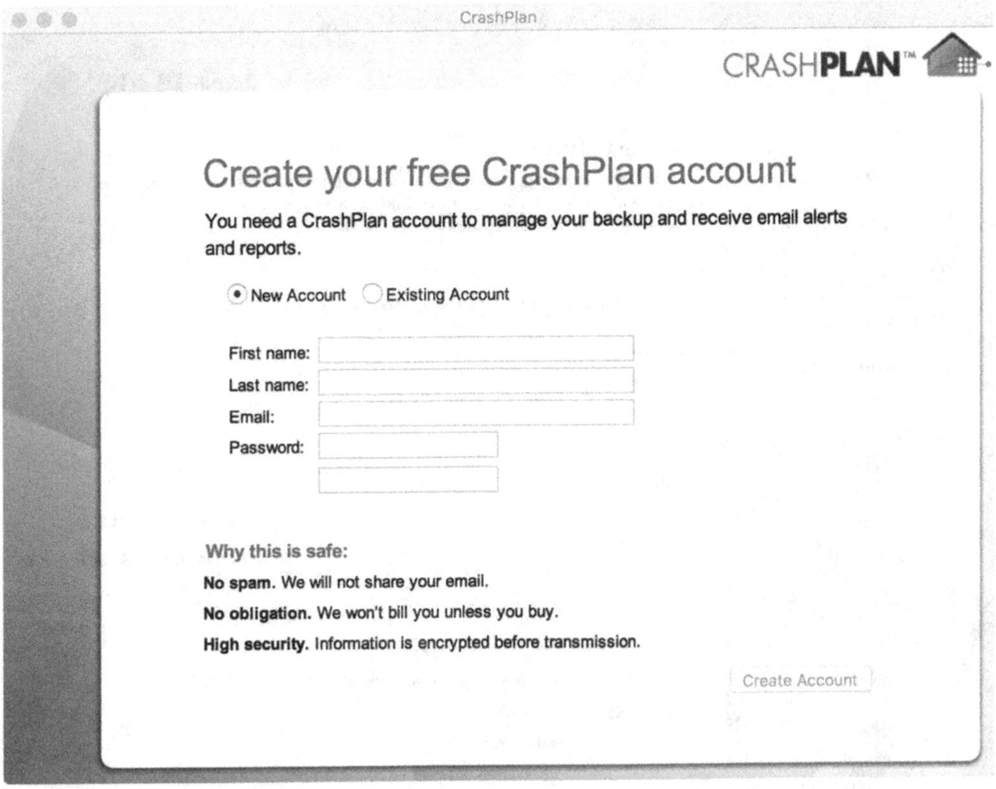

Figure 18-15. Log into your account

Once you are logged in, you can start configuring what you'd like to back up, where you'd like to place your data, and the frequency of your backups.

Configuring a Backup

Once you have installed CrashPlan, you'll want to connect to the cloud and define what should be backed up. To do so, go into your /Applications directory and you will find the CrashPlan icon. Open CrashPlan and click on Backup in the application sidebar. As you can see in Figure 18-16, the screen is divided into three main sections, Destinations, Files and Inbound. Destinations is the target locations you are backing up to. These include the following:

- CrashPlan Central: A subscription.

- Friend: Back up to encrypted files on a friends computer (and they'll usually back up to yours). This option is free.

- Another Computer: Backing up to another computer that signs in using the same account CrashPlan.

- Folder: Backing up to an external disk.

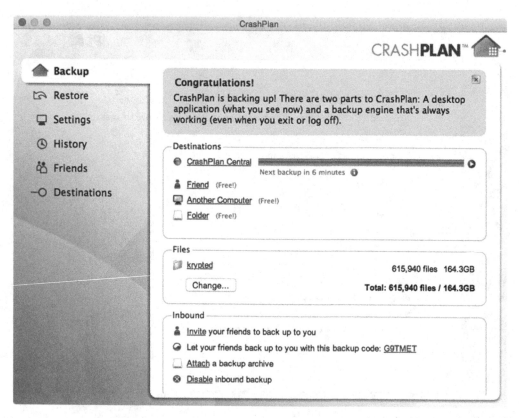

Figure 18-16. Backup with CrashPlan

The quickest and easiest way to get backing up is to just click on the Start button for CrashPlan central. You can then click on the CrashPlan Central link any time to check the status of that backup. Click on the i symbol in any section to see the status of a backup.

> **Note**   I recommend backing up to a Friend or CrashPlan Central and having a local backup. This way, you have an offsite backup in case of a catastrophe as well as an onsite backup for any quick restores.

Next, click on Settings. Here, you can configure a number of General options (shown in Figure 18-17). These include the following:

- Name for this computer: The name that will show up for the computer you're configuring when you look in the CrashPlan web portal.

- Inbound backup from other computes: Configure your computer to accept connections from other computers.

- User is away when not active for: The number of minutes before backups take up more of the CPU and the user is marked as "away".

- When user is away, use up to: Data that needs to be backed up gets compressed before sent to backup destinations, which can be pretty CPU intensive. This is where you can configure the percent of available CPU to use for backups. It should be lower on servers and higher on workstations.

- When user is present, use up to: Amount of the CPU that is used when the user is actively using the computer.

- Stop when battery reaches: The minimum percentage of battery power allowed before backups stop.

- Launch menu bar: Button to start the CrashPlan menu bar item (since you can quit the menu bar app).

- Show full paths on Backup tab: shows the path of files to be backed up in the Files section of the screen.

- Language: The language used in the CrashPlan app.

- Backup Status and Alerts: Configure email alerts so if a backup gets interrupted or missed, you'll be notified.

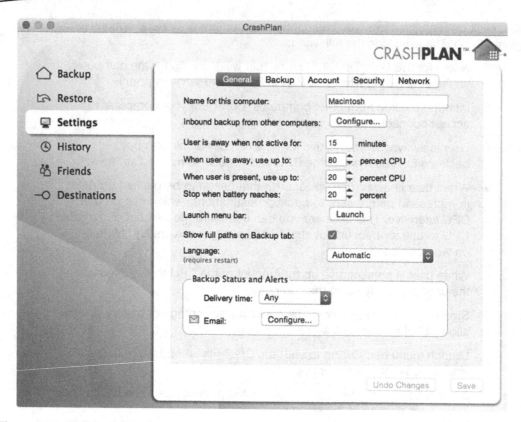

Figure 18-17. Configure Backup Settings

When you're happy with your options, click Save and then click on the Backup tab. Here, you'll see a number of other options, as shown in Figure 18-18. These include the following:

- Backup will run: By default, set to Always but use the Between specified times option to limit the times that backups will run (for example, only at night so work isn't impacted, or only during the hours when the computer is on the local network).

- Verify selection every: Scans the computer for changes to files. Should probably leave this with the default settings.

- Frequency and versions: Define how often CrashPlan backs up and the number of versions of files to keep.

- Filename exclusions: Provide the name of files (or regular expressions for a lot of files) that you'd like to exclude from your backups.

- Advanced settings: Allows for disabling data de-duplication (possibly the coolest feature of CrashPlan, which only backs up the bits that need to be backed up and doesn't create duplicates of entire files. Also allows you to disable encryption, compression and real-time file backup.

- Backup sets: Allows you to backup different files to different locations.

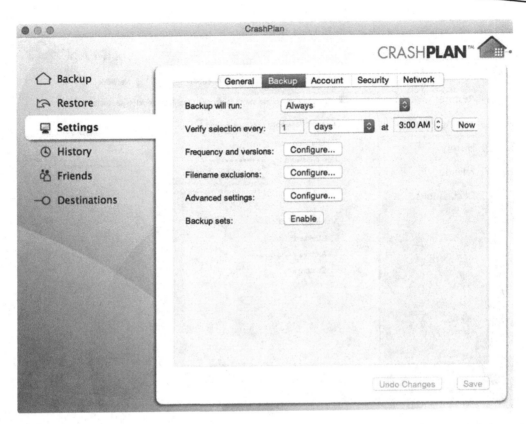

Figure 18-18. Backup Options

You can also switch accounts on a computer and change a password under the Account tab. The Security tab provides great security options to further secure your backups. Here, you can provide a password that will be required in order to open the CrashPlan app in the Account Password section of the screen, as you can see in Figure 18-19. You can also provide deeper levels of encryption with data being backed up. The Archive key password allows you to assign a password to a backup that only you have. The Custom key provides even more encryption and allows you to assign a private key, required to unlock backups.

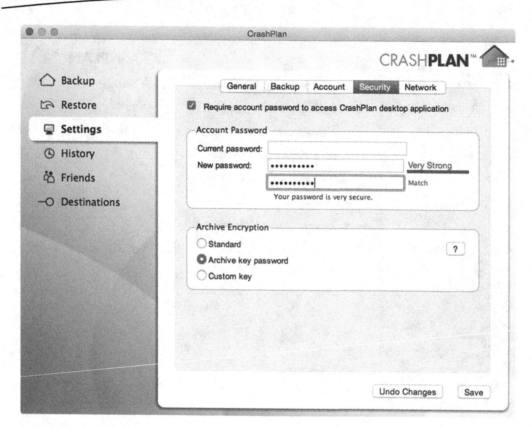

Figure 18-19. Security Options

Finally, click on the Network tab. Here, you can use the Network interfaces and Wireless networks buttons to configure which networks and wireless networks that you'd like backups to use, respectively. You can also define a URL to a PAC file, in order to enable proxying CrashPlan communications (see your network administrator for information regarding your proxy servers). But one of the more interesting features of CrashPlan is the ability to very granularly manage how CrashPlan traffic works. For example, you can decide to limit the rate with which data is sent to other systems over the LAN and WAN, for both when you are marked as present and away. You can also identify buffer sizes for sending and receiving data and define QoS settings for CrashPlan. All of these options are shown in Figure 18-20.

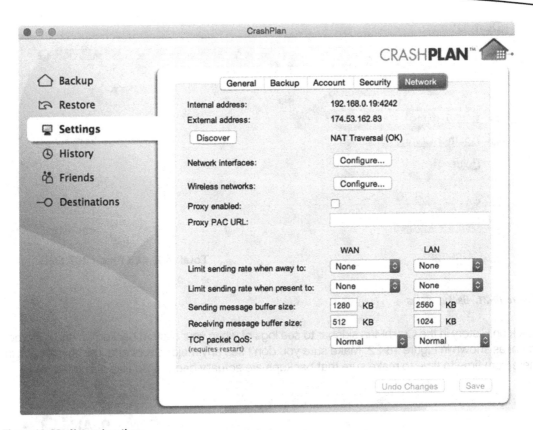

Figure 18-20. Network options

Once you have configured all of the settings appropriately for your environment, click the Save button and then click on Backup in the CrashPlan sidebar. It's likely that you already have some data sitting on your target locations. The Destination that data is backing up to will show the progress that you're making. As Figure 18-21 shows, if you're backing up to a destination not on your local network, it's common for backups to take days, if not weeks for computers with massive amounts of data and/or slow network connections.

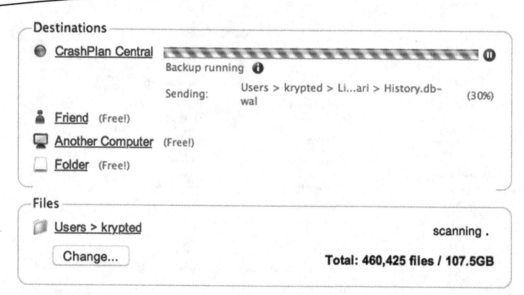

Figure 18-21. Backup status

Click on History in the CrashPlan sidebar to see logs of when your system backed up and restored data, as shown in Figure 18-22. Make sure you don't see any major errors and just check back in here from time to time to make sure that backups are actually backing up files at a good rate.

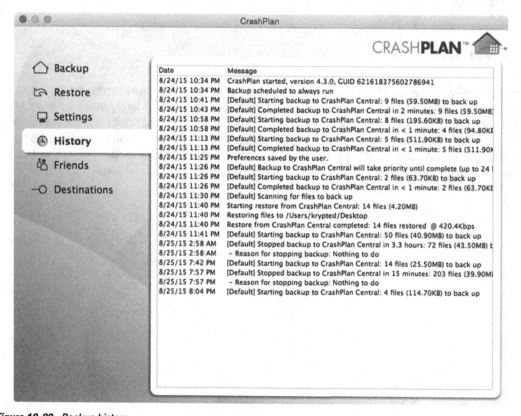

Figure 18-22. Backup history

Once you have configured your backups then it's time to look into restoring your backups.

Restoring CrashPlan data

What's the point of backing up data if you can't restore that data. Let's look at restoring some data that you've backed up. To do so, first click on Restore in the CrashPlan sidebar. Here, you'll see a list of files and folders that are backed up on each of your computers. Use the "Restore files for computer" field to choose the computer you'd like to restore data from (for example, if you want to restore files from your work computer to your home computer, from the computer that had a hard drive fail to the new computer, or from the computer that data was originally backed up from to the same computer).

As you can see in Figure 18-23, we're going to restore the Desktop directory. Below the list of files, you'll see a pretty human readable run-down of exactly what's about to happen. Here, we're going to restore the most recently backed up version of each file using the original permissions to a folder on our hard drive called OLD and rename any existing files so we can complete our restore. Many of these can be changed by clicking on the link and defining a different option for that setting.

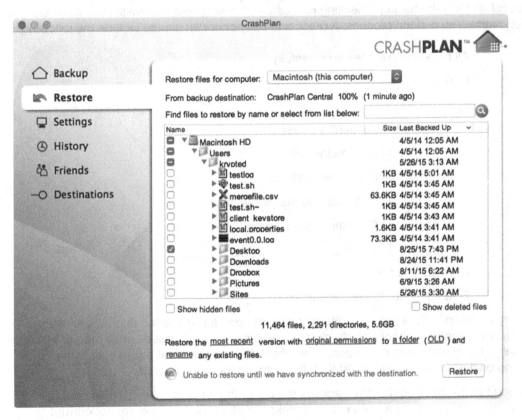

Figure 18-23. Restore CrashPlan data

Once you're finished configuring your restore options, click Restore. The data then slowly but surely appears in the appropriate directory. If you chose to leave the permissions as the original permissions, you may need to take ownership of files once restored.

Once the restore is done, you're finished with your restore. We've now done a basic backup and restore of your computer using CrashPlan.

CrashPlan ProE is a more advanced version of CrashPlan, with finely grained options for configuring directory services memberships, providing your own central location for backed up data, and allows for more than a few devices, which you're not supposed to use if you're using the home edition of CrashPlan.

Checking Your Backups

Once you have configured and started your backups, then it is critical to review their performance. There are typically too many moving pieces to blindly trust that the backups are running as they should and actually backing up all your data in a restorable format.

Many organizations perform checks on their backups daily, weekly, or biweekly. Often, they will also perform a test restore monthly or quarterly. To keep staff (or yourself) from missing critical steps in the backup checking process, it is wise to use a checklist to make sure you don't miss a step in the process. A quick and easy checklist should include the following:

>All backups executed successfully:
>
>[ ] Yes
>
>[ ] No
>
>>If not, please identify cause(s):
>>
>>>[ ] Destination full
>>>
>>>[ ] Source unavailable
>>>
>>>[ ] Error with backup software
>>>
>>>[ ] Operating system error
>>>
>>>[ ] Other: _____
>>
>>Corrective action(s): _____
>>
>>Free space for future backup(s): _____

Every environment will require a different level of need for how often to check backups. Some organizations choose to check their backups on a daily basis, while others will check weekly. No matter what, it is important to check the logs and make sure your systems are being backed up rather than trust that the software has you covered.

In addition to checking that the backups are occurring on schedule, it is also important to occasionally perform a restore just to make sure that the backups are not corrupt or incomplete. Some people choose to restore a folder or a randomly selected file, while others choose to restore an entire volume and check the contents to see whether all the required data has in fact been backed up as it should be. This is strongly suggested, especially if you are backing up to tape or to compressed disk images.

Using Tape Libraries

Crashplan is a great application and fairly simple to use when backing up to a single tape drive with only a few tapes involved in your sets. There are other products that are designed from the ground up with tape libraries in mind. BRU by the Tolis Group, NetVault by Bakbone, PresStor by Archiware, and Time Navigator by Atempo are the primary applications currently used to provide more industrial-strength backups. They are used primarily to back up RAIDs and other larger volumes ranging from a few TB to petabytes in size.

A tape library will typically consist of one or more tape drives and a *hand* (also referred to as a *robot*) that is used to move tapes within the library, placing them in the tape drives Many libraries will also come outfitted with a bar-code scanner in order to quickly find assets within the library. Many tape libraries come with a dedicated slot that is meant to be used for housing a cleaning tape.

> **Tip** Routinely cleaning your drives when they get dirty is critical to ensure that the drives will perform as needed.

Many of these applications will also allow you to "stage" your data onto disk. By staging data to a disk, it is possible to restore data more quickly. Your backups are also compartmentalized because they are being written to a much more efficient storage medium. For example, this could be a Thunderbolt disk or a RAID. The name that many of these programs call this compartmentalization is different, and many vendors will consider it an add-on that requires an additional charge to use it, but when you begin backing up a large amount of data, you will find it to be a lifesaver and well worth the money.

Backup vs. Fault Tolerance

Data backup frameworks don't need to stop at redundant copies of data. Backup and downtime discussions go hand in hand. How long would it take to get a system back online if a primary server with important data went down? How crucial would this be to the organization's operation?

Fault tolerance goes a step beyond the conversation of backing up your data and into the conversation of what you would do if any component of the whole network environment failed. For example, if you are running a mail server and your primary Internet connection goes down, then what is the contingency plan? What if you were to lose the hard drive on the server because of hardware failure? What if the logic board on the server dies? Some organizations go so far as to have a duplicate of every device in their environment. For most, though, it is a matter of analyzing what you can live without in the event of a failure because some fault-tolerant solutions do not have an appropriately high return on investment in case of a failure.

If downtime is a critical factor in keeping a data structure alive, you should consider implementing a failover or *fault-tolerant* solution. In fact, the cost of providing fault tolerance could actually mitigate the cost of downtime in cases where downtime can cause loss of productivity. When configuring OS X Server (or OS X Client as a server) hosting various services, you may choose to provide a fault-tolerant solution when high availability is required.

Fault-Tolerant Scenarios

Fault tolerance comes in two types. The first is *active-passive*. In an active-passive topology, you would maintain a host spare of the service you are load balancing, which is passive (or dormant) until the primary server crashes. Once a primary server comes back online, you manually tell the backup server to stop processing requests and reactivate the primary host. You do not receive any additional benefits other than maintaining a backup server that you would flip to if the primary were to go down. Typically, the backup server will be a less expensive version of the primary server.

The second type of fault-tolerant solution is called *active-active*. In an active-active topology, multiple active servers are used. In this scenario, you will often also engage in load balancing those servers. This gives you the ability to provide increased bandwidth to mission-critical services. The complexity introduced in this scenario is that the data store must be either synchronized with the primary server or shared between the servers, as is the case with using multiple servers as bridgehead servers using a SAN to reshare data. Data in an active-passive topology must be synchronized between the servers, but not as frequently as in active-active environments.

Round-Robin DNS

While active-passive topology traffic reroutes data using the failover daemon (failoverd), in an active-active topology, traffic must be routed between multiple servers on a constant basis. There are two methods predominantly used for doing this. The first is using *round-robin DNS*. Round-robin DNS controls the order in which a load-balanced service forwards traffic across multiple servers. The administrator fills the domain records with multiple address records using the same host name but points to one or more IP addresses that serve the same service. As the DNS request is looking for your DNS server, the web server responds to the client with the next address from the list.

The most basic round-robin DNS setup shapes traffic based on the assumption that each server can handle the same load, which is considered an *equal cost path*. A typical list of A record addresses in your zone file might look like the following if you have three servers:

```
afp  IN  A       10.0.0.7
afp  IN  A       10.0.0.8
afp  IN  A       10.0.0.9
```

You can tell one server to handle more traffic than the others, as is the case with *unequal cost paths*, or paths that send more traffic to one server than the others. You can do this by listing the same server multiple times in the listing of A records for a given address. For example, if you have one server at 10.0.0.4 that is much faster than the others in a six-node cluster of web servers, you might direct traffic using the following entries in a zone file:

```
afp  IN  A       10.0.0.4
afp  IN  A       10.0.0.4
afp  IN  A       10.0.0.5
afp  IN  A       10.0.0.6
afp  IN  A       10.0.0.7
afp  IN  A       10.0.0.8
```

You can use the `rrset-order` command to define how round-robin requests are forwarded. The default `rrset` order is cyclic. There are three different options for record handling:

- Cyclic records are returned in numerical order.

- Fixed records are returned in the same order that they are listed in the file.

- Random records are returned in a random order.

When using round-robin DNS, the traffic is shaped in a static manner and cannot adapt to changes in the servers, such as performance counters and current user load.

Load-Balancing Devices

A *load balancer* can provide many features. Among them is the ability to shape traffic based on multiple factors (IP addresses, port, amount of traffic), automatically failing over to another server when one server becomes unresponsive, and providing a single address for systems to use when requesting a service. The load balancer in most configurations will probably not handle synchronizing data but will perform almost everything else that will be required when architecting this type of solution. Load balancers include Coyote Point Equalizers, F5s/Dell BigIPs, Barracuda Load Balancers, and Cisco Load Directors.

The cost of deploying a solution using round-robin DNS is typically very low compared to the cost of purchasing a load balancer. However, the load balancer will become a more scalable solution over the long run. In cluster environments, the load balancer can become a single point of failure. To build a completely fault-tolerant environment, implement a backup load balancer to automatically go live if there is a problem with the main load balancer. It may seem redundant, but even load balancers can and will fail.

Cold Sites

When discussing redundancy, it is important to explore the physical redundancy of the actual location where your equipment resides. Secondary locations are important for situations where there is a need to be back up and running quickly in the event of a communications error with your primary location. The secondary location, or *cold site*, often consists of a set of servers that are slightly below the speed of your primary site, that are shut down (or offline), and that contain a fairly recent copy of the data stored in your hot site.

Planning is everything when dealing with a secondary location. Much like an evacuation procedure at an office, in the event of a failure at your primary site, a procedure should be written and followed to activate the cold site. These processes often resemble a series of steps that enable you to be online providing the assets that you need quickly and efficiently. An example of this might include a complex flowchart, or it might be as easy as a simple checklist outlining what steps to take.

We cannot stress enough the importance of documenting and testing these mission-critical business processes before you begin to rely on them.

Hot Sites

For locations that require even more redundancy and cannot suffer a performance loss should the primary site go down, a redundant site, or *hot site*, should be implemented. With a hot redundant site, practically a one-to-one ratio of your equipment in the primary location would be available in the secondary site. A hot site is critical for large web sites, such as Amazon.com and Expedia.com, which would lose millions of dollars an hour if users were unable to check the status of accounts, book travel, or purchase music because of an outage.

The goal of any hot site is not to quickly be up and running with a subpar system, as it is with a cold site, but instead to be instantly up and running with an equally powerful system. Many hot sites begin as a redundant location used only in an emergency and often end up running in tandem with various systems in the primary site, allowing any of the systems in the primary site to fail over to the secondary. This can lead to increased throughput capacity for server farms, which might otherwise be sitting idle.

Backing up Services

Finally, it's worth mentioning that each service running on OS X and OS X Server *can* require a special type of backup. These often involve stopping a service and then running a backup, given that some of the data cannot be backed up while the service is running. Many of these services, if provided by Apple, will be fairly straightforward to back up. For example, the settings used in OS X Server are often backed up with tools like Bender, available at `http://robotcloud.screenstepslive.com/s/2459/m/5322/l/94467-bender-automated-backup-of-os-x-server-settings`.

Summary

Whether due to an intrusion, due to a hardware failure, or due to accidental deletion of data (we are our own worse security risks), chances are that at some point you will loose data. In this chapter we looked at backing up OS X so that if you lose data (or have data that is compromised), you will be able to restore that data.

In this chapter, we started out by looking at some backup and storage theory. We then moved on to using Apple's Time Machine, which is built into Mac OS X. Because Time Machine isn't for everyone, we then looked at SuperDuper and Crashplan. Along the way we looked at bringing theory into practice.

Another item that many will look to following an intrusion is data forensics. Therefore, in Chapter 19, we'll look at building an incident response plan and how to do some basic forensics steps in Mac OS X.

InfoSec Acceptable Use Policy

> **Note**   Created by the SANS Institute. Feel free to modify or use for your organization. If you have a policy to contribute, please send e-mail to stephen@sans.edu.

1.0 Overview

InfoSec's intentions for publishing an Acceptable Use Policy are not to impose restrictions that are contrary to <Company Name>. established culture of openness, trust and integrity. InfoSec is committed to protecting <Company Name>'s employees, partners and the company from illegal or damaging actions by individuals, either knowingly or unknowingly.

Internet/Intranet/Extranet-related systems, including but not limited to computer equipment, software, operating systems, storage media, network accounts providing electronic mail, WWW browsing, and FTP, are the property of <Company Name>. These systems are to be used for business purposes in serving the interests of the company, and of our clients and customers in the course of normal operations. Please review Human Resources policies for further details.

Effective security is a team effort involving the participation and support of every <Company Name> employee and affiliate who deals with information and/or information systems. It is the responsibility of every computer user to know these guidelines, and to conduct their activities accordingly.

2.0 Purpose

The purpose of this policy is to outline the acceptable use of computer equipment at <Company Name>.

These rules are in place to protect the employee and <Company Name>. Inappropriate use exposes <Company Name> to risks including virus attacks, compromise of network systems and services, and legal issues.

3.0 Scope

This policy applies to employees, contractors, consultants, temporaries, and other workers at <Company Name>, including all personnel affiliated with third parties. This policy applies to all equipment that is owned or leased by <Company Name>.

4.0 Policy

4.1 General Use and Ownership

1. While <Company Name>'s network administration desires to provide a reasonable level of privacy, users should be aware that the data they create on the corporate systems remains the property of <Company Name>. Because of the need to protect <Company Name>'s network, management cannot guarantee the confidentiality of information stored on any network device belonging to <Company Name>.

2. Employees are responsible for exercising good judgment regarding the reasonableness of personal use. Individual departments are responsible for creating guidelines concerning personal use of Internet/Intranet/Extranet systems. In the absence of such policies, employees should be guided by departmental policies on personal use, and if there is any uncertainty, employees should consult their supervisor or manager.

3. InfoSec recommends that any information that users consider sensitive or vulnerable be encrypted. For guidelines on information classification, see InfoSec's Information Sensitivity Policy. For guidelines on encrypting email and documents, go to InfoSec's Awareness Initiative.

4. For security and network maintenance purposes, authorized individuals within <Company Name> may monitor equipment, systems and network traffic at any time, per InfoSec's Audit Policy.

5. <Company Name> reserves the right to audit networks and systems on a periodic basis to ensure compliance with this policy.

4.2 Security and Proprietary Information

1. The user interface for information contained on Internet/Intranet/
   Extranet-related systems should be classified as either confidential
   or not confidential, as defined by corporate confidentiality guidelines,
   details of which can be found in Human Resources policies.
   Examples of confidential information include but are not limited to:
   company private, corporate strategies, competitor sensitive, trade
   secrets, specifications, customer lists, and research data. Employees
   should take all necessary steps to prevent unauthorized access to
   this information.

2. Keep passwords secure and do not share accounts. Authorized
   users are responsible for the security of their passwords and
   accounts. System level passwords should be changed quarterly, user
   level passwords should be changed every six months.

3. All PCs, laptops and workstations should be secured with a
   password-protected screensaver with the automatic activation
   feature set at 10 minutes or less, or by logging-off (control-alt-delete
   for Win2K users) when the host will be unattended.

4. Use encryption of information in compliance with InfoSec's
   Acceptable Encryption Use policy.

5. Because information contained on portable computers is especially
   vulnerable, special care should be exercised. Protect laptops in
   accordance with the "Laptop Security Tips".

6. Postings by employees from a <Company Name> email address to
   newsgroups should contain a disclaimer stating that the opinions
   expressed are strictly their own and not necessarily those of
   <Company Name>, unless posting is in the course of business duties.

7. All hosts used by the employee that are connected to the <Company
   Name> Internet/Intranet/Extranet, whether owned by the employee
   or <Company Name>, shall be continually executing approved
   virus-scanning software with a current virus database. Unless
   overridden by departmental or group policy.

8. Employees must use extreme caution when opening e-mail
   attachments received from unknown senders, which may contain
   viruses, e-mail bombs, or Trojan horse code.

4.3 Unacceptable Use

The following activities are, in general, prohibited. Employees may be exempted from these restrictions during the course of their legitimate job responsibilities (e.g., systems administration staff may have a need to disable the network access of a host if that host is disrupting production services). Under no circumstances is an employee of <Company Name> authorized to engage in any activity that is illegal under local, state, federal or international law while utilizing <Company Name>-owned resources.

The lists below are by no means exhaustive, but attempt to provide a framework for activities, which fall into the category of unacceptable use.

System and Network Activities

The following activities are strictly prohibited, with no exceptions:

1. Violations of the rights of any person or company protected by copyright, trade secret, patent or other intellectual property, or similar laws or regulations, including, but not limited to, the installation or distribution of "pirated" or other software products that are not appropriately licensed for use by <Company Name>.

2. Unauthorized copying of copyrighted material including, but not limited to, digitization and distribution of photographs from magazines, books or other copyrighted sources, copyrighted music, and the installation of any copyrighted software for which <Company Name> or the end user does not have an active license is strictly prohibited.

3. Exporting software, technical information, encryption software or technology, in violation of international or regional export control laws, is illegal. The appropriate management should be consulted prior to export of any material that is in question.

4. Introduction of malicious programs into the network or server (e.g., viruses, worms, Trojan horses, e-mail bombs, etc.).

5. Revealing your account password to others or allowing use of your account by others. This includes family and other household members when work is being done at home.

6. Using a <Company Name> computing asset to actively engage in procuring or transmitting material that is in violation of sexual harassment or hostile workplace laws in the user's local jurisdiction.

7. Making fraudulent offers of products, items, or services originating from any <Company Name> account.

8. Making statements about warranty, expressly or implied, unless it is a part of normal job duties.

9. Effecting security breaches or disruptions of network communication. Security breaches include, but are not limited to, accessing data of which the employee is not an intended recipient or logging into a server or account that the employee is not expressly authorized to access, unless these duties are within the scope of regular duties. For purposes of this section, "disruption" includes, but is not limited to, network sniffing, pinged floods, packet spoofing, denial of service, and forged routing information for malicious purposes.

10. Port scanning or security scanning is expressly prohibited unless prior notification to InfoSec is made.

11. Executing any form of network monitoring which will intercept data not intended for the employee's host, unless this activity is a part of the employee's normal job/duty.

12. Circumventing user authentication or security of any host, network or account.

13. Interfering with or denying service to any user other than the employee's host (for example, denial of service attack).

14. Using any program/script/command, or sending messages of any kind, with the intent to interfere with, or disable, a user's terminal session, via any means, locally or via the Internet/Intranet/Extranet.

15. Providing information about, or lists of, <Company Name> employees to parties outside <Company Name>.

Email and Communications Activities

1. Sending unsolicited email messages, including the sending of "junk mail" or other advertising material to individuals who did not specifically request such material (email spam).

2. Any form of harassment via email, telephone or paging, whether through language, frequency, or size of messages.

3. Unauthorized use, or forging, of email header information.

4. Solicitation of email for any other email address, other than that of the poster's account, with the intent to harass or to collect replies.

5. Creating or forwarding "chain letters", "Ponzi" or other "pyramid" schemes of any type.

6. Use of unsolicited email originating from within <Company Name>'s networks of other Internet/Intranet/Extranet service providers on behalf of, or to advertise, any service hosted by <Company Name> or connected via <Company Name>'s network.

7. Posting the same or similar non-business-related messages to large numbers of Usenet newsgroups (newsgroup spam).

4.4 Blogging

1. Blogging by employees, whether using <Company Name>'s property and systems or personal computer systems, is also subject to the terms and restrictions set forth in this Policy. Limited and occasional use of <Company Name>'s systems to engage in blogging is acceptable, provided that it is done in a professional and responsible manner, does not otherwise violate <Company Name>'s policy, is not detrimental to <Company Name>'s best interests, and does not interfere with an employee's regular work duties. Blogging from <Company Name>'s systems is also subject to monitoring.

2. Company Name>'s Confidential Information policy also applies to blogging. As such, Employees are prohibited from revealing any <Company> confidential or proprietary information, trade secrets or any other material covered by <Company>'s Confidential Information policy when engaged in blogging.

3. Employees shall not engage in any blogging that may harm or tarnish the image, reputation and/or goodwill of <Company Name> and/or any of its employees. Employees are also prohibited from making any discriminatory, disparaging, defamatory or harassing comments when blogging or otherwise engaging in any conduct prohibited by <Company Name>'s Non-Discrimination and Anti-Harassment policy.

4. Employees may also not attribute personal statements, opinions or beliefs to <Company Name> when engaged in blogging. If an employee is expressing his or her beliefs and/or opinions in blogs, the employee may not, expressly or implicitly, represent themselves as an employee or representative of <Company Name>. Employees assume any and all risk associated with blogging.

5. Apart from following all laws pertaining to the handling and disclosure of copyrighted or export controlled materials, <Company Name>'s trademarks, logos and any other <Company Name> intellectual property may also not be used in connection with any blogging activity

5.0 Enforcement

Any employee found to have violated this policy may be subject to disciplinary action, up to and including termination of employment.

6.0 Definitions

Term Definition

Blogging Writing a blog. A blog (short for weblog) is a personal online journal that is frequently updated and intended for general public consumption.

Spam Unauthorized and/or unsolicited electronic mass mailings.

7.0 Revision History

CDSA

If you are a developer of Mac OS X-based software then there are a few very basic principles that we can impart relating to the security model used when developing software for the Apple platform. While depth is something most developers look for, this is a theory and not a specific technology.

Apple has designed its security around the Common Data Security Architecture (CDSA) model, developed by Intel and open sourced via the Open Group. CDSA is a set of layered security services and a cryptographic framework that provide an interoperable, cross-platform infrastructure for creating security-enabled applications for client-server environments. CDSA covers the essential components to equip applications with security services that provide cryptography, certificate management, trust policy management, and key recovery.

CDSA is defined by a horizontal, four-layer architecture:

- It includes applications such as Mail, Safari, iChat, Disk Utility, Keychain Access, and other applications developed by Apple. For example, 3rd party applications from Tweetie to 1Password take part in the CDSA model, leveraging Keychain services to custom CSSM cryptographic store modules respectively.

- It includes layered services and middleware including the *Application Programming Interfaces (API)s* used by the applications previously listed. An API is a set of definitions that determines how one piece of computer software communicates with another. It is a method of achieving abstraction, usually (but not necessarily) between lower-level and higher-level software. These APIs include interfaces for keychains, file signing, SSL, and certificate management.

- The Common Security Services Manager (CSSM) infrastructure's Cryptographic Services Manager has functions to create and verify digital signatures, generate cryptographic keys, and create cryptographic hashes.

- Security service provider modules, also known as *add-in modules*, are third-party and nonapplication items built using the APIs in the second layer of the CDSA. This allows for extensibility to the framework.

The CDSA is an open source framework, allowing it to closely parallel many of Apple's other initiatives for security and development. It receives peer review from a larger audience than just Apple users; security and development experts contribute to reviewing the CDSA fundamentals. CDSA allows Apple and the community of third-party developers to architect software in a secure manner while still supporting the network features required for the modern applications of today and tomorrow. For more information on the CDSA model, see the Intel CDSA site at http://www.intel.com/ial/security.

Introduction to Cryptography

The word cryptography is derived from the Greek words *kryptos*, meaning "hidden," and *grafein*, meaning "to write." Throughout history, *cryptography* has been used to hide messages inside tradional means of communication that might otherwise be intercepted. Doing so is accomplished by concealing the contents of the message from all except who has the key to unlock it. In modern times, cryptographic techniques are used to protect e-mail messages, information transmitted over the internet, credit card information, and data on corporate networks.

A wide variety of cryptographic techniques are used with computers. They are typically provided for one of two reasons: to protect data while at rest on a computer or to protect data as it is being transferred between two computers or across networks.

Most cryptographic techniques for submitting data over the Internet rely heavily on the exchange of keys; keys easily stored within a Keychain in OS X. Some techniques include:

- *Symmetric-key cryptography* refers to encryption methods where both senders and receivers of data share the same key and data is encrypted and decrypted with algorithms based on those keys. The modern study of symmetric-key ciphers revolves around block ciphers and stream ciphers and how these ciphers are applied.

- *Block ciphers* take a block of plain text and a key and then output a block of cipher text of the same size. DES and AES are block ciphers. AES, also called Rijndael, is a designated cryptographic standard by the U.S. government. AES always uses a key size of 128, 192, or 256 bits as well as a block length of 128 bits. DES is no longer an approved method of encryption as an exhaustive key search attack on a block of DES-encrypted data would take a modern Mac OS X computer a few minutes to decipher. Triple-DES, its variant, remains popular. Triple-DES uses three 56-bit DES keys and is used across a wide range of applications from ATM encryption to e-mail privacy and secure remote access. Many other block ciphers have been designed and released, with considerable variation in quality.

- *Stream ciphers* create an arbitrarily long stream of key material, which is combined with plain text bit-by-bit or character-by-character, somewhat like the one-time pad (or an encryption cipher that is only used once) encryption technique. In a stream cipher, the output stream is based on an internal state, which changes as the cipher operates. That state's change is controlled by the key and, in some stream ciphers, by the plain-text stream as well. When the state doesn't depend on the plain input, two messages encrypted with the same key can be combined to gain information about the plain-text. RC4 is an example of a well-known stream cipher.

- *Cryptographic hash functions* do not use keys but take data and output a short, fixed-length hash in a one-way function. For good hashing algorithms, collisions (two plain texts that produce the same hash) are extremely difficult to find, although they do exist. Collisions must exist, as there are infinite possible inputs to a hash function but only a finite range of outputs.

- *Symmetric-key cryptosystems* typically use the same key for encryption and decryption. A disadvantage of symmetric ciphers is that a complicated key management system is necessary to use them securely. Each distinct pair of communicating parties must share a different key. The number of keys required increases with the number of network members. This requires very complex key management schemes in large networks. It is also difficult to establish a secret key exchange between two communicating parties when a secure channel doesn't already exist between them.

> **Note**   If you don't already have a secure channel, it's *impossible* to establish a shared but secret key. DHX gets around this by creating a transient secure channel.

Whitfield Diffie and Martin Hellman are considered by some to be pioneers of *public-key cryptography*. They proposed the notion of public-key (also called *asymmetric-key*) cryptography, with the Diffie-Hellman key exchange protocol, in which two different but mathematically related keys are used: a public key and a private key. A public key system is constructed so that calculation of the private key is computationally infeasible from knowledge of the public key, even though they are necessarily related. Instead, both keys are generated secretly, as an interrelated pair. In public-key cryptosystems, the public key may be freely distributed, while its paired private key must remain secret. The public key is used for encryption, while the private or secret key is used for decryption.

Who actually invented the first public-key cryptography systems is still up for debate. Ronald Rivest, Adi Shamir, and Len Adleman invented RSA, another public-key system. Later, it was widely held that asymmetric cryptography had been invented by James H. Ellis at GCHQ, a British intelligence organization, even though the Diffie-Hellman and RSA algorithms had been previously demonstrated. In the end, Diffie-Hellman and RSA, were shown to be the first public examples of high quality public-key cryptosystems and are among the most widely used.

In addition to encryption, public-key cryptography can be used to implement digital signature schemes. *Digital signatures* are somewhat like ordinary signatures; they are easy for a user to produce but difficult for anyone else to forge. Digital signatures can also be permanently tied to the content of the message being signed because they cannot be "moved" from one document to another; any attempt would be detectable. In digital signature schemes, there are two algorithms: one for signing, in which a secret key is used to process the message (or a hash of the message or both), and one for verification, in which the matching public key is used with the message to check the validity of the signature. RSA and DSA are two of the most popular digital signature schemes. Digital signatures are central to the operation of public-key infrastructures and to many network security schemes (SSL/TLS, many VPNs, and so on). Digital signatures provide users with the ability to verify the integrity of the message, thus allowing for nonrepudiation of the communication.

Public-key algorithms are most often based on the computational complexity of "hard" problems, often from number theory. The hardness of RSA is related to the integer factorization problem, while Diffie-Hellman and DSA are related to the suitability of an algorithm as the basis of a public-key cryptosystem depends on the difficulty of deriving the private key from the public key. Ideally it would be at least as hard as guessing the private key at random.. More recently, *elliptic-curve cryptography* has developed in which security is based on number theoretic problems involving elliptic curves. Because of the complexity of the underlying problems, most public-key algorithms involve operations such as modular multiplication and exponentiation, which are much more computationally expensive than the techniques used in most block ciphers, especially with typical key sizes, which are frequently exclusive-OR (XOR) operations.. As a result, public-key cryptosystems are commonly "hybrid" systems, in which a fast symmetric-key encryption algorithm is used for the message itself, while the relevant symmetric key is sent with the message, but encrypted using a public-key algorithm. Or, relating back to the introduction of Diffie-Hellman Exchange earlier, two parties use asymmetric encryption to agree on a shared session key. Subsequent communication is symmetrically encrypted using that key. Hybrid signature schemes are also often used, in which a cryptographic hash function is computed, and only the resulting hash is digitally signed.

Cryptography continues to move forward in an almost exponential manner. Although much of the cryptographic data in use today stems from the research done in the 1970s and earlier, new advances and refinements occur all the time. New techniques are emerging today that will change the shape of cryptography 10 to 20 years from now, making the keys, hashes, and algorithms we use today look like child's play. As data grows and computers get faster, though, it is important to have a basic understanding of some of the cryptographic standards you will run into on a regular basis.

Index

■ G

◼ Y, Z

Get the eBook for only $5!

Why limit yourself?

Now you can take the weightless companion with you wherever you go and access your content on your PC, phone, tablet, or reader.

Since you've purchased this print book, we're happy to offer you the eBook in all 3 formats for just $5.

Convenient and fully searchable, the PDF version enables you to easily find and copy code—or perform examples by quickly toggling between instructions and applications. The MOBI format is ideal for your Kindle, while the ePUB can be utilized on a variety of mobile devices.

To learn more, go to www.apress.com/companion or contact support@apress.com.

Printed in the United States
By Bookmasters